W9-DFV-224

AN
OHIO READER
1750 TO THE CIVIL WAR

edited by

THOMAS H. SMITH
Director, Ohio Historical Society

977.1
OHI
v.1
co3

William B. Eerdmans
Publishing Company   Grand Rapids, Michigan

Copyright © 1975 by Wm. B. Eerdmans Publishing Company
All rights reserved
Printed in the United States of America

Library of Congress Cataloging in Publication Data
Main entry under title:

An Ohio reader.

  Includes bibliographical references.
  CONTENTS: v. 1. European settlement to the Civil
War.—v. 2. 1865 to the present.
  1. Ohio—History—Sources. I. Smith, Thomas H.,
1936-
F491.039   977.1   75-11606
ISBN 0-8028-7033-3 (v. 1)

All Ohio State documents reprinted by permission of the Ohio Historical Society.

To Mother

In project - Worlds

C. 3

ACKNOWLEDGMENTS

An effort of this size is never accomplished without help. I would like to thank the library staff of the Ohio Historical Society, especially Conrad Weitzel, the library staff of the Cincinnati Historical Society, and the staff of the Ohio State Library; Professor Harry R. Stevens who offered helpful suggestions and encouragement; Marcia Smith and Bret Smith who helped with the manuscript; Pat Smith who made corrections; and Joanne who watched, waited and typed.

CONTENTS

INTRODUCTION

THIS IS NOT merely a history readings book; it is also a documentary history of the development of a geographical area limited by man-made boundaries—the state of Ohio. The first state to be formed from the Northwest Territory, Ohio struggled from a crude frontier existence to maturity in the modern world. The general movement of the Ohio experience was not unique: it was repeated countless times throughout the Midwest and across the nation; taken by itself, it loses meaning, but considered within the general context of national history, it is reflective of the entire nation's past. Perhaps, if there is a national experience, it is the sum total of all local experiences; and it is through an appreciation of local history that one can discover a patient and tolerant vehicle for understanding matters on a broader scale.

Thus, Ohio history can be seen as a microcosm of national history. Before the coming of Europeans, culturally rich prehistoric Indians had thrived across the state; numerous historic Indians hunted and farmed its productive land and experienced the despair of removal. Like many states, Ohio had its bloody frontier war and muddled through the frustrations of territorial government. Its people developed a stable constitutional government and sought an economic stability upon which Western culture could flourish. Ohioans participated at all levels of western expansion, debated the issues of slavery, and fought to keep the nation one. During the period between the American Civil War and the turn of the century, urbanization and industrialization introduced problems that affected the lifestyle of man and the environment. Ohioans sought a better life, both economic and governmental, and the impact of the state's reform movement extended far beyond its political boundaries. The two world wars in the twentieth century, and the turmoil of reconstruction that followed both, were disruptive and challenging experiences that Ohioans shared with America and the rest of the world. By mid-twentieth century, the issues that faced modern society—including racial strife, educational development, economic expansion, population growth, social welfare, inflation, and governmental finance—were full-blown. Ohioans searched for their own solutions, but not independently of the national experience. Thus, the experiences of Ohioans were shared by Americans of all races, creeds, and political beliefs. What happened in Ohio affected the national scene, and the historical processes at the national level had their impact on the Buckeye State as well.

An Ohio Reader is intended to be many things to many people; its potential uses are numerous and varied. The increasing interest in local history among professional historians over the past twenty years has manifested itself in numerous articles and monographs that have been published on topics limited to specific eras and geographical areas. But the interest goes beyond the needs of the professional. Ohio history has been taught in the public schools of the state at the elementary, secondary, and college level for years, and a genuine fascination with local history has grown among the general public. The current popular search for nostalgia's wonderland in the mass media is one evidence of that fact. The collection of documents and materials in these volumes is intended to be both instructive and interesting to the general reader. At the same time, these volumes are also intended for use in the classroom. Teaching Ohio history for several years and listening to and talking with students and teachers has convinced me of the need for more available sources on local history. Though textbooks currently in use in the state certainly serve a purpose and give students an outline of the flow of events, they fail because of space limitations to provide materials for in-depth study and substantive inquiry.

Four criteria were used to compile the selections in these volumes. First, particular attention was paid to the major issues in Ohio's history that have occupied the time of both historians and laymen. Second, each document selected was intended to stand alone: no reader need have a special expertise in any particular field to understand the meaning of each issue. Consequently, the selections were chosen because they contained both pertinent survey and specific material relative to each topic. Third, a problematic approach was employed when the topic and materials permitted. For instance, during the 1912 Ohio Constitutional Convention the issue of women's suffrage was debated with regularity and vigor; arguments pro and con echoed throughout the convention chamber. The selected segments of the debate from the convention, therefore, air both sides of the women's suffrage issue, which occupied the thoughts of Ohioans for several decades. Fourth, in each instance the documents had to be contemporaneous and represent eyewitness accounts or descriptions of the particular issues that faced each generation. It is only through the participants' record that one can gain an appreciation for historic issues in their own time. Accordingly, each document's authenticity has been preserved, even though many contain archaic spellings and grammatical constructions.

Most of the selections come from state documents and newspaper accounts. The reports made to the governor by the heads of the various state agencies, departments, bureaus, and commissions are taken from the Ohio Executive Documents series. Prior to World War I, these reports were compiled and published as single volumes. Descriptive in construction, they contain data and information found nowhere else. Following World War I, however, the state reports were no longer gathered and published as single volumes but were printed independently by each agency. The majority of these later reports contain informative and descriptive reviews, but they are outlines of the agencies' work for the year. During the Depression of the 1930s, many of the agencies—in order to save money—stopped quality production of their reports and issued mimeographed outlines of their activities. Although printed reports returned during the 1940s, the practice of each agency's printing its own report continued. At the same time, many of the reports became less informative and appeared to be printed for in-house consumption rather than for informing the general public.

Newspaper reporting has also changed substantially since Ohio's early years. In the late nineteenth and early twentieth centuries, newspaper reporters were eyewitnesses to newsworthy events and gave the reading public descriptive accounts of what they observed. This is clearly evident in the articles concerning labor, urban conditions, and bossism. Consequently, newspapers of that period have been highly useful in the compilation of this volume. In the twentieth century, however, newspaper reporting lost much of its narrative dimension in favor of personal interpretations of events. Admittedly, the narrative is still present in modern newspaper reporting; yet the reporter often stands between the reader and the event, and the newspaper becomes a less important source for a collection of this nature.

It may appear to some that the issues and readings selected make for a discouraging picture of the state's history. This may be true, yet the editor believes that the intrinsic meaning of historical processes operates on various levels. While the annual messages of the governors to the general assembly contained glowing accounts of the accomplishments and successes of their respective administrations, the agency reports hit at the problems within the state that had yet to be remedied. To identify a problem at the state executive or legislative level is one thing, but to be personally involved with a problem where it affects the quality of human life on an individual basis is another matter. Consequently, the selections reflect issues that affected the majority of Ohioans at the local level and reveal the most about the particular historical processes at work.

One of the striking themes that emerges from a survey of major documents in the state's history is the similarity of the economic, social, racial, educational, and political issues that faced each generation. The problem of financing education in Ohio was as poignant to the generations during the early 1800s as it was one hundred years later. The effects of industrialization and the exploitation of the state's natural resources on the environment were apparent one hundred years ago; in many instances the solution to these problems is no nearer now than it was then. The problems of intensive urbanization as it affected society are the same in the days of the Office for Economic Opportunity and revenue sharing as they were when George Barnsdale Cox fought for the passage of his own pet ripper bill through the Ohio General Assembly. It is often easy for pessimism to capture the spirit of the historian. The hope persists, however, that at some point an understanding of the past can help clear a path for a greater future.

AN
OHIO READER

1 North of the River Ohio

BEFORE 1788, the area north and west of the Ohio River was a vast wilderness, unexplored and untouched by Europeans, but ripe for exploitation. Fortunes were anticipated by the French, English, and Americans alike from the furs, rich lands, and raw materials that lay within the approximately 250,000 square miles of the Northwest Territory. By the middle of the eighteenth century, and already after three wars, England and France were once again willing to battle for a world empire which included mastery in North America. The Seven Years War, or the French and Indian War (1754 to 1763), witnessed the expulsion of the French from most of the continent and ushered in British dominance over the Ohio Valley and Great Lakes Basin.

Prior to 1750, the English, busily engaged in establishing colonies along the Atlantic coast, paid but cursory attention to the region west of the Allegheny Mountains. Indeed, their knowledge of this area was scant. When George Washington was sent by Virginia's Governor Robert Dinwiddie in 1753 to the famous Forks of the Ohio with orders to expel the French, the young Virginian relied upon French cartography to guide his expedition. During the twenty-five-year period between the close of the French and Indian War in 1763 and the founding of the first permanent settlement in Ohio in 1788, information about the area was anxiously sought. Adventurers, trappers, traders, and surveyors who invaded the pristine wilderness were impressed with the economic potential of the region. Men such as Colonel Henry Bouquet, George Washington, Thomas Hutchins, and others recorded their observations of the natural wealth and speculated about its future development.

It is understandably difficult for twentieth-century man, surrounded by planned obsolescence and engineered waste, to imagine the unspoiled splendor and the abundance of natural resources of the Ohio country. More than three-quarters of what became the state of Ohio was covered by a thick blanket of hardwood forests; here and there over central Ohio were savannas, or prairies, thickly covered with tall grasses. Following the natural drainage patterns, deep and clear streams worked their way east and south to the Ohio River or north to Lake Erie. Wildlife, including the magnificent buffalo, obtained life from the land; many species of birds filled the air, and healthy fish crowded the streams, rivers, and lakes.

All of this was the seedbed for the growth and development of Western civilization as it hurried across the continent. The vast natural resources fed western economic development. Coinciding with a desire for self-government in those settlers who braved the harshness of the wilderness was a dream of economic gain and the accumulation of worldly goods. However, the destruction of the natural environment seemed inherent in Western economics. Forests were leveled to lay open Ohio's rich alluvial soils to the cutting edge of the farmers' plows. Timber not used for building was burned. With the destruction of the forests, topsoil was washed away, the contour of the land was changed, and streams were clogged—all victims of man's advance. Animal life was also destroyed. As the farmers cleared and enclosed their lands into rectangular patterns, there was no longer room for the large animals like the buffalo, elk, or moose. Muskrats, foxes, and squirrels, viewed as enemies by farmers, were trapped and their numbers severely reduced. Predators such as the cougar, black bear, and wolf were systematically destroyed in order to protect livestock, and hunters were rewarded with state-subsidized bounties for their kills.

Of course, those who brought European civilization to the western wilderness were not the first to use the country's natural resources. By 1788, approximately 15,000 Indians of various tribal groups lived within the political boundaries of Ohio and gained their livelihood from the wilderness. The Miami (or Twightwee) lived along the Miami of the Lakes (the Maumee River) and the Wabash River in northwestern Ohio, and were probably the most powerful of the Ohio Indians. In the Scioto River Valley and along its many tributaries lived the Shawnee. This numerically large and aggressive group had settled on the Pickaway Plains in central Ohio after 1758. The Shawnee, under the leadership of such men as Black Hoof, Cornstalk, Blue Jacket, and Tecumseh, represented a continuous resistance to white settlement between 1763 and 1815. Centered in the lower Tuscarawas River Valley and the upper Muskingum Valley were the Delaware. And no less important were the Wyandot, whose villages, by 1783, spread from the southern shore of Lake Erie to the upper Hocking Valley. Their efforts in behalf of the United States during the War of 1812 earned for them land cessions in Ohio, and it was not until 1844 that they relinquished their lands within the state. Small scattered bands of Mingo (or Seneca) lived along the tributaries of the Ohio River in the eastern part of the state.

The descriptions by Lewis Evans and David Zeisberger are accounts of Ohio before Western civilization had crossed the Ohio

River. Evans' account, printed in 1755, was one of the earliest systematic descriptions of the physical features of the Ohio country. While not an eyewitness observer himself, his pamphlet was based on the observations of traders who worked the region, Indians who were familiar with it, and the journal of William Franklin, the son of Benjamin Franklin, who accompanied George Croghan on his trip into the Northwest Territory in 1747.

Probably no one recorded the Ohio wilderness and Indian life with greater sensitivity than the Moravian missionary David Zeisberger. Written from his personal observations between 1745 and 1778, *A History of the Indians* documents the beauty and the harshness of the land and the Indians. His description is not of a static Indian society, but one that had been altered by internal means and by the introduction of European trade goods. Just as the Indians were pushed back by Western civilization, so was the wilderness of the Ohio Valley, and the freshness of its beauty was gone forever.

The Ohio Country

LEWIS EVANS

Muskingum is a fine, gentle River, confined within high Banks, that prevent its Floods from damaging the surrounding Land. It is passable with large Battoes to the Three Legs, and with small Ones to a little Lake at its Head, without any Obstruction from Falls or Rifts. From hence to Cayahóga is a Portage a Mile long. *Cayahóga*, the Creek, that leads from this Portage to Lake Erie is muddy and middling swift, but no where obstructed with Falls or Rifts. As this has fine Land, wide extended Meadows, lofty Timber; Oak and Mulberry fitted for Ship-building; Walnut, Chestnut and Poplar for domestic Services, and furnishes the shortest and best Portage between the Ohio and Lake Erie; and its Mouth is sufficient to receive good Sloops from the Lake; it will in Time become a Place of Consequence. *Muskingum*, though so wide extended in its Branches, spreads all in most excellent Land, abounding in good Springs, and Conveniencies, particularly adapted for Settlements remote from marine Navigation, as Coal, Clay and Freestone. In 1748 a Coal Mine, opposite Lamenshikola Mouth, took Fire, and kept burning above a Twelve-month, where great Quantities are still left. Near the same Place is excellent Whetstone; and about eight Miles, higher up the River, is Plenty of white and blue Clay for Glass Works and Pottery. Though the Quantity of good Land on Ohio, and its Branches, is vastly great, and the Conveniencies attending it so likewise; we may esteem that on Muskingum the Flower of it all.

Hockhocking is passable with Battoes seventy or eighty Miles up; it has fine rich Land, and vast grassy Meadows, high Banks, and seldom overflows. It has Coals about fifteen Miles up, and some Knowls of Freestone.

Now to return to the other Side of Ohio. *Sióto* is a large gentle River, bordered with rich Flats, which it overflows in the Spring; spreading then above Half a Mile in Breadth, though when confined to its Banks it is scarce a Furlong wide. If it floods early, it scarce retires within its Banks in a Month, or is fordable in a Month or two more. The Land is so level that in the Freshes of Ohio the Back-water runs eight Miles up. Opposite the Mouth of this River is the Lower Shawane Town, removed from the other Side, it was one of the most noted Places of English Trade with the Indians. This River, besides vast Extents of good Land, is furnished with Salt on an Eastern Branch, and Red Bole, on Necunsîa Skeintat. The Stream is very

From Lewis Evans, *Geographical, Historical, Political, Philosophical and Mechanical Essays*, (Philadelphia, 1754), pp. 28; 30-31.

gentle, and passable with large Battoes a great Way up, and with Canoes near 200 Miles to a Portage near the Head, where you carry over good Ground four Miles to Sanduski. *Sanduski* is a considerable River, abounding in level rich Land, its Stream gentle all the Way to the Mouth, where it will receive considerable Sloops. This River is an important Pass, and the French have secured it as such; the Northern Indians cross the Lake here from Island to Island, land at Sanduski, and go by a direct Path to the Lower Shawane Town, and thence to the Gap of Ouasioto, in their Way to the Cuttawas Country. This will no Doubt be the Way that the French will take from *Detroit* to *Moville*, unless the English will be advised to secure it, now that it is in their Power.

Little Mineami River is too small to be gone far with Canoes. It has much fine Land, and some Salt Springs; its high Banks, and middling Current, prevent its overflowing much the surrounding Land.

Great Mineami River, Aśśerenîët, or Rocky River, has a very stony Channel, a swift Stream, but no Falls. It has several large Branches, passable with Canoes a great Way; one extending Westward towards the Quiaaghtena River; another towards a Branch of Mineami River (which runs into Lake Erie) to which there is a Portage, and a third has a Portage to the West Branch of Sanduski; besides Mad Creek, where the French have lately established themselves. A Vein of elevated Land, here and there a little stony, which begins in the Northern Part of the Peninsula, between the Lakes Erie, Huron and Michigan, extends across the Lake Mineami River, below the Fork, and Southward along the Rocky River, to Ohio; and is the Reason of this River's being stony, and the Grounds rising a little higher than the adjacent Plains. It is, like all the Land on this River, very rich, and would scarce have been perceived, had not the River worn the Channel down to the Rocks which lie beneath.

. . . .

Into the Western End of Lake Erie falls Mineami River, a considerable Stream, navigable with Canoes to the Portages, which lead to the Quiaaghtena and Rocky River, interrupted with three considerable Rifts below the Forks: But however it is an important River, because of the Portages it furnishes South-Westward.

Life in the Ohio Wilderness

DAVID ZEISBERGER

The North American Indians are of middle size, well built, straight, light-footed, well adapted for travel through the forest, much of which is due to the fact that they do no heavy work, but support themselves by the chase. Their color is brown, but of different shades. Some are light brown, hardly to be distinguished from a brown European, did not their eyes and hair betray them. Again, others are so dark that they differ little from mulattoes.

. . . .

It is very common that they wear a plume of feathers on the middle of the head, rising straight up or hanging downward. They frequently cut the helix of the ear, leaving the upper and lower ends intact and then hang bits of lead to it so that it is stretched. Then this curved border of the auricle is bound with brass wire, distending it considerably, and decorated with silver ornaments. Among Indians who have come in contact with whites this is less often done.

. . . .

The men hunt, secure meat for the household, clothing for their wives and children, getting it in exchange for hides, build houses or huts, and also help their wives clear the land for cultivation and build fences around it. The duties of the women are cooking, finding fire-wood, planting and reaping. They plant corn, principally, making of this their bread, which is baked in the ashes, and preparing with it various dishes. Besides, they raise pumpkins of various kinds, potatoes, beans and other vegetables, which they have learned to know through the whites, such as cabbage, turnips, etc.

. . . .

Food which they prepare must be well cooked and well done; they do not like anything rare or raw. Meat and even fish must be so thoroughly cooked that they fall apart.

Concerning the chase in general, as engaged in by the Indians, it should yet be noticed that, because there is considerable trade in skins, deer are killed mainly for their hides and only so much of the flesh is used as the Indians can consume while on the chase, wherefore, most of the meat is left in the woods for the wild animals,

From David Zeisberger, "History of the Northern American Indians," *Ohio Archaeological and Historical Publications*, **XIX** (1910), 12-132. Reprinted by permission.

which the wolves, especially, seem to know, for these animals take advantage of the hunting season and move in the direction of much shooting; they follow the report of the guns and, when the huntsman has skinned the deer, consume the carcass. The Indians rarely shoot a wolf, the skin of this animal being of little value. As an Indian shoots from fifty to a hundred and fifty deer each fall, it can easily be appreciated that game must decrease.

. . . .

Houses of the Indians were formerly only huts and for the most part remain such humble structures, particularly in regions far removed from the habitation of whites. These huts are built either of bast (tree-bark peeled off in the summer) or the walls are made of boards covered with bast. They are low structures. Fire is made in the middle of the hut under an opening whence the smoke escapes. Among the Mingoes and the Six Nations one rarely sees houses other than such huts built entirely of bast, which, however, are frequently very long, having at least from two to four fire-places; as many families inhabiting such a house as there are fire-places, the families being related. Among the Delawares each family prefers to have its own house, hence they are small. The Mingoes make a rounded, arched roof, the Delawares on the contrary, a high pitched, peaked roof. The latter, coming much in contact with the whites, as they do not live more than a hundred miles from Pittsburg, have learned to build block houses or have hired whites to build them. Christian Indians generally build proper and comfortable houses and the savages who seek to follow their example in work and household arrangement learn much from them.

. . . .

The North American Indians, whom I wish now to describe as well as I have learned to know them, are by nature (I speak of savages) lazy as far as work is concerned. If they are at home and not engaged in the chase they lie all day on their britchen and sleep; when night comes they go to the dance or wander about in disorderly fashion. The old men work a little, chopping wood or doing other things about the house, but the younger do nothing unless driven by dire necessity to build a hut or house or the like. Whatever time is not devoted to sleep is given to amusements, such as ball playing, which they have learned from the whites, as also cards. A game with dice they have themselves invented.

. . . .

They are proud and haughty, even a miserable Indian, capable in no respect, imagines himself to be a great lord. They hold themselves in high regard as if they were capable of great and wonderful things, in which respect they are much encouraged by dreams, held among them to be very significant and, indeed, it would appear that through dreams Satan holds the heathen bound and fettered and in close connection with himself, subjecting them in this fashion to delusion.

. . . .

They are masters in the art of deceit and at the same time are very credulous; they are given over to cheating and stealing, and are not put to shame when caught. Stealing is very common among them. They will steal and sell each other's horses; and, though a thief be caught, little is done to him beyond taking his rifle.

. . . .

They are courageous where no danger is to be found, but in the face of danger or resistance they are fearful and the worst cowards. Hence, in wartime they prefer to attack defenceless whites on plantations, women and children, when they least expect it. Against them they show their heroic courage. They can be very friendly to a white man, give him to eat and act as if they had nothing evil in mind against him and then drive the hatchet into his head.

. . . .

Indians usually treat one another with kindness and civility and in their bearing toward one another are modest. They are communicative but thoughtful. Of empty compliments they know nothing. In meeting it is customary to shake hands, greet one another with the friendly title of Father, Older or Younger Brother, Uncle, Cousin, Grand Son, Grandfather and say "I am glad to see you." Sometimes all this is repeated when the guests have been sometime in the house. Expression of greeting through others is hardly customary, occasionally a gift is sent by way of greeting. Greetings are expressed in all sincerity. If sentiments do not correspond to words and forms, the latter are dispensed with.

. . . .

Their common conversation turns upon hunting or the news of the day. Matter that has no foundation in fact may be drawn into conversation, and even though all may be aware of this, the narration continues uninterrupted. They may laugh now and again but they will listen attentively. No one interrupts another. When one has finished another begins. They never put any one publicly to blush; they are polite to each other and enjoy being politely treated. They like to be regarded as worthy people even though they may be the opposite. They are pleased to know that they are liked.

. . . .

Judged by the mere appearance of the Indians one is surprised how modest and careful they are in relation to each other and imagines that the whites, if they were as free a people and had neither government nor punishment to fear, would not be as united and peaceable as the Indians appear to be. The towns and villages of the latter are not indeed governed by force or law. Each individual is at liberty to live where he pleases, moving from one place to another according to inclination, yet they generally dwell together for the sake of the help they can render each other in building and in fencing up the great field where all may plant and be sure that their pieces of ground will not be molested by cattle.

. . . .

Of violence, murder (except in drunkenness), robbery, theft, one rarely hears among the Indians. They may leave all they have caught in the chase and their utensils in the forest, secured indeed against wild animals such as wolves and bear, but not hidden from the Indians. They often hang their things to trees in the woods where everyone passing by may see them and leave them there for days and weeks, yet they are never molested. Stolen goods may not be easily concealed among them, and whoever has been guilty of theft must restore or repay lest a horse or two or even his gun, which is an Indian's means of sustenance, be taken from him or his friends summoned to make good the injury, even years after the theft has been committed.

. . . .

Their old people, even though they are only able to crawl about and are a source of trouble and have nothing to bequeath to anyone, are faithfully cared for by their friends who seem to wish that their lives should be prolonged. That they are unmerciful and insensible towards the poor and needy may not be said of them. Even strangers who have no friends are given assistance. A poor widow, even though she have children, finds it possible to make a living if she is willing to work. They pay her above the worth of her services in food and clothing; if it is summer she may work on the plantations; in winter she may prepare wood for fire. They are willing to help the poor but always expect them to render some service in return. It has been known that good has been done to prisoners condemned to death, even to whites, though this had to be done secretly.

A few negroes are found among the Indians having been either bought from the whites or secured as prisoners. These are looked upon as of their own kind and allowed full liberty. Indians and negroes intermarry and their mulatto children are as much loved as children of pure Indian blood.

. . . .

That the Indians have some sort of religion and mode of worship whereby they endeavor to please the Deity, cannot be denied. Their worship, however, is unreasoning devotion. It is remarkable that savages who have been cut off from association with other nations for no one knows how many centuries should have so much knowledge of Deity that is handed down from generation to generation.

They believe and have from time immemorial believed that there is an Almighty Being who has created heaven and earth and man and all things else. This they have learned from their ancestors, but where the dwelling place of the Deity is they know not. They have always heard that whoever lives a virtuous life, refrains from stealing, murder and immorality, would at death go to some good place where conditions would be better than here, where there would be a superfluity of everything and a happy life of joy and dancing. On the contrary, whoever lived an evil life would arrive at no good place but have to wander about sad and unhappy. Hence nothing is so terrible and awful to them as death, because they do not know how it will be after this life nor whither they shall go.

They consider the soul to be an invisible being and a spirit. Formerly, they used the word *Wtellenapewoagan* to describe it, meaning the "Substance of a Human Being." Savages use this word to the present day. Now they have accepted the word *Wtschitschank*, that is, "Spirit." They believe also in the immortality of the soul. Some likened themselves to corn which when thrown out and buried in the soil comes up and grows. Some believe their souls to be in the sun and only their bodies here. Others say that when they die their souls will go to God and suppose that when they have been some time with God they will be at liberty to return to the world and be born again. Hence, many believe that their souls have come from God and that they have been in the world before.

. . . .

Concerning the deluge there are some fairly clear traditions among the Indians. According to these, the world was at one time entirely flooded and all men perished. The turtle, however, able to live both on land and sea, had survived and again peopled the world. Hence, the Turtle Tribe is the most important among the Indians. Another tradition is that when the earth was flooded some men and women had seated themselves on the back of a turtle of such great age that moss had already grown on its back. These people commissioned a diver that flew nearby to search for land. After searching in many regions this bird had at last returned with a bit of earth in its mouth. They, then, proceeded on the back of the turtle to where this earth had been procured and found a little spot of dry land, where they settled. Gradually more land appeared, and this was, eventually, peopled by the descendants of those who had on the back of the turtle escaped the general destruction.

. . . .

The following quadrupeds are to be found along the Ohio: In the first place, there are the deer, whose skins are much used in barter and trade by the Indians. Their horns are not straight, but bent toward each other and have prongs. From May until September they are red, after that they lose the red hair and their hide is covered with long, gray hair, which is their winter coat. At about the beginning of the year they shed their horns; new ones grow in spring. These are at first and until they attain their full size, covered with a thin skin, which peels off when the horns harden. The tail is about a foot long and stands up straight when they run. . . .

A large buckskin is valued at a Spanish dollar; two doeskins are regarded as equal in value to one buckskin. . . .

The bear is quite black, has short ears, a thick head and quite a sharp snout. It has but a very short tail and great strong claws on his feet. It can easily climb the trees and bring down chestnuts and acorns. This is done, however, only when these are not ripe and do not, therefore, fall down. They generally break off the branches, throw them down and then climb down to consume the nuts.

Their skins are no great object for trade, hence the Indians prefer to use them for their sleeping places, for which the long hair makes them peculiarly useful. There is likewise a kind of bear, much larger than the common bear, with much hair on the legs, but little on the bodies, which appear quite smooth. The Indians call it the king of bears, for they have found by experience that many bears will willingly follow it.

. . . .

Elk are in my estimation most like the European stag, and I have often thought that they must be the same species and that what is here called the stag is the European fallow deer, but as I have seen neither stag nor fallow deer in Europe I cannot speak authoritatively.

The bucks have long, heavy antlers with many prongs. These they shed each year as do the deer. The tail is quite short. As the skins are very thick and heavy and of no particular value, elk do not tempt the

Indians to the chase. Occasionally, one is shot that happens near an Indian, but most of the flesh is left in the forest for beasts of prey, even though the animals are always fat, in summer as in winter and do not become lean, like the deer.

The buffaloes are dark brown in color, covered with long hair, or rather soft down mixed with hair. Their legs are short, the body is very heavy. They have a hunch upon their backs, just above the shoulders. This diminishes toward the rear, hence, they appear much shorter from the back than from the front. They have a thick head and a long beard depends from the chin. Altogether, they present a terrible appearance. Their horns are short, but thick and quite black. The buffaloes are a good deal heavier and larger than cattle. One that I have seen was a yearling, raised by the Indians and quite tame; even this was the size of a small cow, that has already had calf. At one time these animals appeared in great numbers along the Muskingum, but as soon as the country begins to be inhabited by the Indians, they retire and are now only to be found near the mouth of the above named river. Along the banks of the Scioto and further south, both Indians and whites say that they may be seen in herds numbering hundreds. That is two or three hundred miles from here. If a buffalo cow is shot, its calf, if such it has, will stand quietly by until the huntsman has skinned its dam and then follow him into his hut, stay at his fire and not leave him. That this is true, I have living witnesses enough about me to testify.

The panther has a head and face like a cat, its legs are short and the paws are armed with sharp claws. It is a beast of prey of uncommon strength. Its tail is long, compared with that of the cat. Deer it is able to catch at will. If it spies one and is desirous of capturing it, the panther crawls along the ground behind fallen trees or through the thicket until it is sure of capturing the deer in one leap. Then it springs upon its prey, seizes it with its claws and does not release its hold until the victim is dead.

. . . .

Wild cats, gray in color, are distinguished from the domestic cats in that they have hardly any tail. They are beasts of prey, even invade the hunting lodges of the Indians, when the latter are out and if they find meat devour it.

There are three varieties of fox, red, gray and black.

The raccoon is somewhat larger than a common cat and has a pointed snout. Its forefeet bear some resemblance to hands and are used as such, for it digs up small mussels out of the sand, which form its food when there are no acorns or chestnuts to be had. Its hind legs resemble those of the bear.

. . . .

The beaver was formerly found in great numbers in this region, but since the Indians have learned from the whites to catch them in steel-traps, they are more rarely found. A necessary thing in connection with the beaver-catch is a certain oil or spirit which the Indians prepare of various kinds of bark of trees and other aromatic things, which they place in the traps to decoy the beavers into them. The skins are always of considerable value. They are very industrious animals and for their size, of uncommon strength. Beaver dams of such dimensions are found in creeks, that it might be imagined that they had been built by human hands. Such dams they build when there are many together, for they work harmoniously, at night, in order to dam up the water and often put a considerable piece of land under water in course of their operations.

. . . .

The pole-cat has white and black markings, a gentle and mild countenance. It goes out of the way for no one, and whoever approaches too near is ill rewarded for his curiosity. It has a special gland containing a fluid intolerably foetid. If one approaches too closely, the fluid is discharged and thrown in all directions with the tail. The offensive odor no one can bear and one is ready enough to get away.

. . . .

There are three kinds of squirrels, the black, the grey, and the red. The black are most commonly found, the grey are the largest and the red the smallest in size. Their flesh is tender, and eaten by the Indians in case of sickness or when they are very hungry for meat.

The ground squirrel lives under the ground and is somewhat smaller than a common rat. They do great damage in the fields of the Indians, not only digging out the corn when it has been planted, but also pumpkin and melon seed.

. . . .

Wolves are very numerous, most are gray, some are almost black. As their skins serve no useful purpose and are not much valued, the Indians do not pursue them, unless they catch them tearing skins or devouring meat they have carefully laid away. Sometimes the wolves break into their hunting huts and do much damage. They rarely attack men, never when there are deer to pursue.

. . . .

Wild geese appear here in spring and autumn. Some remain during the winter, others during the summer, the latter hatching their young in this region. Most of them remain long in this country, passing toward winter into a warmer latitude, toward summer to the north, where they build in the neighborhood of the Great Lakes and return in autumn with their young.

Wild ducks are birds of passage like the geese, but there are some varieties that stay during the summer season. One kind, called the tree duck, builds its nest in hollow trees, either hanging over the water or near to it. When the young are hatched, they are thrown into the water and taken elsewhere. The male bird is the most beautiful of the water-fowls and very good to eat.

. . . .

The crane is the largest of the birds of these parts. Standing on its long legs and stretching its neck upwards, it is as tall as a man. Its body is proportionately heavy. When hit by a shot and only wounded, it attacks its pursuer and has great power in striking with its wings.

. . . .

Wild swans are quite like the domestic birds, I have seen in Holland, quite white and of the same size. The Indians declare that their flesh tastes like that of the bear, of which they are particularly fond; and is often so fat that pieces may be cut from the flesh.

Wild turkeys may be seen in the fall in flocks numbering hundreds. In the summer they disperse in the woods, this being the time for hatching the young. In winter their plumage is of a shining black, with white spots on the wings; in summer it changes to a light brown. When the time comes for laying the eggs, the Indians seek them, as they are very fond of them.

Pheasants are not valued by the Indians, though their flesh is palatable. They fall victims, however, to birds of prey.

. . . .

The wild pigeon is of an ash-gray color, the male being distinguished by a red breast. In some years in fall, or even in spring, they flock together in such numbers that the air is darkened by their flight. Three years ago they appeared in such great numbers that the ground under their roosting-place was covered with their dung above a foot high, during one night. The Indians went out, killed them with sticks and came home loaded. At such a time the noise the pigeons make is such that it is difficult for people near them to hear or understand each other. They do not always gather in such numbers in one place, often scattering over the great forests.

The turtle-doves are smaller than the pigeons and are always found in pairs.

Partridges are small, neatly formed birds. In the fall and winter they fly in broods. In the settlements they like to remain near the plantations, as they find the food they like in the fields. The flesh is tender and of a fine flavor. They are favorites with all people, being innocent and harmless birds.

· ·

The eagle has a white head and tail. The wings are black and the body partly black and partly ash-colored. It builds its nest usually in the fork of some lofty and thick tree. It lays the foundation with a great quantity of branches and repairs the nest built there every spring.

· ·

Serpents are so numerous that it is remarkable that Indians who spend much of their time in the forests are not bitten oftener. In stony places or mountains they are found most frequently. The winter they spend underground or in crevices of the rocks. In places where they are numerous, they gather in the fall and lie upon one another and twisted together until spring. Should they be discovered in winter they have to all appearances but little life, being able to move, but not having strength enough to crawl away.

1) Among the most dangerous reptiles are the rattlesnakes. They are yellow in color, marked with black spots. The largest are about four feet long, sometimes more, and about as thick as an arm. The rattles are at the end of their tails, and often betray the snakes when they are not seen. These rattles appear to be a thin, transparent horny substance, arranged in links. From the number of links it is possible to tell the age of the serpent, one being added every year. It is a rare thing to find one with twenty rattles.

· ·

Indians who have been bitten, even if they happen to be quite alone in the forest, know what to do. They seek certain herbs and roots that may be found anywhere and cure themselves of the bite, so that one rarely hears of death occasioned by the bite of this serpent. Horses or cattle bitten in the woods, where it is not possible to render immediate assistance, die in a short time. With proper management these animals may recover in twenty-four hours. With human beings a cure is not effected so quickly, and a curious thing is that the part where a human being has been bitten, becomes spotted like the rattlesnake. The fat of the rattlesnake is used by apothecaries. Here along the Muskingum rattlesnakes are not as numerous as in some regions that are stony or mountainous.

· ·

2) Copperheads, named from the color of the reptiles. Their bite is as venomous as that of rattlesnakes.

3) Vipers have a flat head, are short and thick, black on the back and gray on the belly. When approached, they distend the head and hiss so that it is possible to hear them at quite a distance. Their bite also is venomous.

. . . .

Of fishes, there are doubtless many more varieties than those I have seen in the Ohio. I will, however, confine notice to those I have seen and know.

1) Pike are of uncommon size and generally known.

2) The black-fish, as the Indians call it, has large, brown scales, a small head and a small, round, soft mouth, not armed with teeth. Its shape is not broad, but round. It is reckoned one of the best flavored.

3) The buffalo-fish is thus called by Indians and Europeans because of its being heard sometimes to bellow in the water. Its length is about a foot and a half or even two feet, and its breadth five or six inches. . . .

4) The catfish is without scales and a good fish to eat. In the Muskingum there are no very large specimens of this fish. In the Ohio, on the other hand, they grow to an unusual size. In Pittsburg, a man who had gone fishing at night, having bound the line to his arm and gone to sleep in his canoe, was dragged into the water by the catfish and lost his life. Man and fish were found close together several days later.

5) The sturgeon is the largest of the fish in the Muskingum. The largest caught here were from three to three and a half feet in length.

6) There is a kind of fish with a narrowly formed mouth, armed with sharp teeth, almost like the bill of a duck. It has scales. The Indians do not use it for food.

. . . .

8) The white perch is short and broad. It has scales and is good to eat.

9) The yellow perch is not broad, but longer than the last named, has prickly fins and sharp teeth like those of a pike. It has a yellowish appearance and is one of the most palatable of fishes.

10) Eels are rarely found.

11) There is an other variety of fish, or whatever one may call it, resembling a small catfish, but having four short legs. It has a wide mouth and is about a foot and a half in length. The fins are short.

. . . .

Mosquitoes and sandflies are found in woods in summertime in great numbers. Both sting and a night in the forest would be intolerable without the smoke of a fire. They are particularly annoying in changeable weather. Even horses will make for the fire and stand in smoke to be free of the pests. Great and small gadflies come in July and August and trouble cattle so much that only at night the latter will graze, the gadflies disappearing until dawn of day.

Ticks are to be found in the woods. These will attack one, pierce the skin and suck the blood until they have so swelled that they drop off. Bed-bugs are to be found in the Indian huts at any time and fleas in the summer, not a few.

2 The Northwest Territory

WITH THE ADMISSION of Ohio into the Union in 1803, the United States' transmountain colonial policy proved successful. The vast Northwest Territory created in 1787 served as an experiment in systematic and controlled expansionism, unequaled in the Western world. The people living in what became Ohio, the first state established under this policy, tested the theory that democratic government could evolve during a tutorial period under centralized supervision. Despite eastern state rivalry, political factionalism, foreign intrigues, and Indian warfare, the young American government was able to combine private speculation and federal responsibility in order to control settlement and to provide a governmental structure that insured the westward growth of the country, based on equal rights for states and white citizens.

The Congress of the United States, under the short-lived Articles of Confederation, achieved probably its greatest success when it devised plans for western land division and established a colonial government policy. Control of the public domain, created through compromise, was Congress' responsibility. For it, Congress had to discover schemes acceptable to the eastern states by which the land would be divided for public sale and, once settled, governed. Despite Maryland's insistent demands that the country's western lands be ceded to Congress for the benefit of all the states, the government was already pledged to a paternalistic approach to its public domain by a resolution passed by the Continental Congress in 1780. At the time, Congress resolved to dispose of land ceded to it in a manner that would benefit all the states, and to subdivide those lands into republican states.

Although Congress was working on plans simultaneously to divide the vast Northwest Territory into states and to provide for appropriate land subdivision for settlement, as well as to formulate a policy for colonial government, it reached agreement on land subdivision first. Several land schemes had been proposed, but it was necessary to reach some form of compromise between the New England system of land distribution—the surveying of land into rectangular units—and the Southern method of indiscriminate selection. After months of committee work, lengthy debate, and pressure from land speculators, squatters, and soldiers with land warrants, the members of Congress adopted a land division ordinance on May 20, 1785. Despite the apparent differences between the states over land division, Congress recognized that the western lands provided one key to national unity.

Congress next turned its attention to the establishment of a colonial government. Earlier, in 1784, Congress had accepted a proposal by the resourceful Thomas Jefferson that the territory north of the Ohio River be divided into numerous large states. In classical style, he had given to them names such as Metropotamia, Cherronesus, Pelisipia, Assenisippi, and Polypotamia. Although his plan was criticized and later superseded by the Ordinance of 1787, members of Congress had accepted the principles that the creation of new states would depend on a specific population figure and that each new state would be admitted to the Union as a full and equal partner among the older states. In March 1786, Congress began to search for a new scheme for colonial government. Based on Jefferson's original precepts, James Monroe (then a representative from Virginia), more than anyone else, expanded and refined the details of a territorial government. Throughout the summer of 1786, Congress debated, argued, and delayed the acceptance of a colonial policy. It was not until Manasseh Cutler arrived in New York the following summer, bringing with him a plan for the organization of a colony in the territory, that Congress acted. Faced with financial problems and mindful that it had to provide for settlement north and west of the Ohio River, Congress finally acted on July 13, 1787, to accept the Northwest Ordinance.

The government that was devised and established for the Northwest Territory in 1787 was one of conservative paternalism, although it was based on the republican principles outlined by Jefferson three years earlier. Congress controlled the government through its appointments of a governor, a secretary, and three judges. Even the second stage of government, which allowed for the election of a small legislative council, was closely supervised through exclusive powers granted to the governor. Because of the government's tightly paternalistic stance, friction soon developed between the governor of the territory, Arthur St. Clair, and those he tried to govern. Only the privilege of complete self-government would satisfy the pioneers who first broke the harshness of America's northern frontier.

The events and personalities involved in the creation of the state of Ohio after 1799, when the territory entered into its second stage of government, produced conditions from which emerged the two different political and social philosophies that had had parallel development in the older eastern states. St. Clair, conservative and urbane, became the spokesman for the precepts of Hamiltonianism as expressed in political terms through the Federalist party. His antagonists, Thomas Worthington, Edward Tiffin, Nathaniel Massie, and William Henry Harrison—mostly Virginians—carried their fight against the governor's autocratic rule throughout the territory and into the halls of Congress. Preachers of Jeffersonianism who were allied with the Republican party, they demanded a greater popular participation in the governmental process, knowing that a broadly supported republican government could survive on the frontier. The Jeffersonian Republicans, wise in the practice of politicking, won a victory for self-government. Ohio was admitted into the Union as the seventeenth state on March 1, 1803.

A Government for the Territory

1784

The Committee to whom was recommitted the report of a plan for a temporary government of the western territory have agreed to the following resolutions.

Resolved, that so much of the territory ceded or to be ceded by individual states to the United States as is already purchased or shall be purchased of the Indian inhabitants & offered for sale by Congress, shall be divided into distinct states, in the following manner, as nearly as such cessions will admit; that is to say, by parallels of latitude, so that each state shall comprehend from north to south two degrees of latitude beginning to count from the completion of forty-five degrees north of the equator; and by meridians of longitude, one of which shall pass thro' the lowest point of the rapids of Ohio, and the other through the Western Cape of the mouth of the Great Kanhaway, . . .

That the settlers on any territory so purchased, and offered for sale, shall, either on their own petition, or on the order of Congress, receive authority from them with appointments of time and place for their free males of full age, within the limits of their state to meet together for the purpose of establishing a temporary government, to adopt the constitution and laws of any one of the original states, so that such laws nevertheless shall be subject to alteration by their ordinary legislature; & to erect, subject to a like alteration, counties or townships for the election of members for their legislature.

That when any such State shall have acquired twenty thousand inhabitants, on giving due proof thereof to Congress, they shall receive from them authority with appointment of time and place to call a convention of representatives to establish a permanent Constitution and Government for themselves. Provided that both the temporary and permanent governments be established on these principles as their basis.

. . . .

That whensoever any of the sd states shall have, of free inhabitants, as many as shall then be in any one the least numerous of the thirteen Original states, such State shall be admitted by it's delegates into the Congress of the United States on an equal footing with the said original states: provided the consent of so many states in

From "Report of Government for the Western Territory," April 23, 1784, Gillard Hunt (ed.), *Journals of the Continental Congress*, Vol. XXVI (Washington, 1928), pp. 275-279.

Congress is first obtained as may at the time be competent to such admission. . . . Until such admission by their delegates into Congress, any of the said states after the establishment of their temporary government shall have authority to keep a sitting member in Congress, with a right of debating, but not of voting.

That measures not inconsistent with the principles of the Confedn. & necessary for the preservation of peace & good order among the settlers in any of the said new states until they shall assume a temporary Government as aforesaid, may from time to time be taken by the United States in Congress assembled.

Dividing the Territory

1785

An Ordinance for ascertaining the mode of disposing of Lands in the Western Territory.

Be it ordained by the United States in Congress assembled, that the territory ceded by individual States to the United States, which has been purchased of the Indian inhabitants, shall be disposed of in the following manner:

A surveyor from each state shall be appointed by Congress or a Committee of the States, who shall take an oath for the faithful discharge of his duty, before the Geographer of the United States. . . .

The Surveyors, as they are respectively qualified, shall proceed to divide the said territory into townships of six miles square, by lines running due north and south, and others crossing these at right angles, as near as may be, unless where the boundaries of the late Indian purchases may render the same impracticable, . . .

The first line, running due north and south as aforesaid, shall begin on the river Ohio, at a point that shall be found to be due north from the western termination of a line, which has been run as the southern boundary of the State of Pennsylvania; and the first line, running east and west, shall begin at the same point, and shall extend throughout the whole territory. Provided, that nothing herein shall be construed, as fixing the western boundary of the State of Pennsylvania. The geographer shall designate the townships, or fractional parts of townships, by numbers progressively from south to north; always beginning each range with No. 1; and the ranges shall be distinguished by their progressive numbers to the westward. The first range, extending from the Ohio to the lake Erie, being marked No. 1. The Geographer shall personally attend to the running of the first east and west line; and shall take the latitude of the extremes of the first north and south line, and of the mouths of the principal rivers.

The lines shall be measured with a chain; shall be plainly marked by chaps on the trees, and exactly described on a plat; whereon shall be noted by the surveyor, at their proper distances, all mines, salt-springs, salt-licks and mill-seats, that shall come to his knowledge, and all water-courses, mountains and other remarkable and permanent things, over and near which such lines shall pass, and also the quality of the lands.

The plats of the townships respectively, shall be marked by subdivisions into lots of one mile square, or 640 acres, in the same direction as the external lines, and numbered from 1 to 36; always beginning the succeeding range of the lots with the number next to that with which the preceding one concluded. . . .

. . . And the geographer shall make . . . returns, from time to time, of every seven ranges as they may be surveyed. The Secretary of War shall have recourse thereto, and shall take by lot therefrom, a number of townships . . . as will be equal to one seventh part of the whole of such seven ranges, . . . for the use of the late Continental army. . . .

The board of treasury shall transmit a copy of the original plats, previously noting thereon the townships and fractional parts of townships, which shall have fallen to the several states, by the distribution aforesaid, to the commissioners of the loan-office of the several states, who, after giving notice . . . shall proceed to sell the townships or fractional parts of townships, at public vendue, in the following manner, viz.: The township or fractional part of a township No. 1, in the first range, shall be sold entire; and No. 2, in the same range, by lots; and thus in alternate order through the whole of the first range . . . provided, that none of the lands, within the said territory, be sold under the price of one dollar the acre, to be paid in specie, or loan-office certificates, reduced to specie value, by the scale of depreciation, or certificates of liquidated debts of the United States, including interest, besides the expense of the survey and other charges thereon, which are hereby rated at thirty six dollars the township, . . . on failure of which payment, the said lands shall again be offered for sale.

There shall be reserved for the United States out of every township the four lots, being numbered 8,11,26,29, and out of every fractional part of a township, so many lots of the same numbers as shall be found thereon, for future sale. There shall be reserved the lot No. 16, of every township, for the maintenance of public schools within the said township; also one-third part of all gold, silver, lead and copper mines, to be sold, or otherwise disposed of as Congress shall hereafter direct. . . .

And Whereas Congress . . . stipulated grants of land to certain officers and soldiers of the late Continental army . . . for complying with such engagements, Be it ordained, That the secretary of war . . . determine who are the objects of the above resolutions and engagements . . . and cause the townships, or fractional parts of townships, hereinbefore reserved for the use of the late Continental army, to be drawn for in such manner as he shall deem expedient. . . .

The Northwest Ordinance

1787

An Ordinance for the government of the Territory of the United States northwest of the River Ohio.

Be it ordained by the United States in Congress assembled, That the said territory, for the purposes of temporary government, be one district, subject, however, to be divided into two districts, as future circumstances may, in the opinion of Congress, make it expedient.

Be it ordained by the authority aforesaid, That the estates, both of resident and nonresident proprietors in the said territory, dying

From "An Ordinance for the Government of the Territory of the United States North West of the River Ohio," July 11, 1787, Roscoe R. Hill, (ed.), *Journals of the Continental Congress,* Vol. XXXII, (Washington, 1936), pp. 314-320.

intestate, shall descend to, and be distributed among their children, and the descendants of a deceased child, in equal parts; the descendants of a deceased child or grandchild to take the share of their deceased parent in equal parts among them; and personal property may be transferred by delivery; saving, however to the French and Canadian inhabitants, and other settlers of the Kaskaskies, St. Vincents and the neighboring villages who have heretofore professed themselves citizens of Virginia, their laws and customs now in force among them, relative to the descent and conveyance, of property.

Be it ordained by the authority aforesaid, That there shall be appointed from time to time by Congress, a governor, whose commission shall continue in force for the term of three years, unless sooner revoked by Congress; he shall reside in the district, and have a freehold estate therein in 1,000 acres of land, while in the exercise of his office.

There shall be appointed from time to time by Congress, a secretary, whose commission shall continue in force for four years unless sooner revoked; he shall reside in the district, and have a freehold estate therein in 500 acres of land, while in the exercise of his office. It shall be his duty to keep and preserve the acts and laws passed by the legislature, and the public records of the district, and the proceedings of the governor in his executive department, and transmit authentic copies of such acts and proceedings, every six months, to the Secretary of Congress: There shall also be appointed a court to consist of three judges, any two of whom to form a court, who shall have a common law jurisdiction, and reside in the district, and have each therein a freehold estate in 500 acres of land while in the exercise of their offices; and their commissions shall continue in force during good behavior.

The governor and judges, or a majority of them, shall adopt and publish in the district such laws of the original States, criminal and civil, as may be necessary and best suited to the circumstances of the district, and report them to Congress from time to time: which laws shall be in force in the district until the organization of the General Assembly therein, unless disapproved of by Congress; but afterwards the Legislature shall have authority to alter them as they shall think fit.

The governor, for the time being, shall be commander-in-chief of the militia, appoint and commission all officers in the same below the rank of general officers; all general officers shall be appointed and commissioned by Congress.

Previous to the organization of the general assembly, the governor shall appoint such magistrates and other civil officers in each county or township, as he shall find necessary for the preservation of the peace and good order in the same: After the general assembly shall be organized, the powers and duties of the magistrates and other civil officers shall be regulated and defined by the said assembly; but all magistrates and other civil officers not herein otherwise directed, shall, during the continuance of this temporary government, be appointed by the governor.

For the prevention of crimes and injuries, the laws to be adopted or made shall have force in all parts of the district, and for the execution of process, criminal and civil, the governor shall make proper divisions thereof; and he shall proceed from time to time as circumstances may require, to lay out the parts of the district in which the Indian titles shall have been extinguished, into counties and townships, subject however to such alterations as may thereafter be made by the legislature.

So soon as there shall be five thousand free male inhabitants of full age in the district, upon giving proof thereof to the governor, they shall receive authority, with time and place, to elect representatives from their counties or townships to represent them in the general assembly: *Provided,* That, for every five hundred free male inhabitants, there shall be one representative, and so on progressively with the number of free male inhabitants shall the right of representation increase, until the number of representatives shall amount to twenty-five; after which, the number and proportion of representatives shall be regulated by the legislature: *Provided,* That no person be eligible or qualified to act as a representative unless he shall have been a citizen of one of the United States three years, and be a resident in the district, or unless he shall have resided in the district three years; and, in either case, shall likewise hold in his own right, in fee simple, two hundred acres of land within the same: *Provided, also,* That a freehold in fifty acres of land in the district, having been a citizen of one of the states, and being resident in the district, or the like freehold and two years residence in the district, shall be necessary to qualify a man as an elector of a representative.

The representatives thus elected, shall serve for the term of two years; and, in case of the death of a representative, or removal from office, the governor shall issue a writ to the county or township for which he was a member, to elect another in his stead, to serve for the residue of the term.

The general assembly or legislature shall consist of the governor, legislative council, and a house of representatives. The Legislative Council shall consist of five members, to continue in office five years, unless sooner removed by Congress; any three of whom to be a quorum: and the members of the Council shall be nominated and appointed in the following manner, to wit: As soon as representatives shall be elected, the Governor shall appoint a time and place for them to meet together; and, when met, they shall nominate ten persons, residents in the district, and each possessed of a freehold in five hundred acres of land, and return their names to Congress; five of whom Congress shall appoint and commission to serve as aforesaid; and, whenever a vacancy shall happen in the council, by death or removal from office, the house of representatives shall nominate two persons, qualified as aforesaid, for each vacancy, and return their names to Congress; one of whom Congress shall appoint and commission for the residue of the term. And every five years, four months at least before the expiration of the time of service of the members of council, the said house shall nominate ten persons, qualified as aforesaid; and return their names to Congress; five of whom Congress shall appoint and commission to serve as members of the council five years, unless sooner removed. And the governor, legislative council, and house of representatives, shall have authority to make laws in all cases, for the good government of the district, not repugnant to the principles and articles in this ordinance established and declared. And all bills, having passed by a majority in the house, and by a majority in the council, shall be referred to the governor for his assent; but no bill, or legislative act whatever, shall be of any force without his assent. The governor shall have power to convene, prorogue, and dissolve the general assembly, when, in his opinion, it shall be expedient.

The governor, judges, legislative council, secretary, and such other officers as Congress shall appoint in the district, shall take an oath or affirmation of fidelity and of office; the governor before the president of congress, and all other officers before the Governor. As soon as a legislature shall be formed in the district, the council and house assembled in one room, shall have authority, by joint ballot, to elect a delegate to Congress, who shall have a seat in Congress, with a right of debating but not of voting during this temporary government.

And, for extending the fundamental principles of civil and religious liberty, which form the basis whereon these republics, their laws and constitutions are erected; to fix and establish those principles as the basis of all laws, constitutions, and governments, which forever hereafter shall be formed in the said territory: to provide also for the establishment of States, and permanent government therein, and for their admission to a share in the federal councils on an equal footing with the original States, at as early periods as may be consistent with the general interest:

It is hereby ordained and declared by the authority aforesaid, That the following articles shall be considered as articles of compact between the original States and the people and States in the said territory and forever remain unalterable, unless by common consent, to wit:

ART. 1. No person, demeaning himself in a peaceable and orderly manner, shall ever be molested on account of his mode of worship or religious sentiments, in the said territory.

ART. 2. The inhabitants of the said territory shall always be entitled to the benefits of the writ of *habeas corpus,* and of the trial by jury; of a proportionate representation of the people in the legislature; and of judicial proceedings according to the course of the common law. All persons shall be bailable, unless for capital offences, where the proof shall be evident or the presumption great. All fines shall be moderate; and no cruel or unusual punishments shall be inflicted. No man shall be deprived of his liberty or property, but by the judgment of his peers or the law of the land; and, should the public exigencies make it necessary, for the common preservation, to take any person's property, or to demand his particular services, full compensation shall be made for the same. And, in the just preservation of rights and property, it is understood and declared, that no law ought ever to be made, or have force in the said territory, that shall, in any manner whatever, interfere with or affect private contracts or engagements, *bona fide,* and without fraud, previously formed.

ART. 3. Religion, morality, and knowledge, being necessary to good government and the happiness of mankind, schools and the means of education shall forever be encouraged. The utmost good faith shall always be observed towards the Indians; their lands and property shall never be taken from them without their consent; and, in their property, rights, and liberty, they shall never be invaded or disturbed, unless in just and lawful wars authorized by Congress; but laws founded in justice and humanity, shall from time to time be made for preventing wrongs being done to them, and for preserving peace and friendship with them.

ART. 4. The said territory, and the States which may be formed therein, shall forever remain a part of this Confederacy of the United States of America, subject to the Articles of Confederation, and to such alterations therein as shall be constitutionally made; and to all the acts and ordinances of the United States in Congress assembled, conformable thereto. The inhabitants and settlers in the said territory shall be subject to pay a part of the federal debts contracted or to be contracted, and a proportional part of the expenses of government, to be apportioned on them by Congress according to the same common rule and measure by which apportionments thereof shall be made on the other States; and the taxes for paying their proportion shall be laid and levied by the authority and direction of the legislatures of the district or districts, or new States, as in the original States, within the time agreed upon by the United States in Congress assembled. The legislatures of those districts or new States, shall never interfere with the primary disposal of the soil by the United States in Congress assembled, nor with any regulations Congress may find necessary for securing the title in such soil to the *bona fide* purchasers. No tax shall be imposed on lands the property of the United States; and, in no case, shall non-resident proprietors be taxed higher than residents. The navigable waters leading into the Mississippi and St. Lawrence, and the carrying places between the same, shall be common highways and forever free, as well to the inhabitants of the said territory as to the citizens of the United States, and those of any other States that may be admitted into the confederacy, without any tax, impost, or duty therefor.

ART. 5. There shall be formed in the said territory, not less than three nor more than five States; and the boundaries of the States, as soon as Virginia shall alter her act of cession, and consent to the same, shall become fixed and established as follows, to wit: The western State in the said territory, shall be bounded by the Mississippi, the Ohio, and Wabash Rivers; a direct line drawn from the Wabash and Post Vincents, due North, to the territorial line between the United States and Canada; and, by the said territorial line, to the Lake of the Woods and Mississippi. The middle State shall be bounded by the said direct line, the Wabash from Post Vincents to the Ohio, by the Ohio, by a direct line, drawn due north from the mouth of the Great Miami, to the said territorial line, and by the said territorial line. The eastern State shall be bounded by the last mentioned direct line, the Ohio, Pennsylvania, and the said territorial line: *Provided, however,* and it is further understood and declared, that the boundaries of these three States shall be subject so far to be altered, that, if Congress shall hereafter find it expedient, they shall have authority to form one or two States in that part of the said territory which lies north of an east and west line drawn through the southerly bend or extreme of lake Michigan. And, whenever any of the said States shall have sixty thousand free inhabitants therein, such State shall be admitted, by its delegates, into the Congress of the United States, on an equal footing with the original States in all respects whatever, and shall be at liberty to form a permanent constitution and State government: *Provided,* the constitution and government so to be formed, shall be republican, and in conformity to the principles contained in these articles; and, so far as it can be consistent with the general interest of the confederacy, such admission shall be allowed at an earlier period, and when there may be a less number of free inhabitants in the State than sixty thousand.

ART. 6. There shall be neither slavery nor involuntary servitude in the said territory, otherwise than in the punishment of crimes whereof the party shall have been duly convicted: *Provided, always,*

That any person escaping into the same, from whom labor or service is lawfully claimed in any one of the original States, such fugitive may be lawfully reclaimed and conveyed to the person claiming his or her labor or service as aforesaid.

Be it ordained by the authority aforesaid, That the resolutions of the 23rd of April 1784, relative to the subject of this ordinance, be, and the same are hereby repealed and declared null and void.

Welcome, 1788

ARTHUR ST. CLAIR

On Wednesday the 9th of July 1788 His Excellency Arthur St Clair Esqr Governour & Commander in Chief of the Territory of the United States North West of the River Ohio arrived at Fort Harmar, & on the 15th was published the Ordinance of the honourable Congress for the Government of the Territory—The Commissions of the Governour, the Honourable Judges Samuel H. Parsons, James M. Varnum, and the Secretary's, after which His Excellency addressed the People assembled at Marietta, as follows—

From the Ordinance for the Establishment of Civil Government in this Quarter, that has been just now read, you have a Proof Gentlemen of the Attention of Congress to the Welfare of the Citizens of the United States how remote soever their Situation may be—

A good Government well administered is the first of Blessings to a People—every thing desirable in Life is thereby secured to them, & from the Operation of wholesome & equal Laws, the Passions of Men are restrain'd within due Bounds; their Actions receive a proper Direction; the Virtues are cultivated, & the beautiful Fabric of civilized Life is reared & brought to Perfection.

The Executive Part of the Administration of this Government has been entrusted to me, & I am truly Sensible of the Importance of the Trust, & how much depends upon the due Execution of it—to you

From Arthur St. Clair, address to people at Marietta, July, 9, 1788, in Clarence Carter (ed.), *The Territorial Papers of the United States* II, (1934), pp. 263-266.

Gentlemen, over whom it is to be immediately exercised—to your Posterity! perhaps to the whole Community of America! Would to God I were more equal to the Discharge of it! but my best Endeavours shall not be wanting to fulfil the Desire & the Expectations of Congress, that you may find yourselves happy under it.

. . . .

You will observe Gentlemen, that the System which has been formed for this Country, & is now to take Effect, is temporary only—suited to your infant Situation, & to continue no longer than that State of Infancy shall last: During that Period the Judges, with my Assistance are to select from the Codes of the Mother States such Laws as may be thought proper for you.—This is a very important Part of our Duty, & will be attended to with the greatest Care—But Congress have not intrusted this great Business wholly to our Prudence or Discretion; & here again you have a fresh Proof of their paternal Attention,—We are bound to report to them all Laws that shall be introduced, & they have reserved to themselves the Power of annulling them—so that if any Law not proper in itself, or not suited to your Circumstances, either From our not seeing the whole Extent of its Operation, or any other Circumstance should be imposed it will be immediately repealed. But with all the Care & Attention to your Interest & Happiness that can be taken, you have many Difficulties to struggle with—The subduing a new Country, notwithstanding its natural Advantages, is alone an arduous Task:—a Task however that Patience & Perseverance will Surmount, & these Virtues so necessary in every Situation, but peculiarly so in yours you must resolve to exercise—neither is the reducing a Country from a State of Nature to a State of Civilization so irksome as it may appear from a slight or superficial View—Even very sensible Pleasures attend it;—the gradual Progress of Improvement fills the Mind with delectable Ideas—Vast Forests converted into arable Fields, & Cities rising in Places which were lately the Habitation of wild Beasts give a Pleasure something like that attendant on Creation, if we can form an Idea of it—the Imagination is ravished, & a Taste communicated of even the "Joy of God to see a happy World."—

The Advantages however are not merely imaginary—situated as you are in the most temperate Climate; favour'd with the most fertile Soil; surrounded by the noblest & most beautiful Rivers, every Portion of Labour will meet its due Reward: But you have upon your Frontiers Numbers of Savage and, too often, hostile Nations—against them it is necessary that you should be guarded, & the Measures that may be thought proper for that End, tho' they may a little interrupt your usual Pursuits, I am certain, will be cheerfully submitted to.—One Mode however I will at this Time venture to recommend, which as it is in every Point of View the easiest & most eligible, so I am persuaded it will be attended with much Success—Endeavour to cultivate a good Understanding with the Natives, without much Familiarity Treat them on all Occasions with Kindness & the strictest Regard to Justice—Run not into their Customs & Habits, which is but too frequent with those who settle near them, but endeavour to induce them to adopt yours—Prevent, by every Means, that dreadful Reproach, perhaps too justly brought by them against all the People they have been yet acquainted with, that, professing the most holy & benevolent Religion, they are uninfluenced by its Dictates & regardless of its Precepts—Such a Conduct will produce on their Parts the utmost Confidence—they will soon become sensible of the superior Advantages of a State of Civilization—They will gradually lose their present Manners, & a way be opened for introducing amongst them the Gospel of Peace; & you be the happy Instruments in the Hand of Providence of bringing forward that Time, which will surely arrive, when all the Nations of the Earth shall become the Kingdom of Jesus Christ.

The present Situation of the Territory calls for Attention in various Places, & will necessarily induce frequent Absence both of the Judges & myself from this delightful Spot; but at all Times & Places as it is my indispensable Duty, so it is very much my Desire to do every thing within the Compass of my Power for the Peace, good Order & perfect Establishment of the Settlement—& as I look for, not only a cheerful Acquiescence in, & Submission to, necessary measures, but a cordial Cooperation; so I flatter myself my well meant Endeavours will be accepted in the Spirit in which they are rendered, & our Satisfaction will be mutual and complete.

Dear George Washington

ARTHUR ST. CLAIR

To the President of the United States   *[August, 1789]*
A Memorial respecting the Territory of the united States north west of the River Ohio.—

The Country, generally known by the appellation of the western Territory, is a Tract of Land bounded by the western Limits of

Pennsylvania on the East; by the River Ohio on the South; by the River Missisippi on the West; and by the Line of separation between the United States and the Province of Quebec on the North. This extensive Region is blessed with a fertile Soil and desirable Climate in every part of it which has yet been explored; and the Inhabitants of the neighbouring States, very early discovered a strong Disposition to take Possession of it:—Congress, in order to turn that Disposition to the public Advantage, and to secure to the united States the Benefits that were expected to flow from the right to the Soil, as a fund for discharging the Domestic Debts, gave orders that it should be sold, and established a form of Government for the future Inhabitants: Sales have been made of some considerable Portions of it—A Number of People, from various parts of the United States have been introduced, and the Government has been organized.

. . . .

The Governor and Judges of a Majority of them are to adopt and publish such Laws of the original States, Criminal and Civil, as they judge proper and best suited to the Circumstances of the Territory; and they are to be in force until disapproved by Congress. There are upon the Missisippi and Wabash Rivers a considerable Number of People, the remains of the ancient french Colony, who have been accustomed to be governed by the Laws of France, the Customs of Canada, and the arbitrary Edicts of the british Commandants, after they fell under the Power of Britain:—there are also some People there, who migrated from Virginia after the Cession of the Country to the united States. A Settlement is begun between the great and little Miami composed of Emigrants from Virginia and New Jersey, but principally from the last. The Reservation, for the Virginia Officers, upon the Scioto River, has turned the Attention of many to that part of the Country, and a Settlement will be made there, so soon as it shall be laid open, by People from Virginia and the District of Kentucky where they have been used to the Laws & Customs of Virginia.—Higher up the Ohio comes the Country purchased by the Ohio Company, which being composed of Adventurers, chiefly, from Massachusets, Connecticut and Rhode Island, the first Inhabitants are, and will be, from those States—Above that again are the Ranges of Townships part of which have been sold, and as they are now the Property of Persons in New York, Jersey and Pennsylvania the Settlements will be made by People from those States—to the north of the last is the Connecticut Reservation, which that State is now disposing of—and to the north of the Ohio Companys Tract one of

From Arthur St. Clair to the President, August 1789, Clarence Carter, (ed.), *The Territorial Papers of the United States,* II (1934), pp. 204-212.

the Reservations for the late Army lays.—Laws that are to run thro'
so great an extent of Country, and are to operate upon People who
have very different Habits and Customs require to be very attentively
considered; and it would seem that they should be composed rather
by an intermixture of those of all the original States, than that the
Acts of any one particular State should be adopted—there would
otherwise be a danger of introducing Regulations, proper enough for
a small territory, which would not suit an extensive Country, circumstanced as the western Territory will be with respect to the Habits of
its People. The Laws and Customs of the four New England States
have a great Affinity to each other.—Persons who have lived long
under any System of Law contract a Veneration for it.—The Judges,
who it is to be supposed will always be professional Men, used to
contemplate the Laws of the States where they have lived with a
favorable Eye, and from one point of View only, will see Excellencies in each that are not so obvious to others:—each of them will
have a predilection for those he has been used to:—By discussing the
Principles upon which they have been respectively founded, and
comparing their Operation and Effects, an intermixture that would
suit the whole Country, and tend to make the Inhabitants one
People, would probably be obtained, without shocking too much the
prejudices of any—to that End it seems necessary that the Judges
should be drawn from different parts of the united States. Two of
the three Judges were from New England, and one from New
Jersey—All of them deeply interested, as Proprietors, in the Tracts of
Country that had been sold. It may be a Question whether some
Inconveniencies may not arise from the last Circumstance, (for
Interest often hangs, insensibly to the Persons themselves, a Biass
upon the Minds of very honest and upright Men) and that the
Advantage of a District might be preferred to the Interest of the
Territory.

. . . .

It would be convenient that an express Power should be delegated to the Governor to fix the Seat of Government where the
principal Offices, & particularly that of the Prothonotary of the
supreme Court, should be kept:—without that provision the Judges
may think it belongs to them to determine where the Offices of their
Court shall be; and as two of them are now deeply interested in
particular Districts, it is not probable that a Law which should carry
them, out of one or other of them, to another part of the Country
could be obtained.

The western Territory, taking a comprehensive View of it, is an
interesting and very important Appendage to the united States—The
fertility of the Soil and temperature of Climate seem to point it out

as the Place to which the Emigrations from the Atlantic States should naturally be directed.—The foundation of a great additional Strength may be laid in that Country. Circumstanced as it is in many respects its Growth will probably be astonishingly rapid. It is unnecessary to enquire whether those Emigrations will not be hurtful to the Atlantic States:—the removal of so many of their People suddenly, and much Property with them, must be very sensibly felt for a long time—a regular Account is taken at Fort Harmar of all that pass down the Ohio—it is said an equal number go thro' what is called the Wilderness—The spirit however has gone forth, and cannot now be restrained; but it may well be doubted whether the Peopling that Country will ultimately be of Advantage to the Union; or at least, before any Advantage can accrue from it, whether it may not, by means of that Population, be involved in Difficulties. The Influence of the general Government will not be much felt amongst that People, from the great Distance they are removed from the Seat of it; neither will their connection with, or dependance upon it, be very apparent—

. . . .

With the English Colonies on one side and the Spanish on another, they will be exposed to the Machinations of both those Governments, and in Case of a War with one or both of them (an Event that may not be very far distant) they might be tempted to throw off all Connection with the Parent States, and put themselves under the protection of the one or the other of them. It is not to be doubted that the most alluring Hopes and Promises would be held out to them. It is certain that the British have already had Emissaries amongst the People of the Kentucky District, apparently to stimulate them to Hostilities against the Spaniards, but most probably to cherish the Disposition to revolt, which has appeared there, by intimations that they would be supported from Canada.

. . . .

Spain, also, looks with Jealousy and Discontent at the Growth of the western Country. Her Minister has marked its Progress with Attention, and has probably discovered that, tho it forms at present a part of the united States, the Ligature that binds them together is a weak one; and the Authority of the General Government over it is not well established. It is strongly suspected that he has an Understanding with some leading Characters, and that thro' them, the desire to throw off all Connection both with Virginia and the Union, is spread among the People.

. . . .

Should it be thought an Object, with Congress, to prevent this loss of People and Property (for every Man carries with him more or less of it) it might perhaps be effected by laying open a part of the Western Territory for those who want Land and cannot pay for it immediatly—The Lands upon the Missisippi and Wabash are very inviting and as Settlements are already made upon each of these Rivers would probably be preferred.—They might be set at a moderate rate and an Office opened, where any person might locate them in small Quantities, and where, upon the payment of the purchase Money, which should run upon Interest, they should receive Patents. The People, the loss of whom is the greatest any Country can suffer, would be saved—the Country would be cultivated, and the Union would derive nearly the same Advantage as if the Lands had been paid for in the first Instance; for an Interest would accrue to it, equal to the Interest accruing against it, so far as the appropriations went.

. . . .

Tho', by the above method, a great Number of People, who will otherwise remove into a foreign Country, might be induced to fix within the Territory of the united States, the Danger from their insidious Neighbours would not be at all lessned. Two Things seem necessary to that End viz, that the People of Kentucky should be made easy, by being allowed to erect themselves into a separate State, and being received into the Union as a Member of it—and that the military Establishment in the western Country should be encreased. A handful of Troops, scattered in small Posts from Venango to the Mississippi, without connection or dependance upon each other, can neither awe the one nor restrain the other. It would seem to be necessary that a Force in some Degree respectable should be stationed in that Country, and that Posts much farther advanced than the present ones should be taken.—The British, if they have ill Designs would be kept in some Check, and those Designs be more readily discovered:—Their Influence over the Savages would be lessned, and a very advantageous Trade with them, which now goes to Canada, would be turned into the united States. The People would derive Security, at the same time that they saw and felt that the Government of the Union was not a mere shadow:—their progeny would grow up in habits of Obedience and Respect—they would learn to reverence the Government; and the Countless multitudes which will be produced in that vast Region would become the Nerves and Sinews of the Union.

The Connecticut Reservation is a Tract of Land lying along the western Boundary of Pennsylvania. The Deed of Cession, of Claims to Western Lands, made by that State to the united States takes for a beginning a Line drawn paralel to the western Boundary of Pennsylvania, one hundred and twenty Miles West from it, so that the Space between those lines is impliedly confirmed to Connecticut; and it was understood in Congress when the Cession was accepted, that it would be considered by the State as confirmed, and would be disposed of in what manner that Government might think proper—the Jurisdiction remains with the united States. Judge Parsons has notified the Governor of the western Country that he had contracted with the State of Connecticut to run the outlines of the Tract; but, as the United States were a party in the Business, the line, to be run one hundred and twenty Miles west of Pennsylvania, being a territorial boundary between them and Connecticut, and as it did not appear that they had been consulted, or even had notice of the Intention to ascertain the Boundaries, the Governor did not think proper to permit him to proceed—It may be necessary that He should receive Instructions on that Head, and that the Geographer, or some other Person on the part of the united States should attend the Survey.

I have the honor to be with the utmost Respect Sir Your most obedient and most humble Servant.

Ar St CLAIR

[Endorsed] From Arthur St Clair Esq. Governor of the Western Territory Augt—1789

From the Miami, 1789

JOHN CLEVES SYMMES

Northbend, May the 18th 19th & 20th 1789.

Dear Sir,

I am sure that you begin to be impatient to hear from Miami. I shall therefore give you a short history of my efforts to carry into effect what I had premised before I left New Jersey, in the settleing of this purchase. In doing this I have not succeeded fully to my expectation; but I am very far from despairing.

Whether I was premature and rash in the attempt of so considerable a purchase and settlement, or have not made my calculations on well founded principles; or whether it is, that I have those who endeavour to defeat my views, either from Interested or envious motives I know not, but certain it is, that I have had the mortification to conflict, not only with those from whose malevolent disposition I had no right to expect anything better; but from those in office and power, unexpected obstructions have been thrown in my way. And tho I have not been actually hindered from a settlement, by the United States troops; yet very small has been the support which I have hitherto received. At Muskingum I believe, from two to three hundred men are stationed, tho that post is not to be named in point of danger with the Miami Settlement. On the other hand one Ensign, (Luce) and seventeen rank and file, are all the guards that are allowed me at present, for the protection & defence of this Slaughterhouse, as some in this country (Kentucky) are pleased to term the Miami purchase, on which are three settlements now becoming somewhat considerable, and would have been important beyond my former most sanguine expectations, had I been properly aided as promised with troops of the United States last summer, and permitted to have made my lodgement in September last, when I first explored the purchase. Those with you certainly must have a prediliction in favour of the Ohio company's settlement, or they surely would order a more equal chance on the score of defence. At the City of Marietta they had more than a year the start of the Miami settlers; of course they are much more able to repel an attack, not only from their superior numbers; but from their mode of settlement on the New England plan of connected towns or villages: the settlers with them being restrained by their directors who will not allow them land whereon to settle at pleasure. The different method adopted for settleing Miami, puts it in the power of every purchaser to chuse his ground, and convert the same into a station, village or town at pleasure: and nothing controuls him but the fear of Indians. Therefore whenever ten or twelve men will agree to form a station, it is certainly done. This desultory way of settleing will soon carry many through the purchase, if the savages do not frustrate them.

. . . .

I resolved therefore without loss of time to lay out a number of house-lots in order to form a village on the spot where we were; the ground being very proper for a project of that kind on a small scale.

Forty eight lots of one acre each was accordingly laid off, every

From John Cleves Symmes to Jonathon Dayton, May the 18th, 19th, & 20th, 1789, in Beverly Bond W. (ed.), *The Correspondence of John Cleves Symmes*, (New York, 1926), pp. 53-95.

other one of which I proposed to give away, retaining one for each propriety, upon condition only of the donees building immediately thereon.

These 24 donation lots were soon taken up, and further applications being made, I have extended the village up and down the Ohio, until it forms a front one mile and an half on the river; in which are more than one hundred lots; on forty of which, observing the order of every other lot, there is a comfortable log-cabin built & covered with shingles or clabboards, and other houses are still on hand, so that there remains not three donation lots unappropriated. This village I have called Northbend, from its being situate in the most northerly bend of the Ohio, that there is between Muskingum and the Mississipia. Northbend being so well improved by the buildings already erected and making; and fresh applications every few days being made to me for house lots; I was induced to lay off another village about seven miles up the Ohio from Northbend, being one mile in front on the river. The ground was very eligible for the purpose, and I would have continued further up and down the river, but was confined between two reserved sections. This village I call Southbend from its being contiguous to the most southerly point of land in the purchase. In this village several houses are almost finished, and others begun; and I make no doubt but the whole of the donation lots will soon be occupied if we remain in safety. I have not as yet been able to make a decisive choice of a plat for the City; tho I have found two pieces of ground both eligible for a City; but not upon the present plan of a regular square: on both, a town must, if built, be thrown into an oblong of six blocks, or squares, by four.

One of these plats lies east of this about three miles on the Ohio a little above muddy-creek. The other lies north about the same distance on the bank of the Great Miami, in a large bend of the river which you will observe on the map, about 12 miles up the Miami from its mouth. It is a question of no little moment and difficulty to determine which of these spots are preferable in point of local situation. I know that at first thought most men will decide in favour of that on the Ohio; from the supposition that the Ohio will command more trade & business than the Miami. I will readily grant that more trade will be passing up and down the Ohio, and many more boats constantly plying on a river which is eleven hundred miles in length: But some objections arise to this spot notwithstanding. You must know Sir that a *number* of towns are building on the banks of the Ohio from Pittsburgh to Louisville, and even further down the river. every one of these will be aiming at some importance. When a boat is freighted at any of the upper towns on the Ohio; unless the merchants in our city will give the Orleans price or near it, for their produce or cargoe, the Merchants of the upper towns will not fail to proceed down the river to the highest market. And as merchants will be strewed all along the Ohio, they will have the same advantage of navigation in all respects with ours. But a more important objection lies to this spot on the Ohio from its distance from the Great Miami. The extent of country spreading for many miles on both sides of the G. Miami, is beyond all dispute equal, I believe superior in point of soil, water, & timber, to any tract of equal contents to be found in the United States. From this Egypt on Miami, in a very few years will be poured down its stream to the Ohio, the products of the country, from two hundred miles above the mouth of G. Miami; which may be principally collected at a trading town, low down on the banks of that river: here no rival city or town can divide the trade of the river. The body of Miami settlers will have their communications up and down the G Miami, both for imports & exports. They cannot work their corn and flour boats 8 or 9 miles up the Ohio from the mouth of G. Miami, should the city be built above muddy creek. But were it built on the Miami, the settlers throughout the purchase would find it very convenient.

. . . .

Amazing has been the pains which many in Kentucky have taken to prejudice strangers against the Miami settlements. The cause has principally been owing to the piques of disappointment. Last September many land-jobbers from Kentucky came into the purchase, and applied for lands; and actually pointed out on paper where they wished to take them. I gave them time to the first of November to make payment for one half; and to the present month of May for the other half. The surveying and registering fees was to be paid at the time of the first half.

Some of them agreed to give an advanced price in consideration that I would wait till May come twelve-months for the purchase money. this I was content to do on their paying the surveying fees by the first of November, and allowing interest on the principal sum until paid. After this the greater part of them deserted me when about forty miles up the Miami where I had ventured on their promise to escort me down that river, meandering its courses; which so disobliged me that I have been very indifferent ever since whether one of them came into the purchase or not; as I found them very ungovernable and seditious; not to be awed or persuaded. To the disobedience of these men I impute the death of poor Filson, who had no rest afterwards while with me for fear of the Indians. and at length attempting to escape to the body of men I had left on the Ohio, he was destroyed by the savages.

These pretending purchasers neglecting to pay me one farthing until January, and the surveying business suffering greatly by the want of the fees: I was induced to publish an advertisement in the Lexington gazette; requiring of all those purchasers payment of the surveying fees, by the first of february and of one half of the purchase money by the first of March. and the residue by the first of May ensuing, or I should consider all negociations for land void wherein they did not comply herewith; or give the advanced price on a longer credit. Very few indeed have complied: the others have endeavoured to assperse my character, & throw the reasons of their noncompliance on me. But let the world judge whether it is even probable that they had either intention or ability to accomplish the payment for seventeen townships, the contents of what they had dextriously located as they called it in the space of a very few days.

The truth is, making a few exceptions of very worthy characters from the District of Kentucky, the most of them had no other views than speculation as appeared soon after their return home; from their selling to their neighbours the privilege of taking a part of what they had located, and becoming accountable to me for the purchase money. Finding themselves disappointed in their views, and no longer able to prosecute their plans of selling what they never had an intention of making their own, & driving the same game they had long followed in Kentucky: many have vented their spleen in abuses & calumnies both of me & of the country within the purchase; endeavouring to prevent every person they can from coming to Miami. At Limestone they assert with an air of assurance, that the Miami country is despicable, that many of the inhabitants are killed; the settlers all fled who have escaped the tomhawk: adjuring those bound to the falls of Ohio not to call at the Miamis, for that they would certainly be destroyed by the Indians. With these falsehoods they have terrified about thirty families who had come down the river with a design of settleing at Miami, and prevailed with them to land at Lime-stone & go into Kentucky. But however, they are not able to frustrate the settlements altogether.

. . . .

I will now Sir reassume the subject of the Indians who had been so long impatient to see me at Miami. On my arrival at Miami I found no Indians at the place, they were all out at their Camp about six miles off, and I could not then tarry for an interview. A few days after my arrival at Northbend I had occasion to send my nephew to Columbia in a keel-boat; with him George the interpreter and an old Shawanose called Capt Fog came down to me. Two days after several more Shawanose Indians and some squaws came down by land. And in a few days following, arrived a Shawanose chief with another man of that nation.

The chief communicated to me their wishes to be on friendly

terms: signifying that it would be very much to their advantage to have free intercourse with us, and exchange their peltrys for the articles which they much wanted. To this you will suppose I readily agreed. The chief (the others sitting round him) wished to be informed how far I was supported by the United States, and whether the thirteen fires had sent me hither. I answered them in the affirmative: and spread before them the thirteen stripes which I had in a flag then in my camp. I pointed to the troops in their Uniform (then on parade) & informed the chief, that those were the warriors which the thirteen fires kept in constant pay to avenge their quarrel: and that tho the United States were desirous of peace with them, yet they were able to chastise any agressor who should dare to offend them: and to demonstrate this, I shewed them the seal of my commission, on which the American arms are impressed: Observing that while the Eagle held a branch of a tree as an emblem of peace in one claw; she had strong & sharp arrows in the other; which denoted her power to punish her enemies. The chief who observed the device on the seal with great attention, replied by the interpreter. "That he could not perceive any intimations of peace from the attitude the Eagle was in; having her wings spread as in flight; when folding of the wings denoted rest and peace. That he could not understand how the branch of a tree could be considered as a pacific emblem, for rods designed for correction were always taken from the boughs of trees. That to him the Eagle appeared from her bearing a large whip in one claw, and such a number of arrows in the other, and in full career of flight, to be wholly bent on war & mischief.["]

. . . .

About three weeks previous to this transaction, as several parties of surveyors were surveying in the neighbourhood of Mad-river; Mr John Mills with his party as they were rising out of their camp early one morning were fired upon by a party of Indians, three or four in number: two men; Mr Holman of Kentucky, & Mr Wells of Delaware state were killed: Mr Mills with three others escaped unhurt. This is the only instance wherein violence has been done by the Indians to any man in the purchase since the death of Mr Filson in September last. It remains yet unknown to us of what tribe they were who fired on Mr Mills: those Indians who came in after that tragedy, pretended to be entirely innocent and ignorant of the murders. Some of the settlers at Columbia were for detaining a few of the Indians until the rest would bring in the offenders; but I thought this measure not warrantable and forbid it.

Our living hitherto in the friendly manner we have with the Indians, has excited the jealousy & ill will of many of our neighbours on the Kentucky side of the Ohio: and some even threaten to cross the river and put every Indian to death which they find on the Miami purchase: this however I believe is only threats & will not be executed.

I am very sorry that the people of Kentucky cannot enjoy equal peace and quiet from the savages: perhaps if they would act as moderately towards them, they might live in as much safety as the people of this purchase.

As to the quality of soil throughout the purchase, it is generally good, with a very few exceptions. The military range is held to be equal, if not better land than any range in the tract. There are very few hills after one leaves those of the Ohio: but large bodies of meadow land of excellent quality in many places. It is generally very well watered, as you will perceive by the map; not a stream being laid down therein but what the surveyors noted under oath in their field books as they ran the lines. A variety of stone is met with in the purchase: such as mill-stone-rock, lime-stone, and a gray stone, flat & well formed for building. The timber is in many parts excellent; in some others but indifferent, owing to the soils being too rich. This may seem a paradox to you; but in this country on the richest soil grows the least useful timber. But what I call the beauty of the country is, the many pararies which lie in the neighbourhood of Mad river: these are at once without labour, proper for ploughing or mowing. Mad river itself is a natural curiosity, about six poles wide on an average and very deep, gliding along with the utmost rapidity: its waters are beautifully clear and deep, but confined for the most part within its banks. What can give its current such velocity in the midst of so level a country, is a matter of astonishment to all who beholds it. Some of the surveyors & others who went out about three weeks ago, returned lately to this, and reported to me, that they had explored the country as high as the tenth range; that it was a most agreeable country and tract of land, from one Miami to the other, interspersed with the plats of old Indian Towns, and fine streams of water proper for mill-building. That the head branches of the little Miami were nearly run down by them; being nothing larger than good mill-streams. As to the latitude & climate, I find that we are situate half a degree more northerly than I had imagined, being in 38°-30' North; I am fully of opinion that the climate is an healthy one; there has been no complaint of agues or fevers since the first lodgement was made in November last; very little stagnant water is to be met with; and where the land is a little wet, it may be drained without difficulty.

Ignorant People

ARTHUR ST. CLAIR

December (no date), 1799.

Dear Sir:—Our assembly, at length, is up, and the session has been a very harmonious one, notwithstanding that I was obliged to put a negative upon a good many of their acts.

I have conversed with you on the subject of dividing this Territory into districts and erecting two governments in it. You seemed to think it would be a proper measure, and that nothing made against it but the additional expense it would occasion. To me that has always appeared a small consideration, when compared with the inconveniences that would probably follow from its soon becoming a State; and, if it is not divided, it must become a State very soon. It is even thought by some that the requisite number of inhabitants are now within it, and measures have been taken by the legislature to ascertain it. But no time shall be lost, when it does come about, by directing an annual enumeration.

A multitude of indigent and ignorant people are but ill qualified to form a constitution and government for themselves; but that is not the greatest evil to be feared from it. They are too far removed from the seat of government to be much impressed with the power of the United States. Their connection with any of them is very slender—many of them having left nothing but creditors behind them, whom they would very willingly forget entirely. Fixed political principles they have none, and though at present they seem attached to the General Government, it is in fact but a passing sentiment, easily changed or even removed, and certainly not strong enough to be counted upon as a principle of action; and there are a good many who hold sentiments in direct opposition to its principles, and who, though quiet at present, would then take the lead. Their government would most probably be democratic in its form and oligarchic in its execution, and more troublesome and more opposed to the measures of the United States than even Kentucky. All this, I think, may be prevented by the division of the Territory. Time would be afforded for the cultivation of a disposition favorable to the General Government, as the inhabitants would meet with nothing but friendship and protection from the United States, and the influence of the few wealthy would cease entirely, or scarce be felt, and gratitude and attachment would become fixed habits of the mind. But it is not every division that would answer those purposes,

From Arthur St. Clair to James Ross, December (n.d.) 1799, William Henry Smith, *The St. Clair Papers*, Vol. II, (Cincinnati, 1882), pp. 480-484.

but such a one as would probably keep them in the colonial state for a good many years to come. In a letter, which I wrote to the Secretary of State by the last post, on this subject, I mentioned the proper boundaries to them, but, on further reflection, I think it would not answer; that it would divide the present inhabitants in such a manner as to make the upper or eastern division surely Federal, and form a counterpoise from opposing local interests in the western division to those who are unfriendly to the General Government, I think is certain; but the eastern division is too thinly inhabited, and the design would be too evident. A line drawn due north from the mouth of Eagle Creek, where it empties itself into the Ohio, would answer better. There would then be the counties of Adams, of Ross, of Washington, of Jefferson and Trumbull in the eastern division, and all of them must hereafter be subdivided, and other counties made out of them; and the western division would contain the counties of Hamilton, Wayne, Knox, St. Clair, and Randolph, and each of them would have a sufficient number of inhabitants to continue in the present stage of government—that is, to make laws for themselves by their representatives; whereas, were the Territory divided by the great Miami, the western division must return to the first stage.

. . . .

The division of the Territory, I am persuaded, will be pressed, and I believe it to be a part of Colonel Worthington's business in Philadelphia; and the great Miami, or a line drawn from the mouth of it, will be set forth in the strongest manner as the proper line. The people of Ross are very desirous it should take place. Their views are natural and innocent enough. They look no further than giving consequence to Chillicothe. But I am very much mistaken if their leaders have not other and more extensive views. They think the division in that way would but little retard their becoming a State, and as almost all of them are democrats, whatever they pretend to the contrary, they expect that both the power and the influence would come into their hands, and that they would be able to model it as they please; and it is my fixed belief it would be in a manner as unfriendly to the United States as possible.

Constitution 1802

ARTHUR ST. CLAIR

Mr. President and Gentlemen of the Convention:—You are now an organized body, and I am happy that you are so, in whatever manner it may have been effected. As the act of Congress had not prescribed the mode, I came to clear that difficulty; you got over it without my assistance, and I am perfectly satisfied; but, before you proceed to business, I request to be heard a few words.

When I look around upon this assembly and consider the purpose for which it is convened, and carry back my thoughts for fourteen years, when the affairs of this country were committed to me; when your numbers were only about thirty men; a wilderness before them to subdue, and surrounded by numerous tribes of savages, who, though at peace, were far from possessing friendly dispositions, and soon afterwards at open war—I am filled with astonishment and profound gratitude to the Almighty Ruler of the universe, who led them through all the difficulties they had to encounter, and has made of that small handful a great people, and brought them to that point from which they are to take their station on the theater of America as a nation. To you, gentlemen, as their representatives, it belongs, if you think proper to take it upon yourselves, to form for them that Constitution which, while it secures their political liberty, is to be the foundation of their welfare and respectability. The task is arduous as it is important, and it can not be doubted that you will bring to it patient and candid investigation, true patriotism, and mutual good-will and condescension.

To the present moment, gentlemen, I have looked forward with pleasant hopes, though not without a mixture of fear and anxiety, and my endeavors have not been wanting to lay a foundation for the great work before you, in morals and in regard to the institutions of religion, for it is an eternal truth that without morality there can be no religion, and without religion there can be no happiness.

My feelings, gentlemen, you can appreciate, for most of you are fathers. They have been those of a father who saw the day drawing nigh which was to send a son, over whose education he had long watched with all the varied emotions of parental affection, into a world where dangers awaited him at every step, and where the first would probably be decisive of his future fortune. These cares and anxieties for your constituents, gentlemen, have occupied a considerable portion of my life, and have cost me many a toilsome day and

From Remarks of Governor St. Clair Before the Constitutional Convention, November 3, 1802, William Henry Smith, *The St. Clair Papers*, Vol. II, (Cincinnati, 1882), pp. 592-597.

sleepless night; but the pleasure I have in reflecting that they were not entirely thrown away is very great. It pleased God to favor my endeavors, and make me frequently the instrument of good to them, and of averting the evils that hung over them. It is, gentlemen, too much the fashion of the times to complain of oppression when none is felt. The frame of your present government, it is true, is not so popular as that of the greater part of the United States, or as you may have wished, but it is as much so as it is consistent with the colonial state, and I can with honest pride assert, and for the truth of the assertion I appeal to the whole people, that it has been administered with gentleness, and with one single view, the good of the whole. So far as it depended upon me, the laws have been executed faithfully and without rigor, and by gentle means the spirit of obedience to them, and a love of order, without which civil society can not exist, has been endeavored to be introduced. It was my duty to procure the good of the whole people, and it has been my only ambition to fulfill that duty. Errors, no doubt, I have fallen into. They were errors of the head, not of the heart. They will be judged with candor, and viewed, I trust, with some indulgence. I could indeed have wished, gentlemen, that our political bark had been launched in gentler weather, and under better auspices, for I see a storm approaching in which, if she be not overset, she may at least suffer damage. Party rage is stalking with destructive strides over the whole continent. That baneful spirit destroyed all the ancient republics, and the United States seem to be running the same career that ruined them with a degree of rapidity truly alarming to every reflecting mind. But she is on the waves, and can not now be stopped. . . .

It would be the height of impropriety in me to attempt to direct you in your deliberations, but I may be allowed to offer you some advice. The act of Congress under which you are convened has determined the object on which they are first to be employed, to wit, whether it be or be not expedient, at this time, to form a constitution and frame of government. That being determined in the affirmative, which I presume it will be, you are at liberty to proceed and make that constitution, or to pass an ordinance for the election of representatives for that purpose. But you are further at liberty, gentlemen, to confine the constitution to be made to what is called the eastern division of the Territory, or to extend it to the whole Territory. That the people of the Territory should form a convention and a constitution needed no act of Congress. To pretend to authorize it was, on their part, an interference with the internal affairs of the country, which they had neither the power nor the right to make. The act is not binding on the people, and is in truth a nullity, and, could it be brought before that tribunal where acts of Congress can be tried, would be declared a nullity. To all acts of Congress that respects the United States (they can make no other) in their corporative capacity, and which are extended by express words to the Territory, we are bound to yield obedience. For all internal affairs we have a complete legislature of our own, and in them are no more bound by an act of Congress than we would be bound by an edict of the first consul of France. Had such an attempt been made upon any of the United States in their separate capacity, the act would have been spurned from them with indignation. We, I trust, also know our rights, and will support them, and, being assembled, gentlemen, as a convention, no matter by what means it was brought about, you may do whatever appears to you to be for the best for your constituents as freely as if Congress had never interfered in the matter, and it may be a strong motive to you for so acting, that, by this very act, above five thousand people are divested of the rights they were in possession of without a hearing—bartered away like sheep in a market—transferred to another government, and thrown back into a stage of it which has been loaded with every epithet of opprobrium which the English language affords. But that act holds out certain provisions, which were, no doubt, expected to operate upon you, and, by some, have been thought to be advantageous. The first is, that the section No. 16 in every township shall be granted to the inhabitants of such township for the use of schools. It is to be observed that the section No. 16 in every township is already given for the use of schools in as complete a manner as they could now be granted by the Congress.

All that is wanting is an act to authorize the President to make patents, and that would be wanting were they now to be given by acts of Congress. The grant of these sections was a part of the terms on which the country was settled, and they can not be resumed, because the contract has been complied with on our part; and if the Congress has either granted, sold, or otherwise disposed of any of them, the act is void. The second proposition is, that the salt springs, with the sections which include them, near to the Scioto and Muskingum Rivers, shall be granted to the State for the use of the people, provided the legislature shall never sell or lease the same for a longer term than ten years. It is a happy thing for us that Providence has been pleased to place an article so necessary to the life of man as salt in the bosom of our country. These springs have been worked for a great many years, and, though nothing has been paid for the privilege of working them, salt has always been extremely dear; now, unless the persons to whom they may have been leased pay for their lease, no revenue can be derived from these salt springs, and if they do pay for them, the amount paid, and probably much more, will be laid upon the salt, so that instead of a benefit, this gift would prove an injury, and an injury that would fall unequally. The whole people to whom the rent would accrue, would reap a very small advantage at the expense of those who, from their local situation, must depend on those springs for their salt.

The third is, that the twentieth part of the net proceeds of the lands within the State, sold or to be sold after the 30th of June last, shall be applied to the laying out and making roads from the navigable waters emptying into the Atlantic to the Ohio to the State and through it. This proposition is a mere illusion; it holds out the prospect of an advantage that never will be realized. The application of the money is to be made by Congress, in which we shall have very little weight, at any rate; and it is coupled with conditions that would defeat it, while they insult us. The first condition is, that until another census, that is for nearly nine years to come, we shall submit to have only one member in the House of Representatives of the United States. The next is, that every and each tract of land sold, as aforesaid (the twentieth part of the price of which is to be laid out on roads), shall be exempt from every species of taxation by authority of the State, whether for State, county, township, or any other purpose whatever. The State shall derive no aid as to revenue from those lands, while they may be taxed by Congress for the express purpose of raising a revenue. But those lands are solemnly pledged for the redemption of the public debt, a proportion of which we must pay. The money then pretended to be given by Congress for roads, if Congress had the right to apply it, which they have not, must come from ourselves; but where are we to find it? The reservations amount to a great part of the soil, and are not subject to taxation. The lands sold after the 30th of June last, if you close with this proposition, will not be subject to taxation for five years, and what is there besides, except a very small movable property in a country without trade, from whence our revenue is to be derived, and that movable property taxed already as high as it can possibly bear for county and township purposes. It is evident that the whole expense of the government must be laid upon the lands appropriated before the 30th of June last, for experience has taught us that we have no other resource but a land tax; but such a land tax would fall so unequally, it would never be borne.

But, gentlemen, why are conditions imposed upon us before we can obtain a right which is ours by nature and by compact? Were conditions imposed upon Vermont, or upon Tennessee, before they could be admitted into the Union? There was none attempted. Why, then, this odious distinction in our case? It is past a doubt that the Territory contains the number of people which, by the compact with the United States, or the terms of settlement, is necessary to entitle it to become a State, and a member of the Union on an equal footing with the original States; and the gentlemen in Congress who brought forward these propositions admitted that, if there were not the number at that time, there certainly would be before another session of Congress, and that then was the only time to saddle us with conditions; or, as they termed it, to make a good bargain with us, for, if once we had the necessary number, it would be no longer in their power. Form, then, gentlemen, or direct a new election for the purpose, a Constitution for the whole Territory; assert your right to a full representation in the councils of the nation; direct the legislature forthwith to cause a census to be taken; it will not require much time if set about in earnest. Let your representatives go forward with that in their hands, and demand the admission of the Territory as a State. It will not, it can not be refused. But, suppose it should be refused, it would not affect your government, or any thing you have done to organize it. That would go on equally well, or perhaps better. It was, I think, eight years after the people of Vermont had formed their government, and exercised all the powers of an independent State, before it was admitted into the Union. The government was not retarded a single moment on that account. It would be incomparably better that we should be deprived of a share in the national councils for a session or two, or even for years, than that we should be degraded to an unequal share in them for nine years; but it will not happen. We have the means in our own hands to bring Congress to reason, if we should be forced to use them. If we submit to the degradation, we should be trodden upon, and, what is worse, we should deserve to be trodden upon. I will leave these reflections upon your table, gentlemen, to be made what use of you may think proper.

3 The Ohio Indian Wars, 1790-1795

IT WAS ONE thing for the young American republic to claim the regions west of the Allegheny Mountains and north of the Ohio River through right of conquest; but to hold them was another matter. The Washington administration had to control the westward thrust of settlement into the Northwest Territory, to outline an Indian policy that would provide security for settlement, to provide a sufficient military force to forestall frontier warfare, and to discourage encroachments by foreign powers on the American frontier. The United States had already signed two treaties with the Ohio Indians in an attempt to establish a line separating white settlement from Indian lands: the first in 1785 at Fort McIntosh, and the second at Fort Finney in 1786.

The Ohio Indians were never defeated by American arms during the Revolutionary War, and the United States had gained the vast Ohio Valley through diplomacy rather than on the field of battle. Following the murder of the Shawnee chief Cornstalk at Fort Randolph in 1775, most of the Ohio Indians rallied to the British cause. Congress, in 1783, claimed that those Indians living in the western regions did so at the good will of the United States. However, few of the Indians saw good reasons to relinquish their claims to the Ohio Valley. Americans, encouraged by the dream of economic improvement, scurried to fill what they considered national territory, and thus hostilities grew on the frontier. The struggle for dominance of the Ohio frontier between 1790 and 1795 was critical to American westward expansion, to the Washington administration, and to the St. Clair government in the Northwest Territory. In fact, it was a test for the survival of the federal government itself.

Washington, sensitive to the country's weak financial and military position, was aware that a frontier war could prove disastrous. Consequently, he attempted to reach an accord with the Ohio Indians. These Indians, loosely formed into an Ohio confederacy, were encouraged by the British and the famous Mohawk leader Joseph Brant to resist American encroachments. Although some of the Indians were themselves divided, the resistance to American western advancement centered in the Shawnee and the Miami. Arthur St. Clair, charged with the responsibility of protecting settlements in the Northwest Territory, negotiated two treaties at Fort Harmar on January 9, 1789. The second of these treaties was to re-establish the older Fort McIntosh treaty line of 1785. However, representatives of the two most powerful Ohio tribes, the Shawnee and the Miami, did not attend, and without their support peace was impossible. The rate of bloodletting between whites and Indians increased on the frontier; and in the fall of 1789, Washington, who was determined to hold the western regions and to protect western settlements, authorized the use of military force against the Indians.

Under the command of General Josiah Harmar, Virginia and Pennsylvania volunteers joined a small force of regular troops at Fort Washington. In September 1790, this army began a drive against the Miami villages located where the St. Joseph and St. Mary's rivers join to form the Maumee. However, trouble beset Harmar's command: after reaching its destination and burning villages and supplies, the American force was attacked by Indians and routed on October 21, 1790. Encouraged by this success and responding to the American incursion into their homeland, the Indians increased their raids on the Ohio settlements. The United States was now faced with its first full-scale Indian war.

Confronted by war on the frontier, Congress authorized the formation of a new army in the spring of 1791, this time under the command of St. Clair himself. Washington faced a dilemma. Because of the country's weakness, a war on the frontier might encourage foreign intervention, promote an expanded war, and cost the loss of the West. On the other hand, if no action were taken, the British, allied with the Indians, could control the Ohio Valley and wrest it from the United States. While St. Clair gathered his army, the government attempted to negotiate a settlement with the Miami. The negotiations were fruitless, and the next move was up to the United States.

Harried by numerous problems, St. Clair assembled his army at Fort Washington. Meanwhile, expeditions in June and August of 1791 were directed against the Indians along the Wabash and Eel rivers. Both accomplished little except to further prove American aggressiveness to the Indians. Finally, in September, St. Clair slowly moved his army toward the Miami villages. However, he suffered a complete military disaster along a tributary of the Wabash on November 3, 1791. The casualty list was staggering: 630 officers and men killed, 283 wounded. Never was an American army more soundly defeated by warring Indians. Flushed by success, the Indians demanded that the Ohio River serve as the dividing line between white settlement and Indian territory. The United States attempted to negotiate the differences with the Indians three times in 1792 and 1793. Contemptuous of such weakness, the Indians killed two of the American emissaries in the spring of 1792.

Meanwhile, the command of the western army passed to General Anthony Wayne, the hero of Stony Point. Patient and determined, Wayne prepared his army for a crushing blow against the Indians. After a slow, deliberate march from Hobson's Choice, outside Cincinnati, to the Maumee, Wayne's army defeated the Indians at the Battle of Fallen Timbers on August 20, 1794. Stunned by their defeat and shunned by the British, the Indians signed the Treaty of Greenville on August 10, 1795, which concluded the Ohio Indian wars. Consequently, after a series of setbacks and one demoralizing victory over the Indians, the western army partially opened Ohio to white settlement, and the Northwest Territory was securely part of the United States.

Indians!

RUFUS PUTNAM

Marietta, February 28th 1791

SIR Sence the affair of the 2d of January. Several Wyandot men & women have ben in to Fort Harmer to Trade, they approched with Shyness and in truth our people ware at a loss how to treat them, but on the whole it was thought best, and they ware recived & treated in the Same frindly maner as heretofore: althoe Sculking parties ware at the Same time discovered houvering round Some of our Settlements; the accounts these indians give of the affair at the Big-Bottom, are various—the first reported thet they Saw their Trail on their return & that by mar[ks] they left on certain trees they ware 76 in number & had 20 Scalps—the next account was from one Gevoto a Wyandot man who Said he was told by a man who Saw them, that they consisted of about 30 and that they had Some prisoners as well as Scalps—that they came from a Village on the Tawa river—and another account we have from a Wyandot who Said he Saw the party on their return neer Sandusky, that they ware chiefly Mingos consisted of abut 30 and had 5 prisoners:—the Indians who have ben in, all agree that a great many Indians are going to war, but pretend that the Wyndots & Dellawares are not, and that we must expect a great many here in a few weeks—about ten days ago a Soldier was taken within 60 rods of Fort Harmer but he had the good fortune to make his escape the first night, and the next day came in to the Settlement at Belle-prie, the Sold[ier] Sais thet he was first taken by three and carred a few miles when they came to 4 others, that one of them Spake good English and was very perticuler in his enquierris respecting the number of men at Fort Harmer, Marietta, & Belle-prie the night after the Soldier got into Belle-prie, a party of Indians (Supposed to be the Same who took the Soldier) brook open a number of Deserted houses in the lower part of Belle-prie Settlement, but they did no damage to any of the property except killing one Sheep and two fat hogs a part of which they took of—Our people have nearely compleatd their works of Defence, and I have no great apprehentions for the imediate Saifty of their persons but their forage, Corn & Cattle Still remain exposed as they have not ben able hatherto to remove them to places of Security—

the present crisis appears to me important, not only as it respects the inhabitants of these frontiers but the united States in General— for Should Goverment take efectual measu[res] to bring the natives

From Judge Putnam to the President, February 28, 1791, Clarence Carter (ed.), *The Territorial Papers of the United States*, II (1934), pp. 337-339.

to Submission, & for the protection of those who have Settled under her authorety, She may fairly calculate on a rapid sale of her lands, by which She may Sink many millions of her National Debt—but on the Contrary Should She leve her Citizens to be insulted & murdered by the Savages, I think it dos not require the Spirit of prophecy to foretell the consequence. No more lands will be purchased but will probably be Seized on by privit adventurers who will pay little or no regard to the laws of the United States or the rights of the natives—It is a fact Sir, well known that imediately after the conclusion of the war in 1783 privet adventurers, in a perticuler way, located & by building Cabbens, girdling trees or planting a few hills of Corn, took posetion of all the most valuable land on the Muskingum, Hockhocking, and other rivers as well as on the ohio for Several hundred mils, Nor must it be forgot that numbers of these people ware driven off by the federal Troops at the point of the Bayonet, their houses burnt & corn destroyed—when therefore it Shall be known that Congress have given up the protection of the Country, what are we to expect but these people, with others of like priniples, will return like a flood & Seize the country to them Selves, and Should this be the case is it probable that the United States will ever be able to reduce them to obediance without incuring a much greater expence then the chastizeing the Indians in a proper maner & the necessary establish-[ment] for the protection of the Settlements can posiably amount [to].

all the Settlements in Virginia bordoring on the Ohio in our Neighbourhood are erecting defences—We here that 7 persons ware killed about two [wee]ks ago neer Short Creek the account of which probably reah you before this—Major Sargent I hear is at Fort Pitt—

I have the honour to be with the highest posiable Sentements of Respect Sir your most obedient & most humble Servent

RUFUS PUTNAM

Causes for the War

HENRY KNOX

The Secretary for the Department of War.

[January 26, 1792]
The Causes *of the existing* Hostilities *between the* United States, *and certain Tribes of* Indians *North-West of the* Ohio, *stated and explained from official and authentic Documents, and published in obedience to the orders of the* President *of the* United States.

A Recurrence to the Journals of the United States in Congress assembled, of the early stages of the late war, will evince the public solicitude to preserve peace with the Indian tribes, and to prevent their engaging in a contest in which they were no wise interested.

But although partial treaties or conventions were formed with some of the northern and western tribes, in the years 1775 and 1776; yet those treaties were too feeble to resist the powerful impulses of a contrary nature, arising from a combination of circumstances at that time; and accordingly all the various Indian nations (the Oneidas, Tuscaroras, and a few individuals of the Delawares excepted) lying on our frontiers, from Georgia to Canada, armed against us.

It is yet too recent to have been forgotten, that great numbers of inoffensive men, women and children, fell a sacrifice to the barbarous warfare practised by the Indians, and that many others were dragged into a deplorable captivity.

Notwithstanding that these aggressions were entirely unprovoked, yet as soon as the war ceased with Great-Britain, the United States, instead of indulging any resentments against the Indian nations, sought only how to establish a liberal peace with all the tribes throughout their limits.

Early measures were accordingly taken for this purpose. A treaty was held, and a peace concluded, in the year 1784, with the hostile part of the northern Indians, or Six Nations, at Fort Stanwix.

In January 1785, another treaty was formed with part of the western tribes, at Fort M'Intosh, on the Ohio; to wit, with the Wyandots, Delawares, Ottawas and Chippewas.

. . . .

In January 1786, a treaty was formed with the Shawanese, at the confluence of the Great Miami with the Ohio.

It was not long before certain turbulent and malignant char-

From Statement of Causes of the Indian War, January 26, 1792, Clarence Carter, (ed.), *The Territorial Papers of the United States,* II, (1934), pp. 359-366.

acters, residing among some of the northern and western tribes, which had formed the treaties of Fort Stanwix and Fort M'Intosh, excited uneasiness and complaints against those treaties. In consequence of representations upon this subject, on the 5th of October 1787, Congress directed,

"That a general treaty should be held with the tribes of Indians within the limits of the United States, inhabiting the country northwest of the Ohio and about Lake Erie, as soon after the first of April next as conveniently might be, and at such place and at such particular time as the Governor of the Western Territory should appoint, for the purpose of knowing the causes of uneasiness among the said tribes, and hearing their complaints; of regulating trade, and amicably settling all affairs concerning lands and boundaries between them and the United States."

On the 2d day of July, 1788, Congress appropriated "the sum of twenty thousand dollars, in addition to fourteen thousand dollars before appropriated, for defraying the expences of the treaties which had been ordered, or which might be ordered to be held in the then present year with the several Indian tribes in the Northern Department, and for extinguishing the Indian claims; the whole of the said twenty thousand dollars, together with six thousand dollars of the said fourteen thousand dollars, to be applied solely to the purpose of extinguishing Indian claims to the lands they had already ceded to the United States, by obtaining regular conveyances for the same, and for extending a purchase beyond the limits theretofore fixed by treaty; but that no part of the said sum should be applied for any purpose other than those above mentioned."

Accordingly new treaties were held at Fort Harmar the latter part of the year 1788, and concluded on the 9th day of January, 1789, with a representation of all the Six or Northern Nations, the Mohawks excepted—and with a representation of the following tribes, to wit: the Wyandots, the Delawares, Ottawas, Chippawas, Pattiwatamas, and Sacs.—By these treaties, nearly the same boundaries were recognized and established by *a principle of purchase,* as had been stipulated by the former treaties of Fort Stanwix and Fort M'Intosh.

Thus careful and attentive was the Government of the United States to settle a boundary with the Indians on the basis of fair treaty, to obviate the dissatisfactions which had been excited, and to establish its claim to the lands relinquished on the principle of equitable purchase.

It does not appear that the right of the Northern and Western Indians, who formed the several before mentioned treaties to the lands thereby relinquished to the United States, has been questioned by any other tribes; nor does it appear that the present war has been occasioned by any dispute relatively to the boundaries established by the said treaties.

But on the contrary it appears, that the unprovoked aggressions of the Miami and Wabash Indians upon Kentucky and other parts of the frontiers, together with their associates, a banditti, formed of Shawanese and outcast Cherokees, amounting in all to about one thousand two hundred men, are solely the causes of the war. Hence it is proper that their conduct should be more particularly adverted to.

In the year 1784, when messages were sent to the Wyandots and Delawares, inviting them to meet the Commissioners, first at Cayahoga, and afterwards at Fort M'Intosh, their neighbours the *Miami Indians* were also included in the said invitations; but they did not attend.

In the year 1785 these *invitations were repeated;* but the messengers upon their arrival at the Miami village, had their horses stolen, were otherwise treated with insolence, and *prevented fulfilling their mission.*

In the years 1787 and 1788, new endeavors were used to bring those Indians to treat: they were urged to be present at the treaty appointed to be held at Fort Harmar; but these endeavors proved as fruitless as all the former.

"At the council of the tribes, convened in 1788, at the Miami river, the Miami and Wabash Indians were pressed to repair to the treaty with great earnestness by the chiefs of the Wyandots and Delawares: the Wyandot chiefs particularly presented them with a large belt of wampum, holding one end of it themselves, and offering the other to the hostile Indians, which was refused. The Wyandots then laid it on the shoulders of a principal chief, recommending to him to be at peace with the Americans; but without making any answer, he leaned himself and let it fall to the ground: this so displeased the Wyandots, that they immediately left the council house."

In the mean time the frontier settlements were disquieted by frequent depredations and murders, and the complaints of their inhabitants, (as might be expected) of the pacific forbearance of the government, were loud, repeated, and distressing—their calls for protection incessant—till at length they appeared determined by their own efforts to endeavor to retaliate the injuries they were continually receiving, and which had become intolerable.

In this state of things it was indispensible for the Government to make some decisive exertion for the peace and security of the frontier.

But notwithstanding the ill success of former experiments, and the invincible spirit of animosity which had appeared in certain tribes, and which was of a nature to justify a persuasion that no impression could be made upon them by pacific expedients, it was still deemed adviseable to make one more essay.

Accordingly in April 1790, Anthony Gamelin, an inhabitant of Post Vincennes, and a man of good character, was dispatched to all the tribes and villages of the Wabash river, and to the Indians of the Miami village, with a message purporting, that the United States were desirous of establishing a general peace with all the neighboring tribes of Indians, and of treating them in all respects with perfect humanity and kindness, and at the same time warning them to abstain from further depredations.

The Indians in some of the villages on the lower part of the Wabash, appeared to listen to him, others manifested a different disposition, others confessed their inability to restrain their young warriors, and all referred the messenger to the Indians at the Miami village. At that village some appeared well disposed, but the chiefs of the Shawanese returned the messages and belts, informing the messenger however, that they would, after consultation, within thirty nights, send an answer to Post Vincennes—The promised answer was never received. While the messenger was at the Miami village, two negroes were brought in from our settlements, prisoners; and upon his return to L'Anguille, a chief informed him that a party of seventy warriors, from the more distant Indians, had arrived, and were gone against the settlements.

In three days after his departure from the Miami village, a prisoner was there burnt to death. Similar cruelties were exercised at the Ouittanon towns, about the same time; and in the course of the three months immediately after the last mentioned invitation, upwards of one hundred persons were killed, wounded, and taken prisoners upon the Ohio, and in the district of Kentucky.

It is to be remarked, that previously to the last invitation, the people of Kentucky who, in consequence of their injuries, were meditating a blow against the hostile Indians (as before intimated) were restrained by the President of the United States, from crossing the Ohio, until the effect of the friendly overture intended to be made should be known.

It is also to be observed, that the Wyandots and Delawares, after having frequently and fruitlessly endeavored to influence the Miami and Wabash Indians to peace; upon mature conviction finally declared that force only could effect the object.

As an evidence that the conduct of the hostile Indians has been occasioned by other motives than a claim relatively to boundaries—it is to be observed, that their depredations have been principally upon the district of Kentucky, and the counties of Virginia, lying along the south side of the Ohio, a country to which they have no claim.

It appears by respectable evidence, that from the year 1783, until the month of October, 1790, the time the United States commenced offensive operations against the said Indians, that on the Ohio, and the frontiers on the south side thereof, they killed, wounded and took prisoners, about one thousand five hundred men, women and children; besides carrying off upwards of two thousand horses, and other property to the amount of fifty thousand dollars.

The particulars of the barbarities exercised upon many of their prisoners, of different ages and sexes, although supported by indisputable evidence, are of too shocking a nature to be presented to the public. It is sufficient upon this head to observe, that the tomahawk and scalping-knife have been the mildest instruments of death. That in some cases torture of by fire, and other execrable means have been used.

But the outrages which were committed upon the Frontier inhabitants were not the only injuries that were sustained: repeated attacks upon detachments of the troops of the United States were, at different times, made. The following from its peculiar enormity deserves recital.—In April, 1790, Major Doughty was ordered to the friendly Chickasaws on public business. He performed this duty in a boat, having with him Ensign Sedam, and a party of fifteen men. While ascending the Tenessee river, he was met by a party of forty Indians in four canoes, consisting principally of the aforesaid banditti of Shawanese, and outcast Cherokees. They approached under a white flag, the well known emblem of peace. They came on board the Major's boat, received his presents, continued with him nearly one hour, and then departed in the most friendly manner. But, they had scarcely cleared his oars, before they poured in a fire upon his crew, which was returned as soon as circumstances would permit, and a most unequal combat was sustained for several hours, when they abandoned their design, but not until they had killed and wounded eleven out of fifteen of the boat's crew. This perfidious conduct, in any age, would have demanded exemplary punishment.

All overtures of peace failing, and the depredations still continuing, an attempt at coercion became indispensible. Accordingly the expedition under Brigadier General Harmar, in the month of October, 1790, was directed. The event is known.

After this expedition the Governor of the Western Territory, in order that nothing might be omitted, to effect a peace without further conflict, did, on his arrival at Fort Harmar, in December, 1790, send through the Wyandots and Delawares conciliatory messages to the Miamies, but still without effect.

The Cornplanter, a war Chief of the Senekas and other Indians of the same tribe, being in Philadelphia in the month of February, 1791, were engaged to undertake to impress the hostile Indians with the consequences of their persisting in hostilities, and also of the justice and moderation of the United States.

In pursuance of this design Col. Procter, on the fourteenth of March, was sent to the Cornplanter to hasten his departure, and to accompany him to the Miami village—and messages were sent to the Indians declaratory of the pacific sentiments of the United States towards them. But both Col. Procter and the Cornplanter, although zealously desirous of executing their mission, encountered difficulties of a particular nature, which were insurmountable, and prevented the execution of their orders.

Major General St. Clair, in the month of April, sent messages from Fort Harmar to the Delawares, expressive of the pacific designs of the United States, to all the Indian Tribes.

A treaty was held at the Painted-Post by Colonel Pickering, in June, 1791, with a part of the Six Nations, at which the humane intentions of the General Government toward them particularly, and the Indian tribes generally, were fully explained.

Captain Hendricks, a respectable Indian residing with the Oneidas, appearing zealously disposed to attempt convincing the hostile Indians of their mistaken conduct, was accordingly sent for that purpose, but was frustrated by unforseen obstacles, in his laudable attempts.

The different measures which have been recited must evince, that notwithstanding the highly culpable conduct of the Indians in question, the government of the United States, uninfluenced by resentment, or any false principles which might arise from a consciousness of superiority, adopted every proper expedient to terminate the Indian hostilities, without having recourse to the last extremity; and, after being compelled to resort to it, has still kept steadily in view the re-establishment of peace as its primary and sole object.

Were it necessary to add proofs of the pacific and humane disposition of the General Government towards the Indian tribes, the treaties with the Creeks, and with the Cherokees, might be cited as demonstrative of its moderation and liberality.

The present partial Indian war is a remnant of the late general war, continued by a number of separate banditti, who, by the incessant practice of fifteen years, seem to have formed inveterate and incurable habits of enmity against the frontier inhabitants of the United States.

To obtain protection against lawless violence, was a main object for which the present government was instituted. It is, indeed, a main object of all government. A frontier citizen possesses as strong claims to protection as any other citizen. The frontiers are the vulnerable parts of every country; and the obligation of the government of the United States, to afford the requisite protection, cannot be less sacred in reference to the inhabitants of their Western, than to those of their Atlantic Frontier.

It will appear from a candid review of this subject, that the General Government could no longer abstain from attempting to punish the hostile Indians.

The ill success of the attempts for this purpose, is entirely unconnected with the justice or policy of the measure. A perseverance in exertions to make the refractory Indians at last sensible, that they cannot continue their enormous outrages with impunity, appears to be as indispensible, in the existing posture of things, as it will be adviseable, whenever they shall manifest symptoms of a more amicable disposition, to convince them, by decisive proofs, that nothing is so much desired by the United States as to be at liberty to treat them with kindness and beneficence.

H. KNOX,
Secretary of War.

WAR DEPARTMENT, Jan. 26, 1792.
Philadelphia, Printed by D. C. Claypoole.

With Harmar

EBENEZER DENNY

Agreeably to your directions I present the Court with the following detail of circumstances relative to the campaign carried on by General Harmar against the Maumee Towns.

July 11th 1791 Governor St. Clair arrived at Fort Washington from the Illinois Country, he remained only three days during which time it was determined that General Harmar should carry on an expedition against certain hostile tribes of Indians for which purpose, I understood, he was to have *1000* Militia from Kentucky & *500* from Pennsylvania with all the federal troops on the Ohio.

From "Statement of Lieutenant Ebenezer Denny, September 16, 1791 to Court of Inquiry," Draper Collection, Series U, Vol. 4-7, pp. 25-33.

15th The Governor embarked for New York intending on his way to order out the Militia as soon as possible; I believe the 15th of September was the appointed time for the army to assemble at Fort Washington.

General Harmar began his preparations, and every day was employed in the most industrious manner. The calculations for provisions, horses & stores were immediately made out, & orders given accordingly. Great exertions were used by Cap Ferguson to get in readiness the artillery & military stores, if indeed every officer was busily engaged under the eye of the General in fitting out necessary matters for the expedition, but particularly the quarter master—not a moments time appeared to be lost.

15th & 16th of September—The Kentucky Militia arrived, but instead of seeing active rifle men, such as is supposed to inhabit the frontiers, we saw a parcel of men, young in the country, & totaly unexperienced in the business.

They came upon, so much so, that many of them did not even know how to keep their arms in firing order, indeed their whole object seemed to be nothing more than to see the country, without rendering any service whatever—a great many of their guns wanted repairs, & as they could not put them in order, our artificers were obliged to be employed—a considerable number came without any guns at all—Kentucky seemed as if they wished to comply with the requisitions of Government as ineffectually as possible, for it was evident, that about two thirds of the men served only to swell their number.

19th Sept. A small detachment of Pennsylvania militia arrived.

22nd The Governor returned from New York.

25th Major Doughty with two companies of federal troops joined from Muskingum, & the remains of the Pennsyla militia came this day—The militia last mentioned were similar to the others—*too many substitutes.* The General lost no time in organizing them, tho he met with many difficulties. The colonels were disputing for the command, & the one most popular was least entitled to it. The General's design was to reconcile all parties, which he accomplished after much trouble. The Kentuckians composed three Battalions under the majors; Hall, McMillion & Bhey, with Lt.Col. Toms. Trotter at their head. The Pennsylvanians were formed into one Battalion under Liet.Col. Truby & Major Paul, the whole to be commanded by Colonel John Hardin subject to the order of Gen. Harmar.

26th Sept. The militia marched on the east toward the Indian towns.

30th The General having got forward all the supplies that he expected, he moved out with the federal troops formed into two small Battalions under the immediate command of Major Wyllys & Major Doughty, together with Captain Ferguson's company of artillery & three pieces of ordnance.

October 3rd. General Harmar joined the advanced troops early in the morning, the remaining part of the day was spent in forming the Line of March, the Order of Encampment & Battle, and explaining the same to the militia field officers—General Harmar orders will shew the formations.

4th The army took up the Order of March as is described in the orders.

5th A reinforcement of horsemen & mounted infantry joined from Kentucky. The Dragoons were formed into two troops, the mounted rifle men made a company & this small Battalion of light troops were first under the Command of Major Fontain. The whole of General Harmars command then may be stated thus___

3. Battalions of Kentucky Militia	
1. ditto Penn ditto	1133
1. do light troops mounted ditto	
2. Battalions federal troops	320
Total	1453

The Line of March was certainly one of the best that could be adopted & great attention was paid to keep the officers with their commands in proper order, & the pack horses etc as compact as possible.

The Order of Encampment appeared to be well calculated not only for defense but to preserve the horses & cattle from being lost, however, notwithstanding every precaution was taken, & repeated orders given to the horsemasters to hobble well their horses, and directions to the officers & men not to suffer any to pass through the lines, many of them, owing to the careless of the militia, & the scarcity of food, the great attention was paid in the choice of ground broke loose and strayed through the lines after night & even passed the chain of sentries which encircled the camp, and were lost. Patroles of Horsemen were ordered out every morning by day light to scour the neighboring woods & to bring in any horses that might have broken through the lines, and a standing order directed the picquets to turn out small parties & drive in ever horse. This was done, I believe, to expedite the movement of the army. There was no less attention paid to securing the cattle. Every evening when the army halted [illegible] the guard which was composed of a commissioned officer & 30 or 40 men, built a yard always within the chain of sentries & sometimes in the square of encampment, & placed a sufficient number of sentries round the enclosure, which effectually preserved them. There was not more than 2 or 3 head lost during the whole of the campaign.

13th October. Early in the morning a patrole of horsemen captured a Shawanae Indian.

14th October. Colonel Hardin was detached with 600 light troops to push for the Miami Village. I believe that this detachment was sent forward in consequence of the intelligence gained of the Shawanae prisoner, which was, that the Indians were clearing out as fast as possible, and that if we did not make more hast, the towns would be evacuated before our arrival. As it was impossible for the main body with all their train to hasten their march much, the General thought proper to send on Colonel Hardin in hopes of taking a few before they would all get off. This night the Horses were all ordered to be tied up that the army might start by day light on purpose to keep as near Colonel Hardin as possible. The distance to the Indian towns when the detachment marched a head was about 35 miles.

15th Every exertion was used to get forward the main body. This day we found that the advanced party had gained but very few miles.

16th In the evening met an express from Col. Hardin, who had got into the Village, informing the General that the enemy had abandoned every place.

17th About noon, the army arrived at the small towns.

18th Colonel Trotten was ordered out with 300 men's militia & regulars, to reconnoitre the country & to endeavor to make some discoveries of the enemy; he marched but a few miles when his advanced horsemen came upon 2 Indians & killed them. The Colonel was contented with this victory & returned to camp. Colonel Hardin was displeased because Col. Trotten did not execute his orders & requested the General to give him the command of the party, it was granted, & accordingly Hardin marched next morning, but I believe that he had not two thirds of his number when two miles from camp, for to any certain knowledge many of the militia left him on the march & returned to their companies. Whether he knew it or not I cant tell, but proceeded on with a determination to have some fresh signs of the enemy. I believe the plan was merely to gain some knowledge of the savages. He at length came upon a party not exceeding one hundred, but was worsted, owing entirely as I am informed to the scandilous behaviour of the Militia, many of whom never fired a shot but ran off at the first horse of the Indians, & left the few regulars to be sacrificed. Some of them never halted until they crossed the Ohio. The Army in the main line was employed burning & destroying the houses & corn, shifting their position from one town to another.

1st October. The army having burned five villages besides the capital town & consumed & destroyed near 20,000 bushels of corn in ears, took up the Line of March on out back to Fort Washington & encamped about 8 miles from the enemy. 9 O'Clock p.m. The General ordered out 400 choice men, militia & regulars, under the command of Major Wyllys to return to the Towns—intending to surprize any parties that might be assembled there, supposing that the Indians would collect to see how things were left. The General had felt the enemy, knew their strength, & calculated much upon the success of this enterprize. It was the general opinion that the force of the savages was nothing equal to this detachment, and unless by some such means, there was no possibility of getting any advantage of them. However, the best laid plan was in some measure defeated by the disobeydiance of the militia who ran in pursuit of small parties & left Major Wyllys unsupported, the consequence was that the major with the most part of the regulars were killed & our loss was equal if not greater than the savages.

The intention of the detachment was evident to all the army & would have answered the fullest expectations, provided a due obeydiance had been observed on the part of the militia—to provide against desobeydiance of orders what I believe no one would think of, & had it not been the case, the major might have returned crowned with laurels. The main body waited for the return of the detachment, but to our mortification about 11 O'Clock A.M. of the 22nd a fellow who ran back from the field give some information of Major Wyllys's Misfortune. The General immediately dispatched Major Bhey with his Battalion to the assistance of the parties, but the major did not get the length until he met Colonel Hardin returning to camp with his wounded. I am led to believe that about this time the General lost the confidence he had in the militia, those of them among the dead were of the best men—the effective strength was very much reduced by sickness & otherways—the regular troops did not furnish more than 200. They were very insufficient and I am clearly of the opinion that had the enemy made an attack upon our camp this evening or the morning following, the militia were so pannic struck, that very few of them would have stood. The consequences that would have happened stured every person with horror—the sick & wounded & all the stores artillery &c. would have fallen a prey to the savages. This was also the opinion of several of the principal officers who advised General Harmar of the danger of attempting to return to the Towns, from the time it would take up & the probability that the delay would give the savages time to collect from distant quarters.

22nd October Continued encamped, fixing biers for the wounded, and making repairs.

The frost had destroyed the food early on our march out, & the horses of the army was now very much reduced, so much so, that it was utterly impossible for the main body to perform any thing rapidly, and to get back upon the road which we had so lately passed was attended with difficulty—wherever the greatest attention was paid the little army was kept compact, and vigilance was the word from all who had any reputation to loose. The Militia on the return began to be refractory, showing great signs of a revolt—discharging their pieces in open defiance of the general orders, some of them however were detected & punished which give and was afterwards the cause of many illnatured reports spread, with out any foundations, to injure the Generals reputation.

The army returned by slow marches back to Fort Washington. General Harmars conduct during the campaign was observed to be sober, steady, & attentive to the service, and as my duty required me to be frequently near him should certainly have discovered it had he been at any time intoxicated as has been reported. Every evening as duly as the army halted, the general made his remarks for the day & issued orders for the movement & arrangements for the next, and every morning he was found among the first prepared for the field.

I have the honor to be in
your very humble servant

E. Denny Lieut.
1st Regt. of the US

Fort Washington
September 16th 1796

The honorable
Major General Butler
president of Court of Enquiry

Defeat

ARTHUR ST. CLAIR

Fort Washington, 9th November, 1791.

*Sir:—*Yesterday afternoon the remains of the army under my command got back to this place, and I have now the painful task to give you an account of as warm and as unfortunate an action as almost any that has been fought, in which every corps was engaged and worsted, except the First regiment, that had been detached upon a service I had the honor to inform you of in my last dispatch, and had not joined me.

On the 3d instant, the army had reached a creek about twelve yards wide, running to the southward, which I believe to have been the river St. Mary, that empties into the Miami of the lake; arrived at the village about four o'clock in the afternoon, having marched near nine miles, and were immediately encamped upon a commanding piece of ground in two lines, having the above-mentioned creek in front. The right wing composed of Butler's, Clarke's, and Patterson's battalions, commanded by Major-General Butler, formed the first line; and the left wing, consisting of Bedinger's and Gaither's battalions, and the Second regiment, commanded by Colonel Darke, formed the second line, with an interval between them of about seventy yards, which was all the ground would allow.

The right flank was pretty well secured by the creek, a steep bank, and Faulkener's corps; some of the cavalry and their pickets covered the left flank; the militia were thrown over the creek, and advanced about one quarter of a mile, and advanced in the same order; there were a few Indians who appeared on the opposite side of the creek, but fled with the utmost precipitation on the advance of the militia; at this place, which I judged to be about fifteen miles from the Miami village, I had determined to throw up a slight work, the plan of which was concerted that evening with Major Ferguson, wherein to have deposited the men's knapsacks, and every thing else that was not absolutely necessary, and to have moved on to attack the enemy as soon as the First regiment was come up; but they did not permit me to execute either, for on the 4th, about half an hour before sunrise, and when the men had just been dismissed from the parade (for it was a constant practice to have them all under arms a considerable time before daylight), an attack was made upon the militia. Those gave way in a very little time, and rushed into camp, through Major Butler's battalion, which, together with part of Clarke's, they threw into considerable disorder, and which, notwithstanding the exertions of both those officers, was never altogether remedied, the Indians following close at their heels; the fire, however, of the front line checked them, but almost instantly a heavy attack began upon that line, and in a few minutes it was extended to the second likewise; the great weight of it was directed against the center of each, where the artillery was placed, and from which the

From Arthur St. Clair to Henry Knox, November 9, 1791, William Henry Smith, (ed.), *The St. Clair Papers*, II, (1882), pp. 262-267.

men were repeatedly driven with great slaughter; finding no great effect from our fire, and confusion beginning to spread from the great number of men who were falling in all quarters, it became necessary to try what could be done with the bayonet.

Lieutenant-Colonel Darke was accordingly ordered to make a charge with part of the second line, and to turn the left flank of the enemy. This was executed with great spirit. The Indians instantly gave way, and were driven back three or four hundred yards; but, for the want of a sufficient number of riflemen to pursue this advantage, they soon returned, and the troops were obliged to give back in their turn. At this moment they had entered our camp by the left flank, having pursued back the troops that were posted there.

Another charge was made here by the Second regiment, Butler's and Clarke's battalions, with equal effect, and it was repeated several times, and always with success; but in all of them many men were lost, and particularly the officers, which, with some raw troops, was a loss altogether irredeemable. In that I just spoke of, made by the Second regiment and Butler's battalion, Major Butler was dangerously wounded, and every officer of the Second regiment fell except three, one of whom, Mr. Greaton, was shot through the body.

Our artillery being now silenced, and all the officers killed except Captain Ford, who was badly wounded, more than half of the army fallen, being cut off from the road, it became necessary to attempt the regaining it, and to make a retreat if possible. To this purpose, the remains of the army were formed, as well as circumstances would admit, towards the right of the encampment; from which, by the way of the second line, another charge was made upon the enemy, as if with the design to turn their right flank, but, in fact, to gain the road; this was effected, and as soon as it was open, the militia took along it, followed by the troops, Major Clarke, with his battalion, covering the rear.

The retreat in those circumstances was, you may be sure, a very precipitate one; it was, in fact, a flight. The camp and the artillery were abandoned, but that was unavoidable; for not a horse was left alive to have drawn them off had it otherwise been practicable. But the most disgraceful part of the business is that the greatest part of the men threw away their arms and accouterments, even after the pursuit, which continued about four miles, had ceased. I found the road strewed with them for many miles, but was not able to remedy it; for, having had all my horses killed, and being mounted upon one that could not be pricked out of a walk, I could not get forward myself, and the orders I sent forward, either to halt the front, or to prevent the men parting with their arms, were unattended to. The rout continued quite to Fort Jefferson, twenty-nine miles, which was reached a little after sun-setting. The action began about half an hour before sunrise, and the retreat was attempted at half an hour after nine o'clock.

I have not yet been able to get returns of the killed and wounded; but Major-General Butler, Lieutenant-Colonel Oldham, of the militia, Major Ferguson, Major Hart, and Major Clarke are among the former. Colonel Sargent, my adjutant-general, Lieutenant-Colonel Darke, Lieutenant-Colonel Gibson, Major Butler, and the Viscount Malartie, who served me as an aid-de-camp, are among the latter; and a great number of captains and subalterns in both.

I have now, sir, finished my melancholy tale—a tale that will be felt sensibly by every one that has sympathy for private distress, or for public misfortune. I have nothing, sir, to lay to the charge of the troops but their want of discipline, which, from the short time they had been in service, it was impossible they should have acquired, and which rendered it very difficult, when they were thrown into confusion, to reduce them again to order, which is one reason why the loss has fallen so heavy upon the officers, who did every thing in their power to effect it. Neither were my own exertions wanting; but, worn down with illness, and suffering under a painful disease, unable either to mount or dismount a horse without assistance, they were not so great as they otherwise would, and, perhaps, ought to have been. We were overpowered by numbers; but it is no more than justice to observe that, though composed of so many different species of troops, the utmost harmony prevailed through the whole army during the campaign.

At Fort Jefferson, I found the First regiment, which had returned from the service they had been sent upon, without either overtaking the deserters, or meeting the convoy of provisions. I am not certain, sir, whether I ought to consider the absence of this regiment from the field of action as fortunate or otherwise. I incline to think it was fortunate; for I very much doubt whether, had it been in the action, the fortune of the day had been turned; and, if it had not, the triumph of the enemy would have been more complete, and the country would have been destitute of every means of defense.

Taking a view of the situation of our broken troops at Fort Jefferson, and that there were no provisions in the fort, I called on the field officers, viz.: Lieutenant-Colonel Darke, Major Hamtramck, Major Zeigler, and Major Gaither, together with the adjutant-general, for their advice what would be proper further to be done; and it was their unanimous opinion that the addition of the First regiment, unbroken as it was, did not put the army on so respectable a footing as it was in the morning, because a great part of it was now unarmed; that it had been then found unequal to the enemy, and should they come on, which was probable, would be found so again;

that the troops could not be thrown into the fort, both because it was too small and that there were no provisions in it; that provisions were known to be upon the road at the distance of one, or, at most, two marches; that, therefore, it would be proper to move without loss of time to meet the provisions, where the men might have the sooner an opportunity of some refreshment, and that a proper detachment might be sent back with it to have it safely deposited in the fort. This advice was accepted, and the army was put in motion again at ten o'clock, and marched all night, and the succeeding day met with a quantity of flour; part of it was distributed immediately, part taken back to supply the army on the march to Fort Hamilton, and the remainder—about fifty horse-loads—sent forward to Fort Jefferson. The next day, a drove of cattle was met with for the same place; and I have information that both got in. The wounded who had been left at that place were ordered to be brought here by the return of the horses.

I have said, sir, in a former part of this letter, that we were overpowered by numbers. Of that, however, I have no evidence; but the weight of the fire, which was always a most deadly one, and generally delivered from the ground, few of the enemy showing themselves afoot except when they were charged, and that, in a few minutes, our whole camp, which extended above three hundred and fifty yards in length, was entirely surrounded and attacked on all quarters.

The loss, sir, the public has sustained, by the fall of so many officers, particularly General Butler and Major Ferguson, can not be too much regretted; but it is a circumstance that will alleviate the misfortune, in some measure, that all of them fell most gallantly doing their duty. I have had very particular obligations to many of them, as well as to the survivors; but to none more than to Colonel Sargent. He has discharged the various duties of his office with zeal, with exactness, and with intelligence; and, on all occasions, afforded me every assistance in his power; which I have also experienced from my aid-de-camp, Lieutenant Denny, and the Viscount Malartie, who served with me in the station as a volunteer.

P.S. Some orders that had been given to Colonel Oldham over night, and which were of much consequence, were not executed; and some very material intelligence was communicated by Captain Slough to General Butler, in the course of the night before the action, which was never imparted to me, nor did I hear of it until after my arrival here.

With St. Clair

EBENEZER DENNY

2d.—The army marched at nine o'clock; about twelve o'clock crossed a creek fifteen yards wide, running east. The country very flat and marshy. Joined this afternoon by another Indian path much frequented. Gained eight miles and encamped. Course north twenty-five degrees east this day, and total distance from Fort Washington eighty-nine miles. A scout sent out yesterday fell in with an Indian camp, got some plunder and seven horses branded United States, supposed to have been stolen from Fort Washington. We had a light snow all this day.

3d.—Marched at nine o'clock. The first four miles very flat and wet. About twelve, passed over dry ground, and descended gradually for three miles to a small creek supposed to be a branch of the waters emptying into Lake Erie; proceeded two miles further, and encamped on pleasant, dry ground, on bank of a creek about twenty yards wide, said to be the Pickaway fork of the Omee.* Distance this day about nine miles; general course north-west thirty degrees. Fresh signs of the savages appeared to-day in several places; parties of riflemen detached after them, but without success. It was later than usual when the army reached the ground this evening, and the men much fatigued prevented the General from having some works of defense immediately erected. Major Ferguson, commanding officer of artillery, sent for, and a plan agreed on, intended to be commenced early on to-morrow. The high, dry ground barely sufficient to encamp the army; lines rather contracted. Parallel with the front line runs the creek, about twenty yards wide. On both flanks low, wet ground, and along most part of the rear. Militia advanced across the creek about three hundred yards. Had accompanied the quarter-master in the afternoon on to this ground; it was farther than could have been wished, but no place short of it appeared so suitable. I was much pleased with it; returned and made report; found the army halted and about to encamp on flat land, and with no good water; although it was late, the march was continued till just dark, when we reached the creek.

4th.—Camp on a creek twenty yards wide, supposed to be the Pickaway fork of the Omee, ninety-eight miles from Fort Washington. The frequent firing of the sentinels through the night had disturbed the camp, and excited some concern among the officers.

From Ebenezer Denny's Diary, William Henry Smith, (ed.), *The St. Clair Papers*, II, (1882), pp. 258-262.
*Known since to be a branch of the Wabash.

The guards had reported the Indians to lie skulking about in consider-able numbers. About ten o'clock at night General Butler, who commanded the right wing, was desired to send out an intelligent officer and party to make discoveries. Captain Slough, with two subalterns and thirty men, I saw parade at General Butler's tent for this purpose, and heard the General give Captain Slough very particu-lar verbal orders how to proceed. Myself and two or three officers staid with the General until late, when I returned to the Commander-in-Chief, whose tent was at some distance on the left, and who was unable to be up.

The troops paraded this morning at the usual time, and had been dismissed from the lines but a few minutes, and the sun not yet up, when the woods in front rung with the yells and fire of the savages. The poor militia, who were but three hundred yards in front, had scarcely time to return a shot—they fled into our camp. The troops were under arms in an instant, and a smart fire from the front line met the enemy. It was but a few minutes, however, until the men were engaged in every quarter. The enemy from the front filed off to the right and left, and completely surrounded the camp, killed and cut off nearly all the guards, and approached close to the lines. They advanced from one tree, log, or stump to another, under cover of the smoke of our fire. The artillery and musketry made a tremendous noise, but did little execution. The Indians seemed to brave every thing, and, when fairly fixed around us, they made no noise other than their fire, which they kept up very constant, and which seldom failed to tell, although scarcely heard. Our left-flank, probably from the nature of the ground, gave way first; the enemy got possession of that part of the encampment, but, it being pretty clear ground, they were too much exposed, and were soon repulsed. Was at this time with the General engaged toward the right; he was on foot, and led the party himself that drove the enemy and regained our ground on the left. The battalions in the rear charged several times and forced the savages from their shelter, but they always turned with the battalions and fired upon them back; indeed, they seemed not to fear any thing we could do. They could skip out of reach of the bayonet, and return as they pleased. They were visible only when raised by a charge. The ground was literally covered with the dead. The wounded were taken to the center, where it was thought most safe, and where a great many who had quit their posts unhurt had crowded together. The General, with other officers, endeavored to rally these men, and twice they were taken out to the lines. It appeared as if the officers had been singled out; a very great propor-tion fell, or were wounded, and obliged to retire from the lines early in the action. General Butler was among the latter, as well as several other of the most experienced officers. The men, being thus left with few officers, became fearful, despaired of success, gave up the fight, and, to save themselves for the moment, abandoned entirely their duty and ground, and crowded in toward the center of the field, and no exertions could put them in any order even for defense; perfectly ungovernable. The enemy at length got possession of the artillery, though not until the officers were all killed but one, and he badly wounded, and the men almost all cut off, and not until the pieces were spiked. As our lines were deserted the Indians contracted theirs until their shot centered from all points, and now, meeting with little opposition, took more deliberate aim and did great execution. Exposed to a cross fire, men and officers were seen falling in every direction; the distress, too, of the wounded made the scene such as can scarcely be conceived; a few minutes longer, and a retreat would have been impracticable. The only hope left was, that perhaps the savages would be so taken up with the camp as not to follow. Delay was death; no preparation could be made; numbers of brave men must be left a sacrifice—there was no alternative. It was past nine o'clock, when repeated orders were given to charge toward the road. The action had continued between two and three hours. Both officers and men seemed confounded, incapable of doing any thing; they could not move until it was told that a retreat was intended. A few officers put themselves in front, the men followed, the enemy gave way, and perhaps not being aware of the design, we were for a few minutes left undisturbed. The stoutest and most active now took the lead, and those who were foremost in breaking the enemy's line were soon left behind. At the moment of the retreat, one of the few horses saved had been procured for the General; he was on foot until then; I kept by him, and he delayed to see the rear. The enemy soon discovered the movement and pursued, though not more than four or five miles, and but few so far; they turned to share the spoil. Soon after the firing ceased, I was directed to endeavor to gain the front, and, if possible, to cause a short halt that the rear might get up. I had been on horseback from the first alarm, and well mounted; pushed forward, but met with so many difficulties and interruptions from the people, that I was two hours at least laboring to reach the front. With the assistance of two or three officers I caused a short halt, but the men grew impatient and would move on. I got Lieutenants Sedam and Morgan, with half a dozen stout men, to fill up the road and to move slowly; I halted myself until the General came up. By this time the remains of the army had got somewhat compact, but in the most miserable and defenseless state. The wounded who came off left their arms in the field, and one-half of the others threw theirs away on the retreat. The road for miles was covered with firelocks, cartridge-boxes and regimentals. How fortunate that the pursuit was discontinued; a single Indian might have followed with safety upon either flank. Such a panic had seized the men, that I believe it would not have been possible to have brought any of them to engage again. In the afternoon Lieutenant Kersey, with a detachment of the First regiment, met us. This regiment, the only complete and best disciplined portion of the army, had been ordered back upon the road on the 31st of October. They were thirty miles from the battle-ground when they heard distinctly the firing of the cannon; were hastening forward and had marched about nine miles when met by some of the militia, who informed Major Hamtramck, the commanding officer, that the army was totally destroyed. The Major judged it best to send on a subaltern to obtain some knowledge of things, and to return himself with the regiment to Fort Jefferson, eight miles back, and to secure at all events that post. He had made some arrangements, and as we arrived in the evening, found him preparing again to meet us. Stragglers continued to come in for hours after we reached the fort.

The remnant of the army, with the first regiment, were now at Fort Jefferson, twenty-nine miles from the field of action, without provisions, and the former without having eaten any thing for twenty-four hours. A convoy was known to be upon the road, and within a day's march. The General determined to move with the First regiment and all the levies able to march. Those of the wounded, and others unable to go on, were lodged as comfortably as possible within the fort. Accordingly, we set out a little after ten and continued our route until within an hour of daylight, then halted and waited for day and until the rear came up. Moved on again about nine o'clock; the morning of the 5th we met the convoy. Stopped a sufficiency to subsist us to Fort Hamilton; sent the remainder on to Jefferson under an additional escort of a captain and sixty men; proceeded, and at the first water halted, partly cooked and eat for the first time since the night preceding the action. At one o'clock moved on, and continued our route until nine at night, when we halted and made fires within fifteen miles of Fort Hamilton. Marched again just before day; the General soon after rode on to the fort. Troops reached in the afternoon.

7th.—Fort Hamilton command was ordered off with a small supply for the wounded, etc. About twelve same day, continued our march, and halted before night within fifteen miles of Fort Washington, which place we reached the afternoon of the 8th.

The prediction of General Harmar, before the army set out on the campaign, was founded upon his experience and particular knowledge of things. He saw with what material the bulk of the army was composed; men collected from the streets and prisons of the cities, hurried out into the enemy's country, and with the officers commanding them totally unacquainted with the business in which they were engaged; it was utterly impossible they could be otherwise.

Besides, not any one department was sufficiently prepared; both quartermaster and contractors extremely deficient. It was a matter of astonishment to him that the commanding general, who was acknowledged to be perfectly competent, should think of hazarding, with such people, and under such circumstances, his reputation and life, and the lives of so many others, knowing, too, as both did, the enemy with whom he was going to contend; an enemy brought up from infancy to war, and perhaps superior to an equal number of the best men that could be taken against them. It is a truth, I had hopes that the noise and show which the army made on their march might possibly deter the enemy from attempting a serious and general attack. It was unfortunate that *both* the general officers were, and had been disabled by sickness; in such situation it is possible that some essential matters might be overlooked. The Adjutant-General, Colonel Sargent, an old revolutionary officer, was, however, constantly on the alert; he took upon himself the burden of every thing, and a very serious and troublesome task he had.

Fallen Timbers

ANTHONY WAYNE

No. 83.   *Head Quarters*
                                    Grand Glaize 28th Augt. 1794
Sir
     It's with infinite pleasure that I now announce to you the brilliant success of the Federal army under my Command in a General action with the combined force of the Hostile Indians & a considerable number of the Volunteers & Militia of Detroit on the 20th Instant, on the banks of the Miamis, in the vicinity of the British post & Garrison at the foot of the rapids.
     The army advanced from this place on the 15th & arrived at Roche de Bout, on the 18th. the 19th we were employed in making a

---

From Anthony Wayne to Henry Knox, August 28, 1794, Richard Knopf, ed., *Anthony Wayne: A Name in Arms* (Pittsburgh, 1960), pp. 351-355.

temporary post for the reception of our stores & baggage, & in reconnoitring the position of the enemy who were encamped behind a thick brushy wood and the British Fort. [The "temporary post" was Fort Deposit.]

At 8. OClock on the morning of the 20th the army again advanced in Columns agreeably to the standing order of March—the Legion on the right, its right flank cover'd by the Miamis, One Brigade of Mounted Volunteers on the left, under Brigr General Todd, & the other in the rear under Brigr Genl Barbee, a select Battalion of Mounted Volunteers moved in front of the Legion commanded by Major Price, who was directed to keep sufficiently advanced, so as to give timely notice for the troops to form in case of Action.

It being yet undetermined whether the Indians wou'd decide on peace or war:

After advancing about Five miles, Major Price's corps received so severe a fire from the enemy, who were secreted in the woods & high grass, as to compel them to retreat.

The Legion was immediately formed in two lines principally in a close thick wood which extended for miles on our left & for very considerable distance in front, the ground being cover'd with old fallen timber probably occasioned by a tornado, which render'd it impracticable for the Cavalry to act with effect, & afforded the enemy the most favorable covert for their mode of warfare these savages were formed in three lines within supporting distance of each other & extending near two miles at right angles with the River I soon discover'd from the weight of the fire, & extent of their Lines that the enemy were in full force in front in possession of their favorite ground & endeavoring to turn our left flank, I therefore gave orders for the second line to advance to support the first, & directed Major Genl Scott to gain & turn the right flank of the savages with the whole of the Mounted Volunteers by a circuitous route, at the same time I ordered the front line to advance & charge with trailed arms & rouse the Indians from their coverts at the point of the bayonet, & when up to deliver a close & well directed fire on their backs followed by a br[i]sk charge, so as not to give time to load again I also order'd Capt Mis Campbell who commanded the Legion-ary Cavalry to turn the left flank of the Enemy next the river & which afforded a favorable field for that Corps to act in,

All those orders were obeyed with spirit & promptitude, but such was the impetuosity of the charge by the first line of Infantry—that the Indians & Canadian Militia & Volunteers were drove from all their Coverts in so short a time, that altho every possible exertion was used by the Officers of the second line of the Legion & by Generals Scott, Todd & Barbee of the Mounted Volunteers, to gain their proper position's but part of each cou'd get up in season to participate in the Action, the enemy being drove in the course of One hour more than two miles thro' the thick woods already mentioned, by less than one half their Numbers, from Every account the Enemy amounted to two thousand combatants, the troops actually engaged against them were short of nine hundred; [illegible] Savages with their allies abandoned themselves to flight & dispersed with terror & dismay, leaving our victorious army in full & quiet possession of the field of battle, which terminated under the influence of the Guns of the British Garrison, as you will observe by the enclosed correspondence between Major Campbell the Commandant & myself upon the Occasion

The bravery & Conduct of every Officer belonging to the Army from the Generals down to the Ensigns merits my highest approbation; there were however some whose rank & situation placed their Conduct in a very conspicuous point of view, and which I observed with pleasure & the most lively gratitude, among whom I must beg leave to mention Brigr Genl Wilkinson & Colo Hamtramck the Commandants of the right & left wings of the Legion whose brave example inspired the troops, to them I must add the names of my faithful & Gallant Aids de Camp Captains DeButts & T Lewis & Lieut Harrison who with the Adjt General Major Mills, rendered the most essential services by communicating my orders in every direction & by their Conduct & bravery exciting the troops to press for Victory; Lieut. Covington upon whom the Command of the Cavalry now devolved cut down two savages with his own hand & Lieut Webb one in turn & [illegible] the Enemies left flank.

The wounds received by Captains Slough & Prior & Lieut Campbell Smith (an extra aid de Camp to Genl Wilkinson) of the Legionary Infantry & Capt Van Renselaer of the Dragoons, Captain Rawlins Lieut McKenny & Ensign Duncan of the Mounted Volunteers, bear honorable testimony of their bravery & Conduct.

Captains H Lewis & Brock with their Companies of light Infantry had to sustain an unequal combat for some time which they supported with fortitude, in fact every Officer & soldier who had an Opportunity to come into action displayed that true bravery which will always insure success: & here permit me to declare that I never discover'd more true spirit & anxiety for Action than appeared to pervade the whole of the Mounted Volunteers, & I am well persuaded that had the Enemy maintained their favorite ground but for one half hour longer they wou'd have most severely felt the prowess of that Corps

But whilst I pay this just tribute to the living I must not forget the Gallant dead, among whom we have to lament the early death of those worthy & brave Officers Capt Mis Campbell of the Dragoons &

Lieut Towles of the Light Infantry of the Legion who fell in the first Charge.

Enclosed is a particular return of the killed & Wounded—the loss of the Enemy was more that [than] double to that of the Federal Army—the woods were strewed for a considerable distance with the dead bodies of Indians & their white Auxiliaries, the latter armed with British Muskets & bayonets:

After remaining three days & nights on the banks of the Miamis in front of the Field of battle during which time all the Houses & Corn fields were consumed & destroyed for a considerable distance both above & below Fort Miamis as well as within pistol shot of the Garrison who were compeled to remain tacit spectators to this general devestation & Conflagration; among which were the Houses stores & property of Colo McKee the British Indian Agent & principal stimulator of the War now existing between the United States & the savages

The army returned to this place on the 27th by easy marches laying waste the Villages & Corn fields for about Fifty miles on each side of the Miamis—there remains yet a number of Villages & a great Quantity of Corn to be consumed or destroyed upon Au Glaize & the Miamis above this place which will be effected in the course of a few days, In the interim we shall improve Fort Defiance & as soon as the Escort return[s] with the necessary supplies from Greeneville & Fort Recovery—the Army will proceed to the Miami Villages in order to accomplish the Object of the Campaign.

It is however not improbable that the Enemy may make one more desperate effort against the Army—as it is said that a Reinforcement was hourly expected at Fort Miamis from Niagara, as well as Numerous tribes of Indians living on the Margins & Islands of the Lakes: This is a business rathar to be wished for than dreaded whilst the army remain in force—their Numbers will only tend to confuse the Savages—& the victory will be the more complete & decisive—& which may eventually ensure a permanent and happy peace

Under those Impressions I have the honor to be Your Most Obt & very Huml Sert

ANTY WAYNE

The Honble
Major Genl H Knox
Secretary of War

4 Through Ohio

PEOPLE IN THE EAST had become interested in the vast Northwest Territory. Land speculators, immigrants, and adventurers, as well as men of science who wanted to learn more about nature's wonderland, were hungry for information about the Ohio Valley. During the first three decades of the nineteenth century, published journals and descriptive travel narratives, written both by amateur and trained observers who had journeyed through Ohio, were popular in the United States and Europe. Mostly optimistic about the economic potential for growth of the Ohio Valley, these authors not only gave eyewitness accounts of the state during its frontier period but also added to the cultural heritage of the young republic.

The French had lost their claim to the Ohio Valley in 1763; however, with the publication of Pierre François de Charlevoix's *Historie et Description Generale de la Nouvelle France* in 1744, the first descriptive narrative of the North American continent, their fascination with the region continued. In 1802, for example, François André Michaux, a scientist like his famous father, André Michaux, was sent by the French government to study the vegetation of North America. Michaux's record of his trip, *Travels to the West of the Allegheny Mountains in the States of Ohio, Kentucky, and Tennessee, and Back to Charleston, By the Upper Carolines, . . . in the Year 1802,* first published in 1804, indicated that he was a careful observer of man's fight to bring civilization to the wilderness. After visiting Marietta and Gallipolis and recognizing the success of the Ohio Company's first settlement, he expressed sympathy for his fellow countrymen who were living in the French settlement along the Ohio. Michaux's book is an excellent account of the Ohio frontier on the eve of the state's entry into the Union.

By 1803, when Ohio became the nation's seventeenth state, New Englanders were proud of the success of the Ohio Company's venture on the frontier. Thaddeus Mason Harris, a liberal clergyman from Massachusetts, visited his brother in Marietta. Pleased with the handiwork of his fellow sectionalist who had come to Ohio, Harris, in *The Journal of a Tour into the Territory Northwest of the Allegheny*

Mountains, recorded his prejudices, shared by other New Englanders, against the settlers found in the back counties of Virginia. Harris' journal was popular in the East, and his observations reflect his section's belief that thrift and hard work are the principles upon which a free society is founded.

Two Englishmen, Fortescue Cuming and John Melish, toured Ohio before America's second war with England. Cuming's *Sketches of a Tour to the Western Country . . . 1807-1809,* first published in Pittsburgh in 1810, provided readers with a picture of the famous Zane's Trace, as the author journeyed from the Ohio River through Bainbridge, Chillicothe, and Lancaster during the late summer of 1807. Melish, an unsuccessful English businessman who was interested in the interrelationship between geography and economic development, traveled 2400 miles throughout the United States and recorded his adventures and observations in *Travels in the United States of America, in the Years 1806 & 1807, and 1809, 1810 & 1811.* Although he visited many of the same places Cuming toured, his trips through the Western Reserve in northeastern Ohio provided a splendid account of that section of the state before any substantial economic development had begun. Both men took pains to detail the prospects for economic growth and to explain the circumstances of the people. Melish was particularly impressed with the virtues and quality of life produced by an agrarian society, and his views of American society were similar to those held by Thomas Jefferson.

Of course, not all the observers of Ohio or western society were as optimistic or encouraged by what they saw. The English author Charles Dickens, for instance, visited Ohio in 1842 and recounted his experiences in *American Notes.* His trip from Cincinnati through Columbus to Sandusky, which lasted from April 19 to April 25, was far more trying than the kind of travel to which he was accustomed. Not only was he anxious about protecting the 250 pounds of gold that he carried to finance his trip, but his journey was also physically tiring. On one occasion, the roads were so rough that his wife had to be tied into the coach to prevent her from being thrown to the ground. To be sure, the fact that Dickens was ignored by Ohio's press while he was in the state did not help to improve his impression of the Buckeye State. The *Cleveland Plain Dealer* of April 25, 1842, for example, observed that "the gentlemen and loafers gathered about the dock got a sight of 'the Dickens'—that was all." Dickens' anecdotes, written from memory rather than from notes, represent a view of what the famous English author considered to be the raw side of American life, and thus present a humorous picture of early Ohio.

Along the Ohio

FRANÇOIS A. MICHAUX

Chap. X

Marietta.—Ship building.—Departure for Gallipoli.—Falling in with a Kentucky Boat.—Point-Pleasant.—The Great Kenhaway.

Marietta, the chief of the settlements on the New Continent, is situated upon the right bank of the Great Muskingum, at its *embouchure* in the Ohio. This town, which fifteen years ago was not in existence, is now composed of more than two hundred houses, some of which are built of brick, but the greatest part of wood. There are several from two to three stories high, which are somewhat elegantly built; nearly all of them are in front of the Ohio. The mountains which from Pittsburgh run by the side of this river, are at Marietta some distance from its banks, and leave a considerable extent of even ground, which will facilitate, in every respect, the enlarging of the town upon a regular plan, and afford its inhabitants the most advantageous and agreeable situations; it will not be attended with the inconveniences that are met with at Pittsburgh, which is locked in on all sides by lofty mountains.

The inhabitants of Marietta were the first that had an idea of exporting directly to the Carribbee Islands the produce of the country, in a vessel built in their own town, which they sent to Jamaica. The success which crowned this first attempt excited such emulation among the inhabitants of that part of the Western Country, that several new vessels were launched at Pittsburgh and Louisville, and expedited to the isles, or to New York and Philadelphia. The ship yard at Marietta is situated near the town, on the Great Muskingum. When I was there they were building three brigs, one of which was of two hundred and twenty tons burthen.

The river Muskingum takes its source toward Lake Erie; it is not navigable for two hundred miles from its mouth in the Ohio, where it is about a hundred and sixty fathoms broad.* The country that it runs through, and especially its banks, are extremely fertile.

Near the town of Marietta are the remains of several Indian fortifications. When they were discovered, they were full of trees of the same nature as those of the neighbouring forests, some of which were upwards of three feet diameter. These trees have been hewn

---

From François André Michaux, *Travels to the Westward of the Allegheny Mountains, in the States of Ohio, Kentucky and Tennessee, in the Year 1802*, (London, 1805), pp. 89-102.
*The translation here is faulty. It should be, "it is navigable for only two hundred miles," etc.—Ed.

down, and the ground is now almost entirely cultivated with Indian corn.

Major-General Hart, with whose son I was acquainted at Marietta, gave, in the Columbia Magazine for the year 1787, Vol. I, No. 9, a plan and a minute description of these ancient fortifications of the Indians: the translation of which is given in his Travels in Upper Pennsylvania. This officer, of the most distinguished merit, fell in the famous battle that General St. Clair† lost in 1791, near Lake Eria, against the united savages. When I was at Marietta, General St. Clair was Governor of the State of Ohio, a post which he occupied till this state was admitted in the union. His Excellency coming from Pittsburgh and going to Chillicotha, alighted at the inn where I lodged. As he was travelling in an old chaise, and without a servant, he did not at first attract my attention. In the United States, those who are called by the wish of their fellow-citizens to exercise these important functions do not change their dress, continue dwelling in their own houses, and live like private individuals, without showing more ostentation, or incurring more expense. The emoluments attached to this office varies in every state; that of South Carolina, one of the richest of the union, gives its governor 4280 piastres, while the Governor of Kentucky receives no more than twelve or fifteen hundred. The inhabitants of the State of Ohio are divided in opinion concerning the political conduct of General St. Clair. With respect to talents, he has the reputation of being a better lawyer than a soldier.

. . . .

On the 21st of July we set out from Marietta for Gallipoli, which is a distance of about a hundred miles. We reached there after having been four days on the water. The inhabitants of the country, by putting off from the shore in the night time, would have made that passage in two days and a half or three days. According to the calculation that we made, the mean force of the stream was about a mile and a half an hour; it is hardly to be perceived in those parts where the water is very deep; but as you get nearer the isles, which, as I have said before, are very numerous, the bed of the river diminishes in depth, so that frequently there is not a foot of water out of the main channel. Whenever we came near those shallows the swiftness of the current was extreme, and the canoe was carried away

---

†General Arthur St. Clair was a native of Scotland, who came to America during the French and Indian War, and settled in Western Pennsylvania. He served with much success in the Revolution, and in 1787 was president of the Congress of the Confederation. He was appointed by Washington first governor of the Northwest Territory, and served in that capacity 1788-1802. He was unpopular because of the military defeat here mentioned, and his Federalist principles. On his dismissal, in 1802, he retired to his home in Pennsylvania, and died there in obscurity in 1818.—Ed.

like an arrow, which led us to observe that it was only as we distanced the islands that the bed increases in depth, and that the stream becomes less rapid.

On the day of our departure we joined, in the evening, a Kentucky boat, destined for Cincinnati. This boat, about forty feet long and fifteen broad, was loaded with bar iron and brass pots. There was also an emigrant family in it, consisting of the father, mother, and seven children, with all their furniture and implements of husbandry. The boatmen, three in number, granted us, without difficulty, permission to fasten our canoe to the end of their boat, and to pass the night with them. We intended, by that means, to accelerate our journey, by not putting up at night, as we had before been accustomed to do, and hoped to spend a more comfortable night than the preceding one, during which we had been sadly tormented by the fleas, with which the greater part of the houses where we had slept, from the moment of our embarkation, had been infested. However our hopes were frustrated; for so far from being comfortable, we were still more incommoded. In the course of my travels it was only on the banks of the Ohio that I experienced this inconvenience.

We were on the point of leaving them about two in the morning, when the boat ran aground. Under these circumstances we could not desert our hosts, who had entertained us with their best, and who had made us partake of a wild turkey which they had shot the preceding evening on the banks of the river. We got into the water with the boatmen, and by the help of large sticks that we made use of as oars succeeded in pushing the vessel afloat, after two hours' painful efforts.

Chap. XI

Gallipoli.—State of the French colony Scioto.—Alexandria at the mouth of the Great Scioto.—Arrival at Limestone in Kentucky.

Gallipoli is situated four miles below Point Pleasant, on the right bank of the Ohio. At this place assembled nearly a fourth part of the French, who, in 1789 and 1790, left their country to go and settle at Scioto: but it was not till after a sojourn of fifteen months at Alexandria in Virginia, where they waited the termination of the war with the savages, that they could take possession of the lands which they had bought so dearly. They were even on the point of being dispossessed of them, on account of the disputes that arose between the Scioto Company and that of the Ohio, of whom the former had primitively purchased these estates; but scarcely had they arrived upon the soil that was destined for them when the war broke out afresh between the Americans and Indians, and ended in the destruction of those unfortunate colonies. There is no doubt that, alone and destitute of support, they would have been all massacred, had it not been for the predilection which all the Indian nations round Canada and Louisiana have for the French. Again, as long as they did not take an active part in that war, they were not disturbed: but the American army having gained a signal advantage near the *embouchure* of the Great Kenaway, and crossed the Ohio, the inhabitants of Gallipoli were united to it. From that time they were no longer protected, nor could they stir out of the inclosure of their village. Out of two that had strayed not more than two hundred yards, one was scalped and murdered, and the other carried a prisoner a great distance into the interior. When I was at Gallipoli they had just heard from him. He gained his livelihood very comfortably by repairing guns, and exercising his trade as a goldsmith in the Indian village where he lived, and did not express the least wish to return with his countrymen.

The war being terminated, the congress, in order to indemnify these unfortunate Frenchmen for the successive losses which they had sustained, gave them twenty thousand acres of land situated between the small rivers Sandy and Scioto, seventy miles lower than Gallipoli. These twenty thousand acres were at the rate of two hundred and ten acres to every family. Those among them who had neither strength nor resolution enough to go a second time, without any other support than that of their children, to isolate themselves amidst the woods, hew down, burn, and root up the lower parts of trees, which are frequently more than five feet in diameter, and afterward split them to inclose their fields, sold their lots to the Americans or Frenchmen that were somewhat more enterprising. Thirty families only went to settle in their new possessions. Since the three or four years that they have resided there they have succeeded, by dint of labour, in forming for themselves tolerable establishments, where, by the help of a soil excessively fertile, they have an abundant supply of provisions; at least I conceived so, when I was there.

Gallipoli, situated on the borders of the Ohio, is composed solely of about sixty log-houses, most of which being uninhabited, are falling into ruins; the rest are occupied by Frenchmen, who breathe out a miserable existence. Two only among them appear to enjoy the smallest ray of comfort: the one keeps an inn, and distills brandy from peaches, which he sends to Kentucky, or sells it at a tolerable advantage: the other, M. Burau, from Paris, by whom I was well entertained, though unacquainted with him. Nothing can equal the perseverance of this Frenchman, whom the nature of his commerce obliges continually to travel over the banks of the Ohio, and to make, once or twice a year, a journey of four or five hundred miles through the woods, to go to the towns situated beyond the Alleghany Mountains. I learnt from him that the intermittent fevers, which at first had added to the calamities of the inhabitants of Gallipoli, had not shown itself for upwards of three years. That, however, did not prevent a dozen of them going lately to New Orleans in quest of a better fortune, but almost all of them died of the yellow fever the first year after their arrival.

Such was the situation of the establishment of Scioto when I was there. Though they did not succeed better, it is not that the French are less persevering and industrious than the Americans and Germans; it is that among those who departed for Scioto not a tenth part were fit for the toils they were destined to endure. However, it was not politic of the speculators, who sold land at five shillings an acre, which at that time was not worth one in America, to acquaint those whom they induced to purchase that they would be obliged, for the two first years, to have an axe in their hands nine hours a day; or that a good wood-cutter, having nothing but his hands, would be sooner at his ease on those fertile borders, but which he must, in the first place, clear, than he who, arriving there with two or three hundred guineas in his purse, is unaccustomed to such kind of labour. This cause, independent of the war with the natives, was more than sufficient to plunge the new colonists in misery, and stifle the colony in its birth.

New Englanders

THADDEUS M. HARRIS

Marietta

I soon found that the genial influences of a mild and salubrious climate, aided by habitual exercise, daily improved my bodily strength; while my mind, relieved of its cares, was constantly occupied and amused with the new and interesting scenery and the wonderful antiquities in this neighbourhood; and my spirits were soothed and cheered by the kind attentions of hospitality and friendship.

Thus led to indulge some encouraging prospects of restoration to health, my thoughts turned towards my distant home, which I had never expected to revisit. Taking an affectionate leave of my brother, who inclined to settle in the State of Ohio, and of my much esteemed friends at Marietta, accompanied by Mr. Adams, I set out homewards on Monday morning, June 6th.

I quitted with regret a place where I had passed a few weeks so pleasantly. I shall ever retain a grateful sense of the hospitality with which I was received, and of the respect and attention with which I was honored by the inhabitants of Marietta and Belle Pré.

As we preferred traversing the woods to ascending the river in a boat, we returned to Wheeling on horseback.

The industrious habits and neat improvements of the people on the west side of the river, are strikingly contrasted with those on the east. *Here,* in Ohio, they are intelligent, industrious, and thriving; *there,* on the back skirts of Virginia, ignorant, lazy, and poor. *Here* the buildings are neat, though small, and furnished in many instances with brick chimnies and glass windows; *there* the habitations are miserable cabins. *Here* the grounds are laid out in a regular manner, and inclosed by strong posts and rails; *there* the fields are surrounded by a rough zigzag log fence. *Here* are thrifty young apple orchards; *there* the only fruit that is raised is the peach, *from which a good brandy is distilled!*

I had often heard a degrading character of the Back settlers; and had now an opportunity of seeing it exhibited. The abundance of wild game allures them to be huntsmen. They not only find sport in this pursuit, but supply of provisions, together with considerable profit from the peltry. They neglect, of course, the cultivation of the land. They acquire rough and savage manners. Sloth and independence are prominent traits in their character; to indulge the former is their principal enjoyment, and to protect the latter their chief ambition.

Another cause of the difference may be that, in the back counties of Virginia, every planter depends upon his Negroes for the cultivation of his lands; but in the State of Ohio, *where slavery is not allowed,* every farmer tills his ground Himself. To all this may be added, that most of the "Back-wood's men," as they are called, are emigrants from foreign countries, but the State of Ohio was settled by people from New-England, The Region of Industry, Economy, and Steady Habits.

From Thaddeus Mason Harris, *The Journal of a Tour into the Territory Northwest of the Allegheny Mountains,* (Boston, 1805), pp. 57-59.

Central Ohio

FORTESCUE CUMING

Chapter XXX

Heistant's—Lashley goes on before—Sinking springs—Fatiguing road—Broadley's—Musical shoemaker—Talbot's—Dashing travellers—Bainbridge—Platter's—Irish schoolmaster—Reeves's—Paint creek—Cattail swamp—Rogers's North fork of Paint—Arrival at Chilicothe—Meeker's.

On Tuesday morning the 11th August, we arose with the dawn, and notwithstanding there was a steady small rain, we pursued our journey, having first paid Marshon fully as much for our simple and coarse accommodations, as the best on the road would have cost, but our host I suppose thought his stories and his son's musick were equivalent for all other deficiencies.

The land was poor, and no house on the road until we arrived at Heistant's tavern, four miles from Marshon's, where we met the Lexington stage.

My morning walk had given me an appetite for breakfast, which my fellow traveller not being willing to be at the expence of, declined, and saying that as I walked so much faster than him I would soon overtake him, he went on, intending to satisfy his stomach occasionally with some bread and cheese from his knapsack, and a drop of whiskey from his tin canteen, from which he had made a libation at first setting out, and had seemed surprised at my refusal of his invitation to partake.

Heistant is a Pennsylvania German, and has a good and plentiful house, in a very pleasant situation, called the Sinking springs, from a great natural curiosity near it. On the side of a low hill, now in cultivation, are three large holes, each about twenty feet deep and twenty feet diameter, about sixty paces apart, with a subterraneous communication by which the water is conveyed from one to the other, and issues in a fine rivulet at a fourth opening near the house, where Heistant's milk house is placed very judiciously. The spring is copious and the water very fine.*

After a good breakfast I walked on alone, and at about a mile, I entered on a dreary forest having first passed Irwin's tavern, a pleasant situation where the stage sleeps going towards the S. westward. Three miles from Irwin's, is over very broken, but well timbered hills, to the left of which on Brush creek, I was informed, that

From Fortescue Cuming, *Sketches of a Tour to the Western Country . . . 1807-1809,* (Pittsburgh, 1810), pp. 187-201.
*Sinking Springs is in the southwestern corner of Highland County, Ohio.—Ed.

there is a fine settlement, but it is not in sight of the road. The next two miles was through a beech bottom, which was rendered so miry by the rain that poured on me all the time, that it was most laborious walking through it. About the middle of it, I met three men in hunting shirts with each an axe in his hand. Their appearance in that solitary situation was no ways agreeable; however, we gave each other good day, and they told me that old Lashley had desired them to inform me that he would await me at Bradley's, the next house, but when I came there, he had just departed, so that I might have very soon overtaken him, had I not preferred being alone, to effect which the more certainly, I stopped to rest, as it was a house of private entertainment. Bradley and his wife are about sixteen years from Stewartstown, county Tyrone in Ireland, and have a daughter lately married to a young shoemaker named Irons at the next cabin, where I stopped to get my shoes mended. I here found a dozen of stout young fellows who had been at work repairing the road, and were now sheltering themselves from the increasing storm, and listening to some indifferent musick made by their host on a tolerably good violin. I proposed taking the violin while he repaired my shoes. He consented and sat down to work, and in a few minutes I had all the lads jigging it on the floor merrily; Irons himself, as soon as he had repaired the shoes, jumping up and joining them.

Seeing no prospect of the storm ceasing, I satisfied my shoemaker for his trouble, with something more agreeable to him than my musick, and then set off to reach Talbot's, said to be a good tavern, three miles further.

The road led over the highest hill which I had yet seen since I left the Ohio, and afterwards through a level, well wooded, but thinly inhabited country.

In an hour I was at Talbot's, which is a good two story house of squared logs, with a large barn and excellent stabling, surrounded by a well opened and luxuriant farm, with a fine run of meadow.

The landlord and his family are seven years from Nenagh in the county Tipperary, and is the first Irish settler, I had seen on my tour, from any other part than the north of Ireland. He had kept Ellis's ferry on the Ohio, where Powers now resides, for some years, and has lately rented this house and farm from Mr. Willis of Chilicothe, the contractor for carrying the mail from Wheeling to Lexington.

Observing a new stage wagon in the yard, my host informed me that it was one which Mr. Willis intended in a few days to commence running between Chilicothe and Ellis's ferry, so that it, and the one already established, will each run once a week on different days.

I shifted my wet clothes, and then (there being no doctor nearer than Chilicothe, twenty-four miles) prescribed medicine and regimen for Talbot's little daughter, who was suffering under a severe and dangerous attack of a nervous fever.

Three young men on horseback arrived soon after me, and were shewn into the same room. They talked a little largely, according to a very common custom among young travellers, intimating that they were just returning from the Olympian springs in Kentucky, a place of very fashionable resort, where they had been on a party of pleasure, and where they had attended more to cards, billiards, horse jockeying, &c. than to the use of the waters for medicinal purposes. I am however much mistaken, if they had not been travelling on business, and took the opportunity of visiting those celebrated springs, which are the Bath of Kentucky, and which they now affected to speak of as the sole cause of their journey.† I listened with much amusement to their dashing conversation, knowing tolerably well how to estimate it, in a country where vanity in the young and ambition among the more advanced in life are predominant features. I do not confine this remark to the state of Ohio, where probably there is less of either than in the older states, in which, particularly to the southward of New England, they seem to be national characteristics.

We supped together and were then shewn to our beds by the landlord, who probably thought that the custom of two in a bed was general in America, by his shewing the whole four into a room with two beds: I followed him however down stairs, and soon had a good bed prepared for me in a room by myself.

On Wednesday morning the 12th August, I proceeded through a wilderness of fine land well adapted for cultivation, and finely timbered to Bainbridge, a hamlet of eight cabins, a large stone house building, a blacksmith shop, a post-office, and a store kept by William Daly for Humphrey Fullerton of Chilicothe. Daly told me that he had a good deal of business for the five months he had been here, there being a populous and well cultivated country in the neighbourhood on Buckskin and Paint creeks, at the falls of the latter of which, about a mile to the northward of Bainbridge are some of the best mills in the state, owned by Gen. Massey, who is also proprietor of Bainbridge, which he laid out for a town about a year ago, selling the lots at about thirty dollars each.

The reason assigned for the lands being generally so badly settled along the roads, is, that they belong to wealthy proprietors, who either hold them at a very high price, or will not divide them into convenient sized farms.

From Bainbridge to Reeves's on the bank of Paint creek, is through a fine well wooded level, with hills in sight from every opening in the woods, about a mile distant. I passed a finger post on the left, a mile from Bainbridge, pointing to the westward and

---

†Olympian Springs was in Bath County, Kentucky, a few miles southeast of Owingsburg. Its popularity has declined; in 1880 there were but twenty-five inhabitants at the place.—Ed.

directing to Cincinnatti seventy-three miles, and immediately after I left Platter's tavern and well cultivated farm on the right, a little beyond which is a school-house, where I observed the school-master, an Irish looking old man, with silver grey locks and barefooted, his whole appearance, and that of the cabin which was the school, indicating but little encouragement for the disseminating of instruction.

A mile from Platter's I stopped at Reeves's, where I had been informed I could be well accommodated, although it was not a tavern, and I proved my information to be correct, as I immediately got the breakfast I asked for, excellent bread, and rich milk, neatly served, in a large handsome and clean room, for which it was with difficulty I could prevail on Mrs. Reeves to accept any recompence.

This house is charmingly situated near the bank of Paint creek, and was the best I had seen since I entered the state of Ohio, it being spacious, of two lofty stories, and well built with very handsome stone. It is surrounded on all sides by a noble and well improved farm, which nine years ago, when Reeves came here from Washington in Pennsylvania, was a wilderness. He built his handsome house about five years ago, and at some distance on the bank of the creek, he has a large tanyard and leather shop, from whence one of his men, ferried me across the creek in a canoe.

Paint creek is a beautiful little river about forty yards wide, running easterly to join the Scioto near Chilicothe.

My walk from hence to the north fork of Paint creek, was a most fatiguing one, being thirteen miles, mostly along a very rich bottom, with the creek on the right, and steep hills on the left, over spurs of which the road sometimes leads, which was always a relief to me, after wading for miles through the mud below. This tract is tolerably well settled, the soil being esteemed as rich as any in the state. At eleven miles from Reeves's, is a hamlet of six or seven cabins called Cat-tail swamp, and two miles further I came to Rogers's on the bank of the north fork of Paint.

Reeves's appears to be the best land and the best improved farm on this side the Ohio, but Rogers's, nearly as good a soil, is I think superiour in beauty of situation. The house which is a story and a half high is of square logs, and commodious enough for a farm house. It is on a moderately high bank, from whence they descend to the river by a flight of wooden steps, at the foot of which is a most beautiful spring which flows into a cask sunk on purpose, and from thence is conveyed by a small spout into the river, whose bank is guarded by a natural wall of soft slate, which I think could be easily wrought into good covering for houses. Nature has formed natural stairs of the slate, by which one may descend to any depth into the river for bathing, washing linen, or for any purpose which may be necessary, in proportion as the river rises or falls. A swimmer may also enjoy that invigorating exercise charmingly, as though the river is only about thirty yards wide, it is at this place sufficiently deep, and the current is moderate. Rogers has been here about nine years from Virginia, and was one of the first settlers in this part of the country.

I supped and slept here, and next morning, Thursday the 13th August, after refreshing by swimming in the river, I pursued my way to Chilicothe four miles, the first mile and half of which was over a chain of moderately high and not very steep hills of a tolerably good soil, to colonel M'Arthur's elegant stone house and noble farm.** other two miles and a half was through a level plain, passing a neat house and handsome improvement of Mr. Henry Massey's, just before entering Chilicothe, which I did at eight o'clock, stopping at Muker's tavern, as the breakfast bell rang, which summoned seventeen or eighteen boarders and travellers to an excellent breakfast with good attendance, to which I did ample justice, after my bath and walk.

Chapter XXXI

The Scioto—Chilicothe—Indian monument—Fine prospect—Colonel M'Arthur's—Colonel Worthington's.

Chilicothe, which signifies town in most of the Indian dialects, is most beautifully situated on the right bank of the Scioto, about forty-five miles by land, and nearly seventy following its meanders from the confluence of that river with the Ohio, between Portsmouth and Alexandria. In all that distance the river has a gentle current, and unimpeded navigation for large keels, and other craft for four feet draught of water. It continues navigable for smaller boats and batteaux upwards of one hundred miles above Chilicothe, towards its source to the northward, from whence it glides gently through a naturally rich, level, and rapidly improving country.

**The home of General McArthur was known as "Fruit Hill." Duncan McArthur was of Scotch parentage, born in New York in 1772. Left early to his own resources, he volunteered under Harmar in 1791, worked at the Maysville salt-works, and in 1793 became chain-bearer for General Massie in the latter's survey of Ohio lands. McArthur's industry and capacity soon secured his promotion to the position of assistant surveyor, and by judicious choice of lands he acquired wealth and prominence. Having been major-general of Ohio militia for some years, his services were called for in the War of 1812-15, and he was at Detroit when it was surrendered by Hull. Released on parole, he was elected to Congress, whence he resigned to become brigadier-general in the army, and served in the Western division thereof throughout the war. Later began his political career, consisting of two terms in Congress (1822-26), and the governorship of Ohio (1830). But as an anti-Jacksonian, he failed of re-election, and retired to "Fruit Hill" where he died in 1840.—Ed.

The situation of the town, which is the capital of the state,* is on an elevated and extensive plain of nearly ten thousand acres of as fine a soil as any in America, partly in cultivation and partly covered with its native forests.

This plain is nearly surrounded by the Scioto, which turning suddenly to the N. E. from its general southerly course, leaves the town to the southward of it, and then forms a great bend to the eastward and southward.

Water street, which runs about E. by N. parallel to the Scioto, is half a mile long, and contains ninety houses. It is eighty-four feet wide, and would be a fine street, had not the river floods caved in the bank in one place near the middle, almost into the centre of it. There is now a lottery on foot, to raise money for securing the bank against any further encroachments of the river. Main street, parallel to Water street, is one hundred feet wide, as is Market street which crosses both at right angles, and in which is the market-house, a neat brick building eighty feet long. The court-house in the same street is neatly built of freestone, on an area of forty-five by forty-two feet, with a semicircular projection in the rear, in which is the bench for the judges. It has an octangular belfry rising from the roof, painted white with green lattices, which is an ornament to the town, as is the small plain belfry of the Presbyterian meeting-house, a handsome brick building in Main street; in which street also is a small brick Methodist meeting-house. These are the only places of publick worship in the town, if I except the court-house, which is used occasionally by the Episcopalians and other sects.

The whole number of dwelling houses in Chilicothe, as I counted them, is two hundred and two, besides four brick and a few framed ones now building. I reckoned only six taverns with signs, which small proportion of houses of that description, speaks volumes in favour of the place. There are fourteen stores, a post-office, and two printing-offices, which each issues a gazette weekly.

The scite of the town being on a gravelly soil, the streets are generally clean. The houses are of freestone, brick, or timber clapboarded, the first of which is got in the neighbourhood, is of a whitish brown colour, and excellent for building. They are mostly very good and are well painted.

On the whole I think Chilicothe is not exceeded in beauty of plan, situation, or appearance, by any town I have seen in the western part of the United States.

. . . .

---

*By a law of the last session of the legislature, the seat of the state government was removed to Zanesville, on the Muskingum river.—Cramer.

Chapter XXXII

Congo—Crouse's mill—Pickaway plains—Beautiful prairies—Tarleton and Lybrant's excellent inn—Vestiges of a great fire—River Hockhocking—New Lancaster—Babb's—Jonathan's creek—Springfield—River Muskingum and falls—Zanesville.

We crossed the Scioto at a ferry from the town, the stage and four horses being all carried over in the boat.

The first two miles were over a rich bottom, subject to inundation from the river floods in the winter. We had then three miles of a hilly country to Congo, a fine settlement in and round a beautiful prairie, a mile long to Crouse's mill. This Crouse is a wealthy man, having a good house and offices, a farm of two sections, containing thirteen hundred acres, and an excellent mill house and mill wrought by a creek which crosses the road and falls into the Scioto half a mile on the left. Another mile brought us to Rickey's ·tavern, from whence a road leads to the left to Pickaway Plains, which is a noble and rich prairie, on the west side of the Scioto, fourteen miles long, formerly a principal settlement of the Indians,* and now well inhabited by their white successors, who have a town called Levingston on the Prairie.

From Rickey's to M'Cutchin's tavern is four miles, across a beautiful savanna, variegated with clumps of trees, and fine groves, with farms at every half mile. We here stopped for a few minutes to water the horses, and I exchanged my seat in the stage, with a Mr. Willis of Chilicothe,† who had accompanied us on horseback, on his way to the federal city, Washington, to make some arrangements respecting the mails. The exchange suited us both, as on horseback I had a better view of the country, and his health being delicate, he preferred the stage.

The next six miles were through a thinly wooded but rich plain, with a farm every mile, and a tavern every three miles. The road was so far level but very miry, then another mile and a half over some hilly and broken land brought us to Lybrant's tavern.

Had I not been informed, I should not have known that I was now in the town of Tarleton, as there was but one other house besides the tavern; three or four more were however just going to be

---

*Pickaway Plains, in Pickaway County south of Circleville, was said to contain the richest land in Ohio. It was a noted rendezvous for the Shawnees; from hence started the army that Lewis defeated at Point Pleasant (1774), and here at a camp which he called Camp Charlotte in honor of the queen, Lord Dunmore made the peace that ended the war. Here, also, Chief Logan's famous speech was delivered.—Ed.

†Nathaniel Willis, the grandfather of the poet by that name, was a printer, who prided himself on having been a participant in the Boston Tea-party. During the Revolution, he was proprietor of the Boston *Independent Chronicle*. On peace being declared, he went to Virginia, and at Martinsburg published for a few years the *Potomac Guardian*. Tempted by reports from the new territory, he once more removed and established (probably in 1800) the *Scioto Gazette* at Chillicothe, the third newspaper of the state. He was also, for a time, state printer, and as Cuming informs us connected with the forwarding of the mail.—Ed.

built, and our landlord had no doubt of its soon becoming a smart town. The lots were sold at from sixteen to twenty-five dollars each.

Lybrant's is one of the best and most reasonable inns I had met with in my tour. At one o'clock we set down to a most excellent breakfast of good coffee, roast fowls, chicken pie, potatoes, bread and butter, and cucumbers both sliced and pickled, all not only good, but delicate and fine even to the pastry, which is very uncommon in this country, and our charge was only a quarter of a dollar.

For eight miles from Tarleton, the road runs through low, rich and miry black oak woods, and now and then a small prairie, and settlements not nearer each other than every two miles. The country then rising into hills the road improves, but it continues equally thinly inhabited, the settlements being mostly on what is called the old county road, which runs parallel to the state road about a mile and a half to the northward of it, and is better and shorter by a mile between Chilicothe and New Lancaster.

. . . .

New Lancaster** is a compact little town of one wide street, about six hundred paces long, containing sixty houses, amongst which is a neat little court house of brick, forty-two by thirty-six feet, just built, with a cupola belfry. There are six stores and nine taverns. There is but one brick house, all the rest being of wood, amongst which conspicuously the best is that of Mr. Bucher a lawyer. In most towns in the United States, the best houses are chiefly inhabited by gentlemen of that profession.

After supping at the inn where the stage stopped, I was shewn to bed up stairs in a barrack room the whole extent of the house, with several beds in it, one of which was already occupied by a man and his wife, from the neighbouring country, who both conversed with me until I feigned sleep, in hopes that would silence them, but though they then ceased to direct their discourse to me, they continued to talk to each other on their most private and domestick affairs, as though there had been no other person in the room. In spite of their conversation I at last fell asleep, but I was soon awoke in torture from a general attack made on me by hosts of vermin of the most troublesome and disgusting genii. I started from the bed, dressed myself, spread a coverlet on the floor, and lay down there to court a little more repose, but I was prevented by a constant noise in the house during the whole night, beginning with church musick,

---

**The site of New Lancaster had previously been that of a well-known Indian village called Standing Stone from an eminence in the vicinity. It was the most southwestern town of the Delawares in Ohio, and was also called French Margaret's Town, because a daughter of Madame Montour had at one time resided therein. As an American settlement it was laid out by Zane in 1800; later, "New" was dropped from its title by legislative enactment.—Ed.

among which some sweet female voices were discernible, and ending in the loud drunken frolicks of some rustick guests, who kept Saturday night until late on Sunday morning.

Previous to going to bed I had sauntered round the town, and I observed all the taverns filled with guests in the roughest style of conviviality, from which I infer that the last day of the week is generally devoted to the orgies of Bacchus; by the same classes of people who on the succeeding day, attend with pious regularity the dogmatick lectures of some fanatick dispenser of the gospel. What an heterogeneous animal is man!—sometimes exalted to an approach towards divinity, sometimes debased to lower than brutality:—A perpetual struggle between the essence and the dregs.

The Western Reserve

JOHN MELISH

Chapter XXVIII

Canton,—Canton district,—Connecticut reserve,—Cleveland.

. . . .

Canton was laid out about five years ago, and now consists of 30 dwelling-houses, four taverns, and nine stores. The number of inhabitants is about 250. There are no public buildings.

The inhabitants are composed of farmers and mechanics, and are mostly from Pennsylvania. No manufactures have yet been established except in families, but these are general; and there are a number of mills in the neighbourhood, and several wool carding machines. Sheep thrive remarkably well in the neighbourhood, and it is presumed a manufacture of coarse woollens would succeed.

The price of labour is nearly the same as at Zanesville; common labourers have 50 cents per day and found, masons, carpenters, &c., one dollar per day. The great influx of new settlers consume all the

From John Melish, *Travels in the United States of America in the Years 1806-07-09, 1810-1811,* II (Philadelphia, 1812), pp. 253-263.

surplus provisions, except stock; which is sent to a market at Philadelphia and Baltimore. Flour sells at five dollars per barrel, beef at 3 dollars 50 cents per cwt.

The climate is pretty healthy. Some few cases of fever and ague occur, but they are not very common.

Canton District was lately purchased from the Indians, and extends from the Tuscarawas river about 68 miles to the westward, and from the Connecticut reservation to the north boundary of Zanesville and Chillicothe districts, its average breadth being 28 miles. Its area is about 1800 square miles, or 1,152,000 acres.

The district is nearly all level, and fit for cultivation, but it is in many parts very muddy, a circumstance common in the districts situated on the head waters of the rivers in this state. On this account it is difficult to make good roads, and it requires a pretty thick population to drain the country, and make it agreeable; but there is a sufficient descent for carrying off the water, and this will be a very desirable country some time hence. It is abundantly supplied with springs, and streams of pure water. There is a great deal of prairie or meadow land interspersed through it.

The principal timber is walnut, poplar, ash, elm, oak, sugar maple, and hickory. The soil is well adapted to the culture of grain, grass, tobacco, hemp, &c.

. . . .

We moved on, and came to a little clearing, and a small cabin, where we proposed taking shelter; but the people giving it as their opinion that the storm was over, we went on to a tavern 10 miles from Canton. The family informed us that they had moved from Maryland, and were of German origin; they could still speak German, although their grandfather had left his native country 60 or 70 years ago.

After leaving the tavern about a mile, we saw a tent pitched in the woods a little off the road, and turned aside to make inquiries. This was an emigrant family, consisting of a man, his wife, and two children. They had travelled far in quest of a settlement, and their means being exhausted, they were obliged to stop short at this place, where they meant to *sit down* and clear and cultivate a piece of land. In the language of the country, they were *squatters.* The only visible substance they had, was a tent; a waggon, a horse, a cow, and some bedding. The tent and bedding had been drenched by the rain, but they had a large fire before the door, at which the bedding was hung up to dry, and they sat round it apparently very contented. Little do those who live in cities know of the hardships to be endured by those who subdue and settle the wilderness! and yet perhaps the life of the latter is most to be envied; they are free from all care except that of providing for their families, and the *real* wants of a family are easily supplied; they have no credit *to support* nor bills *to pay;* and they can train up their children in the paths of virtue and of industry, far removed from the evil example of the wicked; no *artificial* circumstance stands between them and their maker: they can behold the bounty of his providence in their flocks, and herds, and in the fields around them; they can work their daily task, confident of a reward; and, blessing the God of mercies, they can repose their heads on the pillow, and enjoy a sweet sleep, the reward of rational labour, and a good conscience.

A little beyond this encampment the country becomes ridgy and barren; we travelled a mile, when we crossed the Tuscarawa, by a wooden bridge. This is now the eighth time that I have crossed this river since leaving Zanesville. Here it is a small stream, quite covered with brush-wood, and its source is in a small lake a few miles to the eastward. We now entered into the *Connecticut Reservation*, at the 41st degree of latitude, and this being the dividing ridge between the northern and southern waters, the same train of reflections occurred as on the top of the Allegany mountains. . . .

After passing the ridge, we came into a fine open plain of fertile land, in which were a great many fields of wheat, and about the middle of it my fellow-traveller and I parted. At the end of this plain, the road winds to the westward, through pretty thick woods, in which I travelled about three miles, and, coming to a small opening, I stopped for the night at the house of a Mr. Bradley.

Mr. Bradley told me he moved from the north-west corner of Connecticut, to Canfield, 35 miles to the eastward, and two years ago he had removed to this place. This township is called Springfield, and has settled up pretty fast within a few years; it now contains 24 families. It has been tolerably healthy this season, but some of the adjoining townships have been very much afflicted with fever and ague. There is a number of tracts of good land in the town, and it is favourable for raising all sorts of small grain, grass, and vegetables. Pumpkins grow to an enormous size, and the people live a good deal upon pumpkin pies.

Mr. Bradley has a thriving family of six sons and one daughter. They have quite the Connecticut appearance. They say they like this country very well.

October 17. I set out from Mr. Bradley's at half past 6 o'clock; the morning was clear, with a little frost. Having travelled about three miles, through a muddy road, I crossed the south branch of the Cayahoga river by a wooden bridge. It is here a dull black stream, covered with brushwood. The north bank rises by a gentle elevation, and is capable of cultivation, but it is poor land. I was now in Tamage township; the country is very thinly settled, and the road deplorably bad. Having passed through Tamage five miles, I entered into Stow, and soon after crossed the main branch of the Cayahoga river, by a shallow ford; the river is about 80 yards broad, and the bottom stony. There are several settlements on its banks, mostly of people from Connecticut. About a mile from the river I stopped to breakfast.

Here I was informed by the family, that they were from Middleton, Connecticut; from whence a good many of the settlers in this town are. The country has suffered a good deal from fever and ague this summer; more, indeed, than in any season they have been in the country, now 10 years. This township contains about 40 families, 20 of whom have settled here within two years. The adjoining towns of Olmstead and Northampton are not well settled, being subject very much to fever and ague, which is the case in a great part of Portage county, and the settlers now move more to the Fire lands. The town of Hudson, to the north, is an old and thriving settlement; the people have fine dairies, and make a great quantity of excellent cheese and butter for the supply of other parts of the country, and for the New Orleans market.

. . . .

At half past 6 I set out out towards Cleveland, now 12 miles distant. I ascended from the creek by a pretty steep path, from whence I travelled a few miles to another creek, having a fall of about 80 feet, and handsome freestone banks. I saw some mills; but they were idle, and appeared to be going to decay. The country appeared poor, and the people sickly.

From Canton to this place, the travelling had been far from agreeable; the roads were muddy, and often deep; and the country was one dull plain, without a single object to exhilarate the imagination, or cheer the spirits; and latterly the people looked pale and sickly. But I was buoyed up with the anticipation of the beauties of Lake Erie, to which I posted with all the alacrity of impatience. I noticed, as I went along, that the country on the banks of the Cayahoga river improved; the road led by a high bank, from whence there was a fine view to the westward; the bottoms on the river were extensive and fertile; though I observed the seeds of disease in its slow, sluggish, winding course, choked up with a vast quantity of vegetable matter undergoing decomposition; and at every settlement I passed, the pale, sickly visages of the inhabitants confirmed the remark. At last, Lake Erie appeared, with a beautiful, blue, placid surface, checkering through the trees. I reached Cleveland; but, without stopping to examine *the city*, I rode on to the bank, where, from an eminence about 70 feet high, I beheld the lake in all its glory. To the northward, no land was to be seen; and to the east and west, the banks were high, and the scenery very picturesque; the view was really sublime. I was delighted with it; and, full of the pleasing sensations which such a view was calculated to excite, I pursued my way to the tavern. But, O! what a contrast was there! the people looked pale, sickly, and dejected. I learned that they had been afflicted with a very severe sickness this season. *It was periodical,* they said, and generally fever and ague; but this season it had been worse than usual, and accompanied with some very severe cases of bilious fever. I found that this had proved a complete check upon the improvement of Cleveland, which, though dignified with the name of a city, remained a paltry *village,* containing a few houses only.

Frontier Ohio

CHARLES DICKENS

We rested but one day at Cincinnati, and then resumed our journey to Sandusky. As it comprised two varieties of stage-coach travelling, which, with those I have already glanced at, comprehend the main characteristics of this mode of transit in America, I will take the reader as our fellow-passenger, and pledge myself to perform the distance with all possible dispatch.

Our place of destination in the first instance is Columbus. It is distant about a hundred and twenty miles from Cincinnati, but there is a macadamised road (rare blessing!) the whole way, and the rate of travelling upon it is six miles an hour.

We start at eight o'clock in the morning, in a great mail-coach, whose huge cheeks are so very ruddy and plethoric, that it appears to be troubled with a tendency of blood to the head. Dropsical it certainly is, for it will hold a dozen passengers inside. But, wonderful to add, it is very clean and bright, being nearly new; and rattles through the streets of Cincinnati gaily.

Our way lies through a beautiful country, richly cultivated, and luxuriant in its promise of an abundant harvest. Sometimes we pass a

From Charles Dickens, *American Notes and Pictures From Italy,* (London, 1966), pp. 187-196.

field where the strong bristling stalks of Indian corn look like a crop of walking-sticks, and sometimes an enclosure where the green wheat is springing up among a labyrinth of stumps; the primitive worm-fence is universal, and an ugly thing it is; but the farms are neatly kept, and, save for these differences, one might be travelling just now in Kent.

We often stop to water at a roadside inn, which is always dull and silent. The coachman dismounts and fills his bucket, and holds it to the horses' heads. There is scarcely ever any one to help him; there are seldom any loungers standing round; and never any stable-company with jokes to crack. Sometimes, when we have changed our team, there is a difficulty in starting again, arising out of the prevalent mode of breaking a young horse: which is to catch him, harness him against his will, and put him in a stage-coach without further notice: but we get on somehow or other, after a great many kicks and a violent struggle; and jog on as before again.

Occasionally, when we stop to change, some two or three half-drunken loafers will come loitering out with their hands in their pockets, or will be seen kicking their heels in rocking-chairs, or lounging on the window-sill, or sitting on a rail within the colonnade: they have not often anything to say though, either to us or to each other, but sit there idly staring at the coach and horses. The landlord of the inn is usually among them, and seems, of all the party, to be the least connected with the business of the house. Indeed he is with reference to the tavern, what the driver is in relation to the coach and passengers: whatever happens in his sphere of action, he is quite indifferent, and perfectly easy in his mind.

The frequent change of coachmen works no change or variety in the coachman's character. He is always dirty, sullen, and taciturn. If he be capable of smartness of any kind, moral or physical, he has a faculty of concealing it which is truly marvellous. He never speaks to you as you sit beside him on the box, and if you speak to him, he answers (if at all) in monosyllables. He points out nothing on the road, and seldom looks at anything: being, to all appearance, thor-oughly weary of it and of existence generally. As to doing the honours of his coach, his business, as I have said, is with the horses. The coach follows because it is attached to them and goes on wheels: not because you are in it. Sometimes, towards the end of a long stage, he suddenly breaks out into a discordant fragment of an election song, but his face never sings along with him: it is only his voice, and not often that.

He always chews and always spits, and never encumbers himself with a pocket-handkerchief. The consequences to the box passenger, especially when the wind blows towards him, are not agreeable.

Whenever the coach stops, and you can hear the voices of the inside passengers; or whenever any bystander addresses them, or any one among them; or they address each other; you will hear one phrase repeated over and over and over again to the most extraordinary extent. It is an ordinary and unpromising phrase enough, being neither more nor less than "Yes, Sir;" but it is adapted to every variety of circumstance, and fills up every pause in the conversation. Thus:—

The time is one o'clock at noon. The scene, a place where we are to stay and dine, on this journey. The coach drives up to the door of an inn. The day is warm, and there are several idlers lingering about the tavern, and waiting for the public dinner. Among them, is a stout gentleman in a brown hat, swinging himself to and fro in a rocking-chair on the pavement.

As the coach stops, a gentleman in a straw hat looks out of the window:

STRAW HAT. (To the stout gentleman in the rocking-chair.) I reckon that's Judge Jefferson, an't it?

BROWN HAT. (Still swinging; speaking very slowly; and without any emotion whatever.) Yes, Sir.

STRAW HAT. Warm weather, Judge.

BROWN HAT. Yes, Sir.

STRAW HAT. There was a snap of cold, last week.

BROWN HAT. Yes, Sir.

STRAW HAT. Yes, Sir.

A pause. They look at each other, very seriously.

STRAW HAT. I calculate you'll have got through that case of the corporation, Judge, by this time, now?

BROWN HAT. Yes, Sir.

STRAW HAT. How did the verdict go, Sir?

BROWN HAT. For the defendant, Sir.

STRAW HAT. (Interrogatively.) Yes Sir?

BROWN HAT. (Affirmatively.) Yes, Sir.

BOTH. (Musingly, as each gazes down the street.) Yes, Sir.

Another pause. They look at each other again, still more seriously than before.

BROWN HAT. This coach is rather behind its time to-day, I guess.

STRAW HAT. (Doubtingly.) Yes, Sir.

BROWN HAT. (Looking at his watch.) Yes, Sir; nigh upon two hours.

STRAW HAT. (Raising his eyebrows in very great surprise.) Yes, Sir!

BROWN HAT. (Decisively, as he puts up his watch.) Yes, Sir.

ALL THE OTHER INSIDE PASSENGERS. (Among themselves.) Yes, Sir.

COACHMAN. (In a very surly tone.) No it an't.

STRAW HAT. (To the coachman.) Well, I don't know, Sir. We were a pretty tall time coming that last fifteen mile. That's a fact.

The coachman making no reply, and plainly declining to enter into any controversy on a subject so far removed from his sympathies and feelings, another passenger says, "Yes, Sir;" and the gentleman in the straw hat in acknowledgment of his courtesy, says "Yes, Sir," to him, in return. The straw hat then inquires of the brown hat, whether that coach in which he (the straw hat) then sits, is not a new one? To which the brown hat again makes answer, "Yes, Sir."

STRAW HAT. I thought so. Pretty loud smell of varnish, Sir?

BROWN HAT. Yes, Sir.

ALL THE OTHER INSIDE PASSENGERS. Yes, Sir.

BROWN HAT. (To the company in general.) Yes, Sir.

The conversational powers of the company having been by this time pretty heavily taxed, the straw hat opens the door and gets out; and all the rest alight also. We dine soon afterwards with the boarders in the house, and have nothing to drink but tea and coffee. As they are both very bad and the water is worse, I ask for brandy; but it is a Temperance Hotel, and spirits are not to be had for love or money. This preposterous forcing of unpleasant drinks down the reluctant throats of travellers is not at all uncommon in America, but I never discovered that the scruples of such wincing landlords induced them to preserve any unusually nice balance between the quality of their fare, and their scale of charges: on the contrary, I rather suspected them of diminishing the one and exalting the other, by way of recompence for the loss of their profit on the sale of spirituous liquors. After all, perhaps, the plainest course for persons of such tender consciences, would be, a total abstinence from tavern-keeping.

Dinner over, we get into another vehicle which is ready at the door (for the coach has been changed in the interval), and resume our journey; which continues through the same kind of country until evening, when we come to the town where we are to stop for tea and supper; and having delivered the mail bags at the Post-office, ride through the usual wide street, lined with the usual stores and houses (the drapers always having hung up at their door, by way of sign, a piece of bright red cloth), to the hotel where this meal is prepared. There being many boarders here, we sit down, a large party, and a very melancholy one as usual. But there is a buxom hostess at the head of the table, and opposite, a simple Welsh schoolmaster with his wife and child; who came here, on a speculation of greater promise than performance, to teach the classics: and they are sufficient subjects of interest until the meal is over, and another coach is ready. In it we go on once more, lighted by a bright moon, until midnight; when we stop to change the coach again, and remain for half an hour or so in a miserable room, with a blurred lithograph of Washington over the smoky fireplace, and a mighty jug of cold water on the table: to which refreshment the moody passengers do so apply themselves that they would seem to be, one and all, keen patients of Dr. Sangrado. Among them is a very little boy, who chews tobacco like a very big one; and a droning gentleman, who talks arithmetically and statistically on all subjects, from poetry downwards; and who always speaks in the same key, with exactly the same emphasis, and with very grave deliberation. He came outside just now, and told me how that the uncle of a certain young lady who had been spirited away and married by a certain captain, lived in these parts; and how this uncle was so valiant and ferocious that he shouldn't wonder if he were to follow the said captain to England, "and shoot him down in the street wherever he found him;" in the feasibility of which strong measure I, being for the moment rather prone to contradiction, from feeling half asleep and very tired, declined to acquiesce: assuring him that if the uncle did resort to it, or gratified any other little whim of the like nature, he would find himself one morning prematurely throttled at the Old Bailey: and that he would do well to make his will before he went, as he would certainly want it before he had been in Britain very long.

On we go, all night, and by-and-by the day begins to break, and presently the first cheerful rays of the warm sun come slanting on us brightly. It sheds its light upon a miserable waste of sodden grass, and dull trees, and squalid huts, whose aspect is forlorn and grievous in the last degree. A very desert in the wood, whose growth of green is dank and noxious like that upon the top of standing water: where poisonous fungus grows in the rare footprint on the oozy ground, and sprouts like witches' coral, from the crevices in the cabin wall and floor; it is a hideous thing to lie upon the very threshold of a city. But it was purchased years ago, and as the owner cannot be discovered, the State has been unable to reclaim it. So there it remains, in the midst of cultivation and improvement, like ground accursed, and made obscene and rank by some great crime.

We reached Columbus shortly before seven o'clock, and stayed there, to refresh, that day and night: having excellent apartments in a very large unfinished hotel called the Neill House, which were richly fitted with the polished wood of the black walnut, and opened on a handsome portico and stone verandah, like rooms in some Italian mansion. The town is clean and pretty, and of course is "going to be" much larger. It is the seat of the State legislature of Ohio, and lays claim, in consequence, to some consideration and importance.

There being no stage-coach next day, upon the road we wished to take, I hired "an extra," at a reasonable charge, to carry us to Tiffin; a small town from whence there is a railroad to Sandusky. This extra was an ordinary four-horse stage-coach, such as I have described, changing horses and drivers, as the stage-coach would, but was exclusively our own for the journey. To ensure our having horses at the proper stations, and being incommoded by no strangers, the proprietors sent an agent on the box, who was to accompany us the whole way through; and thus attended, and bearing with us, besides, a hamper full of savoury cold meats, and fruit, and wine, we started off again in high spirits, at half-past six o'clock next morning, very much delighted to be by ourselves, and disposed to enjoy even the roughest journey.

It was well for us, that we were in this humour, for the road we went over that day, was certainly enough to have shaken tempers that were not resolutely at Set Fair, down to some inches below Stormy. At one time we were all flung together in a heap at the bottom of the coach, and at another we were crushing our heads against the roof. Now, one side was down deep in the mire, and we were holding on to the other. Now, the coach was lying on the tails of the two wheelers; and now it was rearing up in the air, in a frantic state, with all four horses standing on the top of an insurmountable eminence, looking coolly back at it, as though they would say "Unharness us. It can't be done." The drivers on these roads, who certainly get over the ground in a manner which is quite miraculous, so twist and turn the team about in forcing a passage, corkscrew fashion, through the bogs and swamps, that it was quite a common circumstance on looking out of the window, to see the coachman with the ends of a pair of reins in his hands, apparently driving nothing, or playing at horses, and the leaders staring at one unexpectedly from the back of the coach, as if they had some idea of getting up behind. A great portion of the way was over what is called a corduroy road, which is made by throwing trunks of trees into a marsh, and leaving them to settle there. The very slightest of the jolts with which the ponderous carriage fell from log to log, was enough, it seemed, to have dislocated all the bones in the human body. It would be impossible to experience a similar set of sensations, in any other circumstances, unless perhaps in attempting to go up to the top of St. Paul's in an omnibus. Never, never once, that day, was the coach in any position, attitude, or kind of motion to which we are accustomed in coaches. Never did it make the smallest approach to one's experience of the proceedings of any sort of vehicle that goes on wheels.

Still, it was a fine day, and the temperature was delicious, and though we had left Summer behind us in the west, and were fast leaving Spring, we were moving towards Niagara and home. We alighted in a pleasant wood towards the middle of the day, dined on a fallen tree, and leaving our best fragments with a cottager, and our

worst with the pigs (who swarm in this part of the country like grains
of sand on the sea-shore, to the great comfort of our commissariat in
Canada), we went forward again, gaily.

As night came on, the track grew narrower and narrower, until at
last it so lost itself among the trees, that the driver seemed to find his
way by instinct. We had the comfort of knowing, at least, that there
was no danger of his falling asleep, for every now and then a wheel
would strike against an unseen stump with such a jerk, that he was
fain to hold on pretty tight and pretty quick, to keep himself upon
the box. Nor was there any reason to dread the least danger from
furious driving, inasmuch as over that broken ground the horses had
enough to do to walk; as to shying, there was no room for that; and a
herd of wild elephants could not have run away in such a wood, with
such a coach at their heels. So we stumbled along, quite satisfied.

These stumps of trees are a curious feature in American travelling. The varying illusions they present to the unaccustomed eye as it
grows dark, are quite astonishing in their number and reality. Now,
there is a Grecian urn erected in the centre of a lonely field; now
there is a woman weeping at a tomb; now a very commonplace old
gentleman in a white waistcoat, with a thumb thrust into each
arm-hole of his coat; now a student poring on a book; now a
crouching negro; now, a horse, a dog, a cannon, an armed man; a
hunchback throwing off his cloak and stepping forth into the light.
They were often as entertaining to me as so many glasses in a magic
lantern, and never took their shapes at my bidding, but seemed to
force themselves upon me, whether I would or no; and strange to
say, I sometimes recognised in them counterparts of figures once
familiar to me in pictures attached to childish books, forgotten long
ago.

It soon became too dark, however, even for this amusement, and
the trees were so close together that their dry branches rattled
against the coach on either side, and obliged us all to keep our heads
within. It lightened too, for three whole hours; each flash being very
bright, and blue, and long; and as the vivid streaks came darting in
among the crowded branches, and the thunder rolled gloomily above
the tree tops, one could scarcely help thinking that there were better
neighbourhoods at such a time than thick woods afforded.

At length, between ten and eleven o'clock at night, a few feeble
lights appeared in the distance, and Upper Sandusky, an Indian
village, where we were to stay till morning, lay before us.

They were gone to bed at the log Inn, which was the only house
of entertainment in the place, but soon answered to our knocking,
and got some tea for us in a sort of kitchen or common room,
tapestried with old newspapers, pasted against the wall. The bed-
chamber to which my wife and I were shown, was a large, low,

ghostly room; with a quantity of withered branches on the hearth, and two doors without any fastening, opposite to each other, both opening on the black night and wild country, and so contrived, that one of them always blew the other open: a novelty in domestic architecture, which I do not remember to have seen before, and which I was somewhat disconcerted to have forced on my attention after getting into bed, as I had a considerable sum in gold for our travelling expenses, in my dressing-case. Some of the luggage, however, piled against the panels, soon settled this difficulty, and my sleep would not have been very much affected that night, I believe, though it had failed to do so.

My Boston friend climbed up to bed, somewhere in the roof, where another guest was already snoring hugely. But being bitten beyond his power of endurance, he turned out again, and fled for shelter to the coach, which was airing itself in front of the house. This was not a very politic step, as it turned out; for the pigs scenting him, and looking upon the coach as a kind of pie with some manner of meat inside, grunted round it so hideously, that he was afraid to come out again, and lay there shivering, till morning. Nor was it possible to warm him, when he did come out, by means of a glass of brandy: for in Indian villages, the legislature, with a very good and wise intention, forbids the sale of spirits by tavern keepers. The precaution, however, is quite inefficacious, for the Indians never fail to procure liquor of a worse kind, at a dearer price, from travelling pedlars.

It is a settlement of the Wyandot Indians who inhabit this place. Among the company at breakfast was a mild old gentleman, who had been for many years employed by the United States Government in conducting negotiations with the Indians, and who had just concluded a treaty with these people by which they bound themselves in consideration of a certain annual sum, to remove next year to some land provided for them, west of the Mississippi, and a little way beyond St. Louis. He gave me a moving account of their strong attachment to the familiar scenes of their infancy, and in particular to the burial-places of their kindred; and of their great reluctance to leave them. He had witnessed many such removals, and always with pain, though he knew that they departed for their own good. The question whether this tribe should go or stay, had been discussed among them a day or two before, in a hut erected for the purpose, the logs of which still lay upon the ground before the inn. When the speaking was done, the ayes and noes were ranged on opposite sides, and every male adult voted in his turn. The moment the result was known, the minority (a large one) cheerfully yielded to the rest, and withdrew all kind of opposition.

5 The Republican Era

THE BURDEN OF building a state fell mainly to the Jeffersonian Republicans, who were primarily responsible for the construction of Ohio's constitution and its statehood. For nearly thirty years the Republicans, not always working in unison, governed the state. Their leadership guided Ohio along the path from a frontier society to a maturing social and economic community. The founding fathers of the state, fearful of too strong a governor after their experiences with Arthur St. Clair, made sure that the legislative branch of the state government was dominant and that the governor was no more than a figurehead. Young, ambitious, and anxious to have their state's influence felt at the seat of national government, the Republicans not only established laws for Ohio but became involved in issues of national importance, defended the country's western region during an international war, and provided for the economic development of the state's interior.

During the first several legislative sessions, the Ohio General Assembly passed laws that built the government and regulated society. Laws were adopted that established a militia, organized counties and townships, altered tax laws, provided for roads, bridges, and canal locks, and toyed with public education. In order to regulate society, the assembly passed statutes that outlined the provisions for marriage, demanded punishment for bribery and burglary, prescribed "stripes, on his naked back," for the robber, and required twofold restitution to the victim for his property loss. Concerning itself with the morals of society, the assembly forbade Sabbath sporting, gaming, rioting, quarreling, hunting, horse racing, and common labor; and anyone over fourteen years of age heard cursing or swearing was to be fined fifty cents for each offense. Because Ohio was an agrarian state, the farmers' livestock was protected from predators by a bounty on wolves and panthers; and the farmers' grains were defended from gluttonous squirrels by the law's subjection of each person liable to taxation to the responsibility of producing as many as one hundred squirrel scalps or a fine of three cents for each scalp not obtained.

Legislators were also concerned about the free blacks in Ohio. The founders of the state prohibited slavery but failed to confer the rights of citizenship on blacks. Therefore, between 1804 and 1807 the general assembly passed legislation that severely restricted the civil rights of that minority group. Ohio's proximity to two slave states also encouraged its legislators to pass laws that discouraged black migration north of the Ohio River. The so-called black codes remained in force until 1848, when a vocal antislavery movement influenced its repeal.

While busily conducting the state's affairs, the state government supported Republican President Thomas Jefferson in 1806, when he struck out against his political foe Aaron Burr. Excitement ran high throughout the state, especially at Marietta and Cincinnati, where rumors spread that Burr planned to disrupt the Union. Convinced by John Graham, an employee of the State Department, that Burr's vague adventure into the West was treasonable, Governor Edward Tiffin placed the support of the state government behind the President. Calling out the state militia in December 1806, the governor thwarted Burr and his associate, Harman Blennerhassett, in their attempt to gather supplies and boats at Blennerhassett Island, several miles below Marietta on the Ohio River. Ohioans felt satisfied with their actions, and Tiffin was thereafter elected to the United States Senate.

At the time Ohioans were occupied with the Burr episode, the state legislature, guarding its favored position in state government, battled the state's supreme court. While the federal court case *Marbury vs. Madison*, which had been decided the year Ohio entered the Union, had established the principle of judicial review, Ohio had to have its own decision. The question involved was the right granted by the legislature for the state's justices of the peace to render a decision in a civil suit involving fifty dollars or more. In *Rutherford vs. McFaddon*, the Ohio Supreme Court ruled that they did not have that right. Federalist Samuel Huntington's decision upheld the judgment of two lower courts and explained that the act of the Ohio General Assembly violated both the Ohio Constitution and Article VII of the United States Constitution. Moreover, Huntington went further and underscored the principle of judicial review over legislative action, already established by the federal courts. In retaliation, the Ohio General Assembly first tried to impeach the judges who had rendered negative decisions; when that failed, it simply removed them from office through a legislative resolution. While politics played an important role in the affair, the court nevertheless exerted its authority as a partner in state government.

Beginning in the summer of 1812, the nation faced its second war with England. Exposed on the western frontier, Ohioans feared both a British invasion from Canada and a renewal of Indian hostilities. Although they were suspicious that the country was not prepared for a foreign war, the majority of Ohioans patriotically supported the federal government. Ohioans died at the battles of River Raisin, Fort Meigs, Fort Stephenson, and Put-in-Bay; and the few major land successes for the United States during the war were won on Ohio's soil. However, not everyone was enthusiastic about the war with England. The Ohio Federalists, like their eastern cousins, criticized the Madison administration. It was through the pages of the *Ohio Federalist*, edited by Charles Hammond, that opposition to the war was expressed to many Ohioans. Thus, opposition to national policy during a crisis early became part of Ohio's political tradition.

Certainly, Ohioans supported the federal government during the Republican years; however, by 1821, the state was willing to clash with the federal government over control of the Second Bank of the United States. By 1818, two branches of the bank were located in Ohio—one in Cincinnati and a second in Chillicothe. Because the national banks were granted certain favorable benefits by federal legislation, which helped their operations in the state, antagonisms quickly developed between the national bank and local business and political interests. In an attempt to curb this influence, the Ohio General Assembly placed a $50,000 tax upon each branch of the national bank in Ohio and granted the state auditor the right to enter, search, and seize the tax money if the national banks refused to cooperate. However, in the meantime the federal court case *McCulloch vs. Maryland* underscored the constitutionality of the national bank and denied the right of a state to tax the institution. Ignoring this decision, the Ohio General Assembly plunged headlong into a nullification controversy with federal authority. The report made by a joint committee of the Ohio legislature in February 1821 clearly explained the state's case. The controversy ultimately went to the federal courts, and, in *Osbourn vs. Bank of the United States*, Ohio lost its case when Chief Justice John Marshall reiterated his conviction that the power to tax was indeed the power to destroy.

It was also during the Republican era that the rich interior of the state was opened to commerce and development through the construction of a canal system that linked Lake Erie with the Ohio River. Since 1803, men of vision had discussed a canal system in the state, but it was not until Governor Ethan Allen Brown's administration that a canal commission was appointed to study the matter. Encouraged by New York's success with its Erie Canal, Ohio forged ahead with its project, beginning on July 4, 1825. Once completed, the system accelerated Ohio's economic growth and encouraged industrial development.

The Republicans ruled Ohio politics for nearly three decades.

During that time the followers of Jefferson jealously guarded the power of the legislature against the governor and the courts, put the state's constitution into practice, and created a state meant for white Americans. During their ascendancy the state prospered on the country's frontier and moved slowly toward a more settled and mature society.

Ohio's Black Code

1804-1807

An act, to regulate black and mulatto persons.

Sec. 1. *Be it enacted by the general assembly of the state of Ohio,* That from and after the first day of June next, no black or mulatto person, shall be permitted to settle or reside in this state, unless he or she shall first produce a fair certificate from some court within the United States, of his or her actual freedom, which certificate shall be attested by the clerk of said court, and the seal thereof annexed thereto, by the said clerk.

Sec. 2. *And be it further enacted,* That every black or mulatto person residing within this state, on or before the first day of June, one thousand eight hundred and four, shall enter his or her name, together with the name or names of his or her children, in the clerk's office in the county in which he, she or they reside, which shall be entered on record by said clerk, and thereafter the clerk's certificate of such record shall be sufficient evidence of his, her or their freedom; and for every entry and certificate, the person obtaining the same shall pay to the clerk twelve and a half cents: *Provided nevertheless,* That nothing in this act contained shall bar the lawful claim to any black or mulatto person.

Sec. 3. *And be it further enacted,* That no person or persons residents of this state, shall be permitted to hire, or in any way employ any black or mulatto person, unless such black or mulatto person shall have one of the certificates as aforesaid, under pain of forfeiting and paying any sum not less than ten nor more than fifty dollars, at the discretion of the court, for every such offense, one-half thereof for the use of the informer and the other half for the use of the state; and shall moreover pay to the owner, if any there be, of such black or mulatto person, the sum of fifty cents for every day he, she or they shall in any wise employ, harbor or secrete such black or mulatto person, which sum or sums shall be recoverable before any court having cognizance thereof.

Sec. 4. *And be it further enacted,* That if any person or persons shall harbor or secrete any black or mulatto person, the property of any person whatever, or shall in any wise hinder or prevent the lawful owner or owners from retaking and possessing his or her black or mulatto servant or servants, shall, upon conviction thereof, by indictment or information, be fined in any sum not less than ten nor more than fifty dollars, at the discretion of the court, one-half

From Ohio, General Assembly, *Acts,* II (Norwalk, 1901), pp. 63-66. Ohio General Assembly, *Acts,* V (Norwalk 1901), pp. 53-55.

thereof for the use of the informer and the other half for the use of the state.

Sec. 5. *And be it further enacted,* That every black or mulatto person who shall come to reside in this state with such certificate as is required in the first section of this act, shall, within two years, have the same recorded in the clerk's office, in the county in which he or she means to reside, for which he or she shall pay to the clerk twelve and an half cents, and the clerk shall give him or her a certificate of such record.

Sec. 6. *And be it further enacted,* That in case any person or persons, his or their agent or agents, claiming any black or mulatto person that now are or hereafter may be in this state, may apply, upon making satisfactory proof that such black or mulatto person or persons is the property of him or her who applies, to any associate judge or justice of the peace within this state, the associate judge or justice is hereby empowered and required, by his precept, to direct the sheriff or constable to arrest such black or mulatto person or persons and deliver the same in the county or township where such officers shall reside, to the claimant or claimants or his or their agent or agents, for which service the sheriff or constable shall receive such compensation as they are entitled to receive in other cases for similar services.

Sec. 7. *And be it further enacted,* That any person or persons who shall attempt to remove, or shall remove from this state, or who shall aid and assist in removing, contrary to the provisions of this act, any black or mulatto person or persons, without first proving as hereinbefore directed, that he, she or they, is, or are legally entitled so to do, shall, on conviction thereof before any court having cognizance of the same, forfeit and pay the sum of one thousand dollars, one-half to the use of the informer and the other half to the use of the state, to be recovered by action of debt, *qui tam,* or indictment, and shall moreover be liable to the action of the party injured.

ELIAS LANGHAM,
Speaker of the house of representatives.
NATH. MASSIE,
Speaker of the senate.

January 5th, 1804.

An act to amend the act, entitled "An act regulating black and mulatto persons."

Sec. 1. *Be it enacted by the general assembly of the state of Ohio,* That no negro or mulatto person shall be permitted to emigrate into and settle within this state, unless such negro or mulatto person shall, within twenty days thereafter, enter into bond with two or more freehold sureties, in the penal sum of five hundred dollars, before the clerk of the court of common pleas of the county in which such negro or mulatto may wish to reside (to be approved of by the clerk) conditioned for the good behavior of such negro or mulatto, and moreover to pay for the support of such person, in case he, she or they should thereafter be found within any township in this state, unable to support themselves. And if any negro or mulatto person shall migrate into this state, and not comply with the provisions of this act, it shall be the duty of the overseers of the poor of the township where such negro or mulatto person may be found, to remove immediately, such black or mulatto person, in the same manner, as is required in the case of paupers.

Sec. 2. *Be it further enacted,* That it shall be the duty of the clerk, before whom such bond may be given as aforesaid, to file the same in his office, and give a certificate thereof to such negro or mulatto person; and the said clerk shall be entitled to receive the sum of one dollar for the bond and certificate aforesaid, on the delivery of the certificate.

Sec. 3. *Be it further enacted,* That if any person being a resident of this state, shall employ, harbor or conceal any such negro or mulatto person aforesaid, contrary to the provisions of the first section of this act, any person so offending, shall forfeit and pay, for every such offense, any sum not exceeding one hundred dollars, the one-half to the informer, and the other half for the use of the poor of the township in which such person may reside, to be recovered by action of debt, before any court having competent jurisdiction, and moreover be liable for the maintenance and support of such negro or mulatto, provided he, she, or they, shall become unable to support themselves.

Sec. 4. *Be it further enacted,* That no black or mulatto person or persons, shall hereafter be permitted to be sworn or give evidence in any court of record, or elsewhere in this state, in any cause depending, or matter of controversy, where either party of the same is a white person, or in any prosecution, which shall be instituted in behalf of this state, against any white person.

Sec. 5. *And be it further enacted,* That so much of the act, entitled "An act to regulate black and mulatto persons," as is contrary to this act, together with the sixth section thereof be, and the same is hereby repealed.

This act shall take effect and be in force, from and after the first day of April next.

ABRAHAM SHEPHERD
Speaker of the House of Representatives
THOMAS KIRKER
Speaker of the Senate

Jan. 25th 1807

Burr and Blennerhassett

EDWARD TIFFIN

To the General Assembly of the state of Ohio. I now communicate to the representatives of the people such operations as have taken place under the act passed this session, to prevent certain acts hostile to the peace & tranquility of the United States, within the jurisdiction of this State, that they may be fully possessed of what has already occurred, & is still in train.

Immediately upon receiving the law, after its passage, I dispatched an express to Marietta, with orders to arrest the flotilla on the Muskingum river, & the agents engaged in its preparation, & to make due enquiry after such proof as would lead to their conviction; as also to prevent any armaments proceeding, that might be descending the Ohio, if possible. The execution of the operations at Marietta was entrusted to Judge Meigs & Major General Buell, I also dispatched orders to Cincinnati, to plant one or more pieces of artillery on the banks of the Ohio, to keep patroles up the river at proper distances, in order to give notice in due time, of the approach of all boats, either singly or in numbers, & to call out a sufficient force to be able to meet 300 men; the number I expected might probably be with Blennerhassett's & Comfort Tyler's flotillas, if they should effect a junction; & lest they might attempt to pass in detachments of one boat at a time, not to suffer a single boat to pass without an arrest & examination—The execution of these operations were entrusted to generals Gano, Findley & judge Nimmo. I have also given authority to Jacob Wilson esq. of Stubenville to act, if occasion offers for his interposition, in that quarter—and it gives me great pleasure to inform you that I have, last night, received a communication from judge Meigs of Marietta, announcing the complete success of the operations intrusted to him & Gen. Buell, & whose patriotic efforts entitled them both, to my warmest thanks.

It is suspected notice was conveyed to Blennerhassett's island of the passage of the law, & the preparations making here to carry it into immediate effect; for it appears that in the night of the 9th inst., Comfort Tyler passed Marietta with a number (not yet ascertained) of fast rowing boats, with men armed indiscriminately with muskets, pistols & cutlasses, & anchored at the island; & immediately sent an express after Blennerhassett who was hurrying on his flotilla: that upon discovering the movements of our militia they fled full speed to the island, which was guarded at night by sentinals & lighted lanterns at proper distances, & none suffered to pass to it except by countersign or watch word—Spies were also placed at Marietta, to give notice of the movements there; in the mean time Gen. Buell, by direction of Judge Meigs, with a detachment of militia, proceeded up the Muskingum river in the night, & arrested ten of the batteaux as they were descending the river to join Tyler's forces; they were so hurried that four more of the batteaux were not got ready to embark & would also be seized, which is, I believe, the whole of the Muskingum flotilla. There were near 100 barrels of provisions seized on board, & 100 more which had not been put on board; & which I expect he also seized with the same remaining batteaux; these batteaux are each 40 feet long; wide & covered; & calculated each to carry one company of men. It is believed notice was immediately given to the island, of this seizure; for in about three hours afterwards, on the same night, Blennerhasset & Tyler made their escape from the island, & have pushed, it is said, through Kentucky—Col. Phelps of Virginia with a few mounted men are in pursuit of them.

I expect Tyler's boats will descend the Ohio, to meet him & Blennerhasset at some point low down on that river; & I have no doubt but that Gen. Gano will render a good account of them as they attempt to pass Cincinnati.

I also received last night, a communication from the Sec. of War of the United States, by direction of that Government; requiring me without delay, to raise 150 or 200 volunteer militia to be formed in companies with one field officer, one captain two subalterns and 70 men, commissioned officers, privates & musicians to each company, in the pay of the United States; & direct them to march to Marietta, with orders to seize the Muskingum flotilla & prevent it from being removed until further orders from the President. But finding that this service was in part effected, I have ventured from the necessity of the case, to vary in some degree, from these instructions, & which I hope will meet the approbation of the General Government, and also of your's. I have sent on orders last night to Marietta, to raise one company of volunteers, to be composed of one Major, one Capt. two subalterns and 60 men, commissioned officers, privates & musicians, which I have thought sufficient to guard & keep safe the flotilla & stores already arrested; & have also dispatched an express to Cincinnati with orders to raise two companies as above, each—as I thought the most force wanted there to relieve the militia previously ordered out, & to secure Comfort Tyler's flotilla while descending the Ohio, if it was not already done. I have no doubt that these three companies will be instantly under arms, & that this hitherto mysterious enterprise will be completely frustrated; & the intended evil levelled at the peace and tranquillity of the United States, will fall with all its weight on its projectors.

Chillicothe Dec. 15th 1806.   EDWARD TIFFIN.

Rutherford vs. McFaddon

SAMUEL HUNTINGTON

The only question here made is, whether so much of the fifth section of the act, defining the duties of justices of the peace and constables, in criminal and in civil cases, as extends the jurisdiction of justices of the peace in civil cases, to any sum not exceeding fifty dollars, be constitutional, and consequently whether it has any binding force.

Though this is the question put for the court to determine, I shall extend my enquiries and examine into the right of the court to determine upon the constitutionality of an act of the legislature. This is a respect due to the legislative body. It will be satisfactory to the people to know the grounds on which the decision rests. The right has been questioned, and if the court do not possess it, they ought not to enter upon the consideration of the question in the case at bar. It is not matter of surprise, that doubts of this power in the courts of law, have been entertained by those who have not had leisure or opportunity to investigate the subject, or having given it only a hasty and superficial examination: by such persons it has been represented, that the exercise of this power would operate to repeal the laws; that it would be an assumption of legislative authority, and that it would be judging over the head of the legislature.

Let it be distinctly understood, that the court claims no right of altering, repealing or setting aside any law whatever; they do not consider themselves vested with any legislative authority. On the contrary, it is their duty, as well as their aim, to keep the judicial and legislative functions separate and unmixed. It is their duty, peculiarly, to *expound, construe* and *declare* the law; and in discharging this duty, they will not be guilty of the solecism, of declaring a *law* to be unconstitutional; but when the case occurs, they must, on compliance with their duty, compare the legislative *act* with the *constitution,* and if they find such act contrary to the constitution, or prohibited by it, as, in such case, the *act* is, from the beginning, utterly void and of no binding force, it is the duty of the court to declare it *no law.*

For the more correct understanding of the principles upon which the decision of the court is founded, it will be necessary to enquire what is the end and design of a written constitution.

A constitution is defined to be a compact of the people, declaring what form of government they choose to live under; distributing the three great and necessary deposits of delegated authority among

From Samuel Huntington, Chief Justice of the Ohio Supreme Court, opinion in Rutherford vs. McFaddon, *Liberty Hall and Cincinnati Mercury,* November 3, 1807.

the three branches of government, and defining the limits of each. Our constitution, after specifying the powers delegated to each branch and prohibiting the exercise of others, has declared, that "all powers not hereby delegated, remain with the people." The object of every constitution is to secure the liberty of the people, by keeping the legislative, executive and judicial powers separate and distinct from each other, by restraining each within the limits assigned to it, and by preventing all encroachments on each other, or on the rights of individuals. And I shall assume it as an incontested position, that our constitution (allowing it to harmonize with the constitution and laws of the U. States) is the supreme law of the land, and paramount to any legislative act: it follows, that any act in violation of the constitution, or infringing its provisions must be void, because the legislature, when they step beyond the bounds assigned them, act without authority, and their doings are no more than the doings of any other private man. . . .

To the legislature belongs the sole power of making laws; to the judiciary, the sole power of expounding them. So little power is vested in the executive by our constitution, that no danger can be apprehended to our liberties, while the other two branches keep within their constitutional limits: Part of the executive power being committed to the legislature—that of appointing all the high officers in the government, not elected by the people, it has been supposed, that the judiciary received their *authority*, as well as their *appointments* from the legislature; and consequently were bound to carry into effect, their *acts*, whether constitutional or otherwise. This mistake, which I apprehend to be the chief source of the erroneous opinions entertained on this subject, arises from not considering the judiciary, as a co-ordinate branch of the government deriving its authority from the constitution. That instrument, it is true, has empowered the legislature to mark out the jurisdiction, and detail the duties of the several courts; but this power, by no means implies a right to deprive the judiciary of that authority which the constitution vests in it, and requires it to exercise.

The people can never be secure under any form of government, where there is no check among the several departments: in ours, the check upon the executive and judicial officers, for corruption or misbehaviour in office, is an impeachment; there is no check that operates on the *members* of the legislature out of their own body— and all the check upon the *proceedings*, that exists in any other body, arises from the regular exercise of the constitutional powers of the judiciary; for it must be noticed, that the courts can *originate* no question involving the constitutionality of a law, and of course can *decide* no such question, unles it comes legally before them for a judicial decision. . . .

It is contended that the court by taking upon themselves to

decide this question, casts some imputation upon the legislature; that the legislature are as competent to determine the constitutionality of their own acts, as the court, and that a decision against the constitutionality of an act, implies error in the assembly that passed it. No one will contend that the legislature, *may* not, at times, commit mistakes from haste or inattention—the records of every session prove this—the repeal, alteration and amendment of laws, shew the sense of successive assemblies upon this point; and it would seem as probable, that provisions inconsistent with the constitution, might be inadvertently introduced into a law, as that errors of any other description should creep in—in either case the judgment of the court imputes no blame to the legislature:—It frequently happens that two *acts* of the legislature are found in direct hostility with each other, yet, neither expressly repealed; the court is called upon to determine which is the law, as both cannot stand: both are enacted by the same authority; for aught appearing on the face of the laws, both are equally binding on the court; yet the court *must* decide between them—Is it an imputation on the legislature to make this decision? And how does it differ, in application to this point, from a case where a law clashes with the constitution? The most fair and correct position is, that in framing laws, the legislature ought to take into consideration their bearing upon the constitution, as well as upon the existing laws; and that their interference with one or the other, when it happens to take place, should be corrected by the courts in the course of a regular judicial investigation: a contrary principle might not only set our laws and our constitution at variance, but produce the most mischievous confusion in the laws themselves.

If we resort to consequences, to throw further light upon the subject, we will find that going on the ground the legislature *can* pass unconstitutional acts—that they are the sole judges of their constitutionality—and if unconstitutional, that there is no remedy; then indeed is our constitution a blank paper: there is no guarantee for a single right to citizens; your executive and your judiciary, it is true, are bound by the constitution, where it is not made to bend to the laws; but slavery may be introduced; a religious test may be established; the press may be fettered or restrained; the trial by jury may be abolished; *ex post facto* laws may be made; standing armies may be raised, and the whole train of evils against which our constitution meant to provide, may be gradually let in upon us. I speak not of these consequences as likely to follow at present, or altogether; but with a view to point out the necessity of guarding the constitution with the most scrupulous vigilance, and to shew that on the constituted authorities is this duty more peculiarly incumbent.

If we resort to arguments of expediency, either to explain a doubtful clause of the constitution, or to find the true construction of our laws, we shall see that it is of infinitely more importance, to preserve the trial by jury, the great bulwark of our liberties, than to guard against the consequences of a judgment which by setting aside some of the decisions of magistrates, may tend to open disputes, that have been supposed to be settled. This, though an evil to be avoided, where it can be done legally, does not strike at the foundation of any of our rights; it may be an inconvenience to a few individuals, and there the mischief ends; but it should be kept in mind, that in proportion as you encroach on the trial by jury, in the same proportion you take away the rights of the people. You take the right from the many, and bestow it on the few, and whether you build up the power of justices of the peace, or of higher courts upon the ruins of the jury, it is equally a departure from the principles of a republican government, and a step towards a more aristocratic form.

An objection has been stated which is supposed to run parallel with the argument in favor of the extent of trial by jury, as claimed by the counsel of the plantiff in error. It is said, that if the right of trial by jury is extended to all cases, where it might have been claimed at the period of our going into a state government, the chancery jurisdiction of our courts is destroyed, because, sitting in chancery, they proceed to hear & determine cases without a jury, that could not have been tried antecedent to that period, without the intervention of a jury. The three first sections of the third article of the constitution, expressly give the courts jurisdiction in equity, as well as law. This jurisdiction, from its nature, precludes the intervention of a jury in brief cases of chancery: but when certain facts come in issue, even in chancery cases, those facts are ascertained by the verdict of a jury, in a court of law upon an issue directed out of chancery. It is a sufficient answer, however, to the objection, to say, that the same instrument which guarantees the right of trial by jury, also vests in the court the power of trying such causes as came before them, sitting as a court of chancery, according to the known rules and established proceedings of such courts.—I have considered this case as depending upon the construction of our own constitution and laws, without quoting the authority of other decisions, though well aware, that in the first point I am supported by the judgment of the supreme court of the U. S. and of every court of the individual states, which has had the question before them, all of whom have decided that the courts of law possess the power of enquiring into the constitutionality of legislative acts. Notwithstanding the high respect that is due to such authorities, I should not have hesitated to give a different opinion had I been convinced the decisions were erroneous.

Sweeping Resolutions

REPUBLICANS

Resolution on the subject of filling vacancies in office.

Whereas it is provided by the eighth section of the third article of the constitution of this state, "That the judges of the supreme court, the presidents and associate judges of the court of common pleas, shall be appointed by a joint ballot of both houses of the general assembly, and shall hold their offices for the term of seven years, if so long they behave well:" And whereas the first general assembly of this state did appoint judges of the supreme court, presidents and associates of the common pleas, many of whose offices have, at different times, become vacant, and elections have been had to fill such vacancies; and whereas the original term of office is about to expire, and it becomes necessary for the general assembly to provide for that event: Therefore,

Resolved, by the general assembly of the state of Ohio, That the constitution of this state having limited and defined the term of office which the judges of the supreme court, the presidents and associate judges of the court of common pleas, the secretary of state, the auditor and treasurer of state, and also the mode of filling vacancies which may occur in those offices, and that in filling such vacancies by the legislature, it cannot be of right construed to extend beyond the end of the original term for which their predecessors could have constitutionally served, had no such vacancies taken place.

EDWARD TIFFIN,
Speaker of the house of representatives.
DUNCAN M'ARTHUR,
Speaker of the Senate.

From "Resolution on the subject of filling vacancies in office," Ohio, General Assembly, *Acts,* VIII (Chillicothe, 1810), pp. 349-350.

Fort Meigs

WILLIAM HENRY HARRISON

Head Quarters Camp Meigs
9th May 1813

Sir,

I have the honor to inform you that the enemy, having been for several days making preparations for raising the seige of this post accomplished this day, the removal of the last of their Artillery from the opposite Bank and about 12 oclock left their encampment below, were soon embarked and out of sight. I have the Honor to enclose you an agreement entered into between **Genl. Procter** & my self for the discharge of the Prisoners of the Kenty. Militia in his possession—and for the exchange of the officers and men of the Regular Troops which were respectively possessed by us. My anxiety to get the Kentucky Troops released as early as possible induced me to agree to the dissmission of all the prisoners I had. Altho' there was not as many of ours in **Genl. Procters** possession the surplusage is to be accounted for and an eaqual number of ours released from their parole, whenever the Government may think proper to direct it. I am sorroy to inform you that the loss of the Kentucky troops in killed and missing is much greater than I had at first believed it amounts to upwards of Three hundred but of these I hope that many have escaped up the North side of the River to **Fort Winchester**. However much this unnecessary waste of lives may be lamented. It will give you great pleasure to learn that the two actions *on this side* the River on the 5th were infinitely more important and more Honorable to our arms than I had at first conceived & the Sortie made upon the left Flank—**Capt. Nearings** company of the 19th Regt. A Detachment of 12 mos. volunteers under **Majr. Alexander** & Three companies of Kentucky Militia under **Col. Bosswell** defeated at least double the number of Indians & British militia. The sortie on the right was still more glorious, the British Batteries in that direction were defended by the Granidier & Light Infantry companies of the 41st Regt. amounting to two hundred effectives & two Militia companies flanked by a host of Indians. The Detachment sent to attack these consisted of all the off duty belonging to the companies of **Crogham** & **Bradford** of the 17th Regt. **Langham Elliotts**, late **Grahams** and **Nearings** of the 19th above Eighty of Majr. Alexanders volunteers & a single company of Kentucky militia under **Captain Sebry**, amount-

---

From Letter, William H. Harrison to John Armstrong, May 9, 1813, Draper Collection, Series X, Vol. II, p. 44.

ing in the whole to not more than Three hundred & forty yet the end of the action was not a moment doubtful & had not the British troops been covered in their retreat by their allies the whole of them would have been taken.

It is not possible for Troops to have behaved—better than ours did throughout—all the officers exerted themselves to execute my orders and the Enemy who had a full view of our operations from the opposite shore declared that they had never seen so much work performed in so short a time. To all the commandants of Corps I feel particular obligation. These were **Colon. Meller** of the 19th Regt. of Infy. **Col. Mills** of the Ohio Militia **Majr. Stoddard** of the Artillery **Majr. Ball** of the Dragoons & **Majr. Johnson** of the Kentucky Militia. **Captn. Graliott** of the engeneers having been for a long time much indisposed the task of Fortifying this post devolved on **Captn. Wood.** It could not have been placed in better hands. Permit me to recommend to the President and to assure you that any mark of His approbation bestowed on Captn. Wood would be highly gratifying to the whole of the Troops who witnessed his arduous exertions. From **Majr. Hukill** acting Inspector General my aid de camp **Majr. Graham Lieut. Ofallen** who has done the duty of Ass. Ajd. Genl. in the absence of **Majr. Adams** & my volunteer aid de camp **John Johnson** Esq. I received the most useful assistance.

I have the honor to enclose you a list of the killed & wounded during the seige & in the two sorties. Those of the latter was much greater than I had at first expected. Want of sleep & exposure to the continued rains which have fallen almost every day for some time past render me incapable of mentioning many interesting particulars—amongst others a most extraordinary proposition of **Col. Procter's** on the subject of the Indians within our Boundary—these shall form the subject of a communication to be made tomorrow or next day & for which I will provide a safer conveyance than that which caries this. All the prisoners & Deserters agree in saying that the information given to Maj. Stoddard by Ryland of the British having launched a sloop of war this spring is incorrect & the most of them say that the one which is now building will not be launched for many weeks.

I have the honor to be
sir with great respect
Your Hb. Serrt.

Hmb. John Armstrong, Esq.
Secretary of War   WILLM HENRY HARRISON

Fort Stephenson

GEORGE CROGHAN

Defense of Lower Sandusky
Lower Sandusky Aug. 5th 1813

Dr Sir

I have the honor to inform you that the combined force of the Enemy, amounting to at least 500 Regulars & seven or eight hundred Indians under the immediate command of **General Proctor** made its appearance before this place early on Sunday evening last, and so soon as the General had made such disposition of his troops as would cut off my retreat, should I be disposed to make one. He sent **Col. Elliott** accompanied by **Magr. Cambers** with a Flag to demand the surrender of the Fort, as he was anxious to spare the efusion of blood, which he should probably not have in his power to do, should he be reduced to the necessity of taking the place by storm. My answer to the summons was, that I was determined to defend the place to the last extremity and that no force however large should induce me to surrender it. So soon as the Flag had returned, a brisk fire was opened upon us, from the gunboats in the river and from a 5½ Inch Howetzer on shore, which was kept up with little intermission throughout the night. At an early hour the next morning, three sixes (which had been placed during the night within 250 yards of the Picketts) began to play upon us but with little effect. About 4:00 pm discovering that the fire from all his guns was concentrated against the north western angle of the Fort, I became confident that his object was to make a breach and attempt to storm the works at the point, I therefore ordered out as many men as could be employed for the purpose of strengthing that part, which was so effectually secured by means of bags of Flour, sand &c. that the *Picketing* suffered little or no injury. Not withstanding which the Enemy about 5:00 having formed in close column advanced to assault our works at the expected point, at the same time making two feints on the front of Capt. Hunter's lines, the column which advanced against the Northwestern angle consisting of about 350 men, was so completely enveloped in smoke, as not to be discovered until it had approached withing 15 or 20 paces of the lines, but the men being all at their posts & ready to receive it commenced so heavy & galling a fire as to throw the column a little into confusion,

From Letter, George Croghan to William H. Harrison, August 5, 1813, Draper Collection, Series X, Vol. II, p. 31.

being quickly rallied it advanced to the centre works and began to leap into the ditch; just at that moment a fire of Grape was opened from our six pounder, (which had been previously arranged so as to rake in that direction) which together with the Musquetery threw them into such confusion that they were compelled to retire precipitately to the woods. During the assault, which lasted about half an hour our incessant fire was kept up by the Enemies Artillery (which consisted of five *sixes* of a howetzer) but without effect; my whole loss during the seige was one killed and seven wounded slightly. The loss of the Enemy in killed, wounded & prisoners must exceed one hundred & fifty; one Lieut. Col., a Lieut. and fifty rank & file were found in and about the ditch dead or wounded those of the remainder who were not able to escape were taken off during the night by the Indians, seventy stand of Arms and several brace of Pistols have been collected near the works; about three in the morning the Enemy sailed down the river leaving behind them a boat, containing clothing & considerable military stores. Too much praise cannot be bestowed on the officers non commissioned officers & privates under my command for their gallantry & good conduct during the seige,

Yours with respect
(S.C.) G. CROGHAN Majr.
17th US Inft. Comdg.

No War!

CHARLES HAMMOND

I offer myself a candidate, for your suffrages at the ensuing election, to represent you in the state senate. It is known to you that, I am opposed, in opinion, to the present administration of our general government, and to the war, in which they have involved our country. As this is a subject upon which a large number of you entertain different sentiments, I owe it to you, as well as to myself,

From Charles Hammond, "To The Citizens of Belmont County," *Ohio Federalist*, May 11, 1813.

to explain as briefly and as clearly as I can, the grounds upon which my opposition is founded.

I am opposed to the men who now administer our government, because I believe they never entertained just views of the true interests of our common country. I am opposed to them because I believe the whole course of their public conduct has been calculated to injure and depress, instead of cherish and promote the true interest and real happiness of the American people. In opposing them I have been governed by no private or sinister consideration. I have opposed them, and still do oppose them, because the clearest convictions of my understanding compel me to consider their measures destructive to the prosperity and happiness of the nation. In opposing them I am governed by no motive of interest or ambition; I am influenced wholly by a sense of duty. If I preferred my own private interest to the welfare of my country, I would change sides and float with the majority. Like others who have gone before me, I might thus obtain office and official emolument. If I preferred successful ambition to a consciousness of integrity I would regard nothing which was not a mean of securing me popularity and power. If fellow citizens, I regarded your votes rather than your true interests, like others I would flater and cajole you. Like others, I would address myself to your feelings and your prejudices, and endeavour to warm myself into your good opinion for my own profit and advantage. That I do not pursue this course, you can all bear me witness. As the course I pursue leads neither to immediate interest nor popular honor, I submit to your candor that it is unjust to accuse me of interested or dishonorable motives.

I am opposed to this war because I believe it impolitic and oppressive—Impolitic, because it originated in a shameful sacrifice of national honor to French intrigue and perfidy—Impolitic, because there neither was nor now is any reasonable hope of effecting the objects for which it was commenced—Impolitic, because it has given rise to infinitely greater evils than those it pretended to remedy—Impolitic, because it was commenced at a time when division, necessarily attending a presidential election, weakened the national arm—Impolitic, because it was commenced at a time when division, necessarily attending a presidential election, weakened the national arm—broken the national spirit—Impolitic, because it was commenced in a state of preparation which necessarily led to disaster and disgrace—Oppressive, because war always enriches the few at the expence of the many—Oppressive because it is calculated to "depress the peaceable and exalt the turbulent—to discourage industry and invite to rapine—to burden labour for the support of idleness, and to subject virtue to vice."—Oppressive, because carrying on a war, by drafts upon the militia, operates unequally, exacting as much from the poor as the rich—Oppressive, because drafts upon the militia put the rich to but little inconvenience, while it subjects the great body of the people to ruin, misery, and death.

It would exceed the limits of an address like this to adduce arguments in support of all the above reasons for opposing the war; but I will briefly notice a few facts, which need only to be mentioned, to be acknowledged by every man. The impressment of American seamen is a great evil—an outrage which I shall never justify or palliate. But the calling of a sailor is calculated to weaken his attachment to his country and his family:

> "His march is on the mountain wave,
> His home is on the deep."

He does not feel himself as rooted in the soil of his country. His home, his wife, his children are not the whole world to him, nor is he the whole source of their comfort and enjoyments. In such a man his country has not the same interest that she has in her farmers and manufacturers, who form, as it were, a part of the soil itself and take root in it, as the trees of the forest. Can it then be correct policy for the rulers of a country to sacrifice an hundred of her farmers and mechanics, to preserve half a dozen of her seamen from injury and wrong? Do not such rulers act like a man who would tear out his bowels to preserve his extremities from injury?

It is as easy to illustrate the oppressive operation of this war. Who gains by it? Who have obtained offices of honor and emolument? Who are colonels, and majors and captains? The farmers and mechanics of the country? No, fellow citizens, these are not the men. Who are your lieutenants and ensigns, your pay masters, quarter masters, and contractors? Lawyers, doctors, merchants. Idle young men, educated in habits of extravegance, without means of gaining an honest livelihood, without capacity to follow any profession. Such fellow citizens is the description of men who obtain offices. Such is the description of men who will gain by this war. But the farmers and mechanics; what are their gains? They are yoked to the war, like oxen to the plough, driven to perform all the labour and rewarded with a pittance barely sufficient for their existence!

The oppressive character of this war is strongly manifested in the operation of our militia system. The inhabitants of our country are divided into three classes: those who are rich, those who are in comfortable circumstances, and those who have nothing. The great body of people are included in the middle class; to them our militia system presents a most deplorable alternative. A fine of 120 dollars will ruin them. They have no choice but to remain with their families and be stripped of the necessaries of life, or submit to the pangs of separation—endure the fatigues and risks of a campaign, and sustain the difficulties and losses consequent upon their absence from home. To such men the call upon a tour of duty sounds as the death knoll upon all their happiness and prosperity, and it is a chance if either their constitutions or property ever recovers from the shock.

The operation is very different upon the other two classes. He who has nothing to lose can safely set the law at defiance, and the monied man can pay the fine of an 120 dollars without feeling it. Nay, more, the monied man will have it in his power to make money instead of losing. Thousands of dollars worth of property will be brought to sheriff sales, for fines, and he who has money must obtain it at his own price.

These, fellow citizens, are familiar instances of the oppressive character of this war. I oppose it because I believe it adverse to both the honor and interest of the nation. I know you are told that the opponents of this war are the enemies of the country—no doubt there are many honest well meaning men who believe so. But there are also many who say so, who care more for their own aggrandizement than for either the honor or interest of the country. There are men who wish this war to continue, that they may become Excise officers and assessors of land and collectors of taxes. These men have an interest. There are men who wish war to continue that themselves and their friends may retain their military commissions and employments; these men have an interest; but we have all an interest that it should be ended; we all feel its evils, and we all see that these evils must encrease. When you see that some men have a particular interest in supporting this war, and that no man can have a particular interest in opposing it, why should you believe that those who oppose it are enemies to their country? I am an American by birth, and a republican both in principle and feeling. Every sentiment of nature, every attachment of interest, bonds me to the American government, and to the welfare of that people of whom my wife, my children, and myself compose a part. Whoever knows me and pronounces me an enemy to the country, does both himself and me a great injustice.

Federal vs. State Authority: No Bank

THE GENERAL ASSEMBLY

From the papers submitted to the committee, it appears that, in the month of September, 1819, the Bank of the United States exhibited a bill in chancery, before the circuit court of the United States, then sitting at Chillicothe, against Ralph Osborn, auditor of the state of Ohio, and obtained, in that court, an order of injunction against him, prohibiting him, as auditor, from performing the duties enjoined upon him by the "Act to levy and collect a tax from all banks and individuals, and companies and associations of individuals, that may transact banking business in this state, without being authorized to do so by the laws thereof."

It further appears, that the circuit court of the United States, at their last term, adjudged that this act of official duty was a contempt of court; for committing which they awarded a writ of attachment against the auditor, returnable to January term next.

It appears, also, that, at the September term last, upon the application of the Bank of the United States, an order was made, allowing them to file an amended and supplemental bill, making Samuel Sullivan, the treasurer of state, a defendant, "*as present treasurer of Ohio, and in his private and individual character;*" and also making Hiram Mirick Curry, late treasurer, and John L. Harper, the officer that collected the tax, defendants. Upon the filing of which amended and supplementary bill, a further order of injunction was made, prohibiting the treasurer of state from "negotiating, delivering over, or in any manner parting with or disposing of," the money collected for tax, and paid into the state treasury according to law. And it further appears, that, besides these proceedings, an action of trespass at the suit of the Bank of the United States was commenced and made returnable to the last September term of the same circuit court, against Ralph Osborn, John L. Harper, Thomas Orr, James M'Collister, John C. Wright, and Charles Hammond, in which the plaintiffs have filed a declaration, charging, among other things, the taking and carrying away the same sum of money in the proceedings in chancery specified, under color and pretence of the law of Ohio.

Whatever attempt may be made to characterize this proceeding as a controversy between individuals, it is evident that its practical effect is to make the state a defendant before the circuit court of the

From Ohio General Assembly, *Report of the Joint Committee of Both Houses of the General Assembly, Bank of the United States, against The Office of State, in The United States Circuit Court,* February, 1821, *Ohio Executive Documents,* (Columbus, 1822), pp. 5-6; 15-18; 23-25; 30; 32; 34.

United States. In every thing but the name, the state is the actual defendant.

. . . .

The Bank of the United States established an office of discount and deposite at Cincinnati, in this state, which commenced banking in the spring of the year 1817. The legislature met in December following, and, upon the 13th day of December, a resolution was proposed in the House of Representatives, and adopted, appointing a committee to inquire into the expediency of taxing such branches as were or might be established within this state. The committee reported against the expediency of levying such a tax; but the House of Representatives reversed their report by a majority of 37 to 22. A substitute for their report was then offered, asserting the right of the state to levy such a tax, and the expediency of doing it at that time. The constitutional right of the state to levy such a tax was carried by 48 to 12, and the expediency of proceeding to levy the tax, by 33 to 27. A bill assessing a tax was reported to the house, and passed to be engrossed for a third reading and final passage, and, upon the third reading, was postponed to the second Monday of December, 1818.

After this solemn assertion of the right to tax, and when a bill for that purpose was pending before the House of Representatives, the bank proceeded to organize a second office of discount and deposite at Chillicothe, in this state, which commenced banking in the spring of the year 1818. In January, 1819, the legislature enacted the law levying the tax, and postponed its execution until the September following, that the bank might have abundant time so to arrange their business as not to come within the provisions of the taxing law.

At the period of adopting these measures, the constitutional right of the state to levy the tax was doubted by none but those interested in the bank, or those who expected to derive pecuniary advantages for themselves or their friends, by the location of branches. It seemed impossible that a rational, disinterested, and independent mind could doubt. During the existence of the old Bank of the United States, the state of Georgia had asserted this right of taxation, and actually collected the tax. The bank brought a suit to recover back the money in the federal circuit court of Georgia. This suit was brought before the supreme court upon a question not directly involving the power of taxation. The supreme court decided the point before them in favor of the bank, but upon such grounds that the suit was abandoned, and the tax submitted to. When the charter of the present bank was enacted, it was known that the states claimed, and had practically asserted, the power of taxing it, yet no exemption from the operation of the power is stipulated by Congress. The natural inference, from the silence of the charter upon this point, would seem to be, that the power of the states was recognized, and that Congress were not disposed to interfere with it.

The constitution of the United States had distinctly expressed in what cases the taxing power of the states should be restrained. No maxim of legal construction is better settled, and more universally acknowledged, than, that express limitations of power, either in constitutions or in statutes, are distinct admissions that the power exists, and may be exercised in every other case than those expressly limited. With a knowledge of these facts and doctrines in their minds, that a confidence in the power of the state to levy this tax should be almost universal, is what every intelligent man would expect.

But, after the law was enacted that levied the tax, and before the time of its taking effect, the Supreme Court of the United States, in the case of Maryland and M'Culloch, decided, that the states were debarred, by the constitution of the United States, from assessing or levying any such tax. And upon the promulgation of this decision it is maintained, that it became the duty of the state and its officers to acquiesce, and treat the act of the legislature as a dead letter. The committee have considered this position, and are not satisfied that it is a correct one.

It has been already shewn, that, since the 11th amendment to the constitution, the separate states, as parties to the compact of union, are not subject to the jurisdiction of the federal courts, upon questions involving their power and authority as sovereign states. Not being subject to their jurisdiction, no state can be concluded by the opinions of these tribunals: but these are questions, in respect to which there is no common judge, and therefore the state has a right to judge for itself. If, by the management of a party, and through the inadvertence or connivance of a state, a case be made, presenting to the supreme court of the United States for decision important and interesting questions of state power, and state authority, upon no just principle ought the states to be concluded by any decision had upon such a case. The committee are clearly of opinion, that such is the true character of the case passed upon the world by the title of M'Culloch vs. Maryland.

It was once remarked, by a most profound politician, that *words are things;* and the observation is most unquestionably a correct one. This case, dignified with the important and high sounding title of *"M'Culloch* vs. *the state of Maryland,"* when looked into, is found to be an ordinary *qui tam* action of debt, brought by a common informer, of the name of John James; and it is, throughout, an agreed case, made expressly for the purpose of obtaining the opinion of the supreme court of the United States upon the question, whether the states could, constitutionally, levy a tax upon the Bank of the United States. This agreed case was manufactured in the

summer of the year 1818, and passed through the county court of
Baltimore county, and the court of appeals of the state of Maryland,
in the same season, so as to be got upon the docket of the supreme
court of the United States, for adjudication, at their February term,
1819. It is only by the management and concurrence of parties, that
causes can be thus expeditiously brought to a final hearing in the
supreme court.

. . . .

As applied to the question under discussion, however, it has been
shewn, that a power to tax their trade is not a power to *destroy* the
corporation. It is not perceived how a power to diminish the profits
of labor and capital, by exacting a portion of their proceeds for the
support of government, can be construed into a power to destroy
human life, and annihilate capital. The power of taxing the bank is
denied, because it might be so used as to prevent the corporation
from driving a profitable trade, and this is deemed a power to
destroy the charter, which did not originate the trade, but merely
created a facility for conducting it. But what is most singular is this:
that, after arriving at this conclusion, an admission is made, that at
once demolishes the whole doctrine upon which it is founded.

It is conceded that each state may tax the stock owned by its
citizens in this bank. Then it is not a public institution, exempt from
state taxation, upon the great principle that the states cannot tax the
offices, institutions, and operations of the government of the union.
It is not that the states have no power to tax the bank; but that this
power exists only over its capital, and does not extend to its
operations. What then becomes of all the labored doctrines of the
opinion? The government of the union, though supreme within its
sphere of action, removing all obstacles, and so modifying all powers
vested in subordinate governments, as to exempt its own operations
from their influence, cannot, after all, preserve what it can create.
Those who advance this pretension are compelled to admit, that,
upon their own principles, a power to destroy may be wielded by the
state governments.

In its utmost extent, a state tax, upon the operations of the
bank, can produce no other injury than a suspension of its business.
By ceasing to trade, a tax upon business can always be avoided. Not
so a tax upon capital. Should the states of Pennsylvania, New-York,
and Massachusetts, combine to tax the stock in the Bank of the
United States, owned by their citizens, to an amount that must
consume the annual profits, and encroach upon the capital advanced,
the destruction of the bank must be inevitable; for this tax upon
capital may be exacted, whether it be productive or not. The power
of the states to tax the business of the bank, is denied upon the

broad ground, that the power to levy such a tax is tantamount to a power to destroy the bank, and is incompatible with a power in the government of the union to create it. Yet this power to tax the capital, though incontestibly of greater potency to destroy the institution, is admitted to exist. Between the point decided, and the point conceded, there is a palpable contradiction, to which sound argument, and just conclusions, are never subject.

The committee have not deemed it necessary to examine any argument founded upon a supposed abuse of power by the states. As between states, every argument of this sort is inadmissible, because it may be urged with equal force against the exercise of any power by either, and concludes to the destruction of all authority. There can be no doubt, but that the states will, at all times, be ready to encourage rather than repress the introduction and employment of capital within their dominion, where it may probably be of any general advantage. Of this, the state authorities are much more competent judges than capitalists, or their agents at a distance can be. It must always be unwise to force capital into a country against the sense of those who administer the government. That the bank has sustained great losses by sending branches into this state is now notorious; that their trade and loans have been highly injurious to all the best interests of the state, cannot be disputed. This loss on one hand, and injury on the other, would have been avoided, had the bank consulted the authorities of the state, instead of holding counsel with money jobbers and speculators.

The committee have carefully examined the subject, and, without pretending to present it in all the views of which it is susceptible, have urged only those which appear to them most prominent. The result of their deliberations is that the Bank of the United States is, in their opinion, a mere private corporation of trade, and, as such, its trade and business must be subject to the taxing power of the state.

In considering what course the committee should recommend as proper to adopt at this time, one point of difficulty has presented itself. It is urged by many that the tax levied and collected is enormous in amount, and therefore unequal and unjust. It is readily admitted that this allegation is not entirely unfounded, and all must agree that it does not comport with the character of a state to afford any color to accuse her of injustice. Even in the assertion of a right, it is highly derogatory for a state to act oppressively, and all injustice is oppression. It cannot be doubted but that the tax was levied as a penalty, and that it was not supposed the bank would venture to incur it. It was an act of temerity in them to do so, and although, in this view, the tax was justly, and, in the opinion of the committee, legally, collected, yet, under all the circumstances of the case, the committee conceive that the state ought to be satisfied with effecting the objects for which the law was enacted.

At this time the bank can have little object in continuing its branches, except to maintain the point of right, which may not be definitely settled by the controversy. The state, having refused to use the money collected, has no interest but that of character, and an assertion of the right. If an accommodation can be effected without prejudice to the right upon either side, it would seem to be desirable to all parties. With this view, as well as with a view to remove all improper impressions, the committee recommend that a proposition of compromise be made by law, making provision that, upon the bank discontinuing the suits now prosecuted against the public officers, and giving assurance that the branches shall be withdrawn, and only an agency left to settle its business, and collect its debts, the amount collected for tax shall be paid, without interest.

. . . .

For this purpose the committee recommend that provision be made by law, forbidding the keepers of our jails from receiving into their custody any person committed at the suit of the Bank of the United States, or for any injury done to them; prohibiting our judicial officers from taking acknowledgments of conveyances, where the bank is a party, or when made for their use, and our recorders from receiving or recording such conveyances; forbidding our courts, justices of the peace, judges, and grand juries, from taking any cognizance of any wrong alleged to have been committed upon any species of property owned by the bank, or upon any of its corporate rights or privileges, and prohibiting our notaries public from protesting any notes, or bills, held by the bank or their agents, or made payable to them.

The adoption of these measures will leave the bank exclusively to the protection of the federal government, and its constitutional power to preserve it in the sense maintained by the supreme court may thus be fairly, peaceably, and constitutionally tested. Congress must be called to provide a criminal code to punish wrongs committed upon it, and to devise a system of conveyances to enable it to receive and transmit estates; and, being thus called to act, the national legislature must be drawn to the serious consideration of a subject which the committee believe demands much more attention than it has excited. The measures proposed are peaceable and constitutional; conceived in no spirit of hostility to the government of the Union, but intended to bring fairly before the nation great and important questions, which must one day be discussed, and which may now be very safely investigated.

To Bring Prosperity

CANAL COMMITTEE

The committee to whom was referred so much of the governor's message as relates to canals, beg leave to report:

That the superior importance of improving the means of intercourse between different parts of a country, being a well established principle in political economy, it will not be necessary to adduce to the House the evidences of its illustration, which are afforded in the examples of the most illustrious countries of the old world, and in parts of our own; neither have they occasion, in the performance of their present duty to urge with the intelligent members of this body, the peculiar applicability of this doctrine to an agricultural state so remote from the sea as our own. It is a well established fact, that man has not yet devised a mode of conveyance so safe, easy, and cheap, as canal navigation; and although the advantage of easy and expeditious transportation, is not so likely to be perceived when prices are high and trade most profitable, yet the truth is familiar to every person of observation, that the enormous expense of land carriage has frequently consumed nearly, and some times quite, the whole price of provisions at the place of embarkation for a distant market. This is essentially the case in relation to all commodities of a cheap and bulky nature, most of which will not bear a land transportation many miles, and consequently are rendered of no value to the farmer, and are suffered to waste on his hands. The merchant who engages in the exportation of the produce of the country, finding it a loosing commerce abandons it, or is ruined; and crops in the finest and most productive parts of the state, are left to waste on the fields that produced them, "or be distilled to poison and brutalize society."

The profits of agriculture and the reward of labor failing, industry must languish, and the train of evils must succeed, always consequent on such a state of things.

. . . .

From this step the committee conceive there will be no disposition in the General Assembly to recede, if they give due consideration to the honor and interest of the state. The compensation of the Engineer, will form the principal item of expense in this examination, as well as that proposed in the message, and that compensation for the whole season's services would not greatly exceed the cost of a

---

From *Report of the Committee on Canals,* (Columbus, 1822), pp. 1-11.

survey and estimate at the Falls alone—it therefore is in the opinion of the committee, peculiarly desirable, that an examination into the practicability of a navigable communication between Lake Erie and the Ohio river, should be made by the same Engineer, whose compensation for both services would not greatly exceed that for the first alone. A navigable communication across the state, your committee believe, is not forbidden by any natural and insuperable obstacle, but on the contrary, they consider appearances and natural facilities to be highly favorable and inviting.

. . . .

The next consideration that has attracted the attention of your committee, is the profits to result from the Canal. These naturally devide themselves into two heads, namely, the profits to the owners of produce and merchandize by cheapening and facilitating transportation, and those in the light of revenue. Though no contradiction of the premises assumed in the first part of the report is apprehended, it may be excusable to inforce the arguments in favor of the recommendation by calling the attention of the House to some of the particular advantages that may be realized, especially by the agricultural interest, should the contemplated improvement be made. It would operate as another artery in the body politic, not merely beneficial to its neighborhood, but diffusing wealth, activity and vigor to the whole; and it will be allowed us to predict, that if it were once completed, the inhabitants of Ohio would witness its annihilation with as much regret as that of the noble River, or the beautiful Lake, whose waters wash so large a portion of our borders. So long as the produce of our farms shall constitute our staple articles of trade, the market of New York, from its capital, tonnage, commercial situation and climate, will continue preferable to that of New Orleans; and with the aid of the artificial navigation in question, the valley of the Ohio from Pittsburgh to the Falls can realize a sale of its exports much sooner, and the transportation will cost much less, and be attended with less risk, than if a market were sought through the Mississippi. All parts of the western country have felt, and still feel the distructive effects of that climate on our provisions; the experience and observation of all who have been in that trade, can testify to the deleterious influence of the climate on our boatmen and traders, and the sacrifice of life and health at which that commerce is prosecuted.

An adventurer arriving at New Orleans in the spring with a cargo of flour &c. most frequently finds the market overstocked, especially at that season of the year which admits him to descend from the country above the Falls. To leave his property is to abandon it to destruction; to wait for a higher price is to incur the dangers of an unwholesome climate. He must ship his flour or sell at a sacrifice—oftentimes at a price that will not pay freight and charges. It is *fair* therefore to compare the delay, cost, and risk of sending the cargo from the Ohio to some port beyond the Gulph of Mexico, with the time, charges and risk that will be incurred in transporting it to New York by the projected Canal;—and to compare a voyage to New Orleans, by a circuitous and dangerous navigation—through more than ten degrees of latitude—approaching the torid zone—exposed to all the deleterious effects of the climate on the constitutions of persons from a northern latitude, with a safe and expeditious voyage through the heart of our state and that of our sister state, in a healthful climate, and supplied with all the necessaries and comforts which a thickly settled and highly improved country will afford.

. . . .

The views of your committee may be further illustrated by the following exposition, which will apply to all the commerce that would pass the Falls of the Ohio for New Orleans if no other channel for exportation should be opened. At the time of the late rise in the price of flour it was worth at Cincinnati $3.50 per bbl., and at the same time was worth $8.00 in New York, and was purchased at each of these markets for the then expected demand in England. The cost of transporting a barrel of flour from the former to the latter market through the contemplated Canal, is estimated at $1.70 which added to $3.50 the cost at Cincinnati, would make $5.20 the cost at New York—deduct this sum from $8.00 the value at the latter market, and there is left $2.80 the increase in value of a barrel of flour at Cincinnati, produced by the facility of transportation afforded by the proposed Canal.

. . . .

Although the members of this committee have on other occasions, heard much of sectional jealousies, they have lent an unwilling ear to the degrading sentiment; and consider it would be highly derogatory to any part of the state to suspect they would be envious of an immense benefit to a portion of their fellow citizens, procured without expense to themselves, by an operation which cannot fail to enrich the whole community, and place at their disposal most ample resources for education and for every kind of internal improvements.

Your committee in their inquiries on this part of the subject have not been unmindful of the manufacturing interests, which in some part of Europe are thought to receive at least equal benefit with agriculture, from this species of improvement. It is conceived that the advantage of both, from the execution of the project, may be blended in many particulars, and that they may thereby be rendered mutually subservient to each other, and to the best interests of our country.

The probable productiveness of the canal as a source of revenue, comes next to be considered. The committee feel every reasonable confidence in representing that the accomplishment of the noble scheme would more richly reward the undertaking than any other enterprise which the country could promise to the most sanguine adventurer. Computing at the rate of *one cent* per ton per mile, (the rate established on the New York Canal,) for the actual expense of canal transportation, the toll that the commodities so transported, will bear, will be very great; the committee are however content to limit it to *one and a half cents* per ton per mile, (the rates of toll established on the New York Canal,) or in other words, the freight and toll on a ton conveyed the whole length of the canal, would be five dollars—two dollars per ton for transportation, and three dollars per ton for tolls.

. . . .

It has been estimated by the committee, in part from official data, and from sources of information less to be relied on, that in the year 1818—19 there was shipped from Cincinnati and out of the two Miami rivers about 50,000 tons of commodities for a foreign market, the principle part of which it is believed would have found its way to the New York and Montreal markets, if a water transportation could have been had direct to those points. It has also been supposed by the committee that an equal amount would pass through the proposed canal annually from that part of Kentucky which lies above the Falls of the Ohio;—from that part of Indiana which lies above the Falls, and from the parts of Virginia and Pennsylvania which border on the river Ohio, an equal amount; and from that part of the state of Ohio bordering on the river which lies above the Little Miami, an equal amount, making a total thus estimated of 200,000 tons. If these estimates have any foundation, and the committee are of opinion they do not exceed the probable amount, the result will shew the probable amount of commodities which would pass through the proposed canal annually. This amount will increase as the population and improvement of the Western country advances, and as the demand for the produce of our country increases. Estimating the tolls at three dollars per ton, as above shewn, the result will be, a revenue to the owners of the canal stock of $600,000 annually. It may be said this estimate of the amount of transportation through the canal is too great. If so, reduce it one half, allowing only 25,000 tons from each of the divisions, making a total of 100,000 tons, which your committee feel confident is not an over estimate, and the result will be a revenue of $300,000 annually. In order to strengthen these estimates if it be thought necessary, the committee beg leave to call the attention of the House to other sources of transportation: The estimates so far have had reference to the exports of the country only. It is believed that most of the foreign goods and articles imported for the consumption of the states of Ohio, Kentucky, Indiana, Illinois and Missouri would be purchased at New York and transported through the Ohio Canal, which would aid very materially in making good the foregoing estimates.

When the extent of country thus to be supplied with merchandize is taken into view, and when it is recollected that the city of New York will hold forth greater inducements and facilities to the western merchant than any other mart to which the western country can have access; and more especially so when it is recollected that a great proportion of the exports of the western country east of the Falls of Ohio, and some even west of that, will find a market at that city; and that the safety, certainty and cheapness of transportation from that city to the Ohio river, will be such as to hold forth every inducement to merchants to resort to that market for their supplies, it must be admitted that the amount of transportation through the canal from this source will be very considerable. This extent of country is now supplied with most of its importations from Philadelphia and Baltimore by way of the Ohio river. To every mind in the least degree acquainted with the commerce of the western country, it will appear evident, that by opening the proposed communication the channel of that commerce must be changed; that a general revolution in it will take place, and that the proposed canal will be the connecting artery through which the commerce between the whole western country, and the City of New York must pass— that this change in the commerce of the west, thus effected, must essentially promote the interests of our sister states to the south and west; strengthen the bonds of our happy union, and at the same time will enrich our own state by the amount of its tolls; thereby ultimately laying the foundation for an inexhaustable revenue to the state, which will in some degree compensate for the sacrifice made as the price of our early admission into the confederation.

6 To Educate a People

THE FREE PUBLIC educational system enjoyed by Ohioans today was not the outcome of spontaneous genius but rather the net result of many corrected mistakes. Faced with the problems of a frontier society, inadequate finances, moderate interest, and no precedents, the Ohio legislature prior to the Civil War struggled to erect an educational system that would serve the people of the state. No other consideration consumed more legislative time than did education. Despite the lip service politicians paid to the need for good education, the state's school system before 1860 was predicated upon voluntarism and an almost systematic rape of school funds.

Ohio was unique in that it received the first federal aid for education. Manasseh Cutler, the lobbyist for the Ohio Company who strongly believed that the territory north of the Ohio River offered opportunities to create new institutions for mankind, convinced Congress that it should assist in the financing of education. Consequently, the famous Section 16, or 640 acres of land within each surveyed township, was specifically designated by Congress to be used to defray educational expenses. As a result, nearly one thirty-sixth of the land in Ohio was earmarked for the support of education. Without a provision for education within the Ohio constitution, it was left solely to the general assembly to manage the education lands, to establish the purposes for education, and to organize and control a school system. For nearly seventy years the state legislature grappled with these problems in an unconvincing manner. While the concept that land should be reserved to help finance education was brilliant—and the financial potential of these lands, if properly managed, was almost unlimited—the state legislators did not display much enlightenment. Between 1806 and 1850, the legislature, through various methods, divested the state of its vast school land holdings. The money acquired from the sale of these lands was used to establish an educational fund from which the interest earned was to meet local educational needs. However, by 1830, the revenue received by the state from the sale of these school lands was pledged to help pay for the construction of the state's canal system or for other state debts. Education received only the promise of an interest rate, based on the good faith of the state and the whims of future legislatures.

While they were thus getting rid of a major financial source for public education, the numerous legislative bodies refused to commit the state to any kind of concrete system. In the first school law, passed in 1821, the state confessed its responsibility to provide school facilities; at the same time, however, it did not define how a state system would be structured. Pieces of legislation between 1825 and midcentury were marked by decentralization and voluntarism at the local level. It was not until the school act of 1853 that the legislature first established a recognizable statewide system for education. Apparently, what the state legislatures wanted prior to 1850 was truly a free public education system—one without costs.

It would be unfair to condemn everyone who worked toward a state school system during the first half of the nineteenth century. There were those who labored tirelessly to convince several generations that what society gained from public education was worth the cost. Aside from Caleb Atwater of Circleville, who helped to enunciate the purposes of education in a bill passed by the legislature in 1821, the most important individual to promote education in Ohio was Samuel Lewis. A self-educated New Englander who migrated to Ohio, Lewis was appointed state superintendent of common schools in 1837 and began to mirror in the Buckeye State the work of Horace Mann in Massachusetts. Traveling fifteen hundred miles throughout Ohio, Lewis called for the acceptance of an educational policy that included the establishment of a state school fund, the founding of school libraries, and the power for local school districts to borrow money. Unpopular, in poor health, and ahead of his time, Lewis resigned his position in 1839. One of the finest reports made during the first half of the nineteenth century concerning both the structure and substance of education was submitted by Calvin Stowe, the husband of Harriet Beecher. While an instructor at Lane Seminary in Cincinnati, Stowe traveled extensively across Europe and was encouraged by the Ohio General Assembly to observe European educational systems. His report, which recommended a strictly structured system, was issued in 1837 and influenced educational thinking not only in Ohio but across the country.

While the absence of a workable educational system had caused the neglect of many white children in the state, especially in the rural areas, the majority of black children in Ohio had been officially forgotten. Blacks had been placed virtually outside society by the black codes, and few whites were concerned with the education of black youths. Prior to 1848, black children could not attend white schools, and black property owners were not taxed for educational purposes. In several urban areas, however, and in Cincinnati particularly, blacks did attend local schools. Following the repeal of the black codes in 1848, the state legislature pursued a program of quasi-segregation. First authorized by the school act of 1849, and upheld by *State vs. Cincinnati,* segregated schools were to be maintained in districts where a certain number of blacks resided. Although debated without conclusion during the constitution convention of 1850, this principle was continued through the various school acts of 1853, 1864, and 1878. It was not until 1887, when Benjamin W. Arnett, a representative from Xenia, maneuvered House Bill 71 through the general assembly, that segregation in Ohio's schools came to an end.

Despite the unsettled state of education in Ohio and indeed the failure of the legislature to support it, a discernible state school system began to emerge by the end of the nineteenth century. Certainly inequities continued not only in education offered to blacks and whites, but also in that offered in the urban and rural areas. State legislators consumed much time on matters of education during the century, and few would have denied that education provided the foundation for the perpetuation of freedom, patriotism, and the general welfare. The problems emerged in determining what was to be the price and who was to pay.

The First Survey

SAMUEL LEWIS

In compliance with my duty under this law, I proceed to furnish the first Annual Report from this department for the State of Ohio. The fact, that it is the first, and that very little attention has been paid to school statistics in the State, must be my apology for imperfections.

As soon as I received a copy of the law referred to, it became evident that only a commencement could be made the first year, in collecting the official details called for; and that, to understand the subject generally, much traveling and personal observation would be required. A conviction that the expectations of the Legislature and the public could not be realized, led me to consult the Executive of the State on the propriety of accepting the office. A deep interest in the general subject, joined to the advice received, finally determined me to accept, and do what I could, trusting to the indulgence of the Legislature.

My first duty was, to issue circulars to the different county auditors. This was done early in May, so that they must have reached every county in the State by the middle of June. Much difficulty has been found in getting any thing like correct reports. Auditors, though especially requested through the circulars, and required by law, have, in many instances, delayed sending out their circulars until very late, and in some cases, until after the October school elections; and thus the new officers were called upon to report the proceedings of their predecessors without records, or other means of collecting proper information. Of this they very justly complain. In many counties, little or no effort has been made to get the proper information into the different districts; and the first they hear of the requisition is, that the time for their report has almost expired, and they will forfeit their money unless a report be made at once. Under such circumstances, it is not strange if there should be still greater complaints.

. . . .

In addition to the different circulars sent out, my time has been for several months spent in traveling from county to county, chiefly on horseback; occasion has been taken to visit many schools in the country, and to converse with teachers, children, school officers, and parents. My mission has not generally been made known, except to

From Samuel Lewis, "First Annual Report of the Superintendent of Common Schools," January, 1836, *Ohio Executive Documents*, (1837), pp. 3-18.

county auditors, and others with whom I have had official business. This course has given me a better knowledge of the details and practical operation of the system, than could be obtained in any other way. I have traveled in this way more than 1,200 miles, visited forty county seats, and more than 300 schools.

Of the particular enactments required, but few express decided opinions, except the want of funds, in which all agree. The general language is, "We are impatient to see and feel the benefits of the school law, so long promised, and so much praised; we must have common schools made better, and more abundant. The present law, for some reason, does not bring with it the means of education to supply our wants. Let a law be passed that will be felt in its benefits, as well as in its burdens, and we will not complain. We object now to the defects, to the complicated machinery, the inadequacy of the means, the crowded schools, the short time a school is taught. Either leave us to depend wholly on our own efforts, or give us something worth our attention; at present, the law hinders private schools, without supplying public schools." Some say, "If you cannot make the system better, abandon the whole." This is the language of men in every county in our State, all agreeing in the one general and enlightened sentiment; so that we can approach the subject with cheerful confidence, and backed by such a public opinion, profiting by past experience, erect a national institution, that shall be at once our strength, our pride, and our happiness.

The first law assessing a school tax, in 1825, is generally considered the commencement of the system. This was frequently altered, until, in 1836, the present law was passed. The tax, which commenced at half a mill on the dollar, has gradually risen to a mill and a half, and power is given to increase it by townships; some have done so. The history of the different enactments would be tedious, and perhaps of little use. All the legislation on the subject has aimed at the same end, viz: to secure certainly the proper education of all the children in the State, on terms of the greatest possible equality.

It may take some years to secure a perfect uniformity in the system of teaching and conducting school business, with a people so varied in their origin, habits, and prejudices. It is not supposed that any direct legislative enactments can be made, to prescribe rules for the internal regulations of the schools. This would produce great discontent, if at all practicable. These must be left to officers and teachers, in a great degree, after the schools are established. The internal improvement must be effected by those who exercise an influence in the different departments of the work, and it must take time. But as to what shall be taught, there is less difference of opinion. The future fathers and mothers of Ohio, it is agreed, must be so instructed as to enable them to discharge the high and important responsibility of hereditary rulers of a mighty nation. This requires, to be sure—that they learn to *read, and write, and cypher,* according to the old standard. But this, added to the other branches usually required in common schools, is not all; and, while its importance is admitted, it is not the most important:—there are high and noble departments of education, besides merely learning how to make money.

The sound principles of our government are to be taught—that lesson that Washington gave, viz: that "next to our God, we owe our highest duty to our country;" and that this duty does not in chief, consist in splendid efforts in battles or Senates; but that real patriotism consists in a proper cultivation of those arts and principles that adorn society, and make in practice, what we claim in theory, viz: the cottage equal to the palace. The natural impetuosity of unrestricted liberty, is to be tempered by a well grounded conviction that obedience to the law is real liberty. The great point, that majorities must govern by a peaceable expression of opinion, (here for the first time admitted,) must be engraven upon the memory and judgment of all our sons. Patience, until legal and constitutional redress can be had, for all wrongs, public and private, must be inculcated; habits of self-government, economy, and industry, must be enforced. These must all be taught by men who know how to exhibit the proper facts and principles, in all their bearings, and with all their advantages.

It cannot be too deeply impressed on all minds, that we are a christian, as well as republican people: and the utmost care should be taken to inculcate sound principles of christian morality. No creed or catechism of any sect should be introduced into our schools; there is a broad, common ground, where all christians and lovers of virtue meet. On this should every teacher take his stand, and make it a paramount work, to train up the rising generation in those elevated moral principles of the Bible; and here should be taught all the social and relative duties, with proper inducement to correct action.

. . . .

The branches of learning and science to be taught in these schools, will readily occur to every man. They must be such as will qualify our children to perform the different duties of life, that, by the laws of our country, they may be called to discharge, whether public or private; keeping in view, that an early introduction to nature is important in popular education, and that the whole system should be directed to a proper development of the powers of the mind. Nor should we any longer delay the time. Every year's delay is adding mountains of obstacles to be overcome. We need no longer direct public attention to the future—to our children's children—to the third and fourth generation, before the promised blessings are realized. Nothing will be more hurtful than procrastination, in a work like this. If we would render succeeding generations virtuous and happy, we must begin with the present. At the same time, care must be taken to prevent any relaxation of effort on the part of parents, and others interested in the care of the young; and whatever the State does, should, if possible, be so arranged as to increase, rather than diminish, other efforts to effect the same object.

. . . .

In many counties associations are formed of teachers and friends of learning, to promote this object; and the education of the mass, is a marked feature in all discussions and reports. Nothing will rally the people more readily, than the discussion of subjects connected with education. Still, leaving Cincinnati for the present out of the question, there are but very few places in the State, where common school instruction proper, is furnished, approaching near the grade we have supposed; that is, where the means of proper instruction *are free to all, rich and poor, on equal terms.* The city of Cleveland has, within a few months, commenced organizing her free schools, on principles which, if carried out to the extent demanded, in that flourishing place, will distinguish her on the list of free school cities; but even there, the provision is not half enough, and the schools have from 50 to 80 children to the teacher.

As it will be impossible to give a full history of my observations, an example of the several classes must suffice. In one town a free school is taught three months in the year, by one teacher, in a district where more than one hundred children desire to attend; they rush in and crowd the school so as to destroy all hope of usefulnes; the wealthy, and those in comfortable circumstances, seeing this, withdraw their children or never send them; the school thus receives the name of a school for the poor, and its usefulness is destroyed. This example is one that represents nearly all the free schools in the State, as well in the country, as in the cities and towns.

Another and much larger number of the districts, adopt a practice of which the following is an example.

The district has funds which would pay a teacher one quarter or less; but in order to keep up a school as long as possible, it is divided between two or more quarters; the teacher makes his estimate of the amount, besides public money, that must be paid by each scholar, and gets his subscription accordingly. Here none send but those who can pay the balance; of course, the children of the poor, the very intemperate and careless, with sometimes the inordinate lovers of money, are left at home. This mode, though it defeats the primary object of the law, really secures a greater aggregate amount of instruction than the other. Another class proceeds on the same plan, with the exception that the teacher is bound to take the very poor free, if they prove their total inability to pay. This is but little, if any, better than the last, since the poor woman must humble herself, and in effect take the benefit of the poor law, before she can get her children into school; and then, both she and her children must suffer, constantly, deep mortification, which frequently drives from the school some of the most promising children, who (right or wrong) are too proud to brook such humiliating conditions. It effectually banishes the children of those who love money better than learning, as well as those of the intemperate, whose sensibilities are too much vitiated to care for this subject at all. Besides, if the poor go on these terms, it invariably crowds the school to a ruinous extent; and if the teacher cannot instruct all, he will, of course, take care of his patrons first; let him be as honest as he may, he will endeavor to satisfy those that support him; and the poor, whose conscientiousness of poverty always make them jealous and watchful, detect the smallest partiality, and leave the school in disgust, or stay to scatter the seeds of discontent and insubordination. Another part of this class is, where the directors agree with the teacher at so much per month, and, after expending the school money, levy, under the statute, a tax on the scholars for the residue, sometimes admitting the poor, and sometimes rejecting all that are unable to pay the difference.

. . . .

School Teachers

In almost every place, either in town or country, complaints are made that good teachers cannot be had; every opportunity has been improved to become acquainted with the difficulty and its causes; that it exists to a ruinous extent, is certain.

Without intending the least reflection upon good teachers, (and we have many in the profession that are an honor to the State,) it is my duty to say, that many of our common, as well as private school teachers, are unqualified for the task they assume. It is not necessary, in a public document, to repeat more fully what all have heard on this subject. What has been said of systems of instruction may be repeated of teachers. There are found in both public and private schools, every grade, from the most talented, learned, disinterested and energetic, to those of characters entirely opposite. The most general defect is want of learning and energy; and poor teachers are sometimes the most serious obstacles to the introduction of reform in their neighborhoods.

The cause of all this is not hard to find; it is simply that the compensation is not enough to induce men of learning, talent and moral character, to go into the profession, or continue in it. We may speculate as much as we please, pass resolutions, mourn over the defect, establish schools for teachers, and invent an hundred other plans, the more we teach the candidates, the less number of teachers we shall have; for men of learning and talent will not teach, unless the compensation and respectability of the business, are both greatly increased.

Men are, and will be as a general rule, governed by self-interest; and while so wide a field is open for enterprise and learning in other departments, they will not engage in this, unless we make the emoluments in some proportion equal with other professions.

. . . .

While a school is only taught three months in the year, no man qualified will be found willing to engage in it; and to read, and write, and cipher, will be the extent of common school learning, so long as we tax these schools with the support of one-half the students in other professions, or so long as they are taught by a class of men merely because it is easier than making rails; or by those who, having tried every thing else and failed, do this to keep from starving, or, in the language of an examiner who was remonstrated with for giving a certificate, replied: "if the man can't teach he must starve, for he is fit for nothing else under Heaven!"

Still the common school teacher, *good or bad,* holds more of the future destiny of the country in his hands than all other human influences combined, (except the mother;) and as is the teacher, so will be our children.

. . . .

If, then, I am correct in the standard the State has fixed, and in my view of the present condition of the schools, it follows, that something further must be done; and the opinion is fast becoming general with practical men, that common schools, to succeed, must be *free* schools. Whatever means may be adopted to raise the funds, whether by States, counties, townships, or districts, the schools must be opened for all in the district, without charge per scholar, at least one-half the year; in no other way can we induce all to send. These schools must be as good, or better, than private schools, or those in comfortable circumstances will not send to them; and when schools are called "charity," or schools for the poor, it will be their destruction.

We say free schools—not that we would urge the Legislature to supply all the means of instruction without the action of the people; it is generally agreed that this will not do. But the funds must come from legislative and township action combined, so that each township shall feel that the support of its own schools depends on its own action; and what is appropriated by the Legislature—and some appropriation is indispensable, if we wish the work to succeed—should be made to operate as a lever to raise the additional sum required. At the same time, raise the people to action, and excite their interest. This passive assent in favor of education will not answer; the same course in reference to internal improvement would never have made our canals and other public works.

. . . .

Where the schools are kept free in this State, they flourish best. In Cincinnati they have marched steadily forward, overcoming every difficulty, and the people look upon them as the most valuable of their privileges.

The importance of this point must excuse this detail. I will only add, that from my knowledge of public opinion in this State, and especially of practical men, I have no doubt that four-fifths are in favor of this kind of schools, and will heartily approve such measures as may be required to establish and sustain them.

These schools must be made good, we repeat, as well as free. Reason on theories as we may, they will never controvert facts and experience. These prove, that the only way to make free or common schools useful, is to make those who support them interested therein. If the rich man pays his school tax grudgingly, it is because the schools, as he thinks, do him no good; he pays high for tuition in private schools. But make the common school as good as the private, and his interest will induce him to support it. A school not good enough for the rich, will never excite much interest with the poor. They will receive its benefits, if at all, with jealousy; and the effect will be, to build still higher the wall that separates the sympathies of different classes of society.

. . . .

Again, though a great majority of our citizens are enlightened and intelligent, it must be admitted, that quite a number do not regard the education of their children with sufficient interest to induce proper individual action; and unless provision for these, other than parental, be made, they will be even worse situated, in many cases, than the orphan. It is common to say of these, "They could educate their children, if they would": but visits to the houses of many people, in different counties, of whom this was said, would satisfy any man, as it has satisfied me, that if they paid for schooling, it must be taken from the already too scanty fare of an unfortunate wife and poorly provided family. In many cases, you may as well charge fifteen dollars per quarter, as fifty cents. They cannot, if they would, and too many would not, if they could, pay, as individuals, any thing.

. . . .

Whether we regard this subject in reference to *their* interest, or that of the whole people forming the State, it is of too much importance to be passed over lightly, or justify, for a moment, the conclusion that any portion of the rising generation, on whom must devolve the government of the country, can be abandoned to accident or certain ruin. Men may discourse eloquently about family instruction, and fireside education: it is all good; better than orators have spoken, or poets sung. But we must not be misled by eloquence or poetry. The fact is, a large part of our fellow citizens, who depend on their labor for a support, (and they are the majority,) have no time for much of this, if they had ability. If *we* should rise in the morning, and before our little ones were even dressed, hurry to our work, and devote the entire day to it, returning when our fatigued bodies, without other aid, admonished us of approaching night, we should be exceptions to all general rules, if we could undertake the instruction of our sons by candle light. And the cases of three-fifths of our mothers, is still harder. Their labor begins on the first move in the house, nor ends until the last candle is out. They have, emphatically, no time to educate their daughters. Exceptions, we know, there are; persons who have risen above all these obstacles, and educated both themselves and their families. But we must stop until at least one generation shall be educated, before we can expect to make the exceptions, the general rule. We should, in providing for the people, look to their present condition as a body, and not to what they should be according to the perfection of a few characters, perhaps over-drawn, if they ever existed, except in the inventive genius of vivid imaginations. I do not place a low estimate on the capacity of my countrymen; but it is out of their power to do the labor that custom requires of them, and do much toward educating their children at home. A very great number declare they cannot, if they had time.

In this way, only, can we preserve a universal, liberal, republican, christian education. When the different religious societies find that public provision is not to be made sufficient, they will at once set about establishing elementary schools for their own sects; but beyond the poor of their own societies, and the extension of their own influence, they will not voluntarily provide, except in special cases— for the plain reason, that these objects will more than require all their efforts. No imputation is intended to be cast on these societies; the fact is only noted. It exists now to a certain extent, and must increase, unless speedy measures are adopted.

. . . .

The plan I have proposed is general, and includes every class—the poorest equal to the richest child of Ohio. Poverty and pride, it is well said, go together, and so far from condemning the sentiment, we should cherish the laudable aspirations of the young. First furnish proper objects of emulation, and then give a nation's energy, if required, to stimulate them onward to the goal. And if parents should ever in Ohio forget their high responsibilities to their off-spring, we should take them in, give them proper instruction, and by the influence of the child, open a door for the (perhaps) repenting parent to return to the confidence of the world and the affections of his family. These, however, are incidental advantages; the institution to be thus established would include all, benefit all, and, with very few exceptions, save all the rising generation.

SAMUEL LEWIS,
Superintendent of Common Schools.
Columbus, January 9, 1838.

Search for a System

CALVIN STOWE

To his Excellency the Governor and the Honorable The General Assembly of the State of Ohio:

In March, 1836, just before I embarked for Europe, I received a communication from Governor Lucas, with the great seal of the State, enclosing the following resolves of the General Assembly, *to wit:*

"*Resolved by the General Assembly of the State of Ohio,* That C. E. Stowe, Professor in one of the Literary Institutions of this State,

---

From Calvin E. Stowe, "Report on Elementary Public Instruction in Europe," December 19, 1837, *Ohio Executive Documents*, (1837), pp. 2-49.

be requested to collect, during the progress of his contemplated tour in Europe, such facts and information as he may deem useful to the State, in relation to the various systems of public instruction and education, which have been adopted in the several countries through which he may pass, and make report thereof, with such practical observations as he may think proper, to the next General Assembly.

"*Resolved,* That his Excellency the Governor be requested to transmit a certified copy of the foregoing proceedings to Professor Stowe."

In pursuance of the above resolutions, I communicated the intention of the General Assembly to Hon. A. Stevenson, the American Minister near the British Court, and he very readily furnished me with the credentials necessary for the most satisfactory attainment of the object of my inquiries. I am also happy to remark that the communication of Governor Lucas was a ready passport to my free admission to every public institution in Europe to which I applied— and that my endeavors were seconded in the most encouraging manner by all the gentlemen connected with the educational establishments in the several countries through which I passed; and the warmest expressions of approbation were elicited to the zeal manifested by so young a state as Ohio, in the great cause of general education. Particularly in some of the old communities of central Europe, where it happened to be known that I was born in the same year in which Ohio became a sovereign State, it seemed to be matter of amusement as well as gratification, that a man who was *just as old as the State in which he lived,* had come with official authority to inquire respecting the best mode of education for the growing population of his native land; and they remarked that our Governor and Legislators must be very enlightened and highly cultivated men. When in one instance I informed them that our Governor was a plain farmer, and that a majority of our Legislators were of the same occupation, the well known line which a Latin poet applies to husbandmen was applied to us:

"O fortunatos nimium si sua bona norint."
"Oh happy people if they do but appreciate their own blessings."

In the progress of my tour I visited England, Scotland, France, Prussia, and the different States of Germany; and had opportunity to see the celebrated Universities of Cambridge, Oxford, Edinburg, Glasgow, Paris, Berlin, Halle, Leipsic, Heidleberg, and some others; and I was every where received with the greatest kindness, and every desirable facility was afforded me for the promotion of my inquiries. But knowing that a solid foundation must be laid before a durable superstructure can be reared, and being aware that, on this principle, the chief attention of our Legislature is, and for the present must be, directed to our common schools, my investigation of the Universities was comparatively brief—and the most of my time was spent in visiting the best district schools I could hear of, and also the high schools intended for the business education of young men, and the institutions for the education of teachers.

. . . .

In every stage of instruction it is made a prominent object, and one which is repeatedly and strenuously insisted on in all the laws pertaining to education, to awaken a *national spirit*—to create in the youthful mind a warm attachment to his native land, and its institutions, and to fix in his affections a decided preference for the peculiarities of his own country. Indeed the whole plan (which is well understood to have originated in Prussia, when the rapid spread of republican principles first began to threaten the thrones of Europe,) evidently is to unite with the military force which always attends a despotism, a strong moral power over the understanding and affections of the people. In view of this fact, an able English writer denominates the modern kingdom of Prussia, "that wonderful machine of state-craft—as a mere machine the most remarkable in existence—on the model of which most European governments are gradually proceeding to reform themselves." Already has this plan so far succeeded, that there is evidently in these countries a growing disregard for the *forms* of free government, provided the *substance* be enjoyed in the security and prosperity of the people.

Republicanism can be maintained only by universal intelligence and virtue among the people, and disinterestedness and fidelity in the rulers. Republics are considered the natural foes to monarchies; and where both start up side by side it is taken for granted that the one must supplant the other. Hence their watchful jealousy of each other. Now when we see monarchies strengthening themselves in the manner described, are not republics exposed to double danger from vice, and neglect of education within themselves? And do not patriotism and the necessity of self-preservation, call upon us to do more and better for the education of our whole people, than any despotic sovereign can do for his? Did we stand alone—were there no rival governments on earth—or if we were surrounded by despotisms of degraded and ignorant slaves, like those of the ancient oriental world; even *then,* without intelligence and virtue in the great mass of the people, our liberties would pass from us. How emphatically must this be the case *now,* when the whole aspect of things is changed, and monarchies have actually stolen a march upon republics in the promotion of popular intelligence!

. . . .

What faculty of mind is there that is not developed in the scheme of instruction sketched above? I know of none. The perceptive and reflective faculties, the memory and the judgment, the imagination and the taste, the moral and religious faculty, and even the various kinds of physical and manual dexterity, all have opportunity for development and exercise. Indeed, I think the system in its great outlines, as nearly complete as human ingenuity and skill can make it; though undoubtedly some of its arrangements and details admit of improvement; and some changes will of course be necessary in adapting it to the circumstances of different countries.

The entirely practical character of the system is obvious throughout. It views every subject on the practical side, and in reference to its adaptedness to use. The dry technical abstract parts of science are not those first presented; but the system proceeds, in the only way which nature ever pointed out, from practice to theory, from parts to demonstrations. It has often been a complaint in respect to some systems of education, that the more a man studied, the less he knew of the actual business of life. Such a complaint cannot be made in reference to this system, for being intended to educate for the actual business of life, this object is never for a moment lost sight of.

Another striking feature of the system is its moral and religious character. Its morality is pure and elevated, its religion entirely removed from the narrowness of sectarian bigotry. What parent is there, loving his children and wishing to have them respected and happy, who would not desire that they should be educated under such a kind of moral and religious influence as has been described? Whether a believer in revelation or not, does he not know that without sound morals there can be no happiness, and that there is no morality like the morality of the New Testament? Does he not know that without religion, the human heart can never be at rest, and that there is no religion like the religion of the Bible? Every well informed man knows, that, as a general fact, it is impossible to impress the obligations of morality with any efficiency on the heart of a child, or even on that of an adult, without an appeal to some mode which is sustained by the authority of God; and for what code will it be possible to claim this authority if not for the code of the Bible?

But perhaps some will be ready to say, the scheme is indeed an excellent one, provided only it were practicable; but the idea of introducing so extensive and complete a course of study into our common schools is entirely visionary and can never be realized. I answer, that it is no theory which I have been exhibiting, but a matter of fact, a copy of actual practice. The above system is no visionary scheme emanating from the closet of a recluse, but a sketch of the course of instruction now actually pursued by thousands of schoolmasters in the best district schools that have ever been organized. It can be done, for it has been done, it is now done, and it ought to be done. If it can be done in Europe, I believe it can be done in the United States: if it can be done in Prussia, I know it can be done in Ohio. The people have but to say the word and provide the means, and the thing is accomplished; for the word of the people here is even more powerful than the word of the King there; and the means of the people here are altogether more abundant for such an object than the means of the sovereign there. Shall this object, then, so desirable in itself, so entirely practicable, so easily within our reach, fail of accomplishment? For the honor and welfare of our State, for the safety of our whole nation, I trust it will not fail; but that we shall soon witness in this commonwealth the introduction of a system of common school instruction, fully adequate to all the wants of our population.

But the question occurs, *how* can this be done? I will give a few brief hints as to some things which I suppose to be essential to the attainment of so desirable an end.

Means of Sustaining the System

1. Teachers must be skillful, and trained to their business. It will at once be perceived, that the plan above sketched out proceeds on the supposition that the teacher has fully and distinctly in his mind the whole course of instruction, not only as it respects the matter to be taught, but also as to all the best modes of teaching, that he may be able readily and decidedly to vary his method according to the peculiarities of each individual mind which may come under his care. This is the only true secret of successful teaching. The old mechanical method, in which the teacher relies entirely on his textbook, and drags every mind along through the same dull routine of creeping recitation, is utterly insufficient to meet the wants of our people. It may do in Asiatic Turkey, where the whole object of the school is to learn to pronounce the words of the Koran in one dull, monotonous series of sounds; or it may do in China, where men must never speak or think out of the old beaten track of Chinese imbecility; but it will never do in the United States, where the object of education ought to be to make immediately available for the highest and best purposes, every particle of real talent that exists in the nation. To effect such a purpose, the teacher must possess a strong and independent mind, well disciplined, and well stored with every thing pertaining to his profession, and ready to adapt his instructions to every degree of intellectual capacity, and every kind of acquired habit. But how can we expect to find such teachers, unless they are trained to their business?

. . . .

The management of the human mind, particularly youthful mind, is the most delicate task ever committed to the hand of man; and shall it be left to mere instinct, or shall our schoolmasters have at least as careful a training as our lawyers and physicians?

2. Teachers, then, must have the means of acquiring the necessary qualifications; in other words, there must be institutions in which the business of teaching is made a systematic object of attention. I am not an advocate for multiplying our institutions. We already have more in number than we support, and it would be wise to give power and efficiency to those we now possess, before we project new ones. But the science and art of teaching ought to be a regular branch of study in some of our academies and high schools, that those who are looking forward to this profession may have an opportunity of studying its principles. In addition to this, in our populous towns where there is opportunity for it, there should be large model schools, under the care of the most able and experienced teachers that can be obtained; and the candidates for the profession, who have already completed the theoretic course of the academy, should be employed in this school as monitors or assistants, thus testing all their theories by practice, and acquiring skill and dexterity under the guidance of their head master.

. . . .

3. The teachers must be competently supported, and devoted to their business. Few men attain any great degree of excellence in a profession, unless they love it, and place all their hopes in life upon it. A man cannot, consistently with his duty to himself, engage in a business which does not afford him a competent support, unless he has other means of living, which is not the case with many who engage in teaching. In this country especially, where there are such vast fields of profitable employment open to every enterprising man, it is not possible that the best of teachers can be obtained, to any considerable extent, for our district schools, at the present rate of wages.

. . . .

Indeed, such is the state of things in this country, that we cannot expect to find male teachers for all our schools. The business of educating, especially young children, must fall, to a great extent, on female teachers. There is not the same variety of tempting employment for females as for men, they can be supported cheaper, and the Creator has given them peculiar qualifications for the education of the young. Females, then, ought to be employed extensively in all our elementary schools, and they should be encouraged and aided in obtaining the qualifications necessary for this work. There is no country in the world where woman holds so high a rank, or exerts so great an influence, as here; wherefore, her responsibilities are the greater, and she is under obligations to render herself the more actively useful. I think our fair country women, notwithstanding the exhortations of Harriet Martineau, Fanny Wright, and some other *ladies* and *gentlemen,* will never seek distinction in our public assemblies for public discussion, or in our halls of legislation; but in their appropriate work of educating the young, of forming the opening mind to all that is good and great, the more they distinguish themselves the better.

4. The children must be made comfortable in their school; they must be punctual, and attend the whole course. There can be no profitable study without personal comfort; and the inconvenience and miserable arrangements of some of our schoolhouses are enough to annihilate all that can be done by the best of teachers. No instructor can teach unless the pupils are present to be taught, and no plan of systematic instruction can be carried steadily through, unless the pupils attend punctually and through the whole course.

5. The children must be given up implicitly to the discipline of the school. Nothing can be done unless the teacher has the entire control of his pupils in school hours, and out of school too, so far as the rules of the school are concerned. If the parent in any way interferes with, or overrules the arrangements of the teacher, he may attribute it to himself if the school is not successful. No teacher ever ought to be employed to whom the entire management of the children cannot be safely entrusted; and better at any time dismiss the teacher than counteract his discipline. Let parents but take the pains and spend the money necessary to provide a comfortable school-house and a competent teacher for their children, and they never need apprehend that the discipline of the school will be unreasonably severe. No inconsiderable part of the corporate punishment that has been inflicted in schools, has been made necessary by the discomfort of school-houses and the unskilfulness of teachers. A lively, sensitive boy is stuck upon a bench full of knot-holes and sharp ridges, without a support for his feet or his back, with a scorching fire on one side of him and a freezing wind on the other; and a stiff Orbilius of a master, with wooden brains and iron hands, orders him to sit perfectly still, with nothing to employ his mind or his body, till it is *his turn to read.* Thus confined for hours, what can the poor little fellow do but begin to wriggle like a fish out of water, or an eel in a frying pan? For this irrepressible effort at relief he receives a box on the ear; this provokes and renders him still more uneasy, and next comes the merciless ferule; and the poor child is finally burnt and frozen, cuffed and beaten into hardened roguery or

incurable stupidity, just because the avarice of his parents denied him a comfortable school-house and a competent teacher.

6. A beginning must be made at certain points, and the advance towards completeness must be gradual. Every thing cannot be done at once, and such a system as is needed cannot be generally introduced till its benefits are first demonstrated by actual experiment. Certain great points, then, where the people are ready to co-operate, and to make the most liberal advances in proportion to their means, to maintain the schools, should be selected, and no pains or expense spared, till the full benefits of the best system are realized; and as the good effects are seen, other places will very readily follow the example. All experience has shown that governmental patronage is most profitably employed, not to do the entire work, but simply as an incitement to the people to help themselves.

. . . .

There is one class of our population for whom some special provision seems necessary. The children of foreign immigrants are now very numerous among us, and it is essential that they receive a good *English education.* But they are not prepared to avail themselves of the advantages of our common English schools, their imperfect acquaintance with the language being an insuperable bar to their entering on the course of study. It is necessary, therefore, that there be some preparatory schools, in which instruction shall be communicated both in English and their native tongue. The English is, and must be, the language of this country, and the highest interests of our State demand it of the Legislature to require that the English language be thoroughly taught in every school which they patronise. Still, the exigencies of the case make it necessary that there should be some schools expressly fitted to the condition of our foreign immigrants, to introduce them to a knowledge of our language and institutions. A school of this kind has been established in Cincinnati by benevolent individuals. It has been in operation about a year, and already nearly three hundred children have received its advantages. Mr. Solomon, the head teacher, was educated for his profession in one of the best institutions of Prussia, and in this school he has demonstrated the excellencies of the system. The instructions are all given both in German and English, and this use of two languages does not at all interrupt the progress of the children in their respective studies. I cannot but recommend this philanthropic institution to the notice and patronage of the Legislature.

In neighborhoods where there is a mixed population, it is desirable, if possible, to employ teachers who understand both languages, and that the exercises of the school be conducted in both, with the rule, however, that all the reviews and examinations *be in English only.*

These suggestions I have made with unfeigned diffidence, and with a sincere desire that the work which has been so nobly begun by the Legislature of Ohio, may be carried forward to a glorious result. I should hardly have ventured to take such liberty had not my commission expressly authorized me to "make such practical observations as I might think proper," as well as to report facts. I know that I am addressing enlightened and patriotic men, who have discernment to perceive, and good feeling to appreciate, every sincere attempt, however humble it may be, for the country's good; and I have therefore spoken out plainly and directly the honest convictions of my heart; feeling assured that what is honestly meant, will, by highminded men, be kindly received.

All which is respectfully submitted,

C. E. STOWE.

Columbus, Dec. 18, 1837.

Constitutional Debate: Why Educate Blacks?

WILLIAM SAWYER (AUGLAIZE)

The third section was then taken up, and is as follows:

> The General Assembly shall make such provision by taxation and other means (in addition to the income arising from the irreducible fund) as will secure a thorough and efficient system of Common Schools, free to all children in the State.

MR. SAWYER. I move to insert the word "white" between the word "the" and the word "children," so that the section will provide for the education of all the *white* children in the State. That is the only class of children in the State of Ohio for whose education I am willing to make provision in this Constitution.

MR. TAYLOR. I confess, sir, that I am surprised. I did not expect that a motion of this kind would be made by any gentleman

---

From *Report of the Debates and Proceedings of the Convention for the Revision of the Constitution of the State of Ohio, 1850-51,* (Columbus, 1851), II, 11-12.

on this floor. I did not, on the other hand, suppose that any proposition to extend the political rights of the colored citizens of Ohio would be adopted; but I had supposed that a knowledge of the law of self-preservation would have suggested to the gentleman from Auglaize [Mr. Sawyer] and to every gentleman upon the floor, that it would be good policy to give to all within the reach of our laws a good moral and intellectual training. I knew that this Convention was not prepared to increase the political rights of the black man; but I had hoped that all were willing to provide against his becoming the pest of society, by being deprived of all opportunities for education. Shall we not secure protection to ourselves and our children by relieving the colored population of Ohio, from the absolute necessity of growing up in vice and ignorance? Shall we, by the adoption of the amendment of the gentleman from Auglaize, constitute a class who will become the inmates of our poor houses, and the tenants of our jails? I think it must be clear to every reflecting mind that the true policy of the statesman is to provide the means of education, and consequent moral improvement, to every child in the State, the offspring of the black man equally with that of the white man, the children of the poor equally with the rich. But I am told that the Negro belongs to a degraded and inferior race; so much the more reason, sir, for their education and improvement. Leave them to grow up without moral and intellectual training, and they become a positive curse as well as a burthen upon society. Educate them, and they become useful members of the community that has cared for them.

. . . .

MR. SAWYER. I have but a few words to say, sir, upon this subject. I am sure that I would go quite as far as the gentleman from Erie, (Mr. Taylor,) to do justice to the negro race. When he hears my views upon the subject, he may find that we do not differ very widely. Under our present laws, the negro is not taxed for the support of schools to which his children are denied admittance. True, the negro is taxed for school purposes, but it is exclusively for the benefit of his own children, when he desires it should be thus applied. There is therefore no injustice, no inhumanity, if gentlemen choose to place the matter upon that ground. And, sir, I am willing to extend to the negro the same exemption from taxation for the support of white schools, for all time to come. But, sir, while I will oppose any measure for the oppression of the blacks now in the State, I will as strenuously oppose every proposition which, in its practical effect, will tend to encourage the emigration of blacks into the State. And, sir, while I would desire to injure the feelings of no gentleman who holds sentiments opposite to my own, I must say that I rejoice in the passage of the fugitive slave bill; for I believe it will have the effect to rid the free States of the curse of a negro population, intermixed with the whites. Nor shall I be deterred from frankly expressing this opinion of the merits and policy of that measure, because it originated with a whig administration, and has received the emphatic sanction of a whig President. I rejoice at the passage of this bill, because, in the main, it is just,—there may be some wrong features that need repealing—but the general scope and tendency of the law is salutary and politic—it met the exigencies of the times. It has already had the effect to drive thousands of negroes and mulattos into Canada. And I must also rejoice in the fact that the people of those provinces are becoming alarmed at the influx of blacks, which, to quote an expression of one of their newspapers, "is gathering over them like a dark cloud." And why do I exult at what they are beginning to consider as their misfortune? Because, sir, for years they have been inviting this emigration—because they have been encouraging the slaves of the South to desert their masters, not, as I believe, from any love to the blacks, but from a desire to create agitation and disturbance in this Republic. This they have effected too well. The nation is now shaken from centre to circumference by the violent agitation of the question of slavery.

The people of Canada are now reaping the bitter fruits of the seed sown by themselves. They are now overrun with an impover- ished, if not a vicious, negro population. And because the fugitive slave bill has had the effect, in so great a measure, to rid us of the negroes which were everywhere a pest in society, and has accumu- lated them upon the soil of Canada, I rejoice in its passage.

Mr. President, while I sit here, to assist in framing a Constitution for the people of Ohio, I must look first, to the interests of the white race. With this view, I will not encourage the emigration of blacks into this State, nor will I make it so much the interest of that class to remain here, that there will be no disposition for them to emigrate to Liberia. And, in this I am actuated by no hatred of the negro race—no desire to oppress them. I have declared before, and I repeat it now, that I am willing that the negro shall have every privilege and every right that I myself enjoy. I am willing that he shall vote; I am willing that he shall be a justice of the peace, or governor, a judge, or a member of Congress. Aye, sir, I am willing that he shall be President of a Republic. I am willing that the language of our sublime Declaration of Independence, shall apply to the negro as well and as fully as to myself. But sir, I am unwilling that he shall enjoy these privileges in this country, preoccupied as it is, by a different and a higher race. I am willing that he shall enjoy all these rights and privileges in his native country. Is there anything either unjust or inhumane in this?

State Report: To Educate Blacks

Schools for Colored Children

Section 31 of the general school law requires that "The Township Boards of Education in this State, in their respective townships, and the several other Boards of Education and the Trustees, Visitors, and Directors of schools, or other officers having authority in the premises, of each city or incorporated village, shall be, and they are hereby authorized and required to establish within their respective jurisdictions, one or more separate schools for colored children, when the whole number by enumeration, exceeds thirty, so as to afford them, as far as practicable under all the circumstances, the advantages and privileges of a common school education; and all such schools so established for colored children, shall be under the control and management of the Board of Education, or other school officers who have in charge the educational interests of the other schools; but in case the average number of colored children in attendance shall be less than fifteen for any one month, it shall be the duty of said Board of Education, or other school officers, to discontinue said school or schools, for any period not exceeding six months at any one time; and if the number of colored children shall be less than fifteen, the Directors shall reserve the money raised on the number of said colored children, and the money so reserved shall be appropriated for the education of such colored children, under the direction of the Township Board."

Many questions have arisen in regard to the proper interpretation of this section. And to me it seems that the intention of the Assembly which passed the law, does not appear with necessary distinctness. It is sufficiently explicit in regard to those cases where the number of colored children exceeds thirty; less distinct in regard to those cases when the number is less than fifteen; while it makes no manner of provision for those cases which range from fifteen to thirty.

Was this section intended as a prohibition of the admission of colored children into the schools for white children? Or may they be educated with others, in those districts where no special provision is made for their education?

The following case has come to my knowledge. In a certain township there is but a single colored child—a boy of thirteen years. In respect to intelligence, behavior and character generally, he is not inferior to the boys around him. They associate with him in their

From *Sixth Annual Report of the State Commissioner of Common Schools*, (1860), pp. 53-57.

various plays. He resides with a gentleman who pays a higher tax for the support of schools than any other one in the district. This man wishes this boy to attend the common school in that neighborhood. No one objects to his attendance with other children. Now, the question arises, can that boy *legally* attend that school? The former Commissioner, Mr. Barney, decided that he could. Mr. Barney is a lawyer, once in active and successful practice, and during his administration he made the study and interpretation of our school law a specialty. His published opinions have been of great value in operating our school system. In regard to this case, I am *inclined* to the same opinion. For the sake of humanity, I should hope that his opinion is correct. Still I am far from certain that such was the intention of the law. I am not confident that it was intended that colored children should, under any circumstances, be admitted to the common schools of the State. It is my judgment that the law upon this point should be made more definite.

Numerous instances have arisen varying from the one already specified, by the fact that, on the part of a few, objections have been made. Now, does such objection alter the case in respect to its legality? Upon this question popular opinion and practice are not uniform. The law makes no direct reference to such cases.

Great injustice is sometimes done to the colored children of the State by those who should be the guardians of their interests. In illustration of this truth, take the following case, which is a fair sample of some that have been reported to this office. In one of the sub-districts of the State, there reside three colored families, embracing eight enumerated youth. Two of these men—fathers of these colored children—own farms, and pay heavy taxes in that sub-district. But these children are not allowed to attend the public school, though that school is, to some extent, supported by their fathers. No separate school for their benefit has ever been kept up for an hour; nor has their proportion of the school funds been reserved for their instruction in any way. Surely if such wrongs can be practiced upon these people in Ohio, it is high time that we had done speaking of the wrongs that they experience in States further south.

Many of the colored schools are kept in mere sheds and basements; without decent furniture, or anything to render them cheerful and attractive. Their teachers, whether white or colored, are, with few exceptions, poorly qualified, and are employed because they can be had at small salaries. It is, therefore, not strange that but few of the colored children attend these schools. They very properly hold such "seats of learning" in contempt. The number of colored youth enumerated in all the counties except Gallia and Stark, is 12,994; while the number enrolled in colored schools for that year was but 4,888; and the number in average attendance only 2,646.

Doubtless some of these schools are of a better class. And I doubt not that there are many hundreds of colored children in the schools designed chiefly for white children, whether they are *legally* there or not. There are, perhaps, no better public schools in our State than those in Cleveland. Nowhere else does a larger proportion of the youth of the "first families" attend public schools. And yet, the colored children attend these schools, enjoying equal advantages with white children. It is so in many of the rural districts—the question of legality is never raised. Still, there are many places where the necessary instruction of the colored youth of the State is utterly neglected. This fact works not to their injury alone; but also to the injury of all the people of the State. The question is not whether it is desirable that there should be people of this race in our midst. There are already some forty thousand of them scattered through the State; and, to appeal to no higher motive, is it not better that their children should be so taught that they will be intelligent, respectable and useful, rather than be left to grow up in ignorance, and become degraded and dangerous members of society? The fact that many of these people are of low and worthless character, is, to a great extent, the result of their defective and vicious education. Their early training has been under the power of depressing and corrupting influences; and it is as true of the *black* walnut as of the *white* ash, that "as the twig is bent, the tree's inclined." As a matter of mere economy, then, is it not better that the colored children of the State should have facilities for common school instruction?

I speak not as a partisan. I am not here claiming for the colored an equality with white people. Where there are colored children in numbers sufficient, I think it better, as a general rule, for all parties, that there should be separate schools. But since they, like ourselves, are rational and immortal beings,—like us bound to the discharge of important and solemn duties here, and with us journeying into the presence of Him who is no respecter of persons, and who will regard our failure to do justly and kindly to one of the least of these, as a failure to do justly and kindly to Him, I would not, I dare not disregard their rights and interests, precious and sacred to them, as mine are to me. Said the noble-minded Dinter, School Councillor of Prussia, "I promised God that I would look on every Prussian peasant as one who could complain of me before God, if I did not provide for him the best education, both as a man and a Christian, which it was possible for me to provide."

So, it seems to me, should we look upon every child in Ohio; and especially upon the destitute, the neglected, the friendless. Motives of benevolence, motives of duty, should govern all action; public as well as private.

7 The Years of Confusion, 1830-1840

THE PERIOD OF Jacksonian political ascendancy in Ohio was not only a time of growth for the state but also a time of political and economic confusion. Great strides were made in the growth of transportation facilities, as the canal system, started in the mid-1820s, was completed in the 1830s. Railroads were also introduced during this period and within a decade vied with the canals for the carrying trade of merchants and farmers. Population growth brought greater demands for land, and Ohio witnessed wild land speculation.

Politically, the older alliances began to break down; population increases engendered a new political sensitivity for politicians; a redistribution of Congressional seats brought different political influences into government; a new generation of politicians and officeholders introduced broader spectrums of political awareness to the problems of governing; and an expanding economy generated new concerns from both the agrarian and industrial sections of the state. Accompanying these changes was the formation of political parties. Each party competed for strength and life, offering solutions to political and economic problems—solutions that were frustrated by frequent economic depressions affecting all segments of society. Ohio, to be sure, was not alone in these struggles; conditions were unsettled across the nation. Thus the state had drifted into the Jacksonian period reaching for stability.

As the population in the state increased and land prices rose, the lands that had been set aside through treaties with the Indians were coveted by speculators and farmers. Reflecting the general mood of the country—that Indians living in proximity to white society in some way threatened that society—Ohioans began to clamor for the removal of the Indians from northwestern Ohio. Since the Greenville Treaty of 1795, Ottawa, Wyandot, Chippewa, Shawnee, Potawatami, Delaware, Seneca, Miami, and Wea had been living on reservations within Ohio. Beginning with the Treaty of Fort Industry in 1805, the various tribes slowly ceded their lands to the federal government, and the amount of Indian land in the state gradually diminished. No systematic attempt to remove the Indians started until the first

Jackson administration: the first treaty of cession during Jackson's presidency was with the Seneca on February 28, 1831, when the United States acquired their reservation on the Sandusky River just north of Tiffin.

Once the policy of removal was determined, the Ohio tribes quickly gave in, and between February 1831 and February 1833, seven cession treaties were signed with the Indians, removing all the tribes in Ohio with the exception of the Wyandot. The Wyandot held onto two large reservations, one a 147,840 acre tract called the Grand Reserve at Upper Sandusky, and the other consisting of 16,000 acres at Big Spring, between Upper Sandusky and Fort Findlay. However, pressure became great for the removal of the Wyandot from their rich farm lands. In January 1834, the Ohio General Assembly petitioned Congress to act. Accordingly, with authority from the War Department, Robert Lucas, the first Democratic governor of the state, opened negotiations with the Wyandot during the summer of 1834. Frustrated by his failure to reach an agreement, Lucas placed the problems before the legislature. Agitation of the subject continued and finally, on March 17, 1842, the Ohio Wyandot ceded their lands to the federal government and joined their kin west of the Mississippi. Thus, with the final extinction of Indian land claims in Ohio, the northwestern portion of the state was open to speculation and white settlement.

These Indian lands were not the only lands over which Ohio extended its jurisdiction during the Jacksonian period. A controversy that had its roots in the wording of the Ordinance of 1787 erupted into a serious struggle between Ohio and the Michigan Territory for control of a narrow strip of land between the northernmost cape of Maumee Bay and the Indiana border. The issue had been debated for many years, but the crisis was precipitated in 1833, when Michigan applied for statehood. Ohio objected to Michigan's entry into the Union until the border dispute was settled. The issue was embarrassing to Andrew Jackson because the governors of Ohio and the Michigan Territory were both Democrats. Ohio's position was aggressively and ably argued by Robert Lucas at all levels of government. After much rhetoric and muscle-flexing on both sides, Ohio won its case in 1836 and officially gained the disputed territory. The fact that it was an election year and Jackson's Democratic administration needed electoral votes from Ohio far more than verbal support from the Jacksonians in Michigan no doubt had much to do with the final settlement.

Historians studying the Jacksonian period provide two divergent interpretations of its goals and achievements: that the Jacksonians were political idealists who were able to bring together an urban-rural coalition which broadened the base of democracy in the country; or that they were opportunists who were willing to use the political arena for their own personal gain. Central to this controversy was the struggle over the Second Bank of the United States and the banking and monetary structure in the nation. This question was argued in Ohio throughout the Jacksonian period.

Most Ohioans had been opposed to a United States bank. In 1819 the legislature imposed a tax upon both branches of the bank in Ohio and in 1821 placed the banks outside the protection of the laws of the state. Banking conditions in Ohio throughout the 1830s were unsettled. Controversy raged over the extent to which the state should control chartered banks and the issuance of notes, whether there should be a state bank, and over the issue of specie versus paper money. Few understood the role of the banks in the country's economic structure, and by the 1830s the Whigs rallied around the creation of a new federal bank and the termination of specie payment. The Democrats, on the other hand, following the position of the Jacksonians, favored specie payment, worked against the establishment of a national bank, wanted unlimited liability for bank stockholders, and supported an independent treasury system. The Whig position was presented to the state legislature on December 5, 1837, in a speech by Governor Joseph Vance, who blamed the country's depressed economic condition on Democratic fiscal policy. On December 8, 1840, Governor Wilson Shannon, a Democrat who was elected to that office in 1838, argued the Democratic fiscal position in a message to the Ohio General Assembly. This message succinctly outlined his party's economic principles, which were basic to the controversies of the Jacksonian period. The issue of establishing a stable banking system continued to be argued until 1845, when the legislature accepted a conservative banking system, which remained in effect in Ohio until the National Banking Act of 1863.

Remove the Indians

OHIO COMMISSION

· ·

Wyandot Reservation—
Upper Sandusky Sept. 16, 1834

Gov. Lucas, accompanied by John McElvain Esq. Indn agt. & John A. Bryan secry. of the commission, arrived at the agency House this day—The nation is to meet the commissioner for the purpose of entering upon the negotiation on Thursday the 18th, (or rather, as soon after concluding the payment of the annuities, as may be made most convenient to the nation—)

· ·

Friday afternoon, 26th Sept. 1834
½ past 1 Oclk—

The chiefs councillors, Head men &c convened in their council House and coming to order. Tom Long, one of the councillors, rose and gave a general exhortation to the council to preserve order during the interview as it is an occasion that ought to forbid any thing like levity, especially as the chief magistrate of Ohio is one of the parties in this meeting—The Gov. concisely remarked, on opening the negotiation, that he met the chiefs and individuals of this tribe as a commissioner on the part of the united States in a spirit of candor and good will, & would, in what he had to observe in explanation of his views, & in giving those of the government in relation to the welfare and happiness of these Indians, he hoped to use no other than fair arguments—and he assured all who were present, that he would endeavor to consult the best interests of the tribe in what he had to propose to them.

The Gov. then proceeded to explain, in general terms, the views and opinions of the govt—W. Walker, the interpreter, followed, & presented it to the tribe in the Wyandot language.

Upon the conclusion of this statement of the Gov. he enlarged in explanation of the country designed for the Indians, and cited the tribe to the map he submitted for inspection for a knowledge of the country to which the other Indians of the United States, & those from Ohio, have emigrated. The intention is (he said) that each tribe

---

From Dwight L. Smith (ed.), "An Unsuccessful Negotiation for Removal of the Wyandot Indians from Ohio, 1834," *The Ohio State Archaeological and Historical Quarterly,* LVIII (1949), 305-331. Reprinted by permission.

should have exclusive possession of the country they shall select, the united States having a superintending care over the whole country, which all the Indians occupy west of the Mississippi—

. . . .

The Gov. explained further the form of the government designed for the Indians—That a proposition was pending before congress to form a separate and distinct government of their own, & would probably, as soon as they should become sufficiently intelligible [*sic*] & civilised to form a state or territory of themselves, be adopted, and previous to that period they will possess the power of electing a delegate to congress, the same as the other territories of the Union, to take care of their interests and to protect their rights and privileges as a people—After fully and freely explaining all these matters, deemed important to impart a proper knowledge to the tribe, of the benevolent intentions, and the kind, superintending care of the President, and the government of the United States over them, the Gov. read from a Report of the board of commissioners, appointed for the purpose of exploring the country intended for the residence of the united States Indians, who give their views at large on the various subjects connected with the emigration & settlement of all the Indians of the Union east of the Mississippi River.

Succeeding the reading from this document, the Gov. entered at some length in explanation of the advantages to be enjoyed by emigrating to the country designed—He adverted to the extensive range of country from which they could make a selection, the salubrity of the climate, the richness of the soil—the advantages for grasing cattle, horses, sheep &c and the promise held out for realising all the necessaries of life, which the various wants of the Indian now required. He enlarged upon the subject of these advantages, and contrasted the present condition of this nation with their former situation, possessed as they once were of a wide & extended region of country, & now dwindled down to a small and narrow reservation of a few miles in extent, and finding, as it were but a handful of their men & women left, and they dropping off, one after another, loudly speaking to the world that the day of their national prosperity is gone, & pointing them to the West where those remaining might go & where the sprigs of their nation might take root and flourish. Jacko, principal chief, observed, when the Gov. proposed to them to give ample time to consider, (one, two, or four weeks, or such time as they might select, that they would consult together for a while, this evening, and let the Gov. know whether it would be necessary to meet tomorrow—They finally determined to meet tomorrow morning for further consultation—

Saturday, 1 O'clk P.M—
Septr 27—

Thomas Long, one of the chiefs rose and said in behalf of the council, that after some considerable length of time, and hearing the views of one and other of the tribe, and after hearing what the gov. had to say yesterday, they have come to the conclusion to postpone a final decision on the subject—The tribe feel a due sense of the candor and truth with which the Gov. has expressed to them his views and opinions as to a proposed change of their residence—and, taking into consideration his assurance of being their friend, and, that he would do the Indians nothing but Justice in this negotiation,—and further, that the subject should be made plain to their understanding, and be involved in no mystery or uncertainty by him, they have concluded best to postpone the further consideration of the consultation until three weeks from monday next, and he feels happy to remark that there is a [concurrence?] in opinion and feeling between the Gov. and the council as to the time.

. . . .

Journal of Concluding Proceedings

In council, Wednesday ½ past 11 AM. Oct 23d 1834—Jacques principal chief—rose and said that the delay had taken place in consequence non attend. of two or three chiefs. Perhaps circumstances had occurred to prevent their att[endanc]e. He was happy to find the Gov. enjoying usual health, and that they were again permitted to meet together in peace and friend ship to consult on the subject of the negotiation opened for the sale of their lands.

He continued to remark that with regard to the subject that has been submitted to their consideration, that the manner in which the subject has been presented to their consideration was calculated to inspire confidence and to assure them of the entire fairness of the proposition of the govt—That they had viewed the subject in all its bearings in the spirit of candor and truth. That they had convened the nation for these several days to discuss and examine the subject, & had taken the proposition of the govt under their special attention—That from a view of the whole matter they had come to a determination adverse to selling—

further he remarked that in the course of the discussion in the 3 days convention, various propositions were made, one of which was that they would ascertain from the Convt the most favorable terms on which a treaty would be based—The other was whether they w[oul]d consent to sell at all and the first question discussed was whether they w[oul]d emigrate at all—The vote was taken on this latter proposition, and it was decided in the negative—This of course cut off all other questions, and they concluded to close the negotiations, and to end the matter at once—

. . . .

in continuation, (it being intimated by the Gov that he w[oul]d like to hear others who might wish to speak on the subject) said that he recollected very distinctly that you stated in the concluding part of your address that you wished the reasons assigned why we are opposed to selling—

That one [of] the reasons why they were not disposed to sell was that when they contrasted their present situation with the country designed for them in the west he w[oul]d observe that if they emigrated they must necessarily turn agriculturalists and that it was contrary to their general modes and habits of life—That their condition was not calculated for it

on the first day there was a pretty general attend on the 2d day there was less in no. and on the 3d and last day quite a large no. did not attend. That the prevailing sentiment of the nation appears to be adverse to the removal. That it has been so expressed whenever in council, and whenever they have been together on the subject.

. . . .

(Here the Governor made a genl speech)

In his remarks in eluciadation of the views of the govt &c the Gov. asked whether in fact the tribe was as prosperous now as they were five years since? Whether they were not as a tribe generally more involved, and more deeply in debt than they were, four or five years since, and whether they did not think they would be more prosperous and happy should they remove to some chosen spot of their own selection, where they could live under their own laws and regulations?—

After a few moments consulation among themselves, it was concluded to adjourn until after supper, and hold an evening council—

convened agreeably to adjournment—

in reply to the inquiry submitted by the Gov. remarked, that he w[oul]d state, that when the [poll?] of the nation was taken & they had adj[ourne]d they were not authorized to say any thing further than to make known the decision of the nation—They were aware of the difficulties of their nation, and that many of these had been taken into consideration in council and since a final determination was made they have no further power on the subject—

In regard to the extending the laws of the State over them, they have to say that they not only object to selling & removal, but that they object also to the state extending the laws over them—If they do then put them under the laws, why it is a matter beyond their control, and they have only to submit to that when it shall take place—He further remarked that he considered the matter ended, and he should object to meeting on tomorrow—

. . . .

The Indians Must Move

ROBERT LUCAS

A copy of the Resolution of the General Assembly, of the 18th of January last, "instructing our Senators and requesting our Representatives in Congress to use their influence to effect the removal of the Wyandot Indians in this State, by the purchase of their Reservation by treaty; and requesting the appointment of a Commissioner for that purpose," was transmitted to each of our Senators and Representatives in Congress, in conformity to the request of the General Assembly. This subject was promptly acted upon in Congress, and a small appropriation made to defray the expense of the negotiation. By a letter received from the Secretary of War, addressed to me as Governor of Ohio, I was informed that it was the wish of the President of the United States, that I should open a negotiation with those Indians, for the cession of their lands to the United States, and for their removal west of the Mississippi. This duty I performed in accordance with the request of the President.—I had several interviews with the chiefs and head men of the Tribe; and laid fully before them the philanthropic views of the Government, and the advantages that would result to them as a Nation, by accepting the terms offered them. But of these advantages they appeared not to be duly sensible; and a majority of the Chiefs in Council at that time, declined accepting the terms proffered to them.—The terms I was authorized to offer them, I considered to be truly liberal. The Government of the United States was willing to grant them a quantity of land west of the Mississippi, equal to their

---

From Robert Lucas, "Message," *Ohio Executive Documents,* (1836), pp. 3-9.

present Reserve; to provide for their removal and support for one year, at their new residence; and to sell the lands at Sandusky, and apply the whole proceeds to their benefit, excepting only therefrom, the actual expense that might be incurred by the United States in their removal.

The subject of emigrating West, has, as I am informed, been considerably agitated among those Indians; and on which there exists considerable difference of opinion. The present board of Chiefs, I understand, are divided on that subject. Three, I have been informed, are in favor of emigrating; and four are against it.—The former Chiefs, and a majority of the tribe, it is thought, are in favor of emigrating; if so, a change will be effected in the board of Chiefs at their general election, which takes place in January next.—Under this impression, and with a view to give them time to investigate the subject among themselves, I thought it advisable to suspend the negotiation. It will be renewed again whenever I am satisfied that the Nation is willing to treat upon the terms proposed to them.

From personal observation, I am convinced that this tribe cannot long remain as a distinct community. They are getting poorer every year; their numbers are decreasing; and they are sinking deeper and deeper in debt to the white people in the vicinity of the Reserve.— There is but a small portion of the real Indians, that can be said to be in comfortable circumstances. And I have little doubt, were it not for the influence that is exercised over them by individuals who have identified themselves with the tribe, and are in the occupancy of the most valuable lands on the Reserve, that these Indians would at once accept the propositions of Government, and remove, to join their brethren in the West.—These individuals are enjoying all the privileges of Indians: they are permitted by the Chiefs to draw an equal portion of the annuity paid to the tribe; vote with these Indians in their Councils; pay no taxes under our laws; and at the same time claim the privileges of citizens of the State, and vote at our elections.—I am of opinion that the situation of those Indians is entitled to the consideration of the General Assembly. Should they finally determine to remain among us, their interests would require an explanatory law, defining their rights, and protecting them from the many impositions and frauds that they are now subjected to.—I therefore submit this subject to your consideration.

Michigan Border War

ROBERT LUCAS

The Legislature, on the 23d of February last, with but one dissenting vote, passed resolutions, in which it was declared, as the opinion of the General Assembly, that the territory contained within the constitutional limits of Ohio, formed an integral part of the State, of which no power on earth had a right to dispossess her—That measures ought to be taken, immediately, by the Legislative, Executive, and Judicial authorities of Ohio, to cause her jurisdiction to be fully established throughout every part of her territory, as described in her Constitution: and obtain for her laws and public officers that respect and obedience from all persons residing or coming within her boundaries, to which they are properly entitled—that the State had an indisputable right to run out, and designate her northern boundary, in accordance with the provisions of her constitution; and that, without allowing her public works to be longer suspended, or the interest of her citizens to be further jeopardized by the refusal of Congress to unite with her in the work—and that commissioners should be appointed for that purpose, with instructions to run and re-mark the same from the place where a line from the most southerly extreme of Lake Michigan, to the most northerly cape of the Maumee bay crosses her western boundary to the said cape, so that its exact location may be known and recognised by all persons within the State, as well as by those without its limits.

They, on the same day, passed, by the same vote, "An act defining the boundaries of certain counties within the State, and for other purposes;" in which the boundaries of the counties of Wood, Henry and Williams were extended to the line described in the Constitution—two new townships were created in the county of Wood, and elections for Justices of the Peace and other officers were authorized under the laws of Ohio. This Act made it the duty of all officers within the State, civil and military, judicial and ministerial, who were authorised to exercise jurisdiction within these counties, to extend their jurisdiction, respectively, to the line described in said Act. The same Act made it the duty of the Governor to appoint three Commissioners, whose duty it should be to re-mark that part of the said line lying west of Lake Erie, and commonly known as *"Harris's Line,"*—that it should be the duty of the Commissioners, when appointed by the Governor, to proceed, at as early a day as practicable after their appointment, to the discharge of their duties;

From Robert Lucas, "Message," *Ohio Executive Documents,* (1836), pp. 6-7.

and the Commissioners should, in due time, report to the Governor, stating the manner in which their duties had been performed.

. . . .

I also directed the Adjutant General to enclose a number of copies of the Act and Resolutions to Major General John Bell, of the 17th Division, within whose command the counties of Wood, Henry and Williams are situate, with directions to extend his command to the northern boundaries of those counties, as defined in said Act; and to cause all persons, residing therein, that were subject to military duty, under the laws of Ohio, to be enrolled and organized under the laws of this State. All this he promptly effected, and two militia companies were enrolled in Wood county: they met and elected their officers; which have been duly commissioned under our laws, and are now in command. That portion of the disputed territory, that was attached to the counties of Henry and Williams, is now united to the organized militia districts in those counties respectively.

Considering that the most effectual method of executing the Act of the 23d of February, would be to complete the civil organization of that part of the State claimed by Michigan, I determined on attending, in person, in that region of the State at the time the elections were being held; and to take commissions with me to deliver to the various officers that might be elected under our laws; and to meet the Commissioners at Perrysburgh, on the day appointed to commence marking the line; but, on the 20th March, I received a letter from Mr. Forsyth, Secretary of State of the United States, dated the 14th, in which I was told that the President had been informed, by the Acting Governor of Michigan Territory, that a collision was likely to take place between that Territory and Ohio, relative to the extension of our jurisdiction. To that letter I replied at length, on the same day I received it; in which I informed the Secretary of State, that no collision had been anticipated on the part of Ohio, and in no case would it occur, unless resistance were made to our civil authority. I transmitted to him a copy of the Act and Resolutions of last session, at the same time informing him what course Ohio expected to pursue.

. . . .

In accordance with this resolution, I repaired, in company with Cols. Swayne and Andrews and General Niswanger, to Perrysburgh, where we arrived on the 2d of April. The next day I received a note from Richard Rush, Esq. and Col. Howard, Commissioners on the part of the United States, stating that they wished an interview with me. I replied, that I would meet them, either at Toledo or Perrysburgh, as might be most agreeable to them. On the evening of the 6th April they arrived at Perrysburgh, and on the 7th we had an interview on the subject of the conflicting jurisdiction between Ohio and Michigan, and, after mutual explanation, an arrangement was agreed to, which appeared satisfactory on both sides, under which impression we parted; they to Monroe and I to Maumee, on my way to Defiance, in Williams county.

The Commissioners of the U.S. handed to me a document during our conference, as they said, at the request of Mr. Forsyth, which I found to be the opinion of the Attorney General. This opinion, I was fully satisfied on examination, would, in its tendency, counteract the laudable exertions of the President and his Commissioners, which the sequel proved; for it was proclaimed by the authorities of Michigan, as a justification of their acts: And it is a subject worthy of remark, that all the proceedings at Washington were entirely *ex parte;* that the three letters from the Secretary of State were written; the opinion of the Attorney General drawn up; and the Commissioners appointed and had left Washington, before my answer to the Secretary's first letter could have been received, or anything correctly known with regard to the intentions or movements of Ohio. These letters of Mr. Forsyth, and the opinion of the Attorney General, were evidently dictated under feelings highly excited and unfavorable to Ohio, as is manifest from their contents.

The people within the townships of Sylvania and Port Lawrence, had met and held their elections, as authorized by the act of the 23d of February, 1835; and the returns of the elections had been made to the Clerk's office in Wood county. I delivered commissions to six justices of the peace, within said townships, and also appointed and commissioned one Notary Public, in Toledo. I understand a Deputy Sheriff, qualified according to law, with a competent number of township officers and School Examiners, were duly elected and appointed within these townships.

After delivering commissions to the officers in Wood county, I hastened to Defiance, in Williams co. and while at that place I received intelligence of the outrages committed at Toledo by a body of armed men, under pretence of serving civil process, issued against our fellow citizens for acting in obedience to the laws of Ohio. While there, I also received an account of the preparation that was being made in Michigan to arrest our Commissioners while running the line; with a letter from Messrs. Rush and Howard, in which they enclosed to me a copy of a letter addressed by them to the Acting Governor of Michigan, making known to him the wish of the President, that no force should be used in opposition to that measure; a copy of which letter was transmitted to our commissioners on the line, with a request that they would proceed with the line until met by a force to oppose them, and if such force should appear, that they might withdraw to Maumee until a guard sufficient to protect them should be collected. I also issued an order to General Bell to detail a guard for their protection. I then attended the Court in Williams county, and found the organization of that county completed to the line described in the late act, and the jurisdiction of the Court extended accordingly. This is likewise the case in Henry county; and it may be truly said that that part of the State is as completely organized, under the laws of Ohio, as is any other part of the State at this time. But while the authorities of Ohio were thus pursuing a steady, peaceable course, in accordance with the understanding expressed at Perrysburgh in a conference with Messrs. Rush and Howard, (as will be seen in the statement of Cols. Swayn and Andrews,) the authorities of Michigan commenced prosecutions against the citizens of Ohio, in opposition to the advice of the U. States Commissioners, as communicated to the Acting Governor of that Territory (as will be seen by reference to the copy of the letter transmitted to me) with a degree of reckless vengeance, scarcely paralleled in the history of civilized nations. A particular account of those violent proceedings will be found in the letters of Mr. Goodsell, Major Stickney, Colonel Fletcher, and also in the report of the Commissioners, all of which are included in the documents herewith transmitted, and to which I call your particular attention.

It appears to me, the honor and faith of the State is pledged, in the most solemn manner, to protect these people in their rights, and to defend them against all outrages. They claim to be citizens of Ohio. The Legislature, by a solemn Act, has declared them to be such, and has required them to obey the laws of Ohio, which, as good citizens, they have done; and for which they have been persecuted, prosecuted, assaulted, arrested, abducted, and imprisoned. Some of them have been driven from their houses in dread and terror, while others are menaced by the authorities of Michigan. Those things have been all done within the constitutional boundaries of the State of Ohio, where our laws have been directed to be enforced. Are we not under as great an obligation to command respect and obedience to our laws adjoining our northern boundary, as in any other part of the State? Are not the inhabitants of Port Lawrence, on the Maumee Bay, as much entitled to our protection, as the citizens of Cincinnati, on the Ohio river? I feel convinced they are equally as much. Our Commissioners, appointed in obedience to the Act of the 23d February, while in discharge of the duty assigned them, were assaulted, while resting on the Sabbath day, by an armed force from Michigan. Some of the hands were fired on, others arrested, and one of them, Col. Fletcher, is now incarcerated in Tecumseh, (as will be seen by his letter,) and for what? Is it for crime? No, but for faithfully discharging his duty, as a good citizen of Ohio, in obedience to our laws.—These outrageous transgressions demand your most serious consideration; and I earnestly recommend, and confidently hope, that such measures may be adopted as will afford protection to our citizens; provide for the relief of those who have been arrested, and bound under recognizances; and for the liberation of those who are imprisoned; as also for the indemnity of those who have suffered loss in consequence of their obedience to the laws of Ohio; and, in an especial manner, for the more prompt execution of our laws, and the punishment of those who have violated them.

. . . .

The subject of our Northern Boundary has excited considerable attention throughout the nation, and as far as can be learned from the tone of the papers, great exertions are making to raise feelings unfavorable to Ohio, forestalling public opinion to her prejudice, without reference to the merits of our claim, and all principally upon the grounds that Ohio is a great and powerful State, Michigan a weak and small Territory, (while in fact Michigan has a greater extent of territory than Ohio.) This appears to be the substance of every argument, from the beginning to the end of this controversy. We find it in the first letter of Governor Cass to the Surveyor General, so early as 1817, which letter was the beginning of the controversy; we also find it in the arguments of the Ex-President in the last Congress, as well as in all the intermediate arguments. But what is the true state of the case? Ohio has oppressed nobody—she claims no territory more than what is defined in her Constitution: while, on the other hand, we find the territory of Michigan (who can have no legitimate claim to sovereignty, as her government, at any time, may be dissolved by Congress, and the territory, north of Ohio, attached to this State,) exerting all the power of her temporary or territorial Government, to oppress the small village of Toledo, punishing its inhabitants, not for crime, but for claiming their constitutional rights. In this transaction we see the great and powerful city of Detroit, aided by the authorities of the Territory, united to oppress and weaken the small village of Toledo, on the Maumee Bay. But the true parties in the controversy are the United States and the State of Ohio; and let me ask which is the weaker party in this controversy? Surely it will not be contended that the great and gigantic State of Ohio (as she has been tauntingly called) is about to weaken the United States, by claiming her constitutional rights; or that, by enforcing these her just claims, she would be making the weak weaker, and the strong still more powerful, according to the arguments of our opponents. Arguments of this character may suit those who wish to avoid the truth, to shun the light, and carry their point, right or wrong, by their diplomatic management; but, in my view, these arguments are too contracted to meet the approbation of liberal minded statesmen. Is not Ohio a member of the Union? Does she not form a component part of the United States? Will not any measure calculated to promote the prosperity of Ohio, also promote the prosperity of the United States. Why, then, should jealousy be excited against Ohio? Why the extreme exertions of many editors of newspapers, and other individuals, in some of the States, to forestal public opinion, and make impressions unfavorable to Ohio, without examining the justness of our cause? Is this course liberal? is it just? We think not.

. . . .

Very respectfully,
Yours, &c. &c. &c.
ROBERT LUCAS.

Columbus, Ohio.
June 8th, 1835.

Van Buren's Depression

JOSEPH VANCE

The derangements of the currency have brought the subjects of banking and the credit system, as contrasted with a specie circulation, in prominent review before the whole body of our people. The advantages and disadvantages of both systems have been sustained and defended by the ablest men of our country; and we find the whole matter still in the hands of Congress, who alone have the power of settling and putting at rest this distracting question. That the people are ready to abandon the credit system, by prostrating the banks, and establishing what has been called a hard money government, I do not believe. Such a revulsion in the business of the country, would be too oppressive on all classes of society, and more particularly on that active and enterprising portion of our citizens,

From Joseph Vance, "Message," *Ohio Executive Documents*, (1937), pp. 9-16.

who have been the purchasers and venders of our surplus productions, and who have done so much to build up the prosperity of the State, to be for a moment endured.

Let us examine and see what would be the operation of such a hazardous experiment as that of reducing the circulation of the country to specie alone. Every man conversant with the laws of trade, and the effects of currency, must admit, that all articles of merchandise, and all descriptions of property, must fall in proportion to the reduction of the circulation. This, to be sure, is not always its immediate effect, but that it must, in the end, approximate to that standard, is not to be questioned. But its operation will not end here,—it will raise the value of debts in a ratio still more oppressive. Suppose the banks of Ohio were compelled to wind up their business, as they must certainly do, under this exclusive metallic currency, and that after calling in their circulation, there should remain due to them ten millions of dollars. The result would be, that it would take what is now worth forty millions in landed estate, to settle this debt. We may theorize as we please, but all revulsions in trade, when heavy balances remain unsettled, and especially in agricultural States, must in the end be liquidated and paid by a change of property from one hand to another; nineteen-twentieths of which will fall on real estate.—This will prove equally true in winding up the affairs of any other prominent branch of business, as well as that of banking. Stop, for instance, the importation of foreign merchandise— compel the merchants throughout the State to close their business, and the debt due will have principally to be satisfied by real estate. Our whole credit system is in a good degree based upon the security of landed property; and the policy that shall hazard its sacrifice, is destructive to the interest and prosperity of the whole body of our people.

I have tried to understand all the arguments that have been used in favor of this hard money theory; and, after mature reflection, have labored to carry out their results; and I cannot see that there is one human being in the United States to be benefitted by its operations— the men receiving compensations and salaries from the public, and the man of money and of mortgages, excepted. That the destruction of credit will make the rich richer, and the poor poorer, is too plain a proposition to be called in question. The history of our own State is an argument much stronger than any I can make in favor of this position. If there is a single district of country in the United States that owes more to credit than that of any other, it is Ohio. Credit has given us our elevated stand amongst our sister States. Credit has given us one of the most enterprising and active set of business men that have lived in any age or in any country. Credit has given to us an equality of fortune that is not to be found amongst the same number of people in America or elsewhere. Credit has bought our land, made our canals, improved our rivers, opened our roads, built up our cities, cleared our fields, founded our churches, erected our colleges and schools, and put us into the possession of as large a share of rational freedom and solid comfort, as has ever fallen to the lot of any people.

If, then, it is the settled policy of those who administer the affairs of the Government of the Union, to overturn all our previously well established systems of credit, of finance, and of trade, by sinking the whole property and business operations of the country to a specie circulation, why do they not come forward and show their sincerity by the surrender of a portion of their own salaries? Do they suppose that the people will sit quietly by and acquiesce in seeing their land reduced to one-fourth of its present value, whilst the provisions of the same law will add four-fold to the value of the salaries of our public servants? Thus giving to our President annually, instead of twenty-five thousand dollars, (the nominal amount he now receives,) one hundred thousand dollars, and the other federal officers, down to the lowest postmaster, in the same proportion. Does not every person see that, under the prodigal expenditures now making, a few years' appropriations will transfer to the pockets of the officers, agents, contractors, and retainers of the General Government, the whole specie capital of the United States. Is it not now true, that our federal officers are growing rich on the distresses and embarrassments of those who support and sustain them? and are they not at this moment receiving ten per cent over and above that paid to our State officers, where the law gives equal compensation?

One argument used to sustain an exclusive metallic currency is, that it would give stability and uniformity of prices, prevent over-trading, keep down speculation, and save us from embarrassments and revulsions in trade. Can this be true? Would not the evils be as likely to take place under a limited, as under an enlarged circulation? To effect these objects, is it not necessary that we should have, under the control of a well-regulated financial system, a circulation capable of contraction and expansion, so as to meet the wants of the commercial, agricultural, and manufacturing interests of the country? Would not the same embarrassments take place under a circulation sunk down to a specie currency by an unnatural diversion of it from its accustomed channels, that we now have under a redundant currency? or can the amount of circulation control the evil complained of? If you make ten thousand dollars control fifty thousand dollars' worth of property, by sinking the value of property and raising the value of money, I cannot see how there will be less over-trading and greater uniformity in prices in the one case than in the other. I repeat, that it is not the amount of circulation that produces these evils, but the want of power to control, and judgment in the application of our means, by those who have the management of our financial system.

All must agree that both our commercial and agricultural wants require a circulation capable of expansion to-day and contraction to-morrow. The superbundance of our productions in Ohio may this year require five or ten millions of dollars more, to put them into the market, than may be necessary at the next; and one of our sister States may fall short to the same amount; and this state of things may be reversed at the close of each succeeding crop. The capacity of our financial system for the transferring funds from one portion of the Union to another, to meet these fluctuations in trade, is, in my opinion, the only sure remedy.

Different measures have been proposed, to meet the demands of trade, and to regulate exchanges. Eighteen months ago it was positively asserted by the Secretary of the Treasury that this could be effected through the instrumentality of our State banks, with greater advantage to the people than it had ever theretofore been done. We are now told that this experiment has entirely failed, and that there is no other specific than that of a Sub-treasury system, under the direction and control of the Treasury Department.

. . . .

This prosperous condition of our country has passed away, and we are again in the midst of a disordered currency. As yet, this State has felt but partially the withering influence of its effects. The distress and want, that have swept over our commercial cities and manufacturing districts, are but slightly felt by us. How long, and to what extent, we are to be exempt from these afflictions, time alone must disclose; but that they are to reach us in some shape or other, to a much greater degree than we have yet felt, is not to be questioned.

By what has been said, you will perceive, that at the times that our currency has been most deranged, there has been no Bank of the United States, acting as the agent of the Government, in the collection and disbursement of the revenue. In the forty years that this duty was performed by the Bank of the United States, no such embarrassments took place, and the agency of such an institution, it is yet believed by many of our ablest statesmen, is indispensable to the regulation of our exchanges, and the uniformity of our currency.

It has been found that the demands of trade, which may require a large amount of money in New York to-day, and in Charleston, New Orleans, or Mobile, to-morrow, cannot be supplied safely and without hazard of severe pressure in the district from which it is removed, in any other way than by a well founded bank credit through bills of exchange. This, we are aware, cannot be done; we can have no bank capable of performing these functions. On this subject, both Congress and the President have paralyzed themselves, in their attempts to forestal public opinion: and be the wants and the wishes of the people what they may, there is no prospect of immediate relief from that quarter. Our only reliance, then, must be upon the State institutions. That they have the ability to carry out a perfect financial system, so as to meet the demands of commerce, and equalize and reduce the price of exchanges, is what we do not assert;—but of their capacity to approximate it more closely than any other system that has yet been spoken of, (a Bank of the United States excepted) is our sincere belief.

To enable the State banks to give this relief to the country, they must have the aid of Congress and of the State Legislatures. Congress must repeal the Specie Circular, and give credit to the paper of all solvent State institutions, that shall pay specie for their circulation. The State Legislatures must do away all that improvident legislation, that prohibited the issuing and circulating of small bills. Let the condition upon which this relief is offered, be the resumption by the Banks of specie payments, and a relinquishment of any right they may possess to issue notes under the denomination of one dollar. This will bring back our State institutions to the point from which we started when we commenced experimenting upon the currency of the country. Small coin will take the place of your individual and corporation tickets. The man that wants Government lands can easily supply himself—the man that wants specie, will be able to obtain it—confidence will be every where restored—your produce will find a more steady and certain market, and all the operations of business and of trade will revive and prosper.

. . . .

Experience has shown us how dearly we are paying for the war upon the Bank of the United States. Our people are taxed for State, county, canal, road, and school purposes, heavier than the people of any other State in the Union; but for these taxes they have an equivalent. The increase in the price of our productions, and the decrease in the price of our consumption, pay us amply for the tax paid upon roads and canals; whilst the pleasing reflection that our schools are fitting the rising generation to become the defenders of our liberties, and the perpetuators of our institutions, will amply remunerate us for all contributions made to that object. But for the heavy tax that is now paying by the people of this State on exchanges, and the depreciation of money, we have no equivalent. The war upon the Bank was a wanton war, and its fruits are gnawing on the substance of the people, by high premiums on exchanges, exorbitant interest on money, and heavy losses on depreciated paper. The amount of Eastern funds sold by the banks, and by individuals, in this State, as shown in the previous statement, during the last six months, is $6,701,437 59. Double this amount, and you will have the sum sold annually, which will be $13,402,875 18. Two per cent. upon this (which is below the average premium) amounts to $268,057 48: deduct one-fourth, which is the half of one per cent.; the rate paid while we had the Bank of the United States, and you have $201,043 11; which is the tax paid on exchanges alone, by the people of this State, over and above what was paid during the existence of that institution;—and of the loss on depreciated paper, no estimate can be made.

There is also intimately connected with this subject, that of exacting on loans of money, usurious interest. This practice has crept into society by degrees, until it has become an established branch of business in every city and village throughout the State. Leaving the moral of the subject entirely out of view, does not sound policy and the protection of the indulgent creditor call upon you to arrest this crying evil? The history of the last few years furnishes many melancholy examples of persons having wasted their whole property and beggared their families, by paying exorbitant interest on money, to keep up a mercantile or bank credit—when if they had at the commencement of their embarrassments, closed their business, and wound up their affairs, they would have been able to pay all just and legal demands outstanding against them.

. . . .

Money is seductive in its character—it controls property—it ministers to our wants, and gives to us an elevation in society exceedingly flattering to our vanity. These inducements make men risk much to attain its use; and as one principal object of legislation is to protect the unsuspecting, against the wiley and the artful, it is therefore, most respectfully recommended to your consideration, the propriety of passing a law to regulate interest and prevent usury, as well against incorporated companies as against individuals, with such guards and penalties as your wisdom may think right.

The Banking Evil

WILSON SHANNON

Our banks are but a part of a great whole, composed of the various banking institutions of the States, all founded upon, and governed by, the same principles; similar, in some degree, in their organic structure, and bound together and controled by the same general laws of trade and exchange. In seeking, therefore, to remedy the evils of the system in our own State, and to place our currency on a more solid and substantial footing, we may gain much useful information to direct us in the path of duty, by looking at, and understanding the evils of the whole, or any of its various parts. The same consequences which we see resulting from the banking system elsewhere, we may expect to experience here under like circumstances. That there are great evils belonging to, and inherent in, the present banking system of the United States, cannot be successfully controverted. That it has occasionally been instrumental in doing some good, may be admitted. The evils which have been inflicted on the community through the instrumentality of banks of circulation have become so great and alarming, that the question will soon be between reformation and destruction. If they cannot be reformed so as to protect the community from the losses occasioned by their insolvency and mismanagement, the depreciation of their paper, the exorbitant exactions of interest under the disguise of exchanges, and the evils consequent upon their sudden expansions and contractions, the public, for their own protection, will be forced to dispense with the existence of banks of circulation altogether. However difficult it may be to reform these institutions so as to prevent the evils of which we complain, and however doubtful the result of the undertaking may be, I do not think we should despair accomplishing, to a considerable extent, a result so desirable. The object and end to be obtained are at least worthy the effort of the patriot and statesman, who desires to see the industry of the country protected from the plunder and fraud of incorporated wealth.

If the effort to reform our banks should prove unsuccessful, the remedy will be found in the substitution of banks of discount and deposit, for those of circulation.

. . . .

It is obvious, that a paper system, resting mainly on credit or paper, instead of gold and silver—the only basis on which banking can be safely conducted—can neither be safe to the public, or regular

---

From Wilson Shannon, "Message," *Ohio Executive Documents*, (1840), pp. 8-30.

or uniform in its action. Such a paper system will ever be disturbed by the slightest reverses in the trade and business operations of the country, and unable to withstand the shocks to which the trade and business of every commercial community must occasionally be subjected. But its capacity, and inherent tendency, to double the currency at one time and diminish it one half at another—and thus increase or diminish the nominal value of every man's property and labor, one half—is utterly ruinous to every great interest in the country. Whether this irregularity is brought about by those who control the banks, with the view of speculation, or is the necessary and unavoidable operation of the system itself, makes no difference, so far as the effects and consequences to the public are concerned.

Every expansion by the banks, beyond the real wants of the country, must be followed by a corresponding contraction. When they discount freely, and flood the country with their paper, they give to the times a deceptive appearance of prosperity. The merchant is induced to extend his business, contract unnecessary debts, and engage in doubtful speculations. The same remark is applicable, in some degree, to the whole community. We are all liable to be deceived by the appearance of good times. We contract debts more freely, live more extravagantly, and are less disposed to labor. The contraction of the currency, which must of necessity follow, and which we are unable to foresee, finds us involved in debts, which, under a limited circulation, we are unable to pay, and an extended business which we cannot sustain. The consequences are peculiarly severe and unjust, on all the debtor portion of the community. The farmer who contracts to pay a debt of a thousand dollars, when the currency amounts to eight millions, and wheat one dollar a bushel, finds, when the circulation is reduced to four millions, and consequently wheat to fifty cents a bushel, it takes double the produce, and consequently double the labor, to pay the debt, that it would have done if the currency had remained the same. The same principle applies to the whole debtor community. It is true, what one man loses, another may gain; but the loss and gain are unjust. Thus, by creating an uncertain and fluctuating measure of value, contracts between man and man are impaired, and virtually changed.

. . . .

The evils above alluded to are not the only ones entailed on the country by our paper system. There never has been, in any age of the world, a system devised by the ingenuity of man so well calculated to rob labor of its hard earnings, as this. And it is the more dangerous to the interest of the laboring part of community, because its operations cannot readily be seen. The people of the United States pay to the banks, annually, a tax, in the shape of interest and other bank profits, not less than thirty millions. So far as this is paid for the use of their paper, representing real capital, that is, gold and silver, it is legitimate and proper. But the whole amount of specie owned by the banks does not exceed, at most, fifty millions; the interest on which would be three millions, leaving twenty seven millions which are annually paid to the banks, by the people, for the use of their credit, or promissory notes, bearing no interest. This is a heavy tax on the people, and is paid entirely to credit, not to capital, either directly or indirectly, by the labor of the country: for it is unquestionably true, that labor produces all the wealth of the country. Whatever is paid for the support of government, state or general, or to the banks, who create no wealth, is a tax in some shape, on labor. This extraordinary capacity which has been given to mere credit to tax labor, will solve the whole mystery why it is, that those who create the entire wealth of the country, after a life of toil, are, comparatively speaking, poor, while bankers, who have been permitted to use their credit to tax the industry and labor of the country, have grown rich in a few years. As you diminish, therefore, the paper system, you lighten the tax on labor; as you increase it, you add to the burdens labor has to bear. A system of paper credit which is such a heavy tax on the labor and productive industry of the country, should yield some great corresponding advantages to the laboring portion of the community.

. . . .

The insolvency of banks has recently become a common occurrence. Scarcely a week passes but we see it announced that some banking institution has failed to a large amount. Who can estimate the extent of individual misery and suffering, the insolvency, want, and starvation produced by the causes to which I have above alluded? We are daily in the habit (and it is one of the high and responsible duties of those intrusted with the law making power,) of legislating for the protection of the property of the individual citizen, from the depredations of those who are engaged in criminal violations of the right of property. Yet, if all the losses sustained by individuals, by the commission of the various crimes against private property, were added together, the aggregate would fall far short of the losses sustained by the community, in various shapes, through the banking institutions of the country. What difference does it make to the individual citizen, whether he has lost an hundred dollars by the hands of the midnight thief, or by the insolvency of a bank, or the depreciation of its paper? It is true, there may be a great difference in the moral turpitude of the two cases, but the consequence to the individual citizen is the same in both. In each case he has been deprived of the same amount of property without consideration. Are we not as much bound to guard and protect, by our legislation, the property of the individual citizen, from being taken from him without consideration, through the agency of banks, as we are to protect his property from the depredations and acts of the desperate and lawless criminal? The answer would seem to me to be obvious. This is a subject in which we are all deeply interested.

. . . .

I am not opposed, as I have heretofore stated, to a part of our currency being composed of paper, provided it can be made safe; but only to the excess and improper use of paper money. It should not become, (as it has in a great degree,) the exclusive currency of the country, and the measure of value, instead of gold and silver, the standard of value agreed on by the civilized world. It should never be resorted to barely for the purpose of increasing the circulation; and when issued, should be equal to the standard measure of value, and at all times convertible at the will of the holder, into gold and silver. Its advantages are not in furnishing an every day currency to the people, but in facilitating exchanges, aiding commerce, trade, and the heavy business operations of the country. Under these restrictions, and for these purposes and objects, bank paper may be highly useful and advantageous to an extensive, growing, and commercial community, such as we have in the United States. The present system, however, so far from aiding the commerce, trade, exchanges, and heavy business operations of the country, has a contrary influence, and it would seem to have in view, as its main object, to furnish the entire circulating medium of the country, and constitute a new and unsteady measure of value, fluctuating with every expansion and contraction, and subjecting the price of every man's property and labor to the will or caprice of a few irresponsible individuals, who look alone to their own, and not the interest of the public.

How are the evils complained of to be remedied? Not, surely, by the creation of more banks, and the multiplication of bank paper. If I am correct in the view which I have taken of this subject, the difficulties under which the country now labors have been mainly brought about by an inflated and unsteady paper currency. These difficulties would only be enhanced, ultimately, by creating more paper money.

. . . .

The creation of a United States Bank, with a capital of fifty or a hundred millions, is advocated by some as the most effectual means of restoring stability, uniformity, and safety to our currency. Throwing out of view the constitutional objections to such an institution, and viewing it merely as a question of expediency, I am forced to believe that such an institution would but add to the insecurity and evils of our paper system; and, in its political tendency, endanger public liberty. What additional security would belong to an institution deriving its corporate powers and privileges from the general government, over a similar institution deriving the same powers and privileges from a state government? It is not proposed by any one to make the general government, in any event, liable for the debts of the bank, further than as a common stockholder. Is it a matter, then, of any consequence to an institution, whether it derives its corporate powers and privileges from a state or the general government? So far as its real and substantial security is concerned, it can make no difference. In each case its credit must, or ought to depend, on its ability to meet the demands against it, and the skill and integrity with which its affairs have been conducted. In each case the institution has to be controled and managed by individuals subject to the same errors of judgment, the same passions, impulses and feelings that belong to mankind in general. What reason is there, therefore, to hope that a United States Bank would be governed by more wisdom, prudence, and skill than state institutions? What reason have we to believe that it would not be characterized by the same round of alternate expansion and contraction; the same system of hazardous speculation and unsafe banking, that we have witnessed in a large majority of the local banks, as well as in the late bank of the United States? These are evils that appear to be inseparable from the very system itself, and the sources from whence a bank may derive its powers and privileges, can make no difference as to its action or its disposition to do good.

A United States Bank, it is said, would derive a credit from its national name and character. This may be true; but such credit is unreal, unsubstantial, and delusive, and is calculated rather to deceive than to benefit the public. The credit of a bank, like that of an individual, should always rest on something real and substantial; not on a mere name that can be of no service to the creditor or the bank, in the hour of real difficulty. Such fictitious credit as is thrown around a bank by its national character, may give to its paper a wider range of circulation; but this is only calculated to lead to excessive banking and over issues, without furnishing any corresponding ability in the institution to meet the demands against it.

. . . .

The danger to be apprehended from such an institution, in a political point of view, is not to be overlooked or disregarded. Its friends claim, that it would possess the power of regulating the nine hundred and fifty four local banks, with their capital of three hundred and twenty four millions. Admitting that it would possess this power, what would be the political consequences, if it should act in friendly alliance with the National Executive, and wield this vast money power for political purposes? It is claimed, that the patronage of the National Executive is already too great, and dangerous to public liberty. If we add to the already extended executive patronage the entire money power of this country, controled by one common head, it would, indeed, constitute a mass of power, which would make the patriot tremble for the fate of our free institutions. It is in vain to suppose, that such an institution, after its creation has become a party question, would not be political. We but deceive ourselves, when we suppose it would be otherwise.

The most effectual means within the power of the general government, to provide against the abuses and evils above alluded to, are to be found in the provisions of the law establishing the Independent Treasury. This measure, by separating the funds of the government from the banks, and placing them in the custody of the agents of the people, who are prohibited from using them for private purposes, or speculation, under severe penalties, not only increases the security of the public funds, but withdraws that stimulus to overbanking, which they were calculated to create, while possessed and controled by the banks. The evil most to be feared, being excessive banking, the remedy must be something that will restrain the banks. The Independent Treasury law, although it will have but a partial influence in restraining the banks, and consequently will not remedy the evils of the paper system, only to a limited extent, yet, its general influence on the whole currency of the country, in the course of time, must be beneficial.

. . . .

The fears that some entertain, that by requiring the revenues of the general government to be paid in coin, the precious metals would accumulate in the treasury to an injurious extent, are without foundation. It should not be the policy of the general government to collect more money than may be wanted to defray the expenses of an economical administration. In that case the public money would be received one day and paid out the next. It would not and could not accumulate to any considerable extent. It will be paid out not merely to public officers in the shape of salaries; (this constitutes but a small part of the amount disbursed by the general government;) it will be paid out to our seamen in the navy—to our soldiers in the army—to our laborers employed in erecting fortifications, improving our harbors, building ships, and in the various other public works in which the country may engage. It will be paid out to our farmers for their corn, beef, pork and other articles necessary to supply our army and navy. In this way the gold and silver received and paid out by the government will be diffused through the entire community, increasing every year, until, in the course of time, it will form an every day currency for the people, furnish a more extended specie basis for the banks, and enable the legislatures of the States, with more ease, to confine bank paper to its legitimate objects:—heavy business transactions, and the commercial and exchange operations of the country.

. . . .

It does not unfrequently happen that, when a bank fails, the stockholders, or those who manage its affairs, are largely the gainers. This fraud, with impunity, results from the principle, contained in all our bank charters, of a limited liability. The banks, generally, are authorized to issue three dollars of their own notes for every one dollar of capital paid in; and the capital paid in is all that is liable for the payment of their debts. A bank that may be disposed to act fraudulently, can put out three dollars of its own paper for every one that is liable to be applied to the redemption of its notes in circulation. The banker, by breaking, loses the one dollar of stock, but gains the three that were issued upon it. This may not often occur; but it is sufficient to know that it has occurred, and that it may again take place, to authorize the Legislature to guard against it. This limited liability of the stockholders, not only furnishes an opportunity to commit fraud with impunity, but holds out an inducement to engage in excessive banking. The banks are not restrained in their operations, because they know that if successful, they are the gainers; if unsuccessful, the greater part of the loss may be thrown on the public. The inducement should be the other way. The temptation to commit fraud, or to engage in excessive banking, should be taken from them. This can only be done by increasing the personal responsibility of the stockholders, and placing the banker on the same footing, as to liability for the payment of his debts, with the farmer, merchant, manufacturer, or other citizen. Is there any reason why the whole community should be made liable for the payment of their debts, while the banker should alone be exempt?

. . . .

As the subject of a State Bank is again agitated in the public mind, you may be called upon to consider of this measure. I cannot think that such an institution would be calculated to promote the interest of the public. It would have no advantages over the local banks, unless the state would become a stock holder to the amount of the capital stock, or a considerable portion of it. In order to do this, the state debt would have to be increased to the amount of the stock subscribed by the state. When we shall have finished our public works, now under contract, the state debt, on interest, will exceed sixteen millions. The interest on this, will be yearly over nine hundred thousand dollars. This sum will have to be raised, annually, from the tolls on our public works, and by direct taxation. When paid, the greater portion of it will go direct to England, where the larger portion of our state stock is held. Our state will thus be annually drained of at least half a million of coin to pay the holders of our stock in England. This enormous state debt, which has been accumulating for years, has already become burdensome, and its increase should be arrested. The taxes of the people are already oppressive, and instead of being increased should be diminished. Would it, therefore, be wise policy to swell the state debt eight or ten millions in order to engage in the banking business? and thus increase our state stock in the hands of English stockholders, and, consequently, increase the drain of specie out of the state? Such a policy, in my judgment, is deadly hostile to our true interest.

. . . .

What are the acts of which the banks complain, and which they may call on you at this session to repeal? The first is the act to prohibit the banks from issuing, or putting in circulation, notes under the denomination of five dollars. Is there any necessity for repealing this law? Has it come to this, that the banks are unable to do business, profitably, unless they are permitted to issue small notes? I admit that small notes are the most profitable issues a bank can make. By putting them in circulation at a distant point, many of them are worn out or destroyed, and never returned to the bank for redemption. This is so much clear profit to the bank, and is estimated by experienced bankers to be worth fifteen per cent. But what the bank makes in this way is so much of a dead loss to the public. On a small note circulation of two millions, the banks would make, by the loss and destruction of their notes, fifteen per cent., or three hundred thousand dollars. This would be taken from the community without any consideration, and would be unjust and inequitable; and when the issuing of small notes is resorted to with the view of obtaining this profit, it is a gross fraud on the public.

. . . .

The third act objected to, prohibits the banks from issuing bank paper made payable at any other place than where issued, or payable at a future day, or at any other time than on demand, or which is made payable in bank notes, or any thing other than gold or silver; and it makes all notes which on their face are made payable at a future day, payable on demand. Is there any thing in this act which imposes on the banks improper restrictions? Is it not right and proper, in order to preserve a sound currency, to prohibit the banks from flooding the country with their post notes, payable at a distant day, or notes payable at some obscure place, or in a worthless currency?

The fourth act, and the one of which the banks have complained the most, is generally known as the bank commissioner law. These four acts comprise all the principal legislation of the two last sessions, with the view of reforming the banks and the currency. The last named act provides, among other things, for the appointment of three bank commissioners, whose duty it shall be, at least once in every year, to examine thoroughly every banking institution in the state, and oftener, if necessary to the public safety, and to examine the officers of such institutions under oath, as to their affairs. It requires the officers of each banking institution to publish a monthly statement, showing the true situation and condition of the bank. It provides, further, for instituting judicial proceedings against any bank that shall refuse to redeem its notes in gold and silver for more than thirty days in one year, and points out the mode of closing a bank that has become insolvent, and of securing the assets of such institution for the payment of its debts. All these provisions are intended for the security of the public against the insolvency of banks, and they are such as no bank ought to object to.

. . . .

A strict and rigid enforcement of the laws, now in existence, would go far to remedy existing evils. Many of the banks have disregarded all law, and seem to claim the right of acting as sovereign and independent powers. They have disregarded the law against post notes, evaded that passed against small bills, trampled with impunity on the act creating the board of bank commissioners, and closed their doors against officers appointed by the legislature to examine their condition. In short, they have placed themselves above the law, deranged and vitiated the currency, and now deride the efforts of the legislature to reform existing abuses. It is in vain to pass salutary laws, for the reformation of the banks, and the improvement of the currency, if they are permitted to trample on them with impunity, and point to the consequences of their own violation of law, and total disregard of all existing legal enactments, as an argument to prove the utter futility of all attempts at reform. It is for you, who are the guardians, for the time being, of the public interest, to make suitable provisions for the enforcement of the existing laws against the moneyed corporations of the state. The whole subject is one of great importance, and in which the people have a vital interest, and I commend it to your careful and special consideration.

. . . .

8 Ohio and Manifest Destiny

BETWEEN THE PRESIDENTIAL election of 1844 and the close of the Mexican War in 1848, Ohioans debated the country's destiny of sharing the continent with other powers. Encouraged by a growing national consciousness that was accompanied by an ambitious elitism, they however divided sharply along partisan lines on the issue of expansionism. Each party fostered arguments that would satisfy its following, and each made the love of country its test for party loyalty. In the end, the Democrats worked for a compromise to the slave issue, while the Whigs split and by 1854 were finished as a national political force.

The Whigs in Ohio were not anti-expansionists, but were concerned about where expansion would occur. Oregon was acceptable, and a threatened war with Great Britain was not too high a price to pay for the annexation of free territory to the Union. Expansion into the Southwest, which inherently meant the extension of slavery and the growth of southern political influence at the national level, dampened Whig enthusiasm for more land. On the other hand, the Democrats endorsed American expansion and agreed that the "reoccupation of Oregon and the re-annexation of Texas" would not only maintain a sectional balance but also would ensure a national partisan existence. Whig opposition to both the annexation of Texas and the Mexican War was expressed in Congress, the Ohio General Assembly, and by the Ohio executive in speeches, resolutions, and votes. Ohio Whigs objected to the admission of Texas to the Union because, they argued, it was unconstitutional, it violated treaty commitments with Mexico, and it would precipitate a war with a sister republic. Transcending all of their arguments was the issue of slavery. The acquisition of territory in the Southwest, either through annexation or conquest, meant eventual expansion of the power of the Southern slaveholders.

Ohio Whigs controlled both the general assembly and the state's executive during the troubled 1840s. Once war was declared against Mexico in 1846, Whig opposition to the national Democratic party and to the national administration became increasingly vocal. Just as opposition to national foreign policy had surfaced in Ohio through the Federalists during the crisis of 1812, the Whigs spearheaded criticism of the Polk administration and its conduct of the war. National policy was denounced by the Whig-controlled general assembly and by two Whig governors, Mordecai Bartley and William Bebb. The high tide of Whig opposition to the war was reached on February 11, 1847, when United States Senator Thomas Corwin, a Whig from Lebanon, Ohio, synthesized Whig sentiment in what was probably the greatest antiwar speech given in the Senate.

Even while battling the Whigs in state and local elections, the Ohio Democrats were unable to find peace with the Polk administration. Although their opposition certainly never came close to the types of criticism leveled by the Whigs, the Ohio Democrats, while supporting the objectives of national expansion, believed they had been betrayed by Polk. Expansion was to have been a double-fisted thrust, equal in both the North and the South. The promise of the "re-occupation of Oregon" by the national party was accepted by Ohio Democrats at face value. When Polk instead offered the 49th parallel as a compromise line to England, William Allen, who as Ohio's senior senator and chairman of the Senate Foreign Relations Committee had demanded the 54°40' line, resigned his chairmanship in protest. However, disappointment with the national administration neither prevented the Ohio Democrats from supporting Polk's policy during the Mexican War nor thwarted their enthusiasm in branding the Whigs as the party of treason.

The issue of expansion as it affected and was affected by the slavery question was far too great for the Whig party to endure. Founded as a party based more upon its opposition to Democratic rule than on solidifying principles, the Whigs could not find a solution to the agonizing question of what to do about slavery and still remain a national party. The party did not survive the next half decade. On the other hand, the Democrats, with solid support in the South and comfortable strength in the North, sought solutions to the slavery question that were acceptable to its factions and would protect its national image.

Not Texas

SENATE COMMITTEE MAJORITY

The Standing Committee on the Union, to whom was referred that part of the inaugural address of the Governor which relates to the annexation of the republic of Texas to the United States, having considered that subject, now submit the following report—

That the United States is a nation composed of independent States, confederated together for the purposes of mutual protection and convenience. This is proven as well by the history of the country as by the character of the existing compact by which the several States are associated. The government of the United States is one of delegated and limited powers, emanating from the several States which compose the Union, and having no authority except such as has been clearly delegated by the constitution. This may justly be considered the articles of co-partnership, by which the partners, the several States, have agreed that certain affairs of general concernment shall be conducted.

If this exposition of the structure of the General Government be correct—and of its correctness the committee entertain no doubt—it follows, as a necessary consequence, that the Federal Government have no power to form a union with a foreign State, whether great or small, without the consent of all the States now associated together; for none will contend that the power is conferred by the constitution, either on the national Executive, or on Congress, or on both united to form such an union.

A connection with a foreign independent State would emphatically constitute a new firm; one with which the members of the existing firm have never agreed to be connected—a new and different nation.

The fact that Texas is now an inconsiderable State, a country containing a small population—that this population will be merged in the great body of the American people so as scarcely to be known or felt, forms an argument which addresses itself solely to the question of expediency, and in no wise to the constitutionality of the measure.—If the General Government have the power to form a national amalgamation with the republic of Texas, they have the same power to contract a similar union with the Russian Empire, and thus to permit the United States to be swallowed up and lost in the vast ocean of her boundless domain.

From "Report of the Majority of the Standing Committee on the Union Relative to the Annexation of Texas," Ohio General Assembly, Senate, *Journal*, (Appendix), (1845), pp. 12-16.

It is admitted that in the case of the purchase of Louisiana from France, and of Florida from Spain, territory was incorporated with the United States, not previously included within her boundaries.— The peculiar circumstance which governed each of these cases, the obvious necessity of obtaining possession of these provinces, especially of the former, in order to secure to a large proportion of the United States free access to the ocean, through channels obviously designed by nature for that purpose, were such as to illicit at least the tacit assent of all the States then composing the Union. These cases, dissimilar in other respects from the one now under consideration, can not be cited as precedents to justify the proposed annexation of Texas, in opposition to the expressed will of more than one of the United States.

The State of Ohio, then, as one of the members of the present confederacy, has the undoubted right to protest against the admission of the republic of Texas into the United States; nor can such a measure be lawfully consummated without her consent. Ought she to consent to such an union? Your committee believe she ought not, and for the following reasons:

Firstly: Texas is claimed by Mexico as part of her territory, and this claim of Mexico has been unequivocally acknowledged on the part of the United States by solemn treaty. While Mexico still asserts her claim to this territory, the United States cannot extend their jurisdiction over it, without subjecting them, and justly, too, to the imputation of grasping at foreign territory, at the expense of their plighted faith. Nor will the fact that the inhabitants of Texas have successfully asserted their independence, absolve the United States from the merited censure of the civilized world, so long as it is known that the severance of Texas from the republic of Mexico was brought about by citizens of the United States, many, if not all, of whom had left their native land with that avowed intention, and that our government had taken no efficient measures to prevent such movements.

Secondly: A state of actual war now exists between Mexico and Texas, the former still seeking to recover, by force of arms, dominion over her revolted province. The annexation of Texas to the United States while this condition of things continues to exist, necessarily involves this nation in a war with Mexico. Although the weakness of that power may prevent all apprehension of danger on our part, this very circumstance will deepen the stain upon our national honor, for it will be said, at least with the semblance of truth, that we rob the weak, while we fear to provoke the strong. It is pusilanimous to shrink from a righteous and necessary war, however powerful the nation with which we are doomed to engage; but nations, as well as men, may well fear to engage in an unjust contest, however weak their opponent.

Thirdly: Texas owes a large and unascertained debt. If Texas is received into the Union, this debt must be paid by the United States. International law—common honesty requires it. If there can be found no warrant in the constitution for the assumption of the debt of a State by the United States, there surely can be found no such warrant for assuming the debts of foreign nations. Nor ought we to be misled by the fallacious expectation that the unappropriated lands of Texas will remunerate the United States for the moneys advanced to pay her debts. There is too much reason to believe that all the lands within her acknowledged boundaries have already been covered by grants, many of them more than once—that so far from there being a surplussage of land to satisfy these grants, there will be found a great deficiency. That while there will be no lack of certificates of the public debt of Texas, while there is a dollar of money in the Treasury of the United States to satisfy them, there will be found grants and patents sufficient to cover all the territory belonging to Texas, and much of the unappropriated lands now belonging to the United States.

But, lastly: The State of Ohio, which justly prides itself upon being a land of freedom, where equal rights are secured to every citizen, where the elective franchise is guarantied to every white male citizen of full age, where no property qualification is required or permitted to exist, is bound, in justice to herself, to enter her solemn protest against the admission of new territory, to be formed into States, where slavery is to prevail, and where the relative political power of the master is to be increased in proportion to the number of his fellow men whom he holds in bondage, and whom the law recognizes as his property.

Your committee disclaim all wish and all intention to interfere with the institution of slavery, as it now exists in the United States; or with the right of the slaveholding States to count three fifths of their slaves, in determining their share of political power and influence in the councils of the nation. We are aware that this concession, on the part of the free States, was necessary, in order to effect a permanent union of the States; nor are we prepared to say that this union was bought at too dear a price. But we cannot shut our eyes to the fact that the political weight of each citizen of a slaveholding State is increased by this rule of representation, both in Congress and in the election of the national Executive, until, in some instances, it is double that of a citizen of a free State.

. . . .

To this inequality, so far as it now exists, and so far as we are bound to extend it, by the admission of new States to be formed out of territory now belonging to the United States, where the right to hold slaves is guarantied to the inhabitants, we are bound to submit;

for the people of Ohio are among the last to violate their plighted faith, or refuse to abide by a contract fairly made. But we may rightfully object to the admission of new territory, out of which, either in whole or in part, States are to be formed, whose citizens shall have an unequal and undue weight, when compared with the citizens of free States, on all national questions, in consequence of their property in slaves.

Your committee cannot look upon slavery otherwise than a great political as well as moral evil, a calamity in which the free as well as the bound participate; nor are its baneful effects confined to those portions of our country where it actually exists. If the vigor, the healthy action of one part of the body politic are in any degree paralyzed, the whole body will in some way or other, and to some extent, feel its effects. Every part of the Union is therefore interested in preventing the extension of this evil. Let us not deceive ourselves with the belief that an extension of the limits of slavery will have no tendency to increase the number of slaves, or perpetuate the existence of the institution.

. . . .

Your committee are aware that it has been said that the possession of Texas is necessary to enable the United States more easily and effectually to defend their territory. This assumption seems to the committee so preposterous as scarcely to merit serious refutation; how any territory can be made more defensible by extending the line to be defended, by abandoning one provided with natural defences, upon which a defensive force can be rapidly concentrated, and easily sustained, and assuming another presenting fewer obstructions to the advance of a hostile force, and much greater one to that of its defenders, is, to your committee, wholly incomprehensible. Nothing, in their opinion, could have drawn from the advocates of the measure, such an argument but their utter inability to adduce others, having even the semblance of reason.

The extension of the limits over which slavery is to spread its blighting effects, and of the power and political influence of the slaveholding states are undoubtedly the true motives which stimulate to the adoption of this measure. Avarice and a spirit of speculation have but their powerful aid in those sections of the Union where the slaveholding interest does not prevail, party feeling has been to a great extent, made subservient to the same end, and an influence has thus been created, which it seems difficult to withstand.

The General Assembly have once, with entire unanimity, in behalf of the people of Ohio, protested against the proposed measure, and this protest, so far as the same can be done through the ballot box, has been approved by the people, and now, although in danger of being borne down by a combination too powerful to withstand, when our interests are about to be sacrificed—our just influence in the councils of the nation diminished, the moral feeling of our citizens outraged, and our character, as an integral part of the nation, disgraced, we trust that the courage again to express our disapprobation of the measure, and enter our protest against its consummation, will not be found wanting.

ALFRED KELLEY,
Chairman.

Expand in the Southwest

HOUSE COMMITTEE MINORITY

The minority place reluctantly their opinions in opposition to those of the majority. . . . They look upon the arguments and sentiments expressed in the report and resolutions, as improper, and unfit to be adopted by an Ohio Legislature. . . . They rest upon an entire misconception of the motives which prompted a majority of the people of the United States, to sanction the annexation of Texas, and they are unjust to the largest portion of those, who, by their votes sustained that important measure. It really seems to us a great stretch of propriety, to class a majority of the people with stock-jobbers and land speculators, when there are no facts to sustain the imputation. Equally unjust is it, to impute to them a desire to extend and perpetuate slavery, and the minority of your committee think it no more than right, since the majority has so entirely misconceived those motives, to spread before you, what appears to them to have been the true motive of that decision.

One of the first was a patriotic desire to extend the blessings of our free institutions as far as possible, by reincorporating into the Union, a territory alienated from it by misdirected diplomacy, and thus to fulfill the treaty stipulations on the purchase of Louisiana.

From "The Minority of the Committee on Federal Relations, To Whom Were Referred Certain Resolutions on the Annexation of Texas," Ohio General Assembly, House of Representatives, *Journal*, (1844), pp. 114-120.

The second motive was to fortify and strengthen, in a military point of view, the present limits of our territory.

The third was to prevent the designs of a foreign government upon that territory.

And the fourth was to save the people of Texas, sons and daughters of our own soil, from the horrors of a war with a semi-barbarous people.

The extension of slavery had no weight in the minds of the people. The people of the United States would have given an almost unanimous decision in favor of annexation, if slavery did not exist in Texas. The people have through their government decided so often, that the Constitution warrants the admission of new territory into the Union, that it really appears to the minority of the Committee strange that the state of Ohio is to make a party to a protest, which is not only based upon wrong grounds, but whose language and sentiments are so obviously at variance with those of the people of Ohio.

We deem it unnecessary to quote the article of the Constitution, having reference to that subject. That article is so plain, that it needs no implied construction, especially when taken in connection with the fact, that an amendment to that article was negatived in the Convention for the formation of the Constitution, the object of which was to limit the formation of new States, to territory then within the limits of the United States. Every President, and almost every Congress have since, in the most positive manner, through their official action, sanctioned this construction. The treaties for the purchase of Louisiana and Florida were ratified by almost unanimous votes, and the Louisiana treaty was ratified but a few years after the adoption of the Constitution, when its provisions and the discussions upon them were yet fresh in the minds of the people. . . . In short, they ought to settle the constitutional power of the General Government to acquire new territory. The government must either be entrusted with all powers necessary and inherent to all sovereign powers, or else it must be perfectly useless in its most important functions.

. . . .

The constitutional question seem, to the minority of the committee, as decided, and the only question to be asked is, is the annexation of Texas essentially necessary to the prosperity of the whole? The minority of your committee think it is. By the admission of Texas into the Union, we regain a territory unsurpassed for its fertility, which was originally included in the Louisiana purchase, and which is necessary to us for a proper defence of our Southwestern frontier. The fabrics of our people will command a new and extensive market, the waters of the Mississippi as originally designed by Mr. Jefferson, will all be within our limits, and are not these considerations imperiously demanding the annexation?

. . . .

What are the objections urged against it? First, in importance, stands the objection, that it will extend and perpetuate slavery. The minority of your committee beg leave to differ with the majority upon the future consequences likely to flow from annexation. An allwise Providence has hidden from us a view into the future; all predictions as to the consequences arising from the measure under consideration are, therefore, problematical, and the views of the majority, as well as those of the minority, rest upon the same basis. They derive their origin and their hues, no doubt, from the relative position they occupy. The majority has thought proper to present the *dark* side of the picture; be it the lot of the minority to present the *bright.* At the time of the purchase of Louisiana, the same gloomy forebodings were indulged in—the true motives of the government and the people were then, as now, misrepresented, and, strange as it may appear, almost the very identical words used by Governor Slade, and adopted by the majority of your committee, were used by a prominent member of the federal party in opposition to the purchase and admission of Louisiana. It was then claimed to be a virtual dissolution of the Union—it was to absolve the dissenting States from their moral obligations to the Union, and to give them the right to separate from it amicably if they can—forcibly if they must. The prophecies of those days, experience, the best teacher, has proved to be fallacious. The United States being the first to condemn the slave trade as piracy, and Louisiana being thus early, before its full developement, placed within the jurisdiction of the United States, there are now less slaves within its limits than there would have been without the admission.

. . . .

The annexation of Texas will not make one slave more; on the contrary the importations from the West Indies, and elsewhere, must cease when under our jurisdiction. The slave populations of Kentucky, Virginia, Maryland, Delaware, Missouri and Arkansas, will be materially decreased. That decrease will facilitate emancipation. Sooner or later those States will emancipate, and the strict geographical line between the free and slave States will have been passed. Slave property, in the other States, will become unprofitable, and self-interest, that most potent of all arguments, will, instead of as now,

silencing the voice of right and justice, awaken feelings of philanthropy before which slavery must fall.

. . . .

Man proposes—God disposes; and may we not trust to that
Providence which has lately so signally changed the course of our
government; which has so often given us the right men and the right
measures at the proper moment—may we not safely say, that that
Providence will be found on the side of humanity and justice.

The danger of a war with Mexico seems also to haunt the minds
of the majority. The American people dread not war—they justly,
though, dread an *unjust* war; and the question is not whether war
will follow annexation, but it is whether the war would be a just one.
Would we then violate the good faith we owe Mexico by annexing
Texas? Plainly not. Texas is not now, nor was it ever, *owned* by
Mexico. It was even up to the period when it assumed its rank among
the nations of the earth, a free and independent State, bound to
Mexico only by the common ties of the constitution of 1824.
Mexico belonged as much to Texas as Texas to Mexico, and the
majority of the committee should be the last to place Texas skill
with Mexico, when they assert, in their report and resolutions, the
principle, that a violation of the bond of Union gives one of the
States a right to secede. If a violation gives that right, how much
more its entire destruction, as was the case with the constitution of
1824. The people of Texas have but followed our own example in
shaking off a connection which had become irksome and despotic.
They, like ourselves, acted upon that first principle of our government, that the right to govern rests upon the consent of the
governed. The independence of Texas dates, like our own, from their
declaration of independence. It has been acknowledged by ourselves
as well as other powers. There was as much violation of public faith
in that acknowledgment as there is in treating with Texas. It is an old
established principle that we must regard the government in fact and
not the one by claim. Texas is irrevocably lost to Mexico, and the
claim that we violate public faith with a foreign power because we
treat with a part that has separated from it, would lead to the absurd
idea that we were bound to guarantee Mexico her territory. The
present government of France might as well charge us with a violation of public faith, because we purchased Louisiana of Napoleon
and not the Bourbons.

The annexation of Texas is opposed by the majority, in the
abstract; and even "without war and without dishonor," they would
not support the measure. The same seems to be the case with regard
to the public debt of Texas. That debt would be tenfold repaid from
the public domain which would be acquired. Since when has the

party opposed to the annexation of Texas acquired such an aversion to public debts? Public debts have always been regarded by them as public blessings; and even now, in this State, they are soon to form a basis for bank financiering and stockjobbing operations. The whig party would willingly assume the public debt of Texas, if only Texas and her debt could be separated. It is not then, the minority of your committee may safely say, the public debt of Texas which is opposed, but Texas itself. But what shall the minority do with the argument of the majority, where they say, that Texas being an independent state or a revolted province, it makes the case a different one from the purchase of Louisiana? It really seems hardly necessary to refute the argument, for it certainly is the same, whether Louisiana was purchased of Louisiana or of France. The treaty was *with* a foreign power, and the nature of the acquisition is not changed whether it is acquired from the receded part or the original government. And even if there is a difference, that difference is favorable to the present case. Louisiana continued, at the time of the purchase, a different people, with different laws, different language, and a different history from ours.

There remains, then, only one more objection to be considered—it is the danger to be apprehended by too great an extension of territory. The minority of your committee, while they regard some of the other objections as mere sham objections, feel disposed to regard this, as well as the slave argument, as really forming an objection in the minds of the majority. The party to which the majority of your committee belong, has always been distinguished for its opposition to the extension of the influences of our institutions. Here the true distinction between the democratic and the whig party is distinctly brought into view. A democrat always desires the extension of freedom. He would, with an open heart, embrace within its benign influence, every human being, if compatible with our position. A federalist, an aristocrat, a whig, or call him what you please, always wishes to circumscribe the limits of freedom. The federalists of old opposed, instinctively, the purchase of Louisiana, because the circle of freedom and happiness was getting too large for them. The same sentiment has forced the whig party now into opposition to Texas. But how futile have proved all attempts to impede the proud destiny of our Union. Unmoved by their sophistry, the ship of state has prosperously proceeded in its career. Little men, with contracted minds, may be awestruck at the majesty of the proceeding; they may say "hold, enough,"—they may stand aghast at the rapid and steady increase of our resources; but still our nation's course must be onward. The territory belonging to the United States at the formation of the Constitution, is fast filling up. Fifty years ago our own State was but a wilderness. Who even dreamt it would so soon occupy so proud a position? In half a century we have doubled the number of States, doubled our population, and tripled our resources; and for such a people the politician in his chamber would circumscribe limits. The twenty six States now in the Union are now closer united than the original thirteen States; because, in the valley of the Mississippi, all are interested. Yea, they are even, in point of distance, closer together than the original States. Steamboats, railroads, and the inventive genius of our people, has annihilated distance, and New Orleans is now nearer Portland than Baltimore was fifty years ago. Texas was once our own—bungling diplomacy lost it! Shall we not regain it? We shall not only want it for our growing population, but we shall want Oregon besides. The destiny of this Union is so plain, that every attentive mind will have perceived it. *It is to comprise within its limits* the North American continent. That our Union is capable to sustain that territorial extent, the minority of your committee entertain no doubt. There are, no doubt, difficulties to be overcome, for no nation is without them; but who would shrink with childish fear from the future? There always are men who look with gloom to the future. Such men are fit representatives in Hartford conventions—fit speculators about the balance of power; fit sticklers for strict construction when it suits them, and latitudinarians in every thing else. The minority of your committee have no such fears. They believe our free institutions capable of incompassing all within its limits that the good sense of the people will place within them.

These are some of the reasons and the conclusions which have compelled the minority to differ from the majority. In conclusion, the minority would once more appeal to the sense of propriety of this House, whether it is right to class the democratic citizens of Ohio, the Congress, President of the United States, as well as the distinguished individual about, by the free choice of a free people, assuming the office of Chief Magistrate, with stock gamblers, land sharks, and slavemongers. They appeal also to their sense of patriotism, whether they will, from prejudices, be led on to an erroneous construction of the Constitution, to exparte decisions upon collateral issues, and to an unhallowed attack upon the Union. If they do, they may rest assured that the people of Ohio will not support them. Their protest will fall, being unsupported by the people, to the ground; for the people of Ohio are as much opposed to northern nullification as to southern. The blood of the people of Ohio will flow, when necessary, for the *preservation* of this Union—never for its destruction. They may be opposed to Texas; they no doubt regard slavery as an evil, but they look upon it as temporary, which is not decreased by compressing it in a limited space. They require time upon that question; they will not be hurried into a position separate from other States; and they will, in the language of Harrison, *"execrate the hand and the head that could devise and execute a scheme so productive of a calamity so awful."*

All of which is respectfully submitted.
CHARLES REEMELIN,
DAVID H. SWARTZ.

Oregon

DAVID BRINKERHOFF

Mr. Brinkerhoff next obtained the floor, and addressed the committee.

. . . .

Throughout the whole course of this debate here, sir, and in all the discussions on this Oregon question, which have occupied the public press throughout the country, one gratifying fact has manifested itself, and that is, the entire unanimity of Congress and of the country as to the validity of the American title to Oregon.

From the venerable gentleman from Massachusetts, [Mr. Adams,] who has, with so much spirit and energy, advocated giving notice, to the gentleman from South Carolina, [Mr. Rhett,] who with such impassioned vehemence opposed it—on every hand, and upon all sides, it is not only admitted, but insisted, that the American title to Oregon is "clear and unquestionable," indicating that, whatever may be the consequences to arise from our action here, we shall present to the country and to the world a united, an unbroken front.

. . . .

I may say that when, for all the purposes of this debate, it is admitted that Oregon is ours, we may make ourselves easy as

From David Brinkerhoff, "Speech," *Congressional Globe*, Vol. XV, 29th Congress, 1st Session, January 14, 1846, pp. 203-205.

to the consequences that are to follow from the assertion of our title; for, whatever the consequences may be, we, who take the responsibility of that action, may fall back, with consciences quiet and easy, upon the consciousness of having been actuated by a sense of duty, and by a regard to the rights and the honor of the country.

I go for the notice, sir. I have all along been of the opinion that the notice should be given; but I will say that I am extremely gratified to find myself in this position, in the company with which I am surrounded. I was extremely happy to learn, from the report of the debate on this floor, (for I had not the pleasure of listening to the gentleman,) that the venerable gentleman from Massachusetts had taken that position. Firm as are my own convictions, I confess I am glad to fortify them by so high authority; and I am glad, further, that the reproach which had begun so extensively to be insinuated through the country, that all this movement is the result of the action of hair-brained, hot-headed young men, trying to play the statesman, has been removed by the stand which that gentleman has taken upon that question. It is not these hair-brained, hot-headed young men alone that advocate this measure. It has the advocacy of sage experience—of a man, who literally stands in the midst of posterity, whose life is in the past, whose only ambition is not for the future, but for the correct discharge of those responsibilities which attend the close of human existence.

But although it is admitted throughout that the American title to Oregon "is clear and unquestionable," yet the fact of the joint convention of 1827 exists. We have by the terms of that convention admitted Great Britain to a kind of partnership in it; she has a recognised tenancy there which can only be terminated by one year's notice; and the question is not as to the original propriety and policy of this convention. It exists; and the question is, Shall we dissolve this partnership? Shall we get rid of this tenancy, by giving the other party notice to quit? It is said this is a warlike measure. But I repeat what others have said who have spoken before me, that I cannot discover anything of that character in it. We dissolve the partnership, sir; but we do it in strict conformity with the stipulations of the articles of partnership; we give the tenant notice to quit, but it is in accordance with the express provisions of the lease. So far from violating any treaty—which everybody knows would be a cause of war—we are, in giving notice, acting in strict conformity with the provisions of the treaty, and are carrying out a measure, foreseen, anticipated, provided for by the treaty which is to be abrogated. It is not then a warlike, it is a treaty measure, a peace measure, and nothing else.

. . . .

The gentleman from South Carolina, [Mr. Rhett,] in attempting to frighten us and the country from the vigorous exertion of our rights in Oregon, tells us that the cross of St. George waves over thirty British forts in Oregon, and that when you assert these rights you must tear down the cross and place our flag there in its stead. A strange argument this for a gentleman to use who advocates the continuance of this convention! This has occurred under the existence of this convention; it was while this convention has been in force that these forts have been planted, erected, and maintained; and if twenty years have resulted in the erection and manning of thirty British semi-military posts there, while we have not one, what are we to expect from the further continuance of it?

But, sir, there is another reason why this notice should be given. Our people are in Oregon; they demand to be protected there. They have gone there without law; they have none, except such as they have temporarily established. They ask the extension of our laws over them; they ask to be protected in "life, liberty, and the pursuit of" property and "happiness"—to be protected by us. They have hearts of true allegiance towards us; and we cannot deny that request without alienating their affections from us. Can we? I ask any gentleman, whatever his opinion on this subject, to answer me this question: can you continue to retain the allegiance of those settlers in Oregon, if you refuse to protect them? The Hudson Bay Company—we have it officially—are already urging these settlers to set up for themselves, and to declare themselves independent alike of us and of every other nation. Let us delay a little longer, and that appeal will acquire force.

. . . .

The question, then, must be settled, matters must be brought to a crisis—not necessarily or even probably to a warlike crisis, but to a crisis. It must be met. Great Britain is monopolizing the whole trade of that country. Her representative there is the Hudson Bay Company. She is ready to adopt the acts of that corporation, for corporations are the favorite instruments of British aggression, and for the extension of her power. The Hudson Bay Company, then, and the British Government, are, for all the purposes of this debate, one and identical. They have monopolized the trade of the country; they have subsidized the Indians; the half-breeds are under their control; they have military possessions north of the Columbia river, not only between the Columbia river and the parallel of forty-nine degrees, which is the territory actually in dispute, but they have brought down their military posts to within thirty miles of the southern boundary of the American claim in Oregon.

. . . .

"But," say gentlemen, "all this will result in war." War! By whom? By the United States? We begin no war; we declare no war; we propose no war; we deprecate all war; but we assert our rights— rights which we have demonstrated, so far as diplomacy can do it. Great Britain has taken military possession of the country, alike open to us and to her; and if war come from the assertion of our rights, we will not make it. I deny the position of the gentleman from South Carolina, that the war—if war come—will be a war of aggression on our part. It is not so. It would be a war of aggression on her part; and on her would rest the responsibility; upon her the judgment of God and the anathemas of the world.

What do gentlemen on the other side propose to do? The gentle- man from Massachusetts [Mr. Winthrop] has hinted at arbitration. Very well; cannot we arbitrate as well after the notice as before? But I, for one, do not propose to submit the question to arbitration. Is it possible for a crowned head to be impartial between a brother monarch on the one hand and a Republic on the other? Doubtful, sir. But suppose it possible; where will you look for an impartial arbitrator? Louis Philippe, regardless of the sympaties of his people, and intent only on the perpetuation of his dynasty on the throne of France, is sacrificing the dignity of his nation in the cultivation of a "cordial understanding" with her ancient enemy, for the purpose of securing her influence in favor of that dynasty on his own demise. Austria and Prussia, dreading the ambition of France on the west, and the colossal power of Russia on the north, are pursuing the same policy; and Russia herself, having large territory on the northwest coast of America, cannot be impartial, for the reason that she must greatly prefer the British fur-trader and the *Bois brule* for her neighbor, rather than the active, enterprising, indefatigable, and multiplying Yankee. The secondary Powers of Europe are but pup- pets in the hands of the five great Powers; and the Republics of Mexico and South America are in convulsions. I know of no arbiter, therefore, to which the adjustment of this question could be safely committed. We once tried this project of arbitration, sir, in the case of the northeastern boundary; and the award of the King of the Netherlands presented a decision so utterly regardless of treaty stipulations, and so absurd in itself, as to be instantly rejected. We, sir, are ourselves the best guardians of our own rights.

The Committee on Military Affairs, of which I have the honor to be a member, reported a few days since a bill for the raising of two regiments of riflemen, (not mounted;) and on all sides of the House I heard the exclamation, "I go for no such measure." That is the spirit that prevails here. It always will prevail. You never will prepare for war unless war is upon you; and you may postpone it "from July to eternity," and still war will find us unprepared. Shall we therefore

surrender our rights? Shall we therefore expect disaster and defeat?
No. We may experience it as first; but the recuperative energies of
our people, animated by their undying love of country, their attachment to its institutions, their determination to maintain inviolate
every foot of our soil—having within them a burning hatred of the
tyrannies of the Old World, from the galling bonds of which their
forefathers freed themselves—will be sufficient to meet and to bear
us triumphantly out of any emergencies. But that we shall be
technically prepared for war until war comes, no man can believe. We
shall therefore gain nothing, in this respect, by postponement—
nothing at all.

But, said the gentleman from Virginia, [Mr. Hunter,] before you
think of war, you must think of tracking Great Britain with a stream
of fire and blood around the world; you must meet her on every sea,
and in all her possessions—all her colonies, from Aden to the Ionian
Isles, from India to God knows where. We must exhaust and conquer
British power everywhere, before we can expect to take or to keep
either Oregon or Canada. Well, now, I believe in no such doctrine as
that. History teaches no such doctrine; it leads us to no such
conclusion. Great Britain deprived France of all her colonial possessions; she left Napoleon without a solitary colony on the face of the
globe; she confined him to the continent of Europe; and at that very
time he rode triumphant and irresistible over that continent, and
trampled in the dust the subsidized allies of the imperial pirate. Why?
Because there were all his resources. Great Britain may keep her
Chusan, her India, her Mediterranean possessions; she may keep them
all. Does it follow that we cannot beat her on this continent? It does
not; for here are our resources, and hers are distant.

"But," say gentlemen, "this battle for Oregon, if it come at all, is
to be fought in Canada." I believe it; and I am glad that Great Britain
has, in the present conjuncture, an assailable point here, where we
can reach her. And the gentleman takes especial pains to arouse the
jealousy of western men by telling us that "we will get Canada, and
then Oregon must be given up." Now, does any man suppose that the
present Administration, or that any Administration possible, holding
Canada as a conquered pledge, would give up Oregon? I do not. I do
not believe that there is a man in the United States, capable of being
elected President—or of getting there either by "accident," as has
been said of one, or "by the grace of God"—who would be either
such a fool or such a knave. It is impossible. Take Canada, and
Oregon would fall into our hands as a matter of course. But I do not
apprehend any difficulty of this kind. I believe that Great Britain
withholds an amicable settlement because she is satisfied with her
present position. Abrogate the present convention; throw your laws
over your citizens in that territory, and manifest a disposition to

assert and maintain your rights there, and then she will come up to the work of negotiation and settlement in earnest. She is vulnerable, and she knows it, as well as we. War would bring her calamities as great as it would be to us, and greater. We can live without her: she cannot without us. We can do without her manufactures, and have none of her raw material; she depends upon our raw material for her manufactures; it is the very breath of her existence, and without it her people would die from starvation. Where is our fear of war? I have none; and yet I am no advocate for war. God knows, I appreciate its horrors as keenly as any man that lives; for my very earliest recollections are of the scenes war brings—the tears of the young wife, of the mother, of the sister; the partings which break young hearts. These I remember, and I have no wish, as God is my judge, to see them repeated. But yet, looking war calmly in the face, I say, "Be just and fear not." I know the consequences which may result, *perhaps,* (only perhaps, sir)—I know, and I should deprecate the consequences which may perhaps result from the vigorous assertion of American rights. War, if it should be the result, would bring with it the destruction of trade, heavy taxation, heavy losses, the necessity of personal services. You and I, perhaps, might be called to leave the peaceful walks of civil life, and to participate in the hardships and the dangers of the camp and of the tented field. What then? Are we Americans? Are we the descendants of men cotemporary with the youth of the venerable gentleman from Massachusetts? or are we the cowardly, craven wretches, that would not dare to do what our feeble colonies—altogether not equal in strength to the single State of New York at this moment—did to assert and maintain our rights? I think not. That is not the spirit of the people I have the honor to represent. I have not them before me, but I have in my room, resolutions deliberately adopted by a recent convention of that part of the people of Ohio with whom I act politically, declaring the expectations they have of the action of their representatives here, for the vigorous maintenance of our rights to Oregon, and pledging "their lives, their fortunes, and their sacred honor" (such is the language used) to sustain them. Sir, we do not want war, but if we must have it, we would a great deal rather fight Great Britain than some other Powers, for we do not love her. We hear much said about the ties of our common language, of our common origin, and our common recollections, binding us together. But I say we do not love Great Britain at all; at least my people do not, and I do not.

War with Mexico

MORDECAI BARTLEY

Since the last session of the General Assembly the people of the United States have become involved in a sanguinary war with the Republic of Mexico, attended with a loss of life and treasure and that train of calamities incident to a war with a foreign nation. The unfortunate events which have led to this conflict it is not my purpose to discuss, or even to notice in this communication. It is a subject of regret that this collision of arms with the people of a sister Republic has occurred; occupying with us, as they do, the soil of the new world, and in whose protracted and arduous struggle for the establishment of their liberties on the principles of our own government we have heretofore felt a deep interest. The enlightened friends of liberty and humanity had, for some years, indulged the hope that they had found in the liberal and free institutions of America, a fabric of civil government capable of being conducted on the most enlightened and elevated principles of philanthropy and christianity, securing a safe protection to the rights and liberty of every citizen, and affording an asylum, a place of refuge, to the unfortunate of other countries, from the oppressions and devastating wars resulting from their political systems. The belief was entertained that the humane and enlightened public sentiment of this age would soon conduce to the amicable adjustment of all the disputes and controversies of nations, consistent even with the most refined sense of honor, through the intervention of arbitrations and international adjudications; that those restless elements of ambition and jealousy which have so long kept mankind in a state of hostile commotion, might be overcome and brought into submission by an elevated tone of moral sentiment, without a resort to the cruelties of warfare. But existing circumstances threaten disappointment to these hopes and anticipations of the philanthropist. It is evident that we are now approximating great and important events which may exercise a controlling influence over the future destiny of our country. It becomes the true friends of civil liberty, and the improvement of the condition of man, to look with a vigilant and scrutinizing eye to the consequences and enduring influence of the great events which are beginning to open upon us.

On the 20th day of May last, I received through the War Department, a requisition from the President of the United States for three regiments of volunteer Infantry or Riflemen for the service of the

From Mordecai Bartley, "Message," *Ohio Executive Documents*, (1847), pp. 5-8.

United States, in the pending war with the Republic of Mexico. This call of the President was made in obedience to the act of 13th May, 1846, which had passed both branches of Congress, by an almost unanimous vote. The standing forces of the United States then engaged in the war, were believed to be in imminent peril; and the national defence near the seat of war was supposed to require immediate assistance from the volunteer militia of the States. Under the high responsibilities imposed on me, I did not consider myself at liberty to disregard this call upon the patriotism of the State. However much the existence of the war may be deplored, and however great the difference of opinion about the unfortunate events which led to it, when the State was duly called upon, under the authority of the constitution and laws of the United States, for military aid, the solemn injunctions of duty imposed upon me as the Executive officer of the State, as well as every dictate of patriotism, imperatively demanded, as I considered, prompt and energetic action on my part to comply with the call, in the true meaning and spirit of the constitution. If, when a war be actually existing between the United States and a foreign nation and duly recognized by a law of Congress, a State, when called upon by the national authorities, be at liberty to disregard the injunctions of the constitution and judge for itself as to the necessity and expediency of the war, either to withhold its assistance from the United States or to afford only a faltering, unwilling and ineffectual aid, the supremacy of our system of government must soon be at an end, and the constitutional muniments of our national defence prove unavailing. When the emergency of a war with a foreign nation is actually existing, no superficial considerations of temporary inconvenience or pecuniary sacrifice should prevent the performance of those high duties of patriotism which each State of the national confederacy, as well as every citizen of the Republic, owes to the country and to the cause of civil liberty.

Upon the receipt of this call made by the President, prompt and efficient measures were taken to raise the volunteer military force required from this State; and on the 17th day of June, 1846, I delivered over to the authority of the United States, under the command of Brig. Gen. Wool, of the United States Army, three regiments of volunteer troops, duly organized as required by law. These three regiments consisted of thirty full companies, composed chiefly of young men of high promise, whose public spirit and patriotic devotion to the cause of their country is a just ground of pride and gratification to every citizen of the State. They have, upon a sudden call of their country, separated themselves from their homes, their business and their friends, and gone into a distant country to face all the casualties and hardships of a military campaign, in an unfavorable climate and against an enemy long inured to warfare. In every emergency of the service, the Ohio Volunteers will fully sustain the honor of the State and, I doubt not, be found capable of the noblest feats of valor and enterprise.

In collecting and embodying these troops, in subsisting and transporting them to the place of general rendezvous at Cincinnati, and in furnishing them with some essential materials for tents, camp equipage, &c., a very considerable expenditure of money was necessarily incurred. A prompt and faithful compliance with the call of the National Government for volunteers, made this expenditure unavoidable. The call was sudden, and the people of the State had not in anticipation prepared themselves for the emergencies of military life. It was not practicable to collect and organize the volunteer companies and transport them to the general encampment near Cincinnati, without the payment of their necessary incidental expenses; and even then, the volunteers who were separating themselves from their private pursuits and all the attachments of home, were subjected to inconveniencies and difficulties, before they reached Cincinnati, to which our people are but little accustomed.

The Government of the United States has failed thus far to perform its duty in paying this expenditure or refunding the money advanced. The subsistence alone of the thirty companies which were received into the service of the United States, after the time of their arrival at the place of general rendezvous, is all, or nearly all of the expenditure which has been refunded as yet by the General Government.

The Adjutant General of the State is now at Washington, engaged in the settlement of this business with the War Department; and in a short time a special communication will be made, which will bring the subject of these expenditures and the matters connected therewith, fully before you.

The army of the United States is now in possession, by means of conquest, of five of the provinces of Mexico—Tamaulipas, New Leon, Chihuahua, New Mexico and California. The military commander who headed the forces which took possession of New Mexico, has affected to make a formal annexation of this province to the United States, has proclaimed himself Governor of the province, assumed the exercise of civil authority over the people of that country and actually required some of them to take an oath of allegiance to the United States.

If the object of the President of the United States, in sending an army into the interior of Mexico, be solely to compel the government of that country to the terms of a speedy and honorable peace, such proceedings may, perhaps, be excusable, if not entirely justifiable. But if the purpose and effect of this invasion of Mexico, by our armies, be the acquisition of territory, and the annexation of the subjugated provinces to our national confederacy, I have no hesitation in pronouncing it a violation of the fundamental principles of our government and of the spirit and true intent of our national constitution. The Government of the United States has no right to engage in a war of aggression and conquest.

Polk's War

WILLIAM BEBB

Gentlemen of the Senate and of the House of Representatives:

The past history and present condition of the State of Ohio, present interesting subjects for the contemplation and instruction of her legislators and statesmen. Half a century has but just elapsed since the victory of Wayne over the Indians on the Maumee, and the consequent treaty of Greeneville gave to the North Western Territory peace, and to the tenants of its rustic abodes assurance of safety.

This great central valley of the west was then in all its primeval grandeur—its mountains, lakes and gulf, its rivers gliding over cataracts or meandering through vast alluvial plains—its boundless prairies and herds of buffaloes—its forests, unrivalled in extent and variety, and its great tribes of aborigines who, from time unknown, had been the lords of this vast domain. The bold outlines of the scene remain unchanged and unchangeable. The mountains are here and the lakes, the rivers still flow in their channels, but the buffalo have been hunted from the prairies and the deer from the forest. Logan and Tecumseh are no more. The spirit of their race is broken. Their children have sullenly retired beyond the "Father of Waters," and buried the red scalping knife in the ashes of despair. The yells of the war dance, the eloquence of the council, and the incantations of the prophet, are seen and heard no more; but in their stead, halls of legislation, courts of justice, and temples consecrated to Christianity.

From William Bebb, "Message," *Ohio Executive Documents,* (1847), pp. 106-109.

The annals of man present no example where the triumphs of civilization, in so brief a period, have been so brilliant and complete.

. . . .

In contemplating the history of that period, and dwelling upon the difficulties which beset our fathers, in compromising the conflicting interests of the several sections of the Union, how cheering it is, thus to witness the ever living doctrines of the Declaration of American Independence bursting forth into practical operation wherever it was possible to give them immediate efficacy!

And how should a sense of deep humiliation and guilt fall upon us, the descendants of such men, when, with the prosperous career of Ohio and of the other free States of the North Western Territory before our eyes, and with all the lights of this age of Christianity and freedom beaming upon us, we compare or rather contrast the ordinance of 1787 with the constitution of Texas, the one perpetually prohibiting slavery, and the other perpetually prohibiting freedom! How can we reflect upon the motives and means which brought about the annexation of that province with such a constitution!—a constitution fastening slavery forever upon a vast region wherein a neighboring republic had already "broken every yoke and let the oppressed go free."

And how, with the constitution of the United States in our hands, proclaiming that Congress alone shall have power to declare war, can we behold a President of the United States trample that sacred instrument in the dust, deliberately, and without the advice of Congress then in session, involve the country in a foreign war of conquest, and yet not dare give utterance to our indignant condemnation of his unconstitutional acts! Where is the man who does not know and feel that this Mexican war is a *presidential* war! A war which before its commencement Congress would not have declared! A war begun without adequate cause, and without any great, justifiable and commensurate object, compatible with the interests and integrity of the Union. A war conducted without wisdom of design at Washington, and relieved from utter disaster and public odium only by the prudence, bravery and brilliant exploits of General Taylor and his gallant army of regulars and volunteers, who have triumphantly upheld our national banner, and won for themselves imperishable renown, and the gratitude of their country.

In conclusion of this subject, let it never be forgotten, that whilst the freemen of Ohio will in all time to come, as they have in all times past, cheerfully march to the field of battle at the call of the constituted authorities of the country, they will not fail, by word and deed, by the ballot-box, and all other constitutional means in their power, to hold those functionaries to a strict accountability for every violation of the trust committed to their hands, and especially for every infraction of that great Constitution, to which we are indebted, not merely for liberty, but for our national existence, and which is worth infinitely more to us than the conquest of the continent.

Welcome to Hospitable Graves

THOMAS CORWIN

Mr. President: I am not now about to perform the useless task of surveying the whole field of debate occupied in this discussion. It has been carefully reaped, and by vigilant and strong hands; and yet, Mr. President, there is a part of that field which promises to reward a careful gleaner with a valuable sheaf or two, which deserve to be bound up before the whole harvest is gathered. And still this so tempting prospect could not have allured me into this debate, had that motive not been strengthened by another, somewhat personal to myself, and still more interesting to those I represent. Anxious as I know all are to act, rather than debate, I am compelled, for the reasons I have assigned, to solicit the attention of the Senate. I do this chiefly that I may discharge the humble duty of giving to the Senate, and through this medium to my constituents, the motives and reasons which have impelled me to occupy a position, always undesirable, but in times like the present, painfully embarrassing.

I have been compelled, from convictions of duty which I could not disregard, to differ, not merely with those on the other side of the chamber, with whom I seldom agree, but also to separate, on one or two important questions, from a majority of my friends on this side—those who compose here that Whig party, of which I suppose I may yet call myself a member.

Diversity of opinion on most subjects affecting human affairs is to be expected. Unassisted mind, in its best estate, has not yet attained to uniformity, much less to absolute certainty, in matters

From Thomas Corwin, "The Mexican War," *Congressional Globe,* Vol. XVI, (Appendix), 29th Congress, 2nd Session, February 11, 1847, pp. 211-218.

belonging to the dominion of speculative reason. This is peculiarly and emphatically true, where we endeavor to deduce from the present, results, the accomplishment of which reach far into the future, and will only clearly develope themselves in the progress of time. From the present state of the human mind, this is a law of intellect quite as strong as necessity. And yet, after every reasonable allowance for the radical difference in intellectual structure, culture, habits of thought, and the application of thought to things, the singularly opposite avowals made by the two Senators on the other side of the chamber, (I mean the Senator from South Carolina, Mr. Calhoun, and the Senator from Michigan, Mr. Cass,) must have struck all who heard them, as a curious and mournful example of the truth of which I have spoken. The Senator from Michigan, [Mr. Cass,] in contemplating the present aspects and probable future course of our public affairs, declared, that he saw nothing to alarm the fears or depress the hopes of the patriot. To his serene, and as I fear too apathetic mind, all is calm; the sentinel might sleep securely on his watchtower. The ship of State seems to him to expand her sails under a clear sky, and move on, with prosperous gales, upon a smooth sea. He admonishes all not to anticipate evil to come, but to fold their hands and close their eyes in quietude, ever mindful of the consolatory text, "Sufficient unto the day is the evil thereof." But the Senator from South Carolina, [Mr. Calhoun,] summoning from the depths of his thoughtful and powerful mind all its energies, and looking abroad on the present condition of the Republic, is pained with fearful apprehension, doubt, distrust, and dismay. To his vision, made strong by a long life of careful observation, made keen by a comprehensive view of past history, the sky seems overcast with impending storms, and the dark future is shrouded in impenetrable gloom. When two such minds thus differ, those less familiar with great subjects affecting the happiness of nations, may well pause before they rush to a conclusion on this, a subject which, in all its bearings, immediate and remote, affects *certainly* the present prosperity, and *probably* the liberty, of two republics, embracing together nearly thirty millions of people. Mr. President, it is a fearful responsibility we have assumed; engaged in flagrant, desolating war with a neighboring republic, to us thirty millions of God's creatures look up for that moderated wisdom which, if possible, may stay the march of misery, and restore to them, if it may be so, mutual feelings of good-will, with all the best blessings of peace.

I sincerely wish it were in my power to cherish those placid convictions of security which have settled upon the mind of the Senator from Michigan. So far from this, I have been, in common with the Senator from South Carolina, oppressed with melancholy forebodings of evils to come, and not unfrequently by a conviction that each step we take in this unjust war, may be the last in our career; that each chapter we write in Mexican blood, may close the volume of our history as a free people.

. . . .

No, sir; looking at the events of the last twelve months, and forming his judgment of these by the suggestions which history teaches, and which she alone can teach, he would record another of those sad lessons which, though often taught, are, I fear, forever to be disregarded. He would speak of a republic, boasting that its rights were secured, and the restricted powers of its functionaries bound up in the chains of a written Constitution; he would record on his page, also, that such a people, in the wantonness of strength, or the fancied security of the moment, had torn that written Constitution to pieces, scattered its fragments to the winds, and surrendered themselves to the usurped authority of *one man.*

He would find written in that Constitution, *Congress* shall have power to declare war; he would find everywhere in that old charter proofs clear and strong that they who framed it intended that Congress, composed of two Houses, the representatives of the States and the people, should (if any were preëminent) be the controlling power. He would find there a President designated, whose general and almost exclusive duty it is to *execute,* not to *make* the law. Turning from this to the history of the last ten months, he would find that the President alone, without the advice or consent of Congress, had, by a bold usurpation, made war on a neighboring republic; and what is quite as much to be deplored, that Congress, whose high powers were thus set at naught and defied, had, with ready and tame submission, yielded to the usurper the wealth and power of the nation to execute his will, as if to swell his iniquitous triumph over the very Constitution which he and they had alike sworn to support.

If any one should inquire for the cause of a war in this country, where should he resort for an answer? Surely to the journals of both Houses of Congress, since Congress alone has power to declare war; yet, although we have been engaged in war for the last ten months, a war which has tasked all the fiscal resources of the country to carry it forward, you shall search the records and the archives of both Houses of Congress in vain for any detail of its causes, any resolve of Congress that war shall be waged. How is it, then, that a peaceful and peace-loving people, happy beyond the common lot of man, busy in every laudable pursuit of life, have been forced to turn suddenly from these, and plunge into the misery, the vice, and crime which ever have been and ever shall be the attendant scourges of war? The answer can only be, it was by the act and will of the President *alone,* and not by the act or will of Congress, the war-making department of the Government.

. . . .

With these doctrines for our guide, I will thank any Senator to furnish me with any means of escaping from the prosecution of this or any other war, for an hundred years to come, if it please the President who shall be, to continue it so long. Tell me, ye who contend that, being in war, duty demands of Congress for its prosecution all the money and every able-bodied man in America to carry it on if need be, who also contend that it is the right of the President, without the control of Congress, to march your embodied hosts to Monterey, to Yucatan, to Mexico, to Panama, to China, and that under penalty of death to the officer who disobeys him—tell me, I demand it of you—tell me, tell the American people, tell the nations of Christendom, what is the difference between your American Democracy and the most odious, most hateful despotism, that a merciful God has ever allowed a nation to be afflicted with since government on earth began? You may call this free government, but it is such freedom, and no other, as of old was established at Babylon, at Susa, at Bactriana, or Persepolis. Its parallel is scarcely to be found when thus falsely understood, in any even the worst forms of civil polity in modern times. Sir, it is not so; such is not your Constitution; it is something else, something other and better than this.

. . . .

But when I am asked to say whether I will prosecute a war, I cannot answer that question, yea or nay, until I have determined whether that was a necessary war; and I cannot determine whether it was necessary until I know how it was that my country was involved in it. And it is to that particular point, Mr. President—without reading documents, but referring to a few facts which I understand not to be denied on either side of this chamber—that I wish to direct the attention of the American Senate, and so far as may be, that of any of the noble and honest-hearted constituents whom I represent here. I know, Mr. President, the responsibility which I assume in undertaking to determine that the President of the United States has done great wrong to the country, whose honor and whose interest he was required to protect. I know the denunciations which await every one who shall dare to put himself in opposition to that high power— that idol god—which the people of this country have made to themselves and called a President.

But it is my very humility which makes me bold. I know, sir, that he who was told in former times how to govern a turbulent people, was advised to cut off the tallest heads. Mine will escape! Still, holding a seat here, Mr. President, and finding it written in the Constitution of my country that I had the power to grant to the President at his bidding, or not, as I pleased, men and money, I did conceive that it became my duty to ascertain whether the President's request was a reasonable one—whether the President wanted these men and this money for a proper and laudable purpose or not; and with these old-fashioned ideas—quite as unpopular I fear with some on this side of the Chamber as we find them to be on the other—I set myself to this painful investigation. I found not quite enough along with me to have saved the unrighteous city of old.

. . . .

Mr. President, I trust we shall abandon the idea, the heathen, barbarian notion, that our true national glory is to be won, or retained, by military prowess or skill, in the art of destroying life. And, whilst I cannot but lament, for the permanent and lasting renown of my country, that she should command the service of her children in what I must consider wanton, unprovoked, *unnecessary,* and therefore, unjust war, I can yield to the brave soldier, whose trade is war, and whose duty is obedience, the highest meed of praise for his courage, his enterprise, and perpetual endurance of the fatigues and horrors of war. I know the gallant men who are engaged in fighting your battles possess personal bravery equal to any troops, in any land, anywhere engaged in the business of war. I do not believe we are less capable in the art of destruction than others, or less willing, on the slightest pretext, to unsheath the sword, and consider "revenge a virtue." I could wish, also, that your brave soldiers, whilst they bleed and die on the battle-field, might have, (what in this war is impossible) the consolation to feel and know, that their blood flowed in defence of a great right, that their lives were a meet sacrifice to an exalted principle.

. . . .

Your people did go to Texas. I remember it well. They went to Texas to fight for their rights. They could not fight for them in their own country. Well, they fought for their rights. They conquered them! They conquered a peace! They were your citizens—not Mexicans. They were recent emigrants to that country. They went there for the very purpose of seizing on that country, and making it a free and independent republic, with the view, as some of them said, of bringing it into the American confederacy in due time. Is this poor Celtic brother of yours in Mexico—is the Mexican man sunk so low that he cannot hear what fills the mouth and ear of rumor all over this country? He knows that this was the settled purpose of some of your people. He knows that your avarice had fixed its eagle glance on these rich acres in Mexico, and that your proud power counted the number that could be brought against you, and that your avarice and your power together marched on to the subjugation of the third or fourth part of the Republic of Mexico, and took it from her. We knew this, and knowing it, what should have been the feeling and sentiment in the mind of the President of the United States towards such a people—a people, at least in their own opinion, so deeply injured by us as were these Mexicans?

. . . .

Sir, with my opinions as to facts connected with this subject, and my deductions, unavoidable from them, I should have been unworthy the high-souled State I represent, had I voted men and money to prosecute further a war commenced, as it now appears, in aggression, and carried on by repetition only of the original wrong. Am I mistaken in this? If I am, I shall hold him the dearest friend I can own in any relation of life who shall show me my error. If I am wrong in this question of fact, show me how I err, and gladly will I retrace my steps; satisfy me that my country was in peaceful and rightful possession between the Nueces and the Rio Grande when General Taylor's army was ordered there; show me that at Palo Alto and Resaca de la Palma blood was shed on American soil in American possession, and then for the *defence* of that possession, I will vote away the last dollar that power can wring from the people, and send every man able to bear a musket to the ranks of war. But until I shall be thus convinced, duty to myself, to truth, to conscience, to public justice, requires that I persist in every lawful opposition to this war.

While the American President can command the army, thank Heaven I can command the purse. While the President, under the penalty of death, can command your officers to proceed, I can tell them to come back, or the President can supply them as he may. He shall have no funds from me in the prosecution of a war which I cannot approve. That I conceive to be the duty of a Senator. I am not mistaken in that. If it be my duty to grant whatever the President demands, for what am I here? Have I no will upon the subject? Is it not placed at my discretion, understanding, judgment? Have an American Senate and House of Representatives nothing to do but obey the bidding of the President, as the army he commands is compelled to obey under penalty of death? No! The Representatives of the sovereign people and sovereign States were never elected for such purposes as that.

The President has said he does not expect to hold Mexican territory by conquest. Why then conquer it? Why waste thousands of lives, and millions of money, fortifying towns and creating governments, if, at the end of the war, you retire from the graves of your soldiers, and the desolated country of your foes, only to get money from Mexico for the expense of all your toil and sacrifice? Who ever heard, since Christianity was propagated amongst men 'of a nation taxing its people, inlisting its young men, and marching off two thousand miles to fight a people merely to be paid for it in money! What is this but hunting a market for blood, selling the lives of your young men, marching them in regiments to be slaughtered and paid for, like oxen and brute beasts? Sir, this is, when stripped naked, that atrocious idea first promulgated in the President's message, and now advocated here, of fighting on till we can get our indemnity for the past as well as the present slaughter. We have chastised Mexico, and if it were worth while to do so, we have, I dare say, satisfied the world that we can fight. What now! Why, the mothers of America are asked to send another of their sons to blow out the brains of Mexicans, because they refuse to pay the price of the first who fell there, fighting for glory! And what if the second fall too? The Executive, the parental reply is, "we shall have him paid for; we shall get full indemnity!" Sir, I have no patience with this flagitious notion of fighting for indemnity, and this under the equally absurd and hypo-critical pretence of securing an honorable peace. An honorable peace! If you have accomplished the objects of the war, (if, indeed, you had an object which you dare to avow,) cease to fight, and you will have peace. Conquer your insane love of false glory, and you will "conquer a peace." Sir, if your commander-in-chief will not do this, I will endeavor to compel him, and as I find no other means, I shall refuse supplies—without the money of the people, he cannot go further. He asks me for that money; I wish him to bring your armies home, to cease shedding blood *for* money; if he refuses, I will refuse supplies, and then I know he *must*, he will cease his further sale of the lives of my countrymen. May we not, *ought* we not now to do this? I can hear no reason why we should not, except this, it is said that we are in war, wrongfully it may be, but, being in, the President is responsible, and we must give *him* the means *he* requires! He responsible! Sir, we, we are responsible, if, having power to stay this plague, we refuse to do so. When it shall be so—when the American Senate and the American House of Representatives can stoop from their high position, and yield a dumb compliance with the behests of a President, who is for the time being commander of your army; when they will open the treasury with one hand, and the veins of all the soldiers in the land with the other, *merely because* the President commands, then, sir, it matters little how soon some Cromwell shall come into this Hall and say, "the Lord hath no further need of you here." When we fail to do the work "whereunto we were sent," we shall be, we ought to be removed, and give place to others who will.

The fate of the barren fig-tree will be ours—Christ cursed it and it withered.

. . . .

What is the territory, Mr. President, which you propose to wrest from Mexico? It is consecrated to the heart of the Mexican by many a well-fought battle with his old Castilian master. His Bunker Hills, and Saratogas, and Yorktowns, are there! The Mexican can say, "There I bled for liberty! and shall I surrender that consecrated home of my affections to the Anglo-Saxon invaders? What do they want with it? They have Texas already. They have possessed themselves of the territory between the Nueces and the Rio Grande. What else do they want? To what shall I point my children as memorials of that independence which I bequeath to them when those battle-fields shall have passed from my possession?"

Sir, had one come and demanded Bunker Hill of the people of Massachusetts, had England's Lion ever showed himself there, is there a man over thirteen and under ninety who would not have been ready to meet him? Is there a river on this continent that would not have run red with blood? Is there a field but would have been piled high with the unburied bones of slaughtered Americans before these consecrated battle-fields of liberty should have been wrested from us? But this same American goes into a sister republic and says to poor, weak Mexico, "Give up your territory, you are unworthy to possess it; I have got one-half already, and all I ask of you is to give up the other!" England might as well, in the circumstances I have described, have come and demanded of us, "Give up the Atlantic slope—give up this trifling territory from the Alleghany Mountains to the sea; it is only from Maine to St. Mary's—only about one-third of your republic, and the least interesting portion of it." What would be the response? They would say, we must give this up to John Bull. Why? "He wants room." The Senator from Michigan says he must have this. Why, my worthy Christian brother, on what principle of justice? "I want room!"

Sir, look at this pretence of want of room. With twenty millions of people, you have about one thousand millions of acres of land, inviting settlement by every conceivable argument, bringing them down to a quarter of a dollar an acre, and allowing every man to squat where he pleases. But the Senator from Michigan says we will be two hundred millions in a few years, and we want room. If I were a Mexican I would tell you, "Have you not room in your own country to bury your dead men? If you come into mine, we will greet you with bloody hands, and welcome you to hospitable graves."

9 Ohio: White and Black and Gray

BETWEEN 1815, when the first antislavery society was founded in the state, and the outbreak of the American Civil War in 1861, the arguments in Ohio concerning slavery made public similar attitudes across the country. Those motivated by humanitarian considerations believed that slavery within a democratic republic was contrary to the principles of the natural rights proclaimed in both the federal and Ohio constitutions. They were opposed by those who based their defense of slavery on the sanctity of property rights and the rights of individual states to control their internal affairs, including slavery. Within the state's antislavery movement four patterns became clear: the philosophical debate between colonization and abolition; the movement from nonpolitical argumentation into the political arena; the repeal of objectionable state and federal laws; and the willingness not only to use the courts but also to *violate* state and federal statutes to achieve success. The growth of the antislavery movement in Ohio was a lesson in the development of a mass protest movement in a society that tolerated, no matter how reluctantly, the discussion of particularly troublesome questions.

It cannot be denied that the seeds of antislavery sentiment were planted early in Ohio. The Ordinance of 1787 forbade involuntary servitude north of the Ohio River, and the state constitution of 1803 excluded slavery. Early, isolated demands for the freedom of America's blacks became publicized through Benjamin Lundy's efforts in eastern Ohio, the pages of Charles Osborn's *Philanthropist,* and the sermons and tracts of John Rankin, the fiery Presbyterian preacher from Ripley. By 1836, a branch of the American Colonization Society was founded in the Western Reserve, that part of the state which remained the stronghold of antislavery sentiment until the end of the Civil War.

The debate over slavery, in the state as well as the nation, revolved around two divergent principles: colonization, which meant the removal of the blacks from white society; and abolition, which contained the ingredients for amalgamation. At first, the removal of the American black presented a simple and logical solution for a country that propounded the superiority of Anglo-Saxon civilization and the need to protect it from contamination by nonwhite blood. The gap, however, between theory and actual workability was great. Because Ohio's blacks did not want to leave what they considered their home and, at the same time, because whites failed to finance the project, the efforts of the Ohio Colonization Society were unsuccessful. Without doubt, one of the most important events in the antislavery movement was the protracted discussion of the merits of colonization versus abolition during February 1834 at Lane Seminary in Cincinnati. Young, educated, well-meaning, and already deeply involved in the antislavery movement, the Lane students concluded that abolition was the only practical solution to the slavery issue. Similar conclusions were reached elsewhere. Fearful of the repercussions of this judgment, the more conservative elements in both the North and the South sought to quash debate on the issue in order, as they argued, to save the Union from dissolution. Though this restrictiveness was measured by overt acts, including criticism of free expression and attacks upon persons and property, those who advocated abolition became more resolute in their views.

In order to gain support within the mechanisms of government, the antislavery movement had to shift into the political arena. By 1838, Thomas Morris, Democratic senator from Ohio, proclaimed publicly that slavery was wrong "in every country and under every condition of things." Traditionally called the first abolitionist senator, Morris courageously defended the right of petition and challenged the South's attempts to stifle a public airing of the issue. Although he was read out of the Democratic party for his opinion, there nonetheless was an audience of sufficient size that agreed with him. Between 1839 and 1854, the Ohio antislavery movement electioneered for the Liberty party and the Free Soil party before finding a home in the newly formed Republican party in 1856.

Frustrated by the lack of immediate success at the national level, the Ohio antislavery movement agreed to set its own state in order. Because of provisions within the Ohio Constitution of 1803 and the black codes passed by the general assembly between 1804 and 1807, the free blacks living in Ohio, while not literally held in servitude, were for all purposes denied the rights that make men free. Consequently, the repeal of the limiting Ohio black codes became the target for the movement. It was only because of its political involvement that the antislavery movement was able to negotiate the repeal of the black codes in 1848 and subsequently concentrate its attention on matters of national significance.

Through the courts the antislavery movement in Ohio argued its case against federal fugitive slave statutes prior to 1850, the state's own restrictiveness, and the Fugitive Slave Act of 1850. Behind the legal arguments of Salmon P. Chase, the antislavery forces again and again filed their brief against the enforcement of the institution of slavery in a free state. To combat the antiblack posture assumed by the Democratic party through its visible admixture law, the movement argued its case in a court of law to its own satisfaction. The most famous court decision involved the Wellington-Oberlin rescue case, in which members of the antislavery movement willingly ignored federal law in order to achieve their immediate goals.

Thus, while engaged in a complex movement characterized by many differing opinions, the Ohio antislavery forces had a unanimity of purpose. Whether its individuals were motivated for political, civil, or social reasons, the antislavery movement sought personal freedom for the enslaved outside the state and civil liberties for those within.

To Free People from America

OHIO COLONIZATION SOCIETY

At a time when a general effort is making throughout the nation, in behalf of the American Colonization Society, and when a universal appeal is made to the benevolence of community for its support, we owe it to the public, on whose charity our institution, for the present, entirely depends for aid; and especially in the western country, where the operations and objects of the Society are very imperfectly understood, to give a brief sketch of its history, character and claims.

"The *design* of this Society is general—the benefit of the *whole* African race. Its plan of *operation* is specific—*the establishment on the coast of Africa, of a Colony of free people of colour, from America.*"

That the condition of this unhappy race is such as to claim our *sympathies,* and demand our *efforts* for their relief, is very evident. And this is true of them, whether considered as *actual slaves,* or as *nominally free,* in this country; or as the deluded and *ignorant promoters* of the *Slave Trade,* or as its *miserable* and *hopeless victims,* in Africa.

The scheme of the American Colonization Society was devised and adopted by liberal and intelligent men of the *South,* and the *North,* as the plan, and the only one, which could unite these two great divisions of our country, in any efforts for the removal, or even the mitigation, of the greatest evil, and heaviest curse, which afflicts our land.

. . . .

A manumitted slave remains a negro still, and must ever continue in a state of political bondage; and it is obvious that he who is deprived of the inherent rights of a citizen can never become a loyal subject.

Perhaps no argument can better prove the degraded character of the free black population of our country, or more fully show the necessity of forming them into a separate community in a country of their own, than facts which are stated in the first report of the Prison Discipline Society.

"The first cause," says the report, "existing in society, of the frequency and increase of crime, is the degraded character of the coloured population. The facts which are gathered from the Peniten-

From **Ohio State Colonization Society,** *A Brief Exposition of the Views of the Society for the Colonization of Free Persons of Colour, in Africa,* (Columbus, 1827), n.p.

tiaries, to show how great a proportion of the convicts are coloured, even in those states where the coloured is small, show most strikingly the connexion between ignorance and vice."

In Massachusetts less than a *seventieth* part of the population are *coloured.* But of the *convicts,* in the State Prison, nearly *one-sixth* part are persons of colour!

. . . .

This proportion will appear the more alarming, if we apply it to our own population. Suppose a *nineteenth* part of all the inhabitants of Ohio were *convicts,* we should have in our Penitentiary nearly *fifty-thousand* souls!

. . . .

And in our own state of Ohio, where the blacks have been supposed to be in a quite happy condition, even here, where only about the **twelfth* part of our population is coloured, about a *tenth* part of the convicts in the State Prison are persons of colour.

. . . .

But there is another still more important characteristic of the condition of our coloured population, in comparison with which every other circumstance dwindles into insignificance, and from which all that we have already said is only a necessary consequence. We mean Slavery.

That Slavery is an evil no one can deny. All must desire to cure the disease. If the evil be of fearful magnitude now, what will it be fifty years hence? And how much would the danger be aggravated by letting loose a horde of emancipated outlaws in the heart of our country? The mischief then, can only be averted by providing a Colonial settlement; for, in that case, as soon as slaves shall be emancipated, they will become proper subjects of colonization. By thus gradually removing this class of our population, we should not only be liberated from the apprehension of a servile war, at which humanity shudders, but would moreover greatly improve the moral worth of the community.

In this state (Ohio) we are supposed by many not to be at all interested in the prosperity of the Colonization cause; because Slavery is here prohibited by our Constitution and Laws. But the enlightened and liberal will recollect that we were as deeply concerned in the introduction of Slavery into this country, as those who are now the unfortunate holders of slaves—in short, that it was during our colonial existence, without our consent, and in disregard

---

**Should be *one hundred and twenty-fourth.*"

of our oft repeated remonstrances, that the mother country forced upon us this dreadful curse. But though we were all originally innocent of this crime, we all, in whatever part of the Union, become guilty when we refuse to aid, according to our ability, in its removal. And there are many *here,* in Ohio, who notwithstanding their terrible denunciations against slave-holders, are living on the *price of blood.* And it is equally true that thousands who are the holders of slaves, and who have inherited them from their fathers, feel them an impoverishing inheritance and a curse. But what can they do? If they look around them, they find the condition of *free* blacks no better among them than that of the slaves. They find a much greater proportion of them in state prisons, in jails, and on pauper-lists than they do of slaves. Shall they turn them loose on community, regardless of consequences? Let this become universal, and let more than *two millions* of persons be turned out on society without any of the *motives* and *privileges* of freemen, or any of the *restraints* of slavery, and we think that all will admit that our condition and theirs would be made much more wretched by the change. Notwithstanding these considerations, such is the extent of liberal principle, and such the feelings of humanity for the unhappy slave, that hundreds of them are manumitted in slave-holding states every year. This can only be done by sending the liberated slave out of the state, and thus it is done at the expense of *our* safety and happiness in this and other free states. These miserable beings, with all the ignorance and degraded habits of thinking and acting which pertain to slavery, are *flooded* upon us in Ohio and Indiana, in yearly accumulating multitudes, to live among us without any of either the qualifications or privileges of citizens or freemen. The present state of things continuing but a few years, and what by emigration and what by natural increase, we shall have a black population equal to the number of whites. And then, though hundreds of us have fled to Ohio as the asylum of freedom; who will desire her pleasant plains and valleys as a residence? Who would not then prefer a residence in a slave-holding state?

And in the fearful event of a *servile war,* it would not be in the slave-holding states, and among slaves that those schemes of blood and ruin would be laid and ripened into maturity, but here, where they enjoy enough of freedom to feel their chains and to encourage them in an effort to break them off, and are not under the watchful restraints of a master.

In all these views we should regard the black population among us as a great national evil, moral, political, and social; which extends to all parts of our Union, and which tends to the destruction of our happiness and theirs, and which all should labor to remove.

But what can be done to remove the evil, or even to mitigate its ravages? It is now very generally agreed that the only plan which affords any hope of relief on this gloomy subject, either to us or to the degraded blacks, is that of Colonization.

But to the establishment of a Colony in our own country there are insuperable objections; and in the way of colonization in any of the West India Islands, it is believed that there are difficulties which can never be fully overcome. Hence the scheme of colonizing the blacks in Africa, the land of their fathers, is looked upon as the last hope of humanity.

Free the Slaves

THOMAS MORRIS

I take this opportunity to present all these petitions together, having detained some of them for a considerable time in my hands, in order that as small a portion of the attention of the Senate might be taken up on their account as would be consistent with a strict regard to the rights of the petitioners. And I now present them under the most peculiar circumstances that has ever probably transpired in this or any other country. I present them on the heel of the petitions which have been presented by the Senator from Kentucky [Mr. Clay] signed by the inhabitants of this District, praying that Congress would not receive petitions on the subject of slavery in the District, from any body of men or citizens, but themselves. This is something new; it is one of the devices of the slave power, and most extraordinary in itself. These petitions I am bound in duty to present—a duty which I cheerfully perform, for I consider it not only a duty but an honor.

. . . .

Do not suppose, Mr. President, that I feel as if engaged in a forbidden or improvident act. No such thing. I am contending with a

From Thomas Morris, "Speech on Slavery," *Congressional Globe,* Vol. VII, 25th Congress, 3rd Session, February 9, 1839, (Appendix), pp. 167-175.

local and *"peculiar"* interest, an interest which has already banded together a force sufficient to seize upon every avenue by which a petition can enter this chamber, and exclude all without its leave. I am not now contending for the rights of the negro, rights which his Creator gave him and which his fellow-man has usurped or taken away. No, sir! I am contending for the rights of the white person in the free States, and am endeavoring to prevent them from being trodden down and destroyed by that power which claims the black person as *property.* I am endeavoring to sound the alarm to my fellow-citizens that this power, tremendous as it is, is endeavoring to unite itself with the moneyed power of the country, in order to extend its dominion and perpetuate its existence. I am endeavoring to drive from the back of the *negro slave* the politician who has seated himself there to ride into office for the purpose of carrying out the object of this unholy combination. The chains of slavery are sufficiently strong, without being riveted anew by tinkering politicians in the free States. I feel myself compelled into this contest, in defence of the institutions of my own State, the persons and firesides of her citizens, from the insatiable grasp of the slaveholding power as being used and felt in the free States. To say that I am opposed to slavery in the abstract, are but cold and unmeaning words; if, however, capable of any meaning whatever, they may fairly be construed into a love for its existence; and such I sincerely believe to be the feeling of many in the free States who use the phrase. I, sir, am not only opposed to slavery in the abstract, but also in its whole volume, in its theory as well as practice. This principle is deeply implanted within me; it has "grown with my growth, and strengthened with my strength." In my infant years I learned to hate slavery. Your fathers taught me it was wrong in their Declaration of Independence: the doctrines whch they promulgated to the world, and upon the truth of which they staked the issue of the contest that made us a nation. . . . It is, then, because I love the principles which brought your Government into existence, and which have become the corner stone of the building supporting you, sir, in that chair, and giving to myself and other Senators seats in this body—it is because I love all this, that I hate slavery. Is it because I contend for the right of petition, and am opposed to slavery, that I have been denounced by many as an Abolitionist? Yes; Virginia newspapers have so denounced me, and called upon the Legislature of my State to dismiss me from public confidence. Who taught me to hate slavery, and every other oppression? *Jefferson,* the great and the good Jefferson! Yes, *Virginia Senators,* it was your own Jefferson, Virginia's favorite son, a man who did more for the natural liberty of man, and the civil liberty of his country, than any man that ever lived in our country; it was him who taught me to hate *slavery;* it was in his school I was brought up.

. . . .

But, sir, other reasons and other causes have combined to fix and establish my principles in this matter, never, I trust, to be shaken. A free State was the place of my birth; a free Territory the theatre of my juvenile actions. Ohio is my country endeared to me by every fond recollection. She gave me political existence, and taught me in her political school; and I should be worse than an unnatural son did I forget or disobey her precepts. In her Constitution it is declared "That all men are born equally free and independent," and "that there shall be neither slavery nor involuntary servitude in the State, otherwise than for the punishment of crimes." Shall I stand up for slavery in any case, condemned as it is by such high authority as this? No, never! But this is not all. Indiana, our younger Western sister, endeared to us by every social and political tie, a State formed in the same country as Ohio, from whose territory slavery was forever excluded by the ordinance of July, 1787—she, too, has declared her abhorrence of slavery in more strong and emphatic terms than we have done. In her constitution, after prohibiting slavery, or involuntary servitude being introduced into the State, she declares, "But as to the holding any part of the human creation in slavery, or involuntary servitude, can originate only in *tyranny* and *usurpation,* no alteration of her constitution should ever take place, so as to introduce slavery or involuntary servitude into the State, otherwise than for the punishment of crimes whereof the party had been duly convicted." Illinois and Michigan also formed their constitutions on the same principles. After such a cloud of witnesses against slavery, and whose testimony is so clear and explicit, as a citizen of Ohio, I should be recreant to every principle of honor and of justice, to be found the apologist or advocate of slavery in any State, or in any country whatever. No, I cannot be so inconsistent as to say I am opposed to slavery in the *abstract,* in its separation from a human being, and still lend my aid to build it up, and make it perpetual in its operation and effects upon *man* in this or any other country.

. . . .

Yes, this is slavery, boasted American slavery, without which, it is contended even here, that the union of these States would be dissolved in a day, yes, even in an hour! Humiliating thought, that we are bound together as States by the chains of slavery! It cannot be—the blood and the tears of slavery form no part of the cement of our Union—and it is hoped that by falling on its bands they may never corrode and eat them asunder. We who are opposed to, and deplore the existence of slavery in our country, are frequently asked, both in public and private, what have you to do with slavery? It does not exist in your State; it does not disturb you! Ah, sir, would to God it were so—that we had nothing to do with slavery, nothing to fear from its power, or its action within our own borders, that its name and its miseries were unknown to us. But this is not our lot; we live upon its borders, and in hearing of its cries; yet we are unwilling to acknowledge, that if we enter its territories and violate its laws, that we should be punished at its pleasure. We do not complain of this, though it might well be considered just ground of complaint. It is our firesides, our rights, our privileges, the safety of our friends, as well as the sovereignty and independence of our State, that we are now called upon to protect and defend. The slave interest has at this moment the whole power of the country in its hands. It claims the President as a Northern man with Southern feelings, thus making the Chief Magistrate the head of an interest, or a party, and not of the country and the people at large. It has the cabinet of the President, three members of which are from slave States, and one who wrote a book in favor of Southern slavery, but which fell dead from the press, a book which I have seen, in my own family, thrown musty upon the shelf. Here then is a decided majority in favor of the slave interest. It has five out of nine judges of the Supreme Court; here, also, is a majority from the slave States. It has, with the President of the Senate, and the Speaker of the House of Representatives, and the Clerks of both Houses, the army and the navy; and the bureaus, have, I am told, about the same proportion. One would suppose that, with all this power operating in this Government, it would be content to *permit*—yes I will use the word *permit*—it would be content to permit us, who live in the free States, to enjoy our firesides and our homes in quietness; but this is not the case. The slaveholders and slave laws claim that as property, which the free States know only as persons, a reasoning property, which, of its own will and mere motion, is frequently found in our States; and upon which *thing* we sometimes bestow food and raiment if it appear hungry and perishing, believing it to be a human being; this perhaps is owing to our want of vision to discover the process by which a man is converted into a *thing*. For this act of ours, which is not prohibited by our laws, but prompted by every feeling, christian and humane, the slaveholding power enters our territory, tramples under foot the sovereignty of our State, violates the sanctity of private residence, seizes our citizens, and disregarding the authority of our laws, transports them into its own jurisdiction, casts them into prison, confines them in fetters, and loads them with chains, for pretended offences against their own laws, found by willing grand juries upon the oath (to use the language of the late Governor of Ohio) of a perjured villain.

. . . .

Would I could stop here—but I cannot. This slave interest or power seizes upon persons of color in our State, carries them into States where men are property, and makes merchandise of them, sometimes under sanction of law, but more properly by its abuse, and sometimes by mere personal force, thus disturbing our quiet and harassing our citizens. . . . Slave power is seeking to establish itself in every State, in defiance of the constitution and laws of the States within which it is prohibited. In order to secure its power beyond the reach of the States, it claims its parentage from the Constitution of the United States. It demands of us total silence as to its proceedings, denies to our citizens the liberty of speech and the press, and punishes them by mobs and violence for the exercise of these rights. It has sent its agents into free States for the purpose of influencing their Legislatures to pass laws for the security of its power within such State, and for the enacting new offences and new punishments for their own citizens, so as to give additional security to its interest. It demands to be heard in its own person in the hall of our Legislature, and mingle in debate there. Sir, in every stage of these oppressions and abuses, permit me to say, in the language of the Declaration of Independence—and no language could be more appropriate—we have petitioned for redress in the most humble terms, and our repeated petitions have been answered by repeated injury. A power, whose character is marked by every act which may define a tyrant, is unfit to rule over a free people.

. . . .

I again put in a broad denial to this charge, that any portion of these petitioners, whom I represent, seek to excite one portion of the country against another; and without proof I cannot admit that the assertion of the honorable Senator establishes the fact. It is but opinion, and naked assertion only. The Senator complains that the means and views of the Abolitionists are not confined to securing the right of petition only; no, they resort to other means, he affirms, to the Ballot Box; and if that fail, says the Senator, their next appeal will be to the bayonet. Sir, no man who is an American in feeling and in heart, but ought to repel this charge instantly, and without any reservation whatever, that if they fail at the ballot box they will resort to the bayonet. If such a fratracidal course should ever be thought of in our country, it will not be by those who seek redress of wrongs, by exercising the right of petition, but by those only who deny that right to others, and seek to usurp the whole power of the

Government. If the ballot box fail them, the bayonet may be their resort, as mobs and violence now are. Does the Senator believe that any portion of the honest yeomanry of the country entertain such thoughts? I hope he does not.

. . . .

The gentlemen contends that the power to remove slaves from one State to another, for sale, is found in that part of the Constitution which gives Congress the power to regulate commerce within the States, &c. This argument is *non sequiter,* unless the honorable Senator can first prove that slaves are proper articles for commerce. We say that Congress have power over slaves only as persons. The United States can protect persons, *but cannot make them property,* and they have full power in regulating commerce, and can, in such regulations, prohibit from its operations every thing but property; property made so by the laws of nature, and not by any municipal regulations. The dominion of man over things, as property, was settled by his Creator when man was first placed upon the earth. He was to subdue the earth, and have dominion over the fish of the sea, the fowls of the air, and over every living thing that moveth upon the earth; every herb bearing seed, and the fruit of a tree yielding seed, was given for his use. This is the foundation of all right in property of every description. It is for the use of man the grant is made, and of course man cannot be included in the grant. Every municipal regulation then, of any State, or any of its peculiar institutions, which makes man property, is a violation of this great law of nature, and is founded in usurpation and tyranny, and is accomplished by force, fraud, or an abuse of power. It is a violation of the principles of truth and justice, in subjecting the weaker to the stronger man. In a Christian nation such property can form no just ground for commercial regulations, but ought to be strictly prohibited. I therefore believe it is the duty of Congress, by virtue of this power to regulate commerce, to prohibit, at once, slaves being used as articles of trade.

. . . .

But the Senator is not content to entreat the clergy alone to desist; he calls on his countrywomen to warn them, also, to cease their efforts, and reminds them that the ink shed from the pen held in their fair fingers when writing their names to Abolition petitions, may be the cause of shedding much human blood! Sir, the language towards this class of petitioners is very much changed of late; they formerly were pronounced idlers, fanatics, old women, and schoolmisses, unworthy of respect from intelligent and respectable men. I warned gentlemen then that they would change their language; the blows they aimed fell harmless at the feet of those against whom they were intended to injure. In this movement of my country-women I thought was plainly to be discovered the operations of Providence, and a sure sign of the final triumph of *universal emancipation!* All history, both sacred and profane, both ancient and modern, bears testimony to the efficacy of female influence and power in the cause of human liberty. From the time of the preservation, by the hands of woman, of the great Jewish lawgiver, in his infantile hours, and who was preserved for the purpose of freeing his countrymen from Egyptian bondage, has woman been made a powerful agent in breaking to pieces the rod of the oppressor. With a pure and uncontaminated mind, her actions spring from the deepest recesses of the human heart. Denounce her as you will, you cannot deter her from duty. Pain, sickness, want, poverty, and even death itself form no obstacles in her onward march. Even the tender virgin would dress, as a martyr for the stake, as for her bridal hour, rather than make sacrifice of her purity and duty. The eloquence of the Senate, and clash of arms, are alike powerless when brought in opposition to the influence of pure and virtuous woman. The liberty of the slave seems now to be committed to her charge, and who can doubt her final triumph? I do not. You cannot fight against her and hope for success; and well does the Senator know this; hence this appeal to her feelings to terrify her from that which she believes to be her duty. It is a vain attempt.

. . . .

The Senator says, the next or greatest difficulty to emancipation, is the amount of property it would take from the owners. All ideas of right and wrong are confounded in these words: emancipate property, emancipate a horse, or an ox, would not only be an unmeaning, but a ludicrous expression. To emancipate, is to set free from slavery. To emancipate, is to set free a man, not property. The Senator estimates the number of slaves—*men* now held in bondage— at three millions in the United States. Is this statement made here by the same voice which was heard in this Capitol in favor of the liberties of Greece, and for the emancipation of our South American brethren from political thraldom? It is; and has all its fervor in favor of liberty been exhausted upon foreign countries, so as not to leave a single whisper in favor of three millions of men in our own country, now groaning under the most galling oppression the world ever saw? No, sir. Sordid interest rules the hour. Men are made property, and paper is made money, and the Senator, no doubt, sees in these two peculiar institutions a power which, if united, will be able to accomplish all his wishes. He informs us that some have computed the slaves to be worth the average amount of $500 each. He will estimate within bounds at $400 each. Making the amount twelve hundred millions of dollars' worth of slave property. . . . But the assertion has gone forth that we have twelve hundred millions of slave property at the South; and can any man so close his understanding here as not plainly to perceive that the power of this vast amount of property at the South is now uniting itself to the banking power of the North, in order to govern the destinies of this country? Six hundred millions of banking capital is to be brought into this coalition, and the slave power and the bank power are thus to unite in order to break down the present Administration. There can be no mistake, as I believe, in this matter. The aristocracy of the North, who, by the power of a corrupt banking system, and the aristocracy of the South, by the power of the slave system, both fattening upon the labor of others, are now about to unite in order to make the reign of each perpetual. Is there an independent American to be found, who will become the recreant slave to such an unholy combination? Is this another compromise to barter the liberties of the country for personal aggrandisement? "Resistance to tyrants is obedience to God."

. . . .

The Senator tells us that the consequences arising from the freedom of slaves, would be to reduce the wages of the white laborer. He has furnished us with neither data nor fact upon which this opinion can rest. He, however, would draw a line, on one side of which he would place the slave labor, and on the other side free white labor; and looking over the whole, as a general system, both would appear on a perfect equality. I have observed, for some years past, that the Southern slaveholder has insisted that his laborers are, in point of integrity, morality, usefulness, and comfort, equal to the laboring population of the North. Thus endeavoring to raise the slave, in public estimation, to an equality with the free white laborer of the North; while, on the other hand, the Northern aristocrat has, in the same manner, viz: by comparison, endeavored to reduce his laborers to the moral and political condition of the slaves of the South. It is for the free white American citizens to determine whether they will permit such degrading comparisons longer to exist. Already has this spirit broken forth in denunciation of the right of universal suffrage. Will free white laboring citizens take warning before it is too late?

The last, the great, the crying sin of Abolitionists, in the eyes of the Senator, is that they are opposed to colonization, and in favor of amalgamation. It is not necessary now to enter into any of the benefits and advantages of colonization; the Senator has pronounced it the noblest scheme ever devised by man; he says it is powerful but harmless. I have no knowledge of any resulting benefits from the scheme to either race. I have not a doubt as to the real object intended by its founders; it did not arise from principles of humanity and benevolence towards the colored race, but a desire to remove the free of that race beyond the United States, in order to perpetuate and make slavery more secure. The Senator further makes the broad charge, that Abolitionists wish to *enforce* the unnatural system of amalgamation. We deny the fact, and call on the Senator for proof. The citizens of the free States, the petitioners against slavery, the Abolitionists of the free States in favor of amalgamation! No, sir! If you want evidence of the fact, and reasoning in support of amalgamation, you must look into the slave States; it is there it spreads and flourishes from slave mothers, and presents all possible colors and complexions, from the jet black African, to the scarcely to be distinguished white person. Does any one need proof of this fact? let him take but a few turns through the streets of your capital, and observe those whom he shall meet, and he will be perfectly satisfied. Amalgamation indeed! The charge is made with a very bad grace on the present occasion. No, sir; it is not the negro *woman,* it is the *slave* and the contaminating influence of slavery, that is the mother of amalgamation. Does the gentleman want facts on this subject? let him look at the colored race in the free States; it is a rare occurrence there. A colony of blacks, some three or four hundred, were settled, some fifteen or twenty years since, in the county of Brown, a few miles distant from my former residence in Ohio, and I was told by a person living near them, a country merchant with whom they dealt, when conversing with him on this very subject, he informed me he knew of but one instance of a mulatto child being born amongst them for the last fifteen years; and I venture the assertion, had this same colony been settled in a slave State, the cases of a like kind would have been far more numerous. . . .

The Senator, as if fearing that he had made his charge too broad, and might fail in proof to sustain it, seems to stop short, and make the inquiry, where is the process of amalgamation to begin; he had heard of no instance of the kind against Abolitionists; they, (the Abolitionists,) would begin it with the laboring class; and if I understand the Senator correctly, that Abolitionism, by throwing together the white and the black laborers, would naturally produce this result. Sir, I regret, I deplore, that such a charge should be made against the laboring class—that class which tills the ground, and in obedience to the decree of their maker, eat their bread in the sweat of their face—that class as Mr. Jefferson says, if God has a chosen people on earth, they are those who thus labor. This charge is calculated for effect, to induce the laboring class to believe that if emancipation takes place, they will be, in the free States, reduced to the same conditions as the colored laborer. The reverse of that is the truth of the case. It is the slaveholder now, he who looks upon labor as only fit for a servile race, it is him and his kindred spirits who live upon the labor of others, endeavoring to reduce the white laborer to the condition of the slave. They do not yet claim him as property, but they would exclude him from all participation in the public affairs of the country. It is further said, that if the negroes were free, the black would rival the white laborer in the free States. I cannot believe it, while so many facts exist to prove the contrary. Negroes, like the white race, but with stronger feelings, are attached to the place of their birth, and the home of their youth; and the climate of the South is congenial to their natures, more than that of the North. If emancipation should take place at the South, and the negro be freed from the fear of being made merchandize, they would remove from the free States of the North and West, immediately return to that country, because it is the home of their friends and fathers. Already in Ohio, as far as my knowledge extends, has free white labor, (emigrants,) from foreign countries, engrossed almost entirely all situations in which male or female labor is found. But, sir, this plea of necessity and convenience is the plea of tyrants. Has not the free black person the same right to the use of his hands as the white person; the same right to contract and labor for what price he pleases? Would the gentleman extend the power of the Government to the regulation of the productive industry of the country? This was his former theory, but put down effectually by the public voice. Taking advantage of the prejudice against labor, the attempt is now being made to begin this same system, by first operating on the poor black laborer. For shame! let us cease from attempts of this kind.

. . . .

I have endeavored to warn my fellow-citizens of the present and approaching danger, but the dark cloud of slavery is before their eyes, and prevents many of them from seeing the condition of things as they are. That cloud, like the cloud of summer, will soon pass away, and its thunders cease to be heard. Slavery will come to an end, and the sunshine of prosperity warm, invigorate and bless our whole country.

Memorial of Colored Men

SELECT COMMITTEE

The object contemplated by the memorial referred to your committee, is the elevation of colored men to a political equality with the white citizens of the State of Ohio. To secure this object, the memorialists ask that, the legislature take the necessary constitutional steps to strike the word "white" from the first section of the fifth article of the constitution of the State; and they further ask, at your hands, such legislation as will afford to them "the right of trial by their peers," will provide for their admission into public infirmaries and the benevolent institutions of the State, and will allow them equal participations in the benefits of common schools.

The memorialists complain that the prohibition implied by the fifth article of the constitution, is a grievous wrong, and that the legislation which excludes them from any of the benevolent institutions of the State, is unworthy of "our civilization."

The memorial purports to emanate, and does emanate from a convention of colored men, composed of delegates from different parts of the State, respectable for numbers and intelligence, and hence it may reasonably be supposed to indicate the sentiments and feelings of the class there represented.

The formal presentation of a paper, alleging important grievances, and praying for changes in the fundamental law of the State, primarily suggests an inquiry, as to the number, character, and condition of the class involved in these alleged grievances, and requesting so important and radical measures for their relief.

The colored population of this State, in 1850, amounted to 25,279, according to the federal census of that year. The increase of colored population was 7,937 over the preceding census of 1840. Upon the supposition that the ratio of increase remains the same, the present population numbers about 32,000, and will reach nearly to 37,000 by the termination of the present decade. Of the present number less than one-half are of unmixed African descent, while the remainder exhibit the varied characteristics of mixed parentage.

Of the colored population, enumerated in 1850, 12,386 were natives of this State, 12,662 were immigrants from other States of the Union, and the remainder, so far as known, were born in foreign countries. The whole number of blind, deaf and dumb, insane and idiotic, is about seventy-five persons.

A reference to the foregoing statistics your committee deem

From "Report of the Select Committee To Whom Was Referred the Memorial of Colored Men," Ohio General Assembly, Senate, *Journal*, (Appendix), (1857), pp. 528-533.

incidental to the main subject of inquiry referred to them. There are other questions connected with this subject, in the apprehension of many, but which your committee conceive are, more appropriately, matters for abstract speculation, than of practical importance. Of this kind, is the theory which accords separate creations to the different types of the human family, and, in determining their relative position, ascribes to the African mental and physical inferiority. We may, however, before we conclude, have occasion to refer to these questions at more length.

The political condition of the colored population of this State, if not entirely anomalous, is at least strangely incongruous with the theory of a free government. They are amenable to the laws of the State, but in framing these laws they have no representation whatever. All, without exception, who partake of African descent, although its characteristics are almost obliterated by the large preponderance of the caucasian type, are denied the elective franchise, excluded from all public trusts, forbid to serve as jurors, and, finally, when oppressed by poverty or visited with mental disease, or their offspring blind, or deaf and dumb, they are excluded from those institutions which the State has provided for its white citizens, but denied to the black and mulatto, or are only admitted under arbitrary and unequal restrictions.

It is said, in the language of the memorial, that "by a decision of the Supreme Court," a large portion of the colored people "are already in the possession of the elective franchise." Whatever supposed rights may have been exercised under the decision referred to, we are compelled to believe either that the framers of the constitution intended to exclude all colored persons from the elective franchise, or else they intended an absurdly unjust and ridiculous distinction.

With the knowledge, however, that the present political and social condition of the colored population of this State, is familiar to all, your committee will forbear further comment.

The future of this population is of interest to the legislator and the philanthropist. The continued existence of a colored population in our midst may be conceded as fixed, beyond a reasonable doubt. It is vain to expect that any sudden revolution, or the gradual operation of any peaceful cause, will remove them beyond our borders, or materially reduce their number. The existence of a race of different type from the dominant race, inhabiting the same country, is no anomaly. The permanent continuance of the distinct character of the two races, living in the same community, is mainly dependent upon the degree of radical difference of the types which each race represents.

The invaders of a subjugated soil may easily amalgamate with the conquered inhabitants, where no barriers are interposed by difference of complexion or diversity of origin. Natural proclivities of men may produce to some extent the same result, when these barriers do exist, but the process must necessarily be comparatively slow.

The theorist may foresee, by the inevitable laws of population, the ultimate absorption of the weaker race by the more numerous and powerful, but this supposition, however pretending in theory, is not agreeable to the prejudices of the white race, or sufficiently imminent in its practical operation to merit our consideration.

Let the permanent continuance of the colored race, as a part of our population, be conceded, and our next inquiry is, what shall be its condition in the future? This inquiry is formally addressed to this legislature, by the presentation of the memorial now under consideration. To evade or defer decisive action upon this subject, will serve only to procrastinate, and will be unworthy our obligation to the State. Let us look steadily at the difficulties, if any exist, and then afford or deny the relief demanded. If the present policy of the constitution and the laws of Ohio is just and expedient, then no change is necessary. We may then dismiss all further consideration of this whole subject, and practically say to the petitioners, your grievances are imaginary, and your complaints unreasonable murmurs against a just and benificent government. If, however, the policy of our constitution and laws is unjust and oppressive, but expediency demands its perpetuity, then let it be known that our legislature sacrifices justice to expediency, whenever the two seem to conflict.

The first and most important relief asked by the memorialists, is that the elective franchise be accorded to the colored men of the State. It is not, of course, contemplated that the action of the legislature can effect anything in this matter, except merely to submit the proposition to a vote of the people, as an amendment to the constitution; but our action in this event must be based upon a supposed approval of the change proposed, and hence the whole subject is properly before your committee.

Your committee, in the discharge of their duty, unhesitatingly declare their approval of such change in the fundamental law of the State as will abolish color as the criterion for citizenship, and recommend that the necessary steps be taken to submit an amendment for that purpose to a vote of the people.

In assigning a reason for our approval, we are not put upon the defensive. The exclusiveness of the provisions of the constitution, upon this subject, is inconsistent with a democratic theory of government, destructive of political equality, and inconsistent with the principles which gave birth to American freedom, and hence, of itself demands an apology.

The colored men of the State are, with few exceptions, natives of

American soil, they are taxed for the support of government; in war they have borne arms for our defence; the God of equality has given to them the attributes of manhood; why, then, deny to them the rights of men? Is it sufficient to say that they are black, and that the dominant race is white? The policy of our government is opposed to arbitrary rules. Forced inequalities belong to monarchies and despotisms.

But is it said that the safety of our government depends in any way upon the exclusion of the colored men from a participation in its direction? Who believes this? The blacks are capable of patriotic sentiments; many of the colored men of the State, notwithstanding the discouragements and difficulties under which they labor, are educated and enlightened;—all may become so. But when was intellectual superiority made a test for admission to the rights of citizenship? Our constitution and laws do not even require that any inquiry shall be made as to the moral character of the proposed voter. It is sufficient that he be a *white* man. We assert a broader and more democratic doctrine. *It is sufficient that he be a man.*

We admit that the inherent right of self-preservation entitles a State to impose conditions of citizenship. When imposed upon all alike, these conditions may be inexpedient, but not necessarily unjust.

Naturalization laws are designed to test the sincerity of the foreigner's intentions to become an American citizen, and of his allegiance, as well as to secure by previous residence, a knowledge of our government and institutions. Further, the rights of the foreigner are acquired, the rights of the native are born with him—they are his by birth-right.

The apologist predicates the exclusion of the colored men from the elective franchise upon an alleged inferiority of the African type. The justification of African slavery is based upon the same comfortable assurance, and the argument is equally tenable in the one case as in the other. It may be that Providence created the different races of men at different times, and by isolated creations, intending that one race should be crushed, lacerated, and degraded, for the profit, pleasure, or convenience of another race; but the proposition is too monstrous to be adopted practically, without the most conclusive and indisputable evidence.

Reason, the human face, and the human form divine, are letters patent under the hands of the Almighty, which entitle their possessor to all the consideration which belongs to humanity. Practically, color proves nothing. It neither establishes nor disproves capacity to discharge the duties of the citizen. In the actual emergencies of life, it receives no consideration. Experience has demonstrated that the blacks are capable of sustaining a regularly organized government, and that under its auspices, trade, and commerce, and the arts of civilization, have flourished; and although it may be said that the African race do not possess the character to originate civilization, and only partake of advancement by contact, yet it is, after all, reasonable to suppose that all races possess the power of self-culture, and innate elements of character sufficient to advance them to as great a degree of perfectibility as the caucassian race, which we assume to be the most favored type of the human family.

If, however, color be made the test of qualification for citizenship, then an inquiry may naturally arise whether this restriction shall spend its force upon the black alone, or whether it shall include all shades of color. Many colored men approach very nearly to pure Caucassian blood. Is this approach sufficiently near to the proposed standard to entitle him to become an elector, or shall the slightest tinge work his disfranchisement?

If one alternative be adopted, then in your zeal to exclude one-twentieth black, your law may exclude nineteen-twentieths Caucasian. If the other, then are we compelled not to inquire as to the intellectual or moral character of the person, but merely to consult his genealogy. To such absurdities are we led by a false criterion. There is one flagrant injustice resulting directly from the arbitrary restriction of the elective franchise, which your committee think worthy of particular notice here. Our laws tax the property of the colored man equally with the property of the white citizen: taxation, without representation, disguise it as you may, is only legalized plunder—a forced contribution, a badge of despotism. It is true that the black enjoys, to some degree, the protection of our laws, and the safeguards of our institutions. Similar to this, but with greater force, was the reply of the British Government to the complaints of the American colonies, that taxes were imposed upon them without their consent. The rejoinder of the colonists was an appeal to arms, the vocal arguments of booming cannon, and rattling musketry.

We have thus far, in treating of the subject of the memorial, placed the extension of the right of suffrage to the black, upon the broad grounds of justice and equality of human rights. We propose now, briefly to examine it as a question of expediency. We would test the question of expediency, not from present appearances, but by ultimate and inevitable results. Continue our present restrictive policy, and you promise to the black continued degradation and political inequality.

A sense of wrong and injustice will alienate his affections from the government that presses upon him with a heavy hand. He will become indifferent to the interests of a community that denies him political fellowship, and seems only to recognize his manhood in order to strip him by taxation. Discontented, without hopes, without aspirations, he affiliates with vice, and becomes the tenant of your jails and your penitentiary, or only resort to the most menial occupations for a scanty livelihood. Thus will be perpetuated a discontented population, a perpetual gangrene upon the body politic. But change the policy of our constitution and laws; give to the black the rights which belong to him as a man, and you change his destiny; you awaken into life and activity sentiments of patriotism and devotion to country, as natural to the black as to the white. You secure his respect for laws and institutions, which respect his rights; you elevate his entire character, and convert the stubborn malcontent into the useful citizen.

Such your committee believe will be the result of a policy founded upon justice. But fortunately the views of your committee do not rest upon abstract theory; we have the light of the example of other States. Massachusetts has granted the rights of freemen to the blacks within her border. New York gives to them the elective franchise, subject to qualifications, not very onerous.

The constitution of New Hampshire declares that all elections ought to be free, and every inhabitant of the State, having the proper qualifications, (among which color is not included,) has an equal right to elect and be elected into office.

The constitution of Vermont is equally explicit. Its language is: "Every man of the full age of twenty-one years, qualified by a residence of one year, and who is of quiet and peaceable behavior, and who will take the necessary oath, shall be entitled to vote, and to all the privileges of a freeman."

The constitution of Rhode Island, upon this subject, is more equivocal. Connecticut, pursuing the same narrow policy, which applied to a different subject, formerly made her intolerant upon matters of religion, excludes blacks from the polls; and her colored population are proverbially degraded and indolent.

In conclusion, your committee believe there is nothing in the prayer of the memorialists but what is just in theory, and nothing but what the experience of other States has demonstrated as practicable and salutary; and nothing inconsistent with true progress, and the spirit of the age. True humanitarian progress has erased much odious and oppresive legislation from our statute. Our laws once regarded the black as prima facie a slave. When his freedom was sufficiently established, his presence was still regarded as dangerous to society, or which might, by his misfortunes, become burdensome to public charity. Our laws formerly banished him from schools, and made him incompetent as a witness in courts of justice, where a white man was party to the suit. Our laws previously undertook, that as far as possible, the curse pronounced upon Canaan, should be extended to all the descendants of Ham. Who would replace these deformities upon our statute? Not content with the past, your committee propose further progress; and whatever may be the action of this Legislature, they believe that time will accomplish the justice which they recommend. The nineteenth century is remarkable for advancement in every thing that elevates humanity. Its lapse will be more glorious than its morning or its maridian. In every reform truth treads daintily at first, but gathering confidence with every advance, its march is the tread of a conqueror; aged despotisms are as fine dust before it; effete superstitions and prejudices, hoary with age, are scattered and dispelled like hateful shades and shadowy mists before the light of morning.

HERMAN CANFIELD,
O. P. BROWN,
LESTER TAYLOR,
Special Committee.

Resolved, That the committee on the judiciary be instructed to report to the Senate, a bill which shall provide for submitting to the qualified electors of the State, at the next election for senators and representatives, an amendment to the constitution, by which the elective franchise shall be extended to colored men, under the same restrictions, and subject to the same conditions as are imposed upon white citizens.

Resolved, That the committee on benevolent institutions be instructed to inquire and report to the Senate, what legislation, if any, is necessary, in order to extend a participation in the benefits of those institutions, to the colored population.

No Equality

COMMITTEE ON THE JUDICIARY

. . . .

The committee have maturely considered the propositions contained in the memorials referred to them, and have come to the conclusion, that it is inexpedient at this time, to recommend any legislative action on the subject. For this, it is proper, they should submit a few reflections, and they ask for them an attentive consideration.

The philanthropy and honest zeal evinced by the memorialists are fully appreciated. The committee believe that none but disinterested motives prompted the presentation of the memorials; but they feel constrained to say that the time has not yet arrived, if it should ever, when wisdom and common prudence would recommend an alteration in the existing laws, regarding blacks and mulatoes, unless to make them stronger.

. . . .

Ohio, on her southern border, is bounded by two powerful slave holding states. With these states she has ever been on terms of amity, of uninterrupted friendship. Perhaps there are not two states in the Union between which a higher community of feeling exists, (except with regard to slavery,) than between Ohio and Kentucky. Their rise and progress, their present prosperity, and the distinguished stand they have taken among their sister states, have their origin in the same causes. Their territories were won by the strong hand from the barbarous tribes which once overspread them. Shoulder to shoulder, their sons, in the last war, defended from foreign invasion, the frontier of the North West. In all the great measures of the general government, touching commerce, agriculture, manufactures, and the internal improvement of the country, these states have stood side by side. Their interests and their feelings have become intertwined. The beautiful river which marks their separating boundary, is their common highway to the markets of the south, and is their common source of a profitable commerce; their products are much the same, their plans and efforts to effect a permanent system of improvement, to still further advance their power and standing among their sister sovereignties, are of a similar character.

Virginia, like Kentucky, is entitled to our regard, although differing, materially, with us in civil polity, and perhaps, in political feeling. Ohio was once a part of the domain of Virginia, and by a magnanimous cession to the general government by the latter, was enabled to claim and receive the character and standing of an independent state. The question then arises, would it be prudent, or wise, by any act of ours, in the least degree, to disturb the harmony which has so long existed between these powerful states? In the opinion of the committee, it would neither be wise nor prudent. It

---

From "Report of the Committee on the Judiciary, Relative to the Repeal of all Laws Imposing Restrictions and Disabilities on Blacks and Mulattoes," *Ohio Executive Documents,* (1834-35), pp. 1-8.

may be said that the repeal of all laws imposing restrictions or disabilities on negroes and mulattoes, will not tend to interrupt the existing harmony of these states. *Possibly,* this may be the case, but it is thought that every legislative enactment on our part, which would afford to slaves a temptation or inducement to abscond from the service of their masters, and claim protection or attempt a permanent settlement here, *may* lead to a disruption of that fraternity of feeling which it is our interest and duty to cherish.

. . . .

The framers of the constitution foresaw that difficulties might arise by placing the whites and blacks upon an equality; and while they declared that involuntary servitude should not exist in this state, with certain exceptions they withheld from the negro the right of suffrage, and made him incapable, thereby, of holding any office of trust or profit. The object of this disfranchisement was, it is presumed, to prevent the migration hither of that unfortunate race; not from any callous or careless feeling for their unhappy condition, but for the purpose of self preservation, from evils which might arise by the introduction of a class of population degraded and debased in other states, and which from the antipathies of nature and the prejudices of education, operating against them, would necessarily remain so here. The same considerations no doubt prompted the legislature to carry out as far as practicable the views entertained by the Convention of eighteen hundred and two.

Experience has shown that these were not mistaken views. The records of crime in the free states, show a frightful disproportion in the numbers of white and black offenders, and most especially in those states where there are no disabilities or restrictions by law imposed upon the blacks.

. . . .

To account for this disproportion the main argument is, that by the spirit of our institutions, the mind, the capacity of the negro is not developed, that no encouragement is given him to abstain from vice or to prompt him to industry. Without stopping to combat this proposition in detail, the committee deem it sufficient to say, that the history of the race has shown the causes to lie deeper. Nature has forbidden a general amalgamation of the two races; and misfortune, which cannot be at once remedied, has made the black dependent upon, and subservient to the white man.

The free negroes in Ohio, in the aggregate are in no better condition, therefore, than the slaves in Kentucky. They are excluded from social intercourse with the whites, and whatever of education you may give them, will not tend to elevate their standing, to any considerable extent. In those free states where every right has been extended to the negro which the white man claims, it is proven by what is contained in the above statements, that his condition is still worse than in the states where he is under restriction. This may appear singular, indeed, almost unaccountable, but it is nevertheless true.

There are considerations of a still graver character than any presented, which influence the committee, to ask the passage of the resolution appended, such as address themselves to the good sense of every man; challenging deep interest and solicitude, and requiring the calm but firm action of every one who has the weal of his country near his heart. The germ of a faction has sprung into life in the United States, which now but feeble in numerical force, and not extraordinarily distinguished for character or talent, may, if its growth be not checked by the friends of peace and good order, through the medium of individual exertion, or legislative enactment, impair the stability of our Federative Union. It is well known that societies have been formed in different parts of the United States, for the avowed purpose of effecting the immediate emancipation of all the slaves. Any one who will reflect upon this, for a moment, must come to the conclusion, that their efforts contemplate revolution, and necessarily strike at the existence of the Republic. No respect is paid by them to the compact entered into by the States, when the general government was formed. The perseverance which has marked the steps of these visionaries, the increasing establishment of news-papers and periodicals to promulgate their incendiary doctrines; the donations and bequests which these societies have received, from men of fortune, to aid them; and beyond all this, the inculcation of their dangerous principles in the minds of youth in our schools and colleges, give loud warning "that the wolf is upon his walk." Jealou-sies, heart-burnings, and fears have been excited amongst our breth-ren of the south, by the countenance given to these societies by men of respectable standing, and by the efforts made through their agents and emissaries, to inflame the slaves against their masters, and there-by produce revolt and insurrection. Well may Virginia and the Carolinas be indignant at the fanaticism, or the darker motive which prompts this mad interference in their internal concerns. The hor-rible massacre of Southhampton is still fresh in recollection, and the scenes which followed, when the innocent black was sacrificed to appease the manes of the murdered!

. . . .

From a principle of self defence, then, from what experience has taught us of the incapacity of the free blacks to elevate themselves above their present miserable condition, from the enormous amount of crime perpetrated by them, as compared with the crimes committed by the whites or the slaves; and reflecting that there is an insurmountable barrier to their becoming useful or orderly citizens, which does not arise from *casualty, but from fate;* your committee recommend the adoption of the following resolution:

Resolved, That it is inexpedient, at this time, to take any legislative action on the subject matter of the memorials, and that the committee be discharged from the further consideration of the same.

Dred Scott Case

FEDERAL RELATIONS COMMITTEE

Your committee submit that so far as they are able to comprehend the force and effect of said decision, it, among other things, nationalizes slavery: annihilates the heretofore conceded right of the free States to inhibit that institution: asserts that there is no power in Congress, or the people of the United States, or of our territories, to exclude slavery: sanctions the monstrous proposition that man may hold property in man: shuts the courts of justice to hundreds of thousands of native born citizens: assumes that the black man has no civil rights, and dooms every foot of soil to the curse of slavery, and that irrevocably.

Your committee assert that this case has no parallel in wickedness in the history of the world. Verres was content to lay waste a few insignificant provinces. This decision deals with a nation; yea, an entire race. It imbrutes and unhumanizes that race. With a sublime touch of vandalism it ruthlessly strips millions of human beings of rights God-given, and hands them over to be devoured by human beasts of prey. Such is now declared by the highest judicial tribunal in the land, to be the mission of the Constitution of the United States. If so, better far that it had never been written.

However, this decision is contrary to all our preconceived notions of that instrument. The union of States under the Federal compact,

From "Majority Report of the Standing Committee on Federal Relations," Ohio General Assembly, Senate, *Journal,* (Appendix), (1857), pp. 569-570.

has heretofore been regarded as a combination of so many independent sovreignties, for fixed purposes, and definite objects. States upon entering the confederation were not supposed to have surrendered any of their local rights as independent governments. These they cautiously reserved. They delegated to the general government certain powers believed to be in harmony with these reservations. The object desired to be attained, was not a strong overshadowing central government, which should efface State lines, and obliterate State institutions, but one which should effectually secure to all the States, security from foreign aggressions, immunity from domestic depressions, and protect, foster, cherish and perpetuate civil and religious liberty and the rights of all mankind.

These views, as old as the Constitution, are all in detail, dissipated by said decision. It becomes us as citizens of Ohio, calmly, yet firmly to take our position, and abide the consequences. If we ride out the storm, well; if we go down better thus, than tame submission to such consummate wickedness. Three times, once by the ordinance of '87, once by the Constitution of A. D. 1802, and once by our present Constitution, has the territory of our State been forever consecrated to freedom. Now, however, we learn that those instruments were a cheat, a delusion, and a mere rope of sand. We learn that our own Ohio, instead of being, in fact, a free, is in effect, a slave State. The mighty sin against God, and the giant wrong against man, contemplated by that decision, *must not, and shall not, be consummated in Ohio.* It attempts to force upon us an institution, hated, loathed and execrated, by the whole civilized world, and by no portion of the earth with a deeper and more abiding detestation and abhorrance, than by the people of our State.

The men and women of Ohio regard slavery with a loathing which no words yet coined, will express. This accursed institution, may be planted upon our soil and interwoven with our institutions, but not until every valley, every plain and every hill-side, is reddened with the blood, and whitened with the bones of our sons, brothers, husbands and fathers. Sternly to the South and her Northern abettors, we say, in all kindness, that it will take more than one decision fulminated by a jesuitical catholic judge to conquer a free protestant people. We may be deprived of the ability and power to prevent the clanking of the bondsman's chains around our altars, our homes and our fires; but thank God, no human power can prevent our dying in the attempt. We may be unable to protect thousands of our own citizens, in the enjoyment of these civil rights, but long, fierce and desperate, will be the struggle before we yield the point.

We have now seen every department of the general Government subsidized to the support, spread maintainance, and eternalization of slavery. In this mad crusade against our dearest, most sacred and

most cherished rights, we have interposed our most earnest remonstrances, and uttered our most solemn warning. All unheeded and
uncared for has been that remonstrance and that warning. This
decision, if undertaken to be enforced, places us immeasurably
beyond that point, where forbearance is no longer a virtue. Yea, it is
questionable whether it is not even now a crime against both man
and God. Endeavor to enforce that decision in our State, and from
the blue waters of Lake Erie on the North, to the beautiful Ohio on
the South, from the hills of Pennsylvania on the East, to the plains of
Indiana on the West, but one voice will be heard echoing, and
re-echoing, the war cry of the revolution, "Give me Liberty, or give
me Death."

As an indication of the purpose of the General Assembly, and the
people of Ohio, your committee recommend the adoption of the
following resolutions, and the passage of the accompanying act.

O. P. BROWN,
H. CANFIELD,
Committee of the Senate.

RALPH PLUMB,
E. GUTHRIE,
J. H. LITTLER,
GEORGE MYGOTT,
Committee of the House.

Return the Slave

OHIO SUPREME COURT

True, the great principles of natural right asserted in the Declaration of Independence, and lying at the foundation of our institutions, if permitted to operate, would liberate all. But it must be
recollected that negro slavery, existing in some of the states, is an
excepted case, withdrawn from the operation of those great principles, or rather excepted from their action, as matter of compromise

From "The State vs. Hoppesa," *Western Law Journal,* I (1845), 110-115.

as to an existing and admitted evil, necessary to the formation of the union. All and everything may be said in favor of liberty. Nor is it necessary to refer to charts, ordinances, and the written declarations of men, as the foundation and recognition of those natural rights of freedom, inherent in man as the gift of God, and impressed upon our nature by the hand of omnipotence himself. The embodiment of these principles constitutes the base, frame work, and spirit of our system of government, and he who attempts to reconcile it with slavery, assumes a hopeless and impossible task. Slavery is wrong inflicted by force, and supported alone by the municipal power of the state or territory wherein it exists. It is opposed to the principles of natural justice and right, and is the mere creature of positive law. Hence, it being my duty to declare the law, not to make it, the question is not, what conforms to the great principles of natural right and universal freedom—but what do the positive laws and institutions which we, as members of the government under which we live, are bound to recognize and obey, command and direct.

I regret deeply that slavery exists. It is the only blot upon the white pennant of universal liberty, which we have flung upon the free air, for the admiration and imitation of the world. No one can defend it, no one can support it, and it was only tolerated in our system from being combined with circumstances, which appeared to rise above our control.

. . . .

Its existence should not cause bitter and uncharitable feelings towards the people of the states where it is tolerated and continued. For them we should cultivate feelings of kindness and charity. They are not the authors of slavery in this country. It existed among the colonies before our government was formed. It was the chief difficulty in the way of its formation; and in the original draft of the Declaration of Independence, was justly set forth as one of the prominent causes of complaint, that the cupidity and injustice of England made our country a mart for the barter of human flesh, and forced upon her colonies the system of slavery. But once having obtained from the peculiar characteristics of the race enslaved, its removal presents inherent and great difficulties. Had it been the slavery of white men, or men of our race such as slavery existed in Europe, it would have been an easy matter; the moment the shackle dropped or the bond was severed, they would melt away into the community as freemen, unmarked and undistinguishable. Not so with the negro. He stands out just as distinct from our race when free, as when a slave. It is not the badge of slavery but the hand of nature that has marked the difference. The question is, if free what will you do with him? No one scarcely would wish to confer upon him equal political rights, and none certainly would wish for social equality and the amalgamation of the races. So, if all were free, the presence of the negro among our people is a vast evil. If they were to be set free, shall it be at once, or shall it be upon the plan which has already been adopted successfully by many of the states, by gradual abolition? And if set free, shall they be permitted to remain among us? If set free at once, it would be unjust to the old negro, who had worn himself out in the service of his master, and who should receive from him a support, and to the young and helpless, who would have no means of subsistence. And at best it would be at once to throw upon the community the whole slave population, unaccustomed to provide for their support, without property and without the means of support. The question is surrounded with great difficulties, and can only be managed by the wisdom, prudence, and foresight of the state where it exists. Those who are anxious for the abolition of slavery should forbear to aggravate the evil, by suffering their zeal to carry them to the commission of acts which annoy, excite, and awaken the passions, without at all promoting their design. These, instead of breaking, only rivet the fetters. The only power to abolish slavery is with the states where it exists, and if let alone, there is much reason to believe that in time, state after state will find it to be her interest, politically and in all other respects, to abolish slavery, until the evil will eventually disappear. But this is for the states themselves to do.

Upon a subject of so much excitement, all should cultivate a spirit of mildness, candor and neighborly feeling. We should remember that good in life seldom comes unmingled with evil. Those who fix their eye alone upon an evil, and rush forward to remove it, may destroy the good also. We should remember that wisdom above that of man, which directed that the tares be not removed lest the wheat be destroyed also. We should be guided by this wisdom in reference to our government, which tolerated slavery, which was found existing at its formation, to respect and observe in the highest good faith that compromise of a great difficulty, which the wisdom and patriotism of the fathers of the country adjusted and settled, lest we may put to hazard the rich good we enjoy.

It is to be furthermore observed that ours is a government of white men. That our liberties were achieved, and our government formed by white men and for white men. The negro was not included or represented—the hope then was as it now is—that the whole race of negroes should at some future time be removed to a country of their own, to be subject to their own government and laws.

With these views as to the policy, general principles, and intentions of those who gave organization and life to our government, in reference to negro slavery and the negro, as fixing the great outline to govern the doctrines of construction and presumption, sometimes resorted to in the ascertainment of the true meaning of written laws, and the application of general principles, we approach the legal questions directly under consideration.

Questions of higher moment could not be presented to the consideration of a court.

It is claimed that by the treaty with France of 1803, for the cession of Louisiana to the United States, slavery cannot exist within the limits of that territory. That the ordinance of 1787, for the government of the Northwestern Territory, is above the constitution of the state of Ohio, and the constitution of the United States, and confines the recaption of fugitives from labor to the original thirteen states alone, and that by its operation no slave escaping to Ohio, from any of the new states can be reclaimed. That the law of congress providing for the recaption of fugitives from service is unconstitutional. And that the right of enforcing the duty of surrendering up fugitives from service belongs exclusively to the states. That the jurisdiction of the state of Ohio extends to the middle of the Ohio river, or to *ad filum aquae,* and that the moment a master comes, with his slaves, within that line, on the Ohio side, whether by design, force, fraud, mistake, stress of weather, or inevitable accident, or by any means whatever, the slave is free, and cannot be reclaimed. And especially if a boat on which a master with his slave, was navigating the river, should touch the shore on the Ohio side, from whatever cause, either with or without the consent of the master, that the relation of master and slave would cease, and that the slave could not be recaptured.

The treaty with France was for the cession of territory and the change of allegiance. Its object was not to change the relations of persons or the rights of property. Although the *"inhabitants"* of the ceded territory were, by the treaty, secured in all the rights and privileges guaranteed by the constitution of the United States, neither slaves nor Indians were regarded as *inhabitants,* in the sense of that word, as employed in the treaty—and it has never been regarded that the force of that term made freemen of the one, or citizens of the other.

It is claimed by the ordinance of 1787, for the government of the Northwestern Territory, that the right of recaption of fugitives from service escaping into such territory, is confined to fugitives from some one of the original thirteen states. That the ordinance being of the nature of a compact, is of superior binding force to the constitution of the state of Ohio, or the constitution of the United States. That the right of recaption of fugitives from service from any of the new states is prohibited, or at least not granted, and that such right, therefore, does not exist to the new states, whatever may be the provisions of the constitution and laws of the United States.

The Union is composed of states of equal rights and powers. The new states admitted into the Union are subject to the performance of the same duties, and possess the same sovereign, inherent, and guaranteed rights of any of the original states. Hence, the right of recaption of fugitives from labor is secured to the new states under the constitution of the United States, to the same extent that it belongs to the original states. The ordinance was an act of Congress for the government of a territory—and however much I may respect the principles of the ordinance, yet the moment the people of Ohio formed themselves into a state, by the adoption of a constitution, and an admission into the Union, they became clothed with all the rights and powers of an original state, and the constitution of the state became the supreme law of the state, in place of the ordinance governing it as a territory. And it would be strange, indeed, to hold that an ordinance passed by a congress, could be superior to the constitution of the United States, adopted by the people and the states as the supreme law of the land—not subject to alteration by Congress, but only by the power which formed and adopted it. A slave, therefore, owing service, and escaping to Ohio from a new state, is subject to recaption precisely as though the escape had been from one of the original states.

Admixture Unconstitutional

ANDERSON vs. MILLIKIN

This was an action brought by the plaintiff against the defendants, judges of an election, for the refusal of his vote. It was submitted by the parties to the court of common pleas of Butler county, upon an agreed statement of facts, showing: "That the father of the plaintiff was a white man, without any admixture of African blood; that the mother of the plaintiff is a mixture of

From Alfred J. Anderson vs. Thomas Millikin and Others, *Ohio State Reports,* Critchfield, X (1874), pp. 458-467.

three-fourths white and one-fourth African blood; that neither the plaintiff nor his mother ever were slaves or held as such; that the said plaintiff for twenty-five years last past has been a resident of the second ward of the city of Hamilton, in Butler county, in the State of Ohio; and that, in all respects, he was, at the time of the election hereinafter referred to, a qualified voter at said election, in said ward, unless disqualified on account of the admixture of African blood, as aforesaid. That on the 4th of November, A. D. 1856, the said plaintiff, at the polls of the said ward, offered to vote for electors of president and vice-president of the United States, and that said defendants, being then and there the judges of said election, refused to receive the vote of said plaintiff on account of his admixture of African blood, and for no other reason."

. . . .

Gholson, J. The constitution of 1802 contained the following provision as to the persons entitled to the exercise of the elective franchise: "In all elections, all *white male inhabitants* above the age of twenty-one years, having resided in the state one year next preceding the election, and who have paid or are charged with a state or county tax, shall enjoy the right of an elector; but no person shall be entitled to vote, except in the county or district in which he shall actually reside at the time of the election." Art. 4, sec. 1. The use of the word "white," in this section, necessarily excluded those inhabitants of the state, though otherwise qualified, who were not white, and called for a determination of the question, who should be deemed "white," within the meaning of the constitution? This question was answered by repeated judicial decisions. It was considered in view of blood or race, and the rule adopted to meet the obvious difficulty of a mixture of blood or races, was that the white race must predominate. There was a white race and a black race, and the obvious intent was, to exclude the latter from the elective franchise. If an inhabitant of the state had an equal portion of the blood of each race, the exclusion still applied; but if he had a larger proportion of the blood of the white race, he was to be regarded as white, within the meaning of the constitution.

. . . .

In any ordinary case—in any case in which feeling and prejudice did not enter as elements to disturb the judgment—no one would probably claim that a most important right once enjoyed, and, necessarily, in its nature continuous, was abrogated and annulled, unless the intent to do so was clearly and explicitly expressed. Argument and inference from the use of doubtful and indefinite terms, would not be deemed sufficient. We trust that, without influence from any prejudice we might personally feel, or from any which we might suppose to be felt by others, we can, in the language of our official oath, administer justice without respect to persons.

. . . .

But the interest and importance of the question demand from us further remarks. We are bound to presume, that those who framed the present constitution knew what judicial construction the words of the former had received. If we look at the record of their proceedings, published under their authority, we know as a fact that the construction which had been given to the word "white," was expressly and directly brought to their attention. A proposition was made to strike out the word, so as to remove the exclusion of persons not white, and it was contended "that the term 'white' is vague in its signification and has no practical meaning." In answer, it was said: "Such might have been the case, if the word had not received a practical construction for near fifty years; but there is now no question that may with more safety be submitted, to any of our tribunals, from the Supreme Court to the justice of the peace." Mr. Worthington, 2 Debates in Convention, 639. And a member in favor of the proposition, commenting on the decision of the courts as one they had been obliged to make to get over the difficulty from the use of the word "white," expressly stated that decision to be, "that a person having less than half black blood shall have the rights of a white man." Mr. Humphreville, 2 Debates of Convention, 553. In view, then, of this knowledge, presumed and actual, of the construction the word "white" had received in reference to the exercise of the elective franchise, we find the same word in the same connection in the present constitution. By the clear and well-settled rules of construction, we are bound to conclude that the word was used in the same sense, and was intended to include all persons whom the meaning it had received would embrace.

. . . .

If we were satisfied that the framers of the constitution intended to confer the right of suffrage upon a particular description of persons, and, in doing so, used a phrase in a sense which, as then understood, was sufficient for the purpose, and which is shown to be a mistaken one only by subsequent research and newer light, we would still be bound to give effect to the sense in which the phrase was used. The question is not, what the phrase "citizen of the United States" means in the light of the decision in the case of Dred Scott *v.* Sandford, but what the framers of our constitution intended by the use of that phrase, and what, in the connection in which it is found, and with the light and knowledge possessed when it was used, it was intended to mean.

We think it entirely clear, that the phrase "citizen of the United States" was inserted in our constitution with a view to the exclusion of aliens until they should be naturalized, and thus become citizens of the United States. We are confident that the phrase was used with no reference to color, and can not believe that the idea was then entertained that, independent of the word "white," the phrase "citizen of the United States" would operate to exclude any person on account of color, from the exercise of the elective franchise. In truth, it seems too clear for argument, that, had the phrase "citizen of the United States" a then well-understood connotation or signification, that necessarily carried along with it the attribute of whiteness of color, and, much more, of the absence of any admixture whatever of blood or color, the word "white" would have been applied as a qualification to the phrase. "White male citizen of the United States" is the language. Now, if a citizen of the United States must necessarily be, and can only be, a white person, why say *white* citizen of the United States? The very use of the term "white," as applied to a citizen of the United States, necessarily implies that those who used it, supposed and understood that there might be citizens of the United States who were not white.

. . . .

We are aware that the general assembly of the state, by an act passed April 2, 1859, has expressed a view of the meaning of the word "white," in the section of the constitution regulating the elective franchise, in conflict with that which we have stated to be the one intended. There are cases in which subsequent legislation may be properly looked to, as reflecting light on the construction of former laws, though it would not furnish a rule obligatory upon the courts. There are cases involving this very question of color, in which legislative intent would properly be our guide. Such was the case as to the classification of youth entitled to the benefit of the public schools, in which the majority of this court held, that the legislature had expressed an intention that a classification should be made, founded as well upon the visible admixture of color and upon social intercourse, as upon the degree of the blood of the African race. Van Camp *v.* The Board of Education of Logan, ante, 406. But, surely, it can not be claimed, and will not, at this day, be claimed by any intelligent statesman or lawyer that it is within the scope of legislative power to give to the courts an authoritative construction of a provision of the constitution of the state. The simple question with us is, in what sense the word "white" was used in the constitution, and that sense, when ascertained, we suppose to be obligatory both upon us and the general assembly of the state.

The word, we have shown, had received, at the time of the adoption of the present constitution, a clear and settled construction. Doubtless, this construction may not have been satisfactory to many persons; but the time and the opportunity to have expressed dissatisfaction, were during the deliberations of the convention. It was entirely competent for the convention to change the construction which the courts had given, and, we can not doubt, had a change been desired or intended, it would have been made.

In this view, it is obvious that it would be a grave error to suppose that the judges of this court, whatever might be their individual views, have the same right to re-examine the construction given to the word "white," as judges sitting under the old constitution. Indeed, a settled construction, acted upon and acquiesced in for a series of years, is usually obligatory upon judges, whatever doubts they may have of its correctness. But whenever that construction has been acted upon in the framing of laws, and, much more, in the framing of a constitution, to attempt a change might well be regarded a more arbitrary exercise of power, and beyond any legitimate authority of judges.

We are unanimously of the opinion, that the description of persons of which the plaintiff is one, were not deprived by the present constitution of the right to the exercise of the elective franchise, which they enjoyed under the construction which the old constitution had received. The plaintiff, therefore, was entitled, under the constitution, to vote at the election, and was deprived of this constitutional right by the act of the defendants. He is therefore entitled to a judgment in his favor, against the defendants, under the agreed statement of facts.

The Rescue Cases

JOSEPH R. SWAN, C. J.

The affidavits of the relators, without disclosing the cause of their imprisonment, set forth that they were unlawfully imprisoned.

The writs were of course issued upon these affidavits. The returns show that the sheriff of Cuyahoga county holds the relators in custody under a sentence and judgment of the district court of the United States, for the offense of rescuing fugitives from service.

The judgment of the district court is conclusive, and precludes all inquiry on habeas corpus, unless it is a nullity.

Waiving all questions made by counsel as to the power of a state judge, on such a summary proceeding, to declare the sentence of a court of general jurisdiction invalid, it is very clear that we can not go behind the sentence, and revise and review the previous proceedings of the court.

. . . .

Neither the verdict of the jury nor the judgment of the district court can be collaterally impeached, if that court had jurisdiction of the party and offense. The verdicts and sentences of courts in every case would be subject to arbitrary intermeddling, and might be set aside and criminals discharged by any judge who is authorized by statute to issue this writ, if a case could be re-examined and the justice of the verdict and sentence considered on habeas corpus.

. . . .

The only ground, therefore, upon which the relators can be discharged is, to go behind the seventh section of the act, and maintain that Congress never had any legislative power, under the constitution of the United States, to provide punishment for a person who knowingly and intentionally rescues an escaped slave.

This position, if sustained by the court, cuts up by the roots all laws which have been passed, and all laws which may hereafter be passed by Congress, relating to the reclamation of fugitives. It not only disposes of this seventh section of the act of 1850, now under consideration, but the whole of the acts of 1793 and 1850.

Neither the case before us, nor the question thus broadly presented, requires us to consider or determine the powers of the court to appoint commissioners, or the provisions of the law of 1850, which have been the subject of discussion and condemnation, and which have so deeply agitated the public mind.

The question before us is, whether the seventh section of the fugitive law, under which these relators were sentenced, is a nullity, for want of legislative power in Congress, to pass any law whatever relating to fugitives from labor?

. . . .

From *Ex Parte* Simeon Bushnell, *Ex Parte* Charles Langston, *Ohio State Report*, Critchfield, IX (1874), pp. 62-260.

The subjects to which I have alluded, and which are now before us, may have a deep meaning and an exciting interest to these relators and to the public. But they are not in issue, or the proper subjects of discussion or argument in the determination of the question before us. They are, indeed, trifling and evanescent, compared with the consequences which may result from the present action of this court; for, if these relators are discharged, it must be, I repeat, on the ground that the laws of 1783 and 1850 have always been void, and consequently that these and all other laws hereafter passed, of any kind, will now and from henceforth be persistently resisted by the State of Ohio. I say, henceforth persistently resisted, because it will be found, I think, that the same adjudication which determines that Congress have no power to pass any law, determines also a precedent, that the construction of the constitution shall depend upon the shifting private opinions of every judge in every state, who is called upon to give it an interpretation, whatever may be the decision of the Supreme Court of the United States, and other courts of the Union.

. . . .

In the compact of the Union, the framers of the constitution guaranteed to the owners of escaped slaves the right of reclamation. It is made part of the constitution; the whole irrepealable; and to be changed only by the power that made it, in the form prescribed by it.

It was designed to be a practicable and peaceable mode by which a fugitive from service might be delivered up. It can not be extended by implication; the fugitive must not only owe service or labor in another state, but must have escaped from it. This is the extent and the limit of the right of the master.

The constitution of the United States went into operation in March, 1789.

In 1793, the second Congress elected under the constitution of the United States, and composed of many of the members of the convention which framed the constitution, passed an act providing for the rendition of fugitives from justice, and a summary mode for the reclamation of fugitives from labor. By this act, rescuers, obstructers, and harborers of escaped slaves, were to be visited with a penalty not exceeding five hundred dollars.

No jurist will deny, that if Congress can provide a penal forfeiture for an alleged violation of law, as in the act of 1793, they have the legislative power to superadd imprisonment for the same offense, as in the act of 1850. No court can pronounce the one constitutional and the other without legislative authority.

This law of 1793 was passed by Congress without any traces in history of constitutional objection; has been ever since that time, by every department of the government, national and state, not only received and acquiesced in as the law of the land, but in active, practical operation throughout every state in the Union. Enacted at the commencement of our government, it has been in operation for sixty-six years.

It is conceded by the counsel for the relators, that if Congress have no power to legislate on this subject, they never had any power to legislate upon the subject of fugitives from justice. The same reasons for holding that the one is a usurpation of legislative power, is equally fatal to the other. Both stand precisely on the same ground.

The executive departments of the states of the Union have, I believe, acted upon, and I am not aware that any have denied, the constitutionality of the law of Congress for the rendition of fugitive criminals.

It may now be well asked, if such a long period of recognition and acquiescence in the existence of a law is to be disregarded, and the law itself annulled, whether there be anything in our government so settled and stable as not to be liable to attack and overthrow, to vacillation and change; and if, after this lapse of time, a new and yet untried experiment upon this and all other irritating questions of constitutional law is to be entered upon, and a precedent set by the judges of this court, that no question can be put to rest by time or acquiesence, when will the construction of the constitution be settled, and the landmarks of the several departments of the government and the states be permanently fixed?

. . . .

I am of the opinion, and I think the calm judgment of others will concur with me in the opinion, that in view of these decisions of the Supreme Court of the United States settling the power of Congress; in view of the adjudications of the courts of the free states affirming the same power; in view of the acquiescence of all departments of the national and state governments during two generations, the judges of a state court have no judicial right to interpose their own individual opinions upon a question thus disposed of, change the interpretation to what they believe it should be, overrule the adjudications of the Supreme Court of the United States and the state courts, strike down the legislative power of Congress now and from henceforth, resist, and persistently, on the authority of their private judgment and judicial discretion thus assumed over the interpretation of the constitution of the United States, the further exercise of all authority by every department of the national government,

and force upon the State of Ohio and its people the maintenance
of the authority of their own individual opinions as constitutional
law.

. . . .

When will this happy state of friendly litigation in the Supreme
Court of the United States begin, if, in the meantime, the power of
Congress is denied and resisted as a usurpation, by the State of Ohio?
Is the duty of the national government less imperative to enforce her
authority and resist what she believes usurpation than that of the
state government?

But there is a very important political view of this question
which should not be overlooked. No governmental rule can be
evolved by construction from the constitution of the United States
without practically becoming a part of the constitution itself. Thus,
if, in Ohio, no laws of Congress can be operative for the reclamation
of slaves, but laws on that subject may be passed by the general
assembly; and in Illinois, and the other free states which have
acknowledged the decision in the Prigg case, laws enacted by Congress are to be exclusively operative, and the laws of their state
legislatures void; if no tariff law can be operative in South Carolina,
but such law everywhere else valid; if in Mississippi and Alabama the
law against the slave-trade is held unconstitutional and void, and in
every other state enforced, it will be seen that the constitution, by
interpretation, will become somewhat different in the different
states. Now, if this can be done as to one provision of the constitution, it can be done as to all others. If each state may construe it in
its own way, to promote its own local interest, what will the
constitution of the United States become, but a hydra of more than
thirty heads, uttering Babel and conflicting commands, such as each
state in its own jurisdiction may deem it expedient to obey, or party
strife may demand?

. . . .

Now, with respect to the boundary of jurisdiction between the
federal and state governments, I do not desire to say anything but
this, that when Congress has undertaken to enforce, by legislation, a
right guaranteed by the constitution itself, and after the power has
been recognized by all the highest judicial tribunals of the states of
the Union before whom the question has been presented, has been
acquiesced in by the country for sixty-six years; and, superadded to
these circumstances, the federal tribunal, in cases arising under the
constitution, has repeatedly held that Congress have the power, it is

too late for the judges of the courts of Ohio, upon their private judgment, to deny the power.

. . . .

If the individual opinion of every judge is to become the exponent and construction of the constitution of the United States whenever he feels certain that he is right, without regard to the decisions of the highest tribunals of the country, then the individual opinion of every judge is the constitution, not only to himself, but, for the time being, to the country. This, it seems to me, is simply discretion without rule, guide, precedent, or limitation—unstable, capricious despotism.

. . . .

The sense of justice of the people of Ohio has been shocked by some of the unjust provisions of the fugitive acts. It is not the authority of Congress to legislate that they deny, but it is the abuse of the power.

That abuse may be remedied by Congress. And if the power to legislate is denied, the question can be put an end to by repeal—it is the only constitutional mode left; the other alternative is intestine war and resistance of our national government.

All must admit that the owner of escaped slaves is entitled to their reclamation. Good faith to sister states demands it; and there would be no resistance in Ohio to a fair and just law effecting that object. No intense public feeling could be excited upon the question as to who should legislate, Congress or the states, if a proper law were passed by Congress.

For myself, as a member of this court, I disclaim the judicial discretion of disturbing the settled construction of the constitution of the United States; and I must refuse the experiment of initiating disorder and governmental collision, to establish order and even-handed justice.

I do not repeat here the judicial arguments sustaining the power of Congress, which have been pronounced by some of the soundest and wisest judges that have adorned the American bench; for it is my deliberate and confident conviction that the question has by time, acquiescence, and adjudication, passed beyond the reach of judicial consideration of preponderance of argument; certainly beyond the reach of question before this court.

As a citizen, I would not deliberately violate the constitution or the law by interference with fugitives from service. But if a weary, frightened slave should appeal to me to protect him from his pursuers, it is possible I might momentarily forget my allegiance to the law and constitution, and give him a covert from those who were upon his track. There are, no doubt, many slaveholders who would thus follow the impulses of human sympathy; and if I did it, and were prosecuted, condemned, and imprisoned, and brought by my counsel before this tribunal on a habeas corpus, and were then permitted to pronounce judgment in my own case, I trust I should have the moral courage to say, before God and the country, as I am now compelled to say, under the solemn duties of a judge, bound by my official oath to sustain the supremacy of the constitution and the law, *"The prisoner must be remanded."*

10 Ohio and the Rebellion

THE YEARS BETWEEN 1861 and 1865 were turbulent in Ohio. Over the decades, an increasingly large number of Ohioans had become opposed to slavery and the machinations and protestations of the Southern political bloc, and they were relieved to hear of the incident at Fort Sumter. Significant numbers of others, for a myriad of reasons, were fearful of the war and its repercussions. Although it is often tempting to romanticize the glories of the American Civil War and the triumphs of that generation, the war years in Ohio were disruptive, cruel, and vicious.

Ohioans certainly did their part for the war effort. Over one-third of a million (351,418) served in the Union army. From the first battle of the war, an engagement fought at Philippi, Virginia, until Lee's surrender at Appomattox Court House, Ohioans participated in almost every contest. The names of Ohioans in the officer corps is an impressive list indeed: George B. McClellan, Ulysses S. Grant, William T. Sherman, Phil Sheridan, Don Carlos Buell, James B. McPherson, William S. Rosecrans, Jacob D. Cox, Jacob Ammen, and many more. Many Ohioans won the Congressional Medal of Honor, including Jacob Parrot, who was the first to be awarded the citation for his participation in the Andrews Raid through Georgia, and Milton M. Holland, a black from Athens County who was decorated for his bravery at the battle of Chapins Farms, Virginia. Of the Ohioans who served, 35,475 died and over 30,000 were totally or partially disabled.

Not only were Ohioans prominent on the field of battle, but many were influential at the seat of government. Within Lincoln's official family were Salmon P. Chase, Secretary of the Treasury and later Chief Justice of the United States Supreme Court; Edwin M. Stanton, Secretary of War; and William Dennison, Postmaster General. Ohio's senators were Benjamin F. Wade and John Sherman, both significant in American history, while men such as George H. Pendleton, Samuel S. Cox, John A. Bingham, and Clement L. Vallandigham served in the lower house.

Though the state's major racial restrictions had been repealed in

1848, the free blacks in Ohio remained outside official consideration. Anxious to serve the cause of the Union and freedom, however, blacks in Ohio rushed to volunteer following the President's call for troops in 1861. The state refused to enlist blacks for military service, preferring to use them as a labor force. Massachusetts, however, recruited blacks throughout Ohio, and hundreds served for that state. It was not until June 1863 that Ohio began to seek the military service of its own blacks. Although Ohio was credited with having 5,092 of its blacks on active duty, many more participated as cooks, laborers, teamsters, and attendants in the medical service.

The American Civil War, because it was an internal war, was fought bitterly not only on the field of battle but also at home. Ohio was probably as politically divided as any state, and the incriminations and tactics leveled by both the Democrats and the Republicans against each other were restrained by neither moral considerations nor a sense of fairness. The Democrats became ardent states' righters and viewed the Lincoln administration as a powerful alliance between eastern big business and government that threatened the basic fiber of the republic. The Republicans, on the other hand, believed that all who did not actively support the administration and its war effort were in concert with the rebellious South. It was on this point that the two factions railed at each other, as reason gave way to innuendo, vindictiveness, and fear.

Opposition to the war ripened in Ohio. The war, the war aims, and the people conducting the war were openly and vigorously denounced. Resistance to the draft occurred in many localities throughout the state, and this climate produced many eligible candidates for martyrdom. Samuel Medary, Archibald McGregor, Abner Jackson, Edson B. Olds, and others were arrested for making their views public. The story of Clement L. Vallandigham's martyrdom is certainly one of the most absurd in any state's history. Defeated in his bid for re-election to Congress in 1862, Vallandigham became one of the most outspoken critics of the Lincoln administration and its conduct of the war. Because of an inflammatory speech he gave in Mount Vernon on May 1, 1863, the former congressman was arrested under "General Order, No. 38," court-martialed, and exiled to the Confederacy. He eventually reached Canada and from there was the Democratic gubernatorial candidate in 1863, running on a peace platform; however, he was defeated handily by John Brough. What occurred in Ohio during the war underscores the unanswerable questions of the extent to which a free society can quash internal criticism during a national crisis while still remaining a free society.

No Compromise

BENJAMIN WADE

MR. WADE: How is it with the leaders of this modern revolution? Are they in a position to complain of the action of this Government for years past? Why, sir, they have had more than two thirds of the Senate for many years past, and until very recently, and have almost that now. You—who complain, I ought to say—represent but a little more than one fourth of the free people of these United States, and yet your counsels prevail, and have prevailed all along for at least ten years past. In the Cabinet, in the Senate of the United States, in the Supreme Court, in every department of the Government, your officers, or those devoted to you, have been in the majority, and have dictated all the policies of this Government. Is it not strange, sir, that they who now occupy these positions should come here and complain that their rights are stricken down by the action of the Government?

But what has caused this great excitement that undoubtedly prevails in a portion of our country? If the newspapers are to be credited, there is a reign of terror in all the cities and large towns in the southern portion of this community that looks very much like the reign of terror in Paris during the French revolution. There are acts of violence that we read of almost every day, wherein the rights of northern men are stricken down, where they are sent back with indignities, where they are scourged, tarred, feathered, and murdered, and no inquiry made as to the cause. I do not suppose that the regular Government, in times of excitement like these, is really responsible for such acts. I know that these outbreaks of passion, these terrible excitements that sometimes pervade a community, are entirely irrepressible by the law of the country. I suppose that is the case now; because if these outrages against northern citizens were really authorized by the State authorities there, were they a foreign Government, everybody knows, if it were the strongest Government on earth, we should declare war upon her in one day.

But what has caused this great excitement? Sir, I will tell you what I suppose it is. I do not (and I say it frankly) so much blame the people of the South; because they believe, and they are led to believe by all the information that ever comes before them, that we, the dominant party to-day, who have just seized upon the reins of this Government, are their mortal enemies, and stand ready to trample their institutions under foot. They have been told so by our

From Benjamin Wade, "Speech," *Congressional Globe*, Vol. XXX, 36th Congress, 2nd Session, December 17, 1860, pp. 99-107.

enemies at the North. Their misfortune, or their fault, is that they have lent a too easy ear to the insinuations of those who are our mortal enemies, while they would not hear us.

. . . .

Now, Mr. President, I have shown, I think, that the dominant majority here have nothing to complain of in the legislation of Congress, or in the legislation of any of the States, or in the practice of the people of the North, under the fugitive slave bill, except so far as they say certain State legislation furnishes some evidence of hostility to their institutions. And here, sir, I beg to make an observation. I tell the Senator, and I tell all the Senators, that the Republican party of the northern States, so far as I know, and of my own State in particular, hold the same opinions with regard to this peculiar institution of yours that are held by all the civilized nations of the world. We do not differ from the public sentiment of England, of France, of Germany, of Italy, and every other civilized nation on God's earth; and I tell you frankly that you never found, and you never will find, a free community that are in love with your peculiar institution. The Senator from Texas [Mr. Wigfall] told us the other day that cotton was king, and that by its influence it would govern all creation. He did not say so in words, but that was the substance of his remark: that cotton was king, and that it had its subjects in Europe who dared not rebel against it. Here let me say to that Senator, in passing, that it turns out that they are very rebellious subjects, and they are talking very disrespectfully at present of that king that he spoke of. They defy you to exercise your power over them. They tell you that they sympathize in this controversy with what you call the black Republicans. Therefore I hope that, so far as Europe is concerned at least, we shall hear no more of this boast that cotton is king; and that he is going to rule all the civilized nations of the world, and bring them to his footstool. Sir, it will never be done.

But, sir, I wish to inquire whether the southern people are injured by, or have any just right to complain of, that platform of principles that we put out, and on which we have elected a President and Vice President. I have no concealments to make, and I shall talk to you, my southern friends, precisely as I would talk upon the stump on the subject. I tell you that in that platform we did lay it down that we would, if we had the power, prohibit slavery from another inch of free territory under this Government. I stand on that position to-day. I have argued it probably to half a million people. They stand there, and have commissioned and enjoined me to stand there forever; and, so help me God, I will. I say to you frankly, gentlemen, that while we hold this doctrine, there is no Republican, there is no convention of Republicans, there is no paper that speaks for them, there is no orator that sets forth their doctrines, who ever pretends that they have any right in your States to interfere with your peculiar institution; but, on the other hand, our authoritative platform repudiates the idea that we have any right or any intention ever to invade your peculiar institution in your own States.

Now, what do you complain of? You are going to break up this Government; you are going to involve us in war and blood, from a mere suspicion that we shall justify that which we stand everywhere pledged not to do. Would you be justified in the eyes of the civilized world in taking so monstrous a position, and predicating it on a bare, groundless suspicion? We do not love slavery. Did you not know that before today? before this session commenced? Have you not a perfect confidence that the civilized world are against you on this subject of loving slavery or believing that it is the best institution in the world? Why, sir, everything remains precisely as it was a year ago. No great catastrophe has occurred. There is no recent occasion to accuse us of anything. But all at once, when we meet here, a kind of gloom pervades the whole community and the Senate Chamber. Gentlemen rise and tell us that they are on the eve of breaking up this Government, that seven or eight States are going to break off their connection with the Government, retire from the Union, and set up a hostile Government of their own, and they look imploringly over to us, and say to us "you can prevent it; we can do nothing to prevent; but it all lies with you." Well, sir, what can we do to prevent it? You have not even condescended to tell us what you want; but I think I see through the speeches that I have heard from gentlemen on the other side. If we would give up the verdict of the people, and take your platform, I do not know but you would be satisfied with it. I think the Senator from Texas rather intimated, and I think the Senator from Georgia more than intimated, that if we would take what is exactly the Charleston platform on which Mr. Breckinridge was placed, and give up that on which we won our victory, you would grumblingly and hesitatingly be satisfied.

. . . .

Well, Mr. President, I have disavowed all intention on the part of the Republican party to harm a hair of your heads anywhere. We hold to no doctrine that can possibly work you an inconvenience. We have been faithful to the execution of all the laws in which you have any interest, as stands confessed on this floor by your own party, and as is known to me without their confessions. It is not, then, that Mr. Lincoln is expected to do any overt act by which you may be injured; you will not wait for any; but anticipating that the Government may work an injury, you say you will put an end to it, which means simply, that you intend either to rule or ruin this Government. That is what your complaint comes to; nothing else. We do not like your institution, you say. Well, we never liked it any better than we do now. You might as well have dissolved the Union at any other period as now, on that account, for we stand in relation to it precisely as we have ever stood: that is, repudiating it among ourselves as a matter of policy and morals, but nevertheless admitting that where it is out of our jurisdiction, we have no hold upon it, and no designs upon it.

Then, sir, as there is nothing in the platform on which Mr. Lincoln was elected of which you complain, I ask, is there anything in the character of the President elect of which you ought to complain? Has he not lived a blameless life? Did he ever transgress any law? Has he ever committed any violation of duty of which the most scrupulous can complain? Why, then, your suspicions that he will? I have shown that you have had the Government all the time until, by some misfortune or maladministration, you brought it to the very verge of destruction, and the wisdom of the people had discovered that it was high time that the scepter should depart from you, and be placed in more competent hands; I say that this being so, you have no constitutional right to complain; especially when we disavow any intention so to make use of the victory we have won as to injure you at all.

This brings me, sir, to the question of compromises. On the first day of this session, a Senator rose in his place and offered a resolution for the appointment of a committee to inquire into the evils that exist between the different sections, and to ascertain what can be done to settle this great difficulty! That is the proposition, substantially. I tell the Senator that I know of no difficulty; and as to compromises, I had supposed that we were all agreed that the day of compromises was at an end. The most solemn compromises we have ever made have been violated without a whereas. Since I have had a seat in this body, one of considerable antiquity, that had stood for more than thirty years, was swept away from your statute-books. When I stood here in the minority arguing against it; when I asked you to withhold your hand; when I told you it was a sacred compromise between the sections, and that when it was removed we should be brought face to face with all that sectional bitterness that has intervened; when I told you that it was a sacred compromise which no man should touch with his finger, what was your reply? That it was a mere act of Congress—nothing more, nothing less—and that it could be swept away by the same majority that passed it. That was true in point of fact, and true in point of law; but it showed the weakness of compromises. Now, sir, I only speak for myself; and I say that, in view of the manner in which other compromises have been heretofore treated, I should hardly think any two of the

Democratic party would look each other in the face and say "compromise" without a smile. [Laughter.] A compromise to be brought about by act of Congress, after the experience we have had, is absolutely ridiculous.

But what have we to compromise? Sir, I am one of those who went forth with zeal to maintain the principles of the great Republican party. In a constitutional way we met, as you met. We nominated our candidates for President and Vice President, and you did the same for yourselves. The issue was made up; and we went to the people upon it. Although we have been usually in the minority; although we have been generally beaten, yet, this time, the justice of our principles, and the maladministration of the Government in your hands, convinced the people that a change ought to be wrought; and after you had tried your utmost, and we had tried our utmost, we beat you; and we beat you upon the plainest and most palpable issue that ever was presented to the American people, and one that they understood the best. There is no mistaking it; and now, when we come to the Capitol, I tell you that our President and our Vice President must be inaugurated, and administer the Government as all their predecessors have done. Sir, it would be humiliating and dishonorable to us if we were to listen to a compromise by which he who has the verdict of the people in his pocket, should make his way to the presidential chair. When it comes to that, you have no Government; anarchy intervenes; civil war may follow it; all the evils that may come to the human imagination may be consequent upon such a course as that. The moment the American people cut loose from the sheet anchor of free government and liberty—that is, whenever it is denied in this Government that a majority fairly given shall rule—the people are unworthy of free government. Sir, I know not what others may do; but I tell you that, with the verdict of the people given in favor of the platform upon which our candidates have been elected, so far as I am concerned, I would suffer anything to come before I would compromise that away.

. . . .

I say, then, that so far as I am concerned, I will yield to no compromise. I do not come here begging, either. It would be an indignity to the people that I represent if I were to stand here parleying as to the rights of the party to which I belong. We have won our right to the Chief Magistracy of this nation in the way that you have always won your predominance; and if you are as willing to do justice to others as to exact it from them, you would never raise an inquiry as to a committee for compromises. Here I beg, barely for myself, to say one thing more. Many of you stand in an attitude hostile to this Government; that is to say, you occupy an attitude

where you threaten that, unless we do so and so, you will go out of
this Union and destroy the Government. I say to you, for myself,
that, in my private capacity, I never yielded to anything by way of
threat, and in my public capacity I have no right to yield to any such
thing; and therefore I would not entertain a proposition for any
compromise; for, in my judgment, this long, chronic controversy that
has existed between us must be met, and met upon the principles of
the Constitution and laws, and met now.

. . . .

There is one other subject about which I ought to say something.
On that side of the Chamber, you claim the constitutional right, if I
understand you, to secede from the Government at pleasure, and set
up an adverse Government of your own; that one State, or any
number of States, have a perfect constitutional right to do it. Sir, I
can find no warrant in the Constitution for any doctrine like that. In
my judgment, it would be subversive of all constitutional obligation.
If this is so, we really have not now, and never have had, a Government; for that certainly is no Government of which a State can do
just as it pleases, any more than it would be of an individual. How
can a man be said to be governed by law, if he will obey the law or
not just as he sees fit? It puts you out of the pale of Government,
and reduces this Union of ours, of which we have all boasted so
much, to a mere conglomeration of States, to be held at the will of
any capricious member of it. As to South Carolina, I will say that she
is a small State; and probably, if she were sunk by an earthquake
to-day, we would hardly ever find it out, except by the unwonted
harmony that might prevail in this Chamber. [Laughter.] But I think
she is unwise. I would be willing that she should go her own gait,
provided we could do it without an example fatal to all government;
but standing here in the highest council of the nation, my own
wishes, if I had any, must be under the control of my constitutional
duty.

. . . .

I acknowledge, to the fullest extent, the right of revolution, if
you may call it a right, and the destruction of the Government under
which we live, if we are discontented with it, and on its ruins to erect
another more in accordance with our wishes. I believe nobody at this
day denies the right; but they that undertake it, undertake it with
this hazard: if they are successful, then all is right, and they are
heroes; if they are defeated, they are rebels. That is the character of
all revolution: if successful, of course it is well; if unsuccessful, then

the Government from which they have rebelled treats them as traitors.

. . . .

I say that is the way it seems to me, as a lawyer. I see no power in the Constitution to release a Senator from this position. Sir, if there was any other, if there was an absolute right of secession in the Constitution of the United States when we stepped up there to take our oath of office, why was there not an exception in that oath? Why did it not run "that we would support the Constitution of the United States unless our State shall secede before our term was out?" Sir, there is no such immunity. There is no way by which this can be done that I can conceive of, except it is standing upon the Constitution of the United States, demanding equal justice for all, and vindicating the old flag of the Union. We must maintain it, unless we are cloven down by superior force.

Well, sir, it may happen that you can make your way out of the Union, and that, by levying war upon the Government, you may vindicate your right to independence. If you should do so, I have a policy in my mind. No man would regret more than myself that any portion of the people of these United States should think themselves impelled, by grievances or anything else, to depart out of this Union, and raise a foreign flag and a hand against the General Government. If there was any just cause on God's earth that I could see that was within my reach, of honorable release from any such pretended grievance, they should have it; but they set forth none; I can see none. It is all a matter of prejudice, superinduced unfortunately, I believe, as I intimated before, more because you have listened to the enemies of the Republican party and what they said of us, while, from your intolerance, you have shut out all light as to what our real principles are. We have been called and branded in the North and in the South and everywhere else, as John Brown men, as men hostile to your institutions, as meditating an attack upon your institutions in your own States—a thing that no Republican ever dreamed of or ever thought of, but has protested against as often as the question has been up; but your people believe it. No doubt they believe it because of the terrible excitement and reign of terror that prevails there. No doubt they think so, but it arises from false information, or the want of information—that is all. Their prejudices have been appealed to until they have become uncontrolled and uncontrollable.

Well, sir, if it shall be so; if that "glorious Union," as we all call it, under which the Government has so long lived and prospered, is now about to come to a final end, as perhaps it may, I have been looking around to see what policy we should adopt; and through that gloom which has been mentioned on the other side, if you will have it so, I still see a glorious future for those who stand by the old flag of the nation. There lie the fair fields of Mexico all before us. The people there are prejudiced against you. They fear you intend to overrun and enslave them. You are a slavery propaganda, and you are fillibusters. That has raised a violent antagonism between you and them. But, sir, if we were once released from all obligation to this institution, in six months they would invite us to take a protectorate over them. They owe England a large debt, and she has been coaxing and inviting us to take the protectorate of that nation. They will aid us in it; and I say to the commercial men of the North, if you go along with me, and adopt this policy, if we must come to this, you will be seven-fold indemnified by the trade and commerce of that country for what you lose by the secession. Talk about eating ice and granite in the North! Why, sir, Great Britain now carries on a commerce with Mexico to the amount of nearly a hundred million dollars. How much of it do we get? Only about eight million. Why so? Because, by our treatment of Mexico, we have led them to fear and to hate us; and they have been compelled, by our illiberal policy, to place themselves under the shadow of a stronger nation for their own protection.

The Senator from Illinois [Mr. Douglas] and my colleague [Mr. Pugh] have said that we Black Republicans were advocates of negro equality, and that we wanted to build up a black government. Sir, it will be one of the most blessed ideas of the times, if it shall come to this, that we will make inducements for every free black among us to find his home in a more congenial climate in Central America or in Lower Mexico, and we will be divested of every one of them; and then, endowed with the splendid domain that we shall get, we will adopt a homestead policy, and we will invite the poor, the destitute, industrious white man from every clime under heaven, to come in there and make his fortune. So, sir, we will build up a nation, renovated by this process, of white laboring men. You may build yours up on compulsory servile labor, and the two will flourish side by side; and we shall very soon see whether your principles, or that state of society, or ours, is the most prosperous or vigorous. I might say, sir, that, divested of this institution, who doubts that the provinces of Canada would knock at our doors in a day? Therefore, my friends, we have all the elements for building up an empire—a Republic, founded on the great principles of the Declaration of Independence, that shall be more magnificent, more powerful, and more just than this world has ever seen at any other period. I do not know that I should have a single second for this policy; but it is a policy that occurs to me, and it reconciles me in some measure to the threatened loss or secession of these States.

But, sir, I am for maintaining the Union of these States. I will sacrifice everything but honor to maintain it. That glorious old flag of ours, by any act of mine, shall never cease to wave over the integrity of this Union as it is. But if they will not have it so, in this new, renovated Government of which I have spoken, the 4th of July, with all its glorious memories, will never be repealed. The old flag of 1776 will be in our hands, and shall float over this nation forever; and this Capitol, that some gentlemen said would be reserved for the southern republic, shall still be the Capitol. It was laid out by Washington; it was consecrated by him; and the old flag that he vindicated in the Revolution shall still float from the Capitol. [Applause in the galleries.]

The PRESIDING OFFICER: The Sergeant-at-Arms will take proper measures to preserve order in the gallery or clear it.

Mr. WADE: I say, sir, I stand by the Union of these States. Washington and his compatriots fought for that good old flag. It shall never be hauled down, but shall be the glory of the Government to which I belong, as long as my life shall continue. To maintain it, Washington and his compatriots fought for liberty and the rights of man. And here I will add that my own father, although but a humble soldier, fought in the same great cause, and went through hardships and privations sevenfold worse than death, in order to bequeath it to his children. It is my inheritance. It was my protection in infancy, and the pride and glory of my riper years; and, Mr. President, although it may be assailed by traitors on every side, by the grace of God, under its shadow I will die.

The Ohio Army

ADJUTANT GENERAL

History of the Formation of the Ohio Army.

The commencement of the present year found the country on the brink of a war in many respects, unexampled in the history of the world. With the exception of the short and inconsiderable war with Mexico, the nation had been, for nearly fifty years, in a state of profound peace. No one dreamed that a war could arise, demanding the utmost energies of the country, without a sufficient note of warning to afford opportunity for at least some preparation. Resting in this fancied security, the people of Ohio lost all interest in military matters, so that they not only neglected to cultivate among themselves anything like military taste and education, but had come to consider every effort in that direction as a fit subject for ridicule. Hence, on the breaking out of the present war, the State was found to be comparatively without arms, organization or discipline, to prepare her for the part it became her to take in the fearful struggle. Of the many thousand muskets received by the State from the Federal Government, with which to arm and drill the militia, nearly all had been lost or sold for a trifle. The cannon had been used for firing salutes, and left exposed to the weather, until rust and decay had rendered them and their equipments worthless.

A few volunteer companies had been formed from time to time, and after a spasmodic existence for two or three years, had most of them been disbanded or had dwindled to nothing.

Almost the entire organization of the militia was merely nominal. Very many of the high offices were vacant, and the system, if it could be called so, had no working power. The only bright spots in this melancholy picture were, less than a dozen independent companies of Volunteer Infantry, and seven or eight gun squads of Artillery, called by law, companies. Six of these called a Regiment, but really composing a single Battery, under the command of Col. James Barnet, took the field at once as then organized, and during the three months service, proved most efficient in the early part of the campaign in Western Virginia. One section of this Battery, under Lieut.-Col. Sturges, had the honor of opening war in that region, at the attack and capture of Phillippi.

Still it may be said with truth, that the war found the State in no condition whatever to meet its requirements. When the President of the United States demanded thirteen Regiments from Ohio to commence the work of putting down the rebellion, not one was ready to go into the field in a condition fit for service. There was no lack of willingness however on the part of the people, to volunteer for the defence of the Government. Within two weeks, instead of thirteen thousand, nearly thirty thousand had offered their services to meet the call of the President. So eager were they all to take part in the high duty of maintaining the integrity of the government, and the majesty of the law, that it became a task of serious and embarrassing difficulty, to decide which should be the favored ones. After the

From "Annual Report of the Adjutant General, 1861," *Ohio Executive Documents*, (1862), pp. 153-168.

thirteen Regiments originally called for were selected, the Legislature decided that ten thousand more of the men, who had so promptly offered themselves to the country, should be retained in the service of the State, to defend her against invasion should it be threatened by the rebels.

Four thousand more were held in reserve in organized companies, under command of their respective captains, drilling and preparing to meet the next call. The remainder were disbanded.

Of the thirteen Regiments called for by the President for three months, two, viz. the First and Second, were ordered to Washington immediately. Within two days after receiving the proclamation of the 15th April, they were on their way to the field. They were, under an imperative order from the War Department, reluctantly sent without arms or clothing, except that with which they left their homes. After many delays, they finally reached Washington, and received their supplies of arms and uniforms, and served out their time in the army of the Potomac, participating in the battle of Bull's Run. Immediately after that battle, they were ordered home and mustered out of service, as their term of enlistment had expired. The other eleven Regiments were directed to rendezvous at Camp Dennison, and while there, by order of the President, were re-organized for three years, instead of three months. To effect this organization was a matter of considerable difficulty. By the State law, as three months men, they had elected their own officers. Under the order of the President, the officers were to be appointed by the Governor of the State; and the difficulty was to determine whether to break up the old organization and appoint officers without regard to their former positions, or to take the Regiments as they were, and confirm all the old commissions. It was at length decided to retain the general organization of the Regiments, together with the numbers, and to effect the change in the service as quietly as possible. Measures were taken to ascertain who would volunteer for three years, and the officers of the Regiments were appointed with due regard to their wishes. The vacancies, occasioned by the refusal of many of the three months men to enter the three years service, were filled by recruiting, for which purpose officers were sent out into the neighborhood, where the companies were originally raised.

When their recruits began to come in, it was found that the presence of the three months men, who had declined to re-enlist, was the cause of much inconvenience, and greatly tended to demoralize the entire force. The quarters were crowded, jealousies sprung up, doubts arose as to the rights of the different classes of troops, ill feeling was engendered, and general insubordination in most regiments was the result. It became absolutely necessary to separate the three months men from the others. Instead of mustering them out of the service however, as would seem to have been the proper method, no directions were received from the War Department as to the disposition to be made of them, though sought by the Governor and officers often and earnestly. At length the Colonels of the Regiments took the responsibility of sending these three months men home on furlough until further orders.

The results of this unfortunate step on the subsequent recruiting service, became apparent in a few weeks to a lamentable extent. Some two or three thousand men were scattered over the State, discontented and complaining because they were not paid. These feelings were participated in by their friends, until very many were led to believe that the promises of the Government were worthless, and bitterness and wrath succeeded to suspicion and disappointment. The influence of such men on the recruiting service may be easily imagined, and will account in part for the want of success in rapidly filling the regiments organizing in July and August. In the meantime, the troops had to be retained in Camp Dennison until the new recruits were drilled, and the whole clothed and armed for the field. This did not take place until the latter part of June, and even then two of the regiments were incomplete as to numbers, when they took the field in Western Virginia.

The general officers appointed under the act of April 23d, 1861, for the three months troops, were: Geo. B. McClellan, Major-General; Joshua L. Bates, J. D. Cox, and Newton Schleich, Brigadiers-General. Of these, Brigadier-General Cox remained in the three years service, under the appointment of the President, and General McClellan was transferred to the regular army.

The other nine regiments, authorized by the act of April 26, 1861, retained in the service of the State, were promptly clothed and armed, and about the 20th of May—a little more than one month after the fall of Sumter—were pouring into Western Virginia. It was wisely determined that the best way to defend the State against invasion, was to keep the invaders at a distance.

These troops were placed by the Governor under command of Major-General McClellan, who treated them in all respects as United States troops. They were placed under United States general officers, Brigadier-General Hill being the only State officer of that grade. The work done by these State troops in opening the campaign, and contributing so largely to the important victories gained at that time, will not soon be forgotten.

These services were promptly acknowledged by the Federal Government, who adopted these troops into the United States service, *ab initio,* and undertook the charge of mustering them out and paying them off. At the expiration of their term of enlistment, they were ordered home for that purpose, and then appeared another instance of want of foresight on the part of the authorities at Washington, that produced most serious damage to the service. When these troops arrived, by regiments, had there been due preparation, they could have been mustered out and paid off in a few days, and at a trifling expense. But there were neither mustering officers, pay-masters, muster-rolls, nor money, although the Governor had person-ally visited Washington, given special notice of the necessity for making proper arrangements, and made provision for the necessary funds. Hence the troops had to be sent home after a hard campaign, without pay, and with a very uncertain prospect as to when they would receive it. Many of them believed it never would come, and all considered themselves ill treated, and the ardor of their patriotism was considerably cooled by the reflection that they had been fighting for a Government whose promises were not to be trusted. There may have been good reasons for this apparent neglect, but the results were none the less deplorable.

These nine thousand men were now scattered over the State, and instead of re-enlisting for the war, as most of them would have done (and had actually promised before leaving Virginia), after a few days of rest, and providing for their families from their three months' pay, they very naturally declined to enter the service again until they received what they had so well earned. The difficulty of re-collecting them and their officers, and getting their muster and pay rolls prepared, after they had become scattered, and remained so for several weeks, needs not to be described. With a very limited supply of paymasters, and the uncertainty attending the time required to do the work, it was no small task to notify the men of the time and place of payment. They had to be collected by companies in the small towns, in the neighborhood of which most of the men of each company were enlisted. Many were necessarily absent, the process was slow, and some two or three months were consumed in doing what ought to have been done in two weeks.

Thus, many thousands of men were kept for the whole summer out of the ranks at a time when they were much needed, and by their experience already acquired, could have been of most essential bene-fit to the country. Nor was this all. Disappointed and disgusted with the treatment they had received, they aggravated to a tenfold degree the mischief produced by the three months men sent home from Camp Dennison. At the same time, the difficulty of finding and paying off these latter, was even greater than that of the State troops. Their officers had in many cases gone with their regiments, and carried with them the muster-rolls and accounts, so that nothing was left by which to identify them but their certificates of furlough, which told nothing of their time of service or of the state of their accounts. It is therefore not to be wondered at, that recruiting came almost to a stand, and the prospect of raising troops in Ohio was for a time very discouraging.

. . . .

When the President called for these troops, no digested plan for raising them was presented by the War Department. The Governor was simply requested to furnish so many Regiments, organized in a specific manner, and to be commanded by officers of his appointment. Companies were to be completed before being mustered into service, and a regiment before the Field and Staff officers might be mustered, and its organization completed. No provision was made for the transportation nor subsistence while organizing, nor any authority given their officers to command them until they were filled and mustered. Field officers appointed to take charge of camps, to instruct, drill, and discipline the men, had no legal authority to enforce obedience to their commands. No provision was made for the clothing of recruits, or furnishing them with blankets, until the company was full; nor indeed until the last of August, could a Quartermaster be appointed and mustered into service, to provide for the wants of regiments, until a complete organization was perfected. Nothing was allowed as compensation to the men during the time they were awaiting the completion of their companies, nor to those who, by great exertions, and often at considerable expense, were endeavoring to recruit companies and regiments. Nor was any defined power given to the Governor to regulate the recruiting service, except that incidentally derived from the power to appoint officers. Indeed, it seemed as though the War Department supposed that companies would spontaneously flock together and organize themselves into regiments, and ask to be received into service. In the beginning the ardent patriotism of the people answered every purpose, but presently the work of organization and preparation became more difficult and protracted.

These difficulties had to be met as best they might. Many of these expenses, including clothing, subsistence, and transportation, were met by the State, expecting to be reimbursed by the General Government. Authority had to be assumed, for which there was no warrant, and men submitted to orders from a natural instinct to obedience, or because they knew no better. But still serious and continued evils were the result. Men came into camp poorly clothed, expecting to be immediately uniformed; instead of which they were often not even furnished a blanket; and the chilly nights of September, with a hard plank, or it might be even the damp ground, for a bed, deprived them of all relish for a soldier's life. Having nothing to bind them to the service, they deserted by scores, and checked the disposition of others to enlist, by their sad stories of suffering and neglect. If they remained in camps, they soon found that they were their own masters, and bid defiance to all discipline. Before the Quartermaster at Cincinnati could furnish their supplies, whole companies would disappear, the men either returning to their homes, or joining other companies, until the officers, discouraged and disgusted, would abandon the seemingly hopeless attempt, preferring rather to sacrifice their time and expenses, than submit to so much of mortification and disappointment.

. . . .

Other States have probably felt the difficulties less, for several reasons. It fell to the lot of Ohio to furnish the entire quota of her soldiers to the most disagreeable service in North-western Virginia, a service not made more enticing by the fact, that while Ohio furnished the great majority of the men, other States, in an immense proportion, furnished the Generals; this, in conjunction with studied misrepresentation of our own State, induced thousands to go into service in other States, many of whom are now daily importuning us to interfere for their transfer to Ohio regiments. Ohio, in this way, has furnished at least ten thousand men, who have gone to the credit of other States. Entire regiments have thus been formed, the officers of which, defying our authority, and thwarting our plans, have filled the ranks of their own companies by maligning the officers of Ohio, and disseminating dissatisfaction and distrust. Many of the difficulties under which we have labored, we dare not, for the good of the service, make public, and defend ourselves by explaining; for it was better that individuals should be traduced, than that the public service should suffer. Trouble that we had been struggling to avoid or to extricate ourselves from, were indignantly represented to us as though we alone of all the State, were ignorant of their existence. Many of these difficulties arose from causes over which we had no control, and which we were making the most strenuous efforts to overcome, others were inherent in the magnitude of the work itself. Ohio has not meted out its contributions to the National forces with a stingy hand. Ohio has not inquired how much she was bound to do, and paused at that. The State owed 57,000 men to the service, our recruits number nearly 80,000. Ohio did not go into this war with arsenals filled, and materials provided. The preparations necessary for war had been studiously avoided, and she had nothing but her sons to offer, all else had to be created. The work was no small one, but it has been accomplished. It may now be said with pride, that in all that goes to constitute an army, in its personnel as well as its material, the regiments of Ohio are second to none others in the army. . . .

On to Washington

GEORGE W. McCOOK

Columbus, June 5, 1861.

Governor:—I have the honor to submit the following statement as to the condition, clothing, equipment and arms of the First and Second Ohio Regiments:

As the troops, by directions from Washington, were ordered forward in companies, before muster, without uniforms or arms, which were to be furnished there, you requested me to precede them, make arrangements for quarters, organize the Regiments, supervise the election of field officers, and have them properly mustered into the service of the United States. For these purposes I had your authority to command; the officers were directed to me for orders, I was furnished with your letter of credit for ten thousand dollars, and I expected to report to you in person in ten days.

Nothing but the pressing emergency which then existed would have justified you in adopting this course, and when I made objections to moving the troops without equipments of any kind, they were silenced by the production of a telegraphic despatch to you which no man could question—"if it is possible, two Regiments should reach here yet this week; arms, equipments, etc., will be furnished here.*" I had no authority to purchase anything, except for the necessary subsistence of the troops on their arrival at Washington, and I was to reach that point some hours in advance of the foremost companies. At Pittsburg I met C. P. Wolcott, who was going to New York to make purchases for the State, and was introduced to Mr. James M. Brown, who was going forward for the same purpose.

Ascertaining at Harrisburg that the railway routes were broken up, I remained there to await the troops, as it was impossible for them to go forward. As I wished to be aided by the advice of Mr. Wolcott, he stopped with me, and Mr. Brown was directed to proceed by the first train to Philadelphia, to purchase blankets, absolutely necessary, as we understood the men had none with them. As the original expectation of equipment at Washington was thus defeated, Mr. Wolcott, who had your general authority for purchasing, communicated with you on the subject of supplying these Regiments. The great object was an immediate supply for the protection of the health of the men, and resort was first had to Gov. Curtin

---

From "Report of George W. McCook, Agent with First and Second Ohio Regiments," *Ohio Executive Documents,* (1862), pp. 413-416.
*Washington.

to furnish clothing from the State establishment in Philadelphia, upon terms which were communicated to you by Mr. Wolcott, and which met your approval. This arrangement was abandoned by Mr. Wolcott upon inquiry at Philadelphia, because a day could not be fixed when the clothing would be delivered, and on the 22d of April he telegraphed me from Philadelphia that "he had made arrangements independent of the State clothing department of Pennsylvania for outfits, consisting of the articles mentioned in my message to Gov. Dennison." Under this arrangement, whch was made with Mr. Brown, the clothing for the troops was furnished. The purchases had to be made in great haste, as it was impossible to know at what time the troops might be ordered to march to points where no supply could be obtained, and until they reached Philadelphia, there was no time when it was certain they would remain the next day in the same camp.

There was furnished by Mr. Brown, to each man, a blanket, overcoat, blouse, a pair of pantaloons, two flannel shirts, two pairs of socks, one pair of shoes, and a hat, and when I learned that drawers had not been included in the order, I requested him to furnish two pairs for each man.

. . . .

The night the troops arrived in the wet camp, near Philadelphia, I required Mr. Brown to collect all the over-coats which were finished, and send them to camp, where nearly six hundred were issued to the men, between nine and eleven o'clock at night. But I did understand that the material from which the clothing was made, was examined before, at the time of purchase, by competent persons, and I attach a copy of a letter to me from Capt. Woods, ninth infantry, an officer of the U.S. Army, from Ohio, who was on duty in Philadelphia at the time. And I now believe that with the exception of a portion of the pantaloons, the articles furnished were of a good material, and as well made as could be expected under the circumstance attending the purchase and manufacture of the goods. And I know that whilst the troops were marching to Washington, they passed a Pennsylvania Regiment commanded by officers from Philadelphia, who had not yet succeeded in getting over coats for their men.

When we arrived in Washington, an effort was made by the proper officers to obtain regulation pantaloons from the government, but no requisition would be filled except in behalf of troops mustered for three years.

. . . .

The equipments of the two Regiments, for which, up to the last, we had relied upon the Government to furnish, were, with the exception of canteens only, supplied by the State. The knapsacks and haversacks were purchased by Mr. Wolcott and there are certainly none better in the service. The belts, cartridge-boxes, bayonets, scabbards, &c, were selected by me, and delivered on your order, from those made by Schuyler, Hartley & Graham, of New York, under their contract with the State. A requisition for these was approved at Washington, but as it was impossible to ascertain when they could be supplied from the arsenal at Philadelphia, resort was again had to your purchases for the troops in Ohio.

Camp kettles for cooking were supplied by the Government *the day after* our arrival at Philadelphia, and tents were sent with us to Washington, and there delivered.

. . . .

Arms were at first procured by order of General Wool from a lot sent to Governor Curtin, of Pennsylvania; they were the old flint-lock musket altered to percussion, but these were turned in at Washington, and percussion muskets of the last pattern obtained in their stead. The arms are undoubtedly good, and it would be a source of great gratification if all the regiments in the State were, in this respect, as well supplied.

. . . .

There is no "demoralization" of the regiments, as has been reported to their prejudice. Their hardships were those incident to the life of the soldier, trying, I admit, to men leaving comfortable homes, but not greater than those endured by their comrades in Ohio. There were, on Thursday evening last, only three sick men in the hospital; very few would accept a discharge if tendered to them, and neither regiment would exchange lots with any others of the State. It is strange, indeed, if troops whose evening drills were the attraction of Philadelphia, although their camp was six miles from the city, and whose soldierlike appearance and march extorted reluctant commendation from papers in Baltimore, and who have more than once shown their bronzed faces when marching through Pennsylvania Avenue, should in four days have become demoralized.

. . . .

The heavy cloth uniforms, so much admired, are not, in my judgment, suited for a campaign in June and July, if troops are for use and not show, and no soldier ought to be compelled to button one over his breast or pack it upon his back. The hat is better than the jaunty cap, the shoe is better than the boot, the loose blouse is better than the coat; and the forced march and the battles of the summer will satisfy every one who does not know this already. These troops are not kept in the back ground for want of proper equipment. New arms were given them because they *were fit for service,* and unless intentions are strangely changed within four days, there will be no serious affair near Washington in which they will not bear a part.

I am, Governor,
Very respectfully,
GEO. W. McCOOK.

Governor William Dennison,
Columbus, Ohio.

Morgan's Raid

DAVID TOD

Columbus, July 16, 1863.

To the People of the State:

The exciting and important events which have transpired within the past two weeks make the present moment a fitting one for the Chief Executive to address you.

Late in the night of the 12th instant I received reliable information that a well organized rebel force of cavalry and artillery, supposed to exceed five thousand in number, under the lead of the notorious John Morgan, was about to enter the southwestern portion of our State. Availing myself of the power given me by the Constitution and laws, I at once, by proclamation, called out for the defense of the State that portion of its organized militia forces residing within the counties supposed to be in danger. As these organizations were only consummated by the election of company officers on the 4th instant, but few returns had been made; hence it was quite uncertain what the actual number embraced in the call would be. The route the enemy would take was also uncertain. It was believed, however, that the capital of our State was altogether the most

From "Governor Tod to the People of Ohio," July 26, 1863, *Ohio Executive Documents,* (1864), pp. 232-234.

attractive point for the enemy. This point afforded a richer field for plunder than any other within his reach, and, in addition to this, there were at Camp Chase over a thousand rebel prisoners, many of whom, including his Chief of Staff, had been captured from Morgan's band. Hence to this point was ordered a larger force of the militia than to any other.

The other points named, outside of Cincinnati, for the assemblage of the militia, were Camp Dennison, Chillicothe, Portsmouth, and Marietta. The response to the call, at all the points, was most gratifying. With but very few individual exceptions, the men called into service, forgetting everything but duty, promptly and cheerfully repaired to the camps assigned them, and when en route for camp, while there, and when returning to their respective homes, conducted themselves in a manner most creditable. The people of the State should ever hold in grateful remembrance the men who thus won so much character for our State. The few who endeavored to escape a full performance of duty will be frowned upon and despised by all good citizens, and this is the severest punishment that can be inflicted upon a fellow citizen.

The large militia force assembled near Columbus kept the enemy from attempting an attack upon this place. All the other points indicated for the assemblage of the militia were felt of by the enemy, and, but for their presence, would have been sacked and pillaged.

From these several points large numbers of the militia moved promptly out and participated with the Federal forces in the numerous skirmishes and engagements that took place with the enemy; and in every instance, save one, behaved with great gallantry and bravery. The exception referred to was the surrender of about three hundred and fifty, under command of Col. Sontag, near Portsmouth. The men comprising this command are all indignant at the conduct of their commanding officer, and are in nowise responsible for the disgrace that attaches to the surrender. The conduct of Col. Sontag, although a volunteer officer without appointment or commission, shall be inquired into. I am not now in possession of information which would enable me to do justice to all the officers in command of these various organizations.

. . . .

The enemy entered the State on the night of the 12th instant, in the northwest corner of Hamilton county, closely pursued by a large Federal force, and passing through the counties of Butler, Warren, Clermont, Brown, Adams, Pike, Jackson, Gallia, Meigs, Vinton, Hocking, Athens, Washington, Morgan, Muskingum, Guernsey, Belmont, Harrison, and Jefferson, was finally captured near New Lisbon, in Columbiana county, this day, about 3 o'clock P.M. More or less skirmishing and fighting took place all along the route, but the two principal engagements were near Buffington's Island, in Meigs county, on the 19th instant, and near Salineville, Columbiana county, this morning at 8 o'clock. At the first of these engagements, our forces, consisting of a cavalry and artillery force of regular troops, and of the militia there assembled, were under the command of Generals Hobson and Shackleford, aided materially by a naval force on the river at that point. At the second engagement, near Salineville, our forces, consisting of the 9th Michigan Cavalry, and our militia forces, were under command of Major Way.

In the first of these engagements the enemy lost, in killed, wounded, and prisoners, about twenty-five hundred; in the second, about three hundred. The final surrender to General Shackleford took place without an engagement, and embraced Morgan himself and the remnant of his command, the number not now known. Thus was captured and destroyed one of the most formidable cavalry forces of the rebels, a force that has been a terror to the friends of the Union in Tennessee and Kentucky for about two years. Well may every loyal heart be proud of this achievement.

The losses upon our side have been trifling, so far as numbers are concerned; but I am pained to be compelled to announce that a few gallant spirits have been taken from us. Prominent among the number is the brave Major Daniel McCook, the honored father of the heroic boys who bear his name, and who have won so much glory and renown for our arms in this great struggle. Major McCook, although advanced in years, has periled his life, as a volunteer, upon many of our battle-fields. Believing that he could be of service in ridding the State of her invaders, he volunteered, with his trusty rifle, as a private, and fell in the engagement near Buffington's Island. His memory will be cherished by all, and the sincere sympathies of all true patriots will be given to his widow and children.

Throughout the entire contest I was in constant communication, both night and day, with Maj.-Gen. Burnside, who had command of the entire forces; and I take great pleasure in testifying to the zeal, fidelity, and ability with which he has conducted the campaign.

The damage to property will necessarily be large in dollars and cents, but insignificant when contrasted with the beneficial results to our State and country.

Prompt measures have been taken to ascertain the names of the sufferers, and the amount of damage sustained, all of which will be communicated to the next General Assembly. Steps have also been taken to adjust and pay for all service rendered by the militia, ample provision for which was made by the last General Assembly.

And now, fellow-citizens, do not for a moment doubt but that this raid of Morgan will ultimately prove a benefit to us as a people. It has taught an insolent foe that however so well provided, or however so large, he cannot with impunity invade our State. It has demonstrated to ourselves that, when acting in concert, the people of Ohio are a tower of strength. Remember that our military organization had never mustered; the officers were not even yet commissioned; still, thus fresh and unknown to each other, they were able to do such efficient service.

Let me say, then, to the military forces of Ohio, both volunteer and militia, go vigorously forward with your organizations. This raid has taught you the lesson that you have something to do, and that your trainings are not mere idle ceremonies. You are to be the conservators of peace. Upon you the people of the State depend to maintain law and preserve quiet and order in every neighborhood. Be prepared at once to do your duty fully.

In some of our sister States serious riots, resulting in the loss of many lives and large destruction of property, have occurred on account of the efforts of the Federal authorities to enforce the laws for the preservation of our government.

I am happy to announce to the people of the State that there is no just cause for apprehending such disturbances within our border; but, be this as it may, ample provision has been made to quell any such disturbance, should any be attempted.

Thank God, we have but few bad men in Ohio; and the good and virtuous of every neighborhood are able to preserve the peace and dignity of the State.

The State authorities have but little to do, directly, with the enforcement of the draft. They have looked to it, however, in season, that honest and faithful agents, citizens of the State, have been selected by the Federal authorities to execute the draft. Fairness and justness, therefore, are guaranteed to every citizen. Additional troops are required to maintain our glorious government. Our brave and gallant boys in the field require assistance in men from home, and they must have it. I have, therefore, cheerfully given to the Federal authorities all aid in my power to enforce the draft soon to be made; and I earnestly implore the assistance of all good men throughout the State in this necessary work.

The brilliant achievements of our forces during the present month, resulting in the destruction and capture of over a hundred thousand of the enemy, together with their strongholds, give us the hope that the war will soon terminate; the drafted man, therefore, need not anticipate a three years' campaign. He may safely depend upon his neighbors at home, and the law-making power of the State, to take care of those dependent upon him during his absence.

Let us all then, fellow-citizens, with one heart and with one voice, cheerfully stand by our government in this its hour of trouble. The reflection, hereafter, that we have done so, will cheer and sustain us on our way through life; our children will love us and cherish our memories, and God will bless us for so doing.

DAVID TOD,
Governor.

The Ohio Boys

SURGEONS' REPORTS

OHIO—SIXTH DISTRICT. Extracts from report of Dr. David Noble.

The number of men examined by me for military service and for the purpose of exemption, as nearly as can be ascertained, is four thousand five hundred. A very large number of these, especially those who wished to be exempted, were able-bodied; about twenty per cent. of those claiming exemption were stricken from the rolls; and about fifteen per cent. of those offering themselves as recruits and substitutes were rejected. Soldiers discharged on account of physical disability swell the amount of rejections considerably.

The district is composed of the counties of Highland, Brown, Clermont, Clinton, and Fayette, and contains about four thousand five hundred and fifty square miles.

. . . .

Diseases.—In this county, (Fayette,) intermittents are very prevalent during the fall months; the patients frequently continuing to have the chills during the winter months; the cause evidently being marsh miasmata. The tertian and quartan type of the disease is the most prevalent during the winter months. Occasionally, cases of ague are found on the streams, although it yields very readily to treat-

From J. H. Baxter, (comp.), *Statistics, Medical and Anthropological of the Provost-Marshal-Generals Bureau, Derived from Records of the Examination Board*, Vol. I, (Washington, 1875), pp. 401-409.

ment; however, in the early history of this disease—say twenty-five years ago—the inhabitants of the lowlands bordering on the large streams were subject to intermittent fever during the fall and winter months, and the disease often proved fatal to the people residing near the Little Miami River.

. . . .

Inhabitants.—The people of the district are principally farmers, and composed of different nationalities, Irish, French, German, English, and Scotch. The natives are generally Virginians or their descendants, are an industrious, frugal, and (before the war) a peaceable people. No large manufacturing establishments are found in this district. All the cereals are raised in abundance, and large quantities of wine are manufactured in the southern part of Brown County, the soil of which is well adapted to the successful cultivation of the grape.

Causes of exemptions.—So many exemptions occurring under paragraph 85, sections 31 and 32, may be attributed to wounds received in felling the trees of the forest; this country being heavily timbered and comparatively new. The greater ratio per thousand exempted under section 9 may be accounted for from the fact that functional diseases of the liver, heart, kidneys, and pancreas are common here. A general cachectic condition of the system, produced either from unwholesome food or solitary vice, producing muscular tenuity, anaemia, lack of physical power, are all embraced under that section, (No. 9.)

. . . .

The frauds that are most frequently practiced by enrolled men seeking exemption, and by drafted men, are the placing of irritating substances in the eyes and feigning ophthalmia, or by extracting the teeth. The first can be detected by the character of the inflamed surface after asking the duration of the disease; the second by the alveolar process not being absorbed. A man presented himself before the board for exemption on account of loss of teeth; on being asked how long they had been *out,* he said "two weeks;" and, thrusting his hand down to the bottom of a long pocket in his jeans pantaloons, exhibited *twelve sound teeth* that had been recently extracted, thus settling the question that a man may stand the steel, but fear the powder and lead.

. . . .

The best physically developed men I have examined in this district are of Celtic origin. Perhaps my experience here is not a fair test, as quite a number of foreigners presented themselves as substitutes, and claimed to come from Ireland or Canada very lately. As a general thing, they were men who led a kind of peripatetic life, attached to circuses and other traveling exhibitions. A great many could perform acrobatic feats, in which they would rival the best performers attached to any circus. But, for good fighting material, I think the Western Americans can excel any nationality. The cause may be found in their early habit of handling a gun, their unerring aim bringing down a squirrel from the loftiest tree. Nor is this opinion based upon any preconceived notion as to my particular locality, being a foreigner myself, but from actual observation on the battle-field; having served during the years 1862 and 1863 as surgeon to an Ohio regiment in active field-service. Their occupation, being principally farming, has a tendency to develop their physical system, and pure air and healthy invigorating exercise render them capable of enduring hard and fatiguing marches.

The pure-blooded African is every way *physically* equal to the European; and, when a free man from the North, or even a contraband from the South—if a house-servant, and intelligent, and not brutalized by the lash of a hard overseer or master—from his imitative qualities, would, I presume, be readily taught the manual of arms. Negroes are easily molded to the will of their superiors when well treated, and as subordination and discipline are the qualities that characterize the true soldier, I would venture the opinion that they are inferior to no other as common soldiers, and are eminently well fitted for military service. Their mixture with the white race deteriorates very much from their physical development.

. . . .

DAVID NOBLE,
Surgeon Board of Enrollment Sixth District of Ohio.

Ohio—Seventh District. Extracts from report of Dr. M. Lemen.

The Seventh Congressional District of Ohio is composed of the counties of Franklin, Madison, Greene, and Clark, and is situated near the center of the State; Franklin County occupying the central portion, Madison, Greene, and Clark Counties joining, and extending in a westward and southwestwardly direction. It lies in latitude forty degrees north and longitude six degrees west from Washington, D.C. Its population, according to the census of 1860, numbered one hundred and fourteen thousand eight hundred and seventy-three, and it contains one thousand seven hundred and fourteen square miles.

The frauds most successfully practiced by recruits and substitutes in order to get into the service, and the most difficult sometimes to discover, are the concealment of epilepsy, and misrepresentation of age. Induced by high local bounties, great numbers of boys, some of them scarcely sixteen years of age, and, on the other hand, men often exceeding forty-eight or fifty years, have enlisted at the different recruiting-offices, and have attempted to pass an examination at this office. Many of these boys, whose youthful appearance at once betrayed their unripe age, were not even allowed to strip, but were sent out of the room without even having their names recorded. Many of those over age would resort to the trick of coloring their hair and shaving their faces, the better to pass an examination, not so much with the view of getting into the service, as of getting the large bounty.

That we have been, in some instances, deceived is probably enough; and the wonder is that we have not been oftener deceived, considering that the number rejected for under and over age exceeds all the other causes of rejection together.

Boys that have been rejected at one office often apply to another, and I have frequently examined boys and old men who, by their own acknowledgment, had been rejected by the examining-surgeons in various districts of other States as well as of this State.

While the recruit or substitute makes it his business to conceal any existing disqualification in order to get into the service, the drafted or enrolled man, by an exaggeration of some real or pretended disability, endeavors to keep out of it. Chronic rheumatism, old and long-forgotten injuries, sprains, slight pleuritic adhesions and weakness of breast, previous attacks of sickness, deafness, near-sightedness, sore eyes, and physical disability are some of the most frequent claims by which he expects to escape the service.

Such are some of the most successful frauds practiced by recruits, substitutes, drafted and enrolled men; and there is no remedy I know of that will entirely obviate the difficulty.

The greatest physical aptitude for military service is unquestionably, as far as my observation extends, found in the American-born, especially in men of the Northwestern States.

My experience as to the physical qualifications of the colored race for military service has as yet been very limited, not having examined to exceed three hundred of them; yet, as far as my observation goes, I think their physical qualifications equal to those of the white race. Those that I have examined were generally healthy, stout, and exceedingly well physically developed.

.   .   .   .

Ohio—Eleventh District. Extracts from report of Dr. O. C. Miller

I was appointed surgeon of the board of enrollment for the eleventh district of Ohio on the 28th day of December, 1864, and entered upon the discharge of my duties on the 7th day of January, 1865.

. . . .

The district is composed of the counties of Lawrence, Scioto, Jackson, Vinton, Gallia, and Adams, and is situated in that part of the State of Ohio included in the great bend of the Ohio River southwardly, and embraces the most southern point in the State. The district is almost entirely included in the arc of the semicircle produced by the great bend in the river before mentioned, and has a river-boundary on the south of one hundred and sixty miles, while the diameter of the semicircle within which the district is situated is less than one hundred miles. The district embraces the great iron and coal belt as it passes through the State, and is especially known in the State and elsewhere as the "mineral region of the State of Ohio." In Adams County, one of the counties of the district, the first furnace in the West for the manufacture of pig-iron from the ore was constructed.

. . . .

The population connected with the furnaces and founderies above alluded to are a hardy, industrious, and necessarily frugal people, largely of Virginia origin, until within a few years past, since which a foreign element has been introduced, modifying to a very considerable extent the habits and customs of that class of the inhabitants. That portion of our population of southern origin either kept aloof entirely or entered very reluctantly into the military service upon the call of the President for troops to put down the now extinct rebellion, while the foreign element, especially the Germans and Welsh, entered freely and voluntarily, and aided materially to fill the quotas required from the district. It is with no little pride that I mention in this connection the fact that on every call for troops our quota has been promptly filled, and to a very large extent without draft. Even under the last call, or call of December, 1864, the quota assigned to our district was almost entirely filled when the order was received to suspend recruiting, while, in addition, very large numbers have enlisted from this and been credited to other States and districts. Almost one entire regiment, the Second Virginia Cavalry, was made up from recruits from this district, and very many have gone to other regiments and have been credited to other localities.

I have alluded to this to show how fully the laboring population of the country appreciated the nature of the contest in which we were engaged, and how essentially necessary it was to the people of this, a border district, that at all hazard, and at any cost, the rebellion should be crushed, and that speedily.

With the 5th U.S. Col'd Troops

MILTON M. HOLLAND

Norfolk, Va., Jan. 19, 1864.

Dear Messenger:—You will be reminded of the company of colored soldiers raised by myself in the county of Athens, and taken to Camp Delaware, 25 miles north of Columbus, on the Olentangy. It has since been mustered into the service in the 5th Reg't U. S. Colored Troops. The regiment is organized, and has been in active service for three months. Our company is C—the color company—in which you may remember of the flag presentation, made by the kind citizens of Athens, through Mr. Moore, at which Mr. Langston was present and received it, pledging in behalf of the company, that they would ever be true to that flag, though it might be tattered and torn by hard service, it should never be disgraced. I am happy to say that those colors have been used as the regimental colors for several months, and we had the honor of forming the first line of battle under their floating stars. We now have new regimental colors, and the old ones are laid away in my cabin, and I am sitting now beneath them writing.

The regiment, though young, has been in one engagement. The men stood nobly and faced the cowardly foe when they were hid in the swamp firing upon them. They stood like men, and when ordered to charge, went in with a yell, and came out victorious, losing four killed and serveral wounded. The rebel loss is large, as compared with ours. As for company C she played her part admirably in the charge. Our 4th sergeant, Charles G. Stark, is said to have killed the picket guard while in the act of running away.

I must say of the 5th, that after twenty days hard scouting, without overcoats or blankets, they returned home to camp, which the soldiers term their home, making twenty-five and thirty miles per day. Several of the white cavalry told me that no soldiers have ever done as hard marching through swamps and marshes as cheerfully as we did, and that if they had to follow us for any length of time it would kill their horses. During that raid, thousands of slaves belonging to rebel masters were liberated. You are aware that the colored man makes no distinction in regard to persons, so I may say all belonging to slaveholders were liberated. We hung one guerrilla dead, by the neck, by order of Brig. Gen. Wilder, a noble and brave man, commanding colored troops—"the right man in the right place." He

---

From Letter, Milton M. Holland to Editor, *Athens Messenger,* January 19, 1864, in *Athens (Ohio) Messenger,* February 4, 1864.

has but one arm, having lost his left one at the battle of Antietam;
but with his revolver in hand, he was at the head of our regiment
cheering us on to victory.

One of the boys belonging to Co. D was captured and hung. He
was found by our cavalry pickets yesterday, and is to be buried
to-day. We hold one of their "fair daughters," as they term them, for
the good behavior of her husband, who is a guerrilla officer, toward
our beloved soldiers. The soldier was found with a note pinned to his
flesh. Before this war ends we will pin their sentences to them with
Uncle Sam's leaden pills.

The boys are generally well, and satisfied that though they are
deprived of all the comforts of sweet home, and laboring under great
disadvantages as regards pay, and having families to support upon less
wages than that of white soldiers, still trust that when they do return
they will be crowned with honors, and a happier home prepared for
them, when they will be free from the abuses of northern and
southern fire-eaters. Though we should fall struggling in our blood
for right and justice, for the freedom of our brothers in bondage, or
fall in defence of our national color, the Stars and Stripes, our home
and fireside will ever be protected by our old friend Gov. Tod, by the
loyalty of Abraham Lincoln, our Moses, and the all-wise God that
created us. Friends at home be cheerful, cast aside all mercenary
compensation. Spring forth to the call, and show to the world that
you are men. You have thus far shown, and still continue to show
yourselves worthy of freedom, and you will win the respect of the
whole nation. There is a brighter day coming for the colored man,
and he must sacrifice home comforts, and his blood if necessary, to
speed the coming of that glorious day. I will close my letter in the
language of the immortal Henry—"Give me liberty, or give me
death!"

Yours truly,
MILTON M. HOLLAND,
O. S. Co. C, 5th U. S. C. T.

Arrest the Traitor

JAMES L. VALLANDIGHAM

On the next day, the first day of May, Mr. Vallandigham addressed a very large assemblage at Mt. Vernon, and as this was the occasion on which he made the speech for which ostensibly he was arrested, we will give a fuller account of the meeting than would otherwise be necessary; and for this account we are indebted principally to James T. Irvine, Esq., one of the secretaries. After speaking of the assemblages of the people at various places in the fall of 1862 and the spring of 1863, he says:—

"The meetings I have referred to were purely voluntary and spontaneous; indeed the Democracy were solicitous for them all over the State. They proceeded from the people themselves in their several localities, and were not appointed or called for by State Central Committees or organizations. Mr. Vallandigham regarded these demonstrations of popular opinion as favorable signs of the times—as manifestations of such an overwhelming popular sentiment in behalf of the old system of government according to the Constitution and laws as would oblige the Lincoln Administration to observe the established requirements of 'the best government the sun ever shone upon.' In conversation with friends, including the writer, Mr. Vallandigham expressed strongly his opinion that such meetings and keeping them up were necessary to maintain, preserve and perpetuate the spirit of liberty among the people at large, and thus save it from being utterly destroyed in this country by the despotism and tyranny of the ruling powers. And not only Mr. Vallandigham, but many others of our leading men believed and held that the vindication, by these meetings and the speeches addressed to them, of the right of the people to peaceably assemble and discuss public affairs and petition for a redress of grievances, was what secured that right then and thereafter from being forever stricken down. And it is a conviction in the minds of the Democracy of Ohio to-day that their manly nomination and support by speech, press and votes, and with their lives if necessary to an exercise of their right to do so, of Mr. Vallandigham for Governor in 1863, did more than anything since the American Revolution of 1776 to establish the right of freemen to speak and vote their opinions on questions of common interest and concern.

"The immense mass-meeting held at Mount Vernon, Ohio, on

From James L. Vallandigham, *A Life of Clement L. Vallandigham*, (Baltimore, 1872), pp. 247-258.

May-day, 1863, was not, however, held on Mr. Vallandigham's suggestion, but at the instance of the Democracy of Knox County, of which Mount Vernon is the county seat. The Democratic people of the county called for the meeting with one accord. Hon. C. L. Vallandigham, Hon. Geo. H. Pendleton, Hon. S. S. Cox, and many other eminent speakers (including, I think, Hon. D. W. Voorhees, of Indiana), were specially invited by the local committee.

. . . .

"Although I cannot recollect Mr. Vallandigham's words in his speech to the meeting, I have a distinct impression of the fact that he counselled the people to be firm but temperate in their protests against the unwarrantable proceedings of the men temporarily invested with absolute power, and to trust to the sober second-thought and the might of the people through the ballot-box to vindicate their true principles and outraged representatives.

"Other speakers at the meeting used stronger terms of denunciation than Mr. V., and hence there was much surprise that he was singled out for tyrannic vengeance. From the false allegations of the infamous spies and informers on which he was arrested, the summary trial by a packed military commission, the so-called 'conviction' contrary to the weight of evidence, and the sentence and exile, considered together, the inference was irresistible, in the minds of his friends at least, that his removal from before the people, to prepare the way for the complete intimidation and forcible and fraudulent crushing out of the people's views and votes which followed in the State and Presidential elections of 1863 and 1864, had been deliberately resolved upon as a political necessity."

. . . .

The following account of the meeting we take from the *Democratic Banner* of May 9th, published in Mount Vernon:

"Friday, May 1st, 1863, was a proud and glorious day for the faithful and unconquerable Democracy of old Knox, and one that will long be remembered by them with high and patriotic pleasure. Early in the morning the people began to come to town in wagons, carriages, and on horseback. Between ten and eleven o'clock the processions from the several townships arrived, and took the places assigned them by the Marshals. The processions were composed of wagons, carriages, buggies, &c., filled with people of both sexes and all ages, and of numerous horsemen. A remarkably large number of national flags, with *all* the stars of the Union as it was, on hickory poles, formed a very prominent and pleasing feature in each of these processions. A profusion of butternuts and liberty or copperhead pins, Union badges, and other appropriate emblems of Liberty and Union, were also distinguishable features.

. . . .

"One of the most noticeable and pleasing incidents of the procession and meeting, was a very large wagon drawn by six horses, from Wayne township, containing thirty-four young ladies representing the thirty-four States of the Union. The wagon was tastefully shaded with evergreens, in which the thirty-four young ladies were embowered.

"The principal stand from which Messrs. Vallandigham, Cox, and Pendleton spoke, was canopied by large and beautiful American flags, and surrounded by various banners and emblems, all betokening the undying principles of the Democratic party.

"The first speaker introduced to the audience was the bold and fearless patriot and statesman, Hon. C. L. Vallandigham, who was received with such a shout of applause as fairly made the welkin ring. He proceeded to deliver one of the ablest and most inspiring true Union addresses ever made, in which he also evinced his unfaltering devotion to Liberty and the Constitution. Manliness, candor, genuine patriotism, and true statesmanship were manifested in the speaker throughout. If any of his lying detractors were present, it must have struck them with overwhelming force, and caused them to wince with a sense of their foul slanders. Mr. V. spoke for about two hours, and was listened to with the greatest attention, accompanied with tremendous shouts of applause."

. . . .

The day after the meeting at Mt. Vernon Mr. Vallandigham returned home, and immediately heard rumors of his intended arrest. Such rumors he had often heard before. To an arrest on process from legal authority he did not object; nay more, he would have been pleased to appear before a civil tribunal and answer to any charges that might be brought against him. But a forcible, illegal, military arrest he was determined to repel, and when on a former occasion he had reason to apprehend it, he had made preparation to resist by thoroughly arming himself and stationing armed guards of his friends within his house and without; and for weeks at a time he sat up all night or lay down in his day-clothes in readiness to meet the minions of despotism, should they attempt to violate the sanctity of his dwelling.

. . . .

It was under these circumstances that on the evening of the 4th of May, Mr. Vallandigham and his family, consisting at that time of his wife, son, his wife's sister, and a young nephew of his own, and two domestics, females both, retired to rest at their accustomed hour. At half-past two o'clock in the morning they were rudely awakened from slumber by a violent knocking upon the front door. Arising, Mr. Vallandigham, who did not immediately suspect that it was a force coming to arrest him, went to the front window of the room over the parlor. As he approached it he heard the tramp of armed men, the low voice of command given by officers, the rattling of arms, and mutterings and whispering of many people. Looking out, lights were seen gleaming amidst the shrubbery in the yard below, and the glittering of many bayonets shone bright from the gas-light near the house. As he threw open the shutters the sounds struck upon his wife's ears, and she screamed with affright. He demanded what was wanted. Captain Hutton, an officer of General Burnside's staff, who was in command, answered that he had been sent by that General to arrest him, and that he might as well come down and surrender. Mr. Vallandigham replied that he would not; that he, Captain Hutton, had no right to arrest him, and that General Burnside had no right to issue an order for his arrest. To this a threat was made that unless he would come down he would be shot. He answered this in a defiant manner, and then shouted for the police. By this time the whole household was up; his wife and sister-in-law, both very nervous, timid women, were weeping, nearly crazed by terror, and begging him to come away from the window; the servant girls were equally alarmed. After repeated threats to shoot, inter-mingled with entreaties, the officer in command ordered the front door to be forced; but it was found too strong, and a door in the rear was then attacked. The house now shook with the violent blows of axes upon the door, and the horrid clamor filled the hearts of the women with an agony of fear. At last the door gave way, and the rattling of ramrods and bayonets, as well as the half-suppressed oaths of the men as they rushed into the back parlor, arose clearly and distinctly in the night air. Mr. Vallandigham still determined he would not surrender whilst there was any hope of rescue. He desired to delay the soldiery until some organised effort could be made by his friends outside to drive off his assailants. He had dressed himself whilst the soldiers were bursting open the door below; and he arranged with his nephew, who had served in the Union army, to open fire on the soldiers as soon as they should be attacked from the outside. Another demand to surrender was sternly refused, and the soldiers mounted the stair and commenced battering away at the door of the room in which he stood. He then retired into another room which communicated with the one now attacked. In a few moments the second door was broken in, but lo! the victim was not yet brought to bay. A short interval of silence followed, and Mr. V.

endeavored to soothe the affrighted ladies whilst he anxiously listened for the sound of footsteps coming to his aid; nothing, however, but the measured tread of the sentinels could be heard on the outside. The third door was now attacked, and as there was no chance of successful resistance, he concealed his revolver and calmly awaited the entry of the troops. The house was full of soldiers, though the officer in command had not entered, and directly the third door gave way the soldiers broke into the room where he stood, and half a score of muskets were pointed instantly at him. Thereupon he said: "You have now broken open my house and overpowered me by superior force, and I am obliged to surrender." The muskets were lowered, and hastily though not roughly he was torn from the arms of his devoted wife and weeping child and hurried down stairs. Leaving his wife stupefied in agony of grief and alarm, he passed through the shattered panels of his doors into the street. The bugles sounded the recall, and surrounded by soldiery he was marched rapidly to the depot, and thence carried by the special train to Cincinnati, where after daylight he was taken to the military prison, Kemper Barracks.

. . . .